Steve Wellum is my favorite  integrates exegesis, biblical theology, and practical theol again in this book on *solus C*

Andy N

and theology at Bethlehem College & Seminary in
Minneapolis; elder of Bethlehem Baptist Church

"Christ alone" is the glue and centerpiece of the five great *solas* of the Reformation according to this magnificent work by Steve Wellum. We see the centrality of Christ in both his person and his work, for the work of Christ is effective because of who he is. Wellum makes his case from both biblical and systematic theology, and he shows he is well versed in philosophy as well. I believe this book is going to be read and quoted for many years to come.

Thomas R. Schreiner, James Buchanan Harrison Professor of
New Testament, The Southern Baptist Theological Seminary

In *Christ Alone—The Uniqueness of Jesus as Savior*, Stephen Wellum reminds us that "Christ alone" is not only the center of the five Reformation *solas*, but that it stands as the central doctrine of systematic theology. Without it we cannot fully understand the doctrines of the Trinity, humanity, or salvation. "Christ alone," argues Wellum, "must connect all the doctrines of our theology because Christ alone stands as the cornerstone of all the purposes and plans of God himself." Consequently, if we get "Christ alone" wrong, Wellum reminds us, "all other doctrines will likely suffer." So take up this book, read it, and think on the person and work of Christ in order that you may know, worship, and proclaim the same Christ as the Reformers, who is none other than the Christ of Scripture.

Juan R. Sanchez, senior pastor of High Pointe
Baptist Church, Austin, Texas

5 Solas

Sola SCRIPTVRA - Scripture

Sola Deo Gloria - ~~Glory~~ Glory to God

Sola Fide - Faith alone

Sola gratia - Grace alone

Sola CHRISTUS - CHRIST Alone

Christ

ALONE

THE UNIQUENESS OF
JESUS AS SAVIOR

The Five Solas Series

Edited by Matthew Barrett

Books in Series:

God's Word Alone—The Authority of Scripture
   by Matthew Barrett

Christ Alone—The Uniqueness of Jesus as Savior
   by Stephen Wellum

Grace Alone—Salvation as a Gift of God
   by Carl Trueman

Faith Alone—The Doctrine of Justification
   by Thomas Schreiner

God's Glory Alone—The Majestic Heart of Christian Faith and Life
   by David VanDrunen

Christ
ALONE

THE UNIQUENESS OF
JESUS AS SAVIOR

What the Reformers Taught
. . . and Why It Still Matters

STEPHEN WELLUM

MATTHEW BARRETT, SERIES EDITOR
FOREWORD BY MICHAEL REEVES

ZONDERVAN

Christ Alone—The Uniqueness of Jesus as Savior
Copyright © 2017 by Stephen Wellum

This title is also available as a Zondervan ebook.

Requests for information should be addressed to:
Zondervan, 3900 *Sparks Dr. SE, Grand Rapids, Michigan 49546*

ISBN 978-0-310-51574-6

Cover design: Christopher Tobias/Outerwear for Books
Interior design: Denise Froehlich

Printed in the United States of America

17 18 19 20 21 22 23 24 25 26 27 /DCI/ 15 14 13 12 11 10 9 8 7 6 5 4

To Kirk, Colin, and Jonathan,
My brothers by nature and by sovereign grace.
Each of you in your own way has encouraged me
to glory and rest in Christ Alone.

Contents

A Note from the Series Editor 11

Foreword, Michael Reeves 13

Acknowledgments 15

Abbreviations 17

Introduction 19

Part 1: Christ Alone: The Exclusivity of His Identity

1. The Biblical Identity of Jesus Christ 31

2. The Self-Witness of Christ: God the Son Incarnate 55

3. The Apostolic Witness to Christ: God the Son Incarnate . . 83

4. From Incarnation to Atonement: An Exclusive
   Identity for an All-Sufficient Work 107

Part 2: Christ Alone: The Sufficiency of His Work

5. The Threefold Office of Christ Alone: Our Prophet,
   Priest, King 127

6. The Cross-Work of Christ in Historical Perspective 157

7. The Cross of Our All-Sufficient Savior:
   Penal Substitution, Part 1 193

8. The Cross of Our Glorious Redeemer:
   Penal Substitution, Part 2 221

Part 3: Christ Alone in the Reformation and Today

9. Chalcedonian Unity: Agreement on Christ's Exclusive
   Identity in the Reformation 249

10. The Sufficiency of Christ: The Reformation's
    Disagreement with Rome. 257

11. The Loss of Christ's Exclusivity: Our Current Challenge . 275

12. Reaffirming Christ Alone Today 297

Conclusion 311

Bibliography. 315
Scripture Index 329
Subject Index 337

A Note from the Series Editor

What doctrines could be more foundational to what it means to be an evangelical Protestant than the five *solas* (or *solae*) of the Reformation? In my experience, however, many in evangelical churches today have never heard of *sola Scriptura* (Scripture alone), *sola gratia* (grace alone), *sola fide* (faith alone), *solus Christus* (Christ alone), and *soli Deo gloria* (glory to God alone).

Now it could be that they have never heard the labels but would recognize the doctrines once told what each *sola* means. At least I pray so. But my suspicion is that for many churchgoers, even the content of these five *solas* is foreign, or worse, offensive. We live in a day when Scripture's authority is questioned, the exclusivity of Christ as mediator as well as the necessity of saving faith are offensive to pluralistic ears, and the glory of God in vocation is diminished by cultural accommodation as well as by individual and ecclesiastical narcissism. The temptation is to think that these five *solas* are museum pieces of a bygone era with little relevance for today's church. We disagree. We need these *solas* just as much today as the Reformers needed them in the sixteenth century.

The year 2017 will mark the 500th anniversary of the Reformation. These five volumes, written by some of the best theologians today, celebrate that anniversary. Our aim is not merely to look to the past but to the present, demonstrating that we must drink deeply from the wells of the five *solas* in order to recover our theological bearings and find spiritual refreshment.

Post tenebras lux

Matthew Barrett, series editor

Foreword

Five hundred years on from the Reformation, there is much to encourage and much to trouble those of us who count ourselves among the heirs of the Reformers. At the same time that the key principles of the Reformation are being forgotten, derided, and attacked at large, we see Reformational teaching faithfully and clearly expounded by an impressive regiment of scholars and preachers.

Yet for all the fresh re-exposition of Reformation theology in our day, there is a danger that it could be distorted into a theological system abstracted from Jesus Christ. The principle of Christ alone (*solus Christus*) remains as a critical bulwark against that danger—a guardian of the essence of that for which the Reformers fought.

Solus Christus expresses the biblical conviction that there is "one mediator between God and men, the man Christ Jesus" (1 Tim 2:5 ESV), and that therefore "there is salvation in no one else, for there is no other name under heaven given among men by which we must be saved" (Acts 4:12 ESV). Christ's identity is absolutely exclusive and his work entirely sufficient. We have no need, then, for any other prophet to provide us with a new revelation, any other priest to mediate between us and God, or any other king to rule Christ's church. Christ alone stands at the center of God's eternal purposes, Christ alone is the object of our saving faith, and therefore Christ alone must stand at the very center of our theology. Stephen Wellum is therefore perfectly right when he argues here that *solus Christus* is the linchpin of Reformation theology and the center of the other four principles or *solas* of the Reformation.

Solus Christus is the principle that, if followed, will ensure that we today are as robustly and thoroughly *Christian*—as anchored in Christ—as the Reformers. It protects us from becoming what Martin Luther termed "theologians of glory" who assume fallen human ideas of God, grace, faith, and Scripture. *Solus Christus* can keep us instead as epistemically faithful and humble "theologians of the cross."

In particular, *solus Christus* protects us when we think of grace alone (*sola gratia*) from thinking of grace as a blessing or benefit that can be abstracted from Christ. (That was very much the problem with medieval Roman Catholic conceptions of grace, and remains a problem today where justification and sanctification are divorced.) *Solus Christus* protects us when we think of faith alone (*sola fide*) from thinking of faith as a merit in itself or as a mystical mood or thing without an object. Faith is only that which grasps Christ, in whom is all our salvation. *Solus Christus* is the interpretative key to Scripture so that as we accept Scripture alone (*sola Scriptura*) as our supreme authority, we know how to read it. And *solus Christus* ensures that it is the glory of the *living*, *triune* God we seek when we assert that we think and do all for the glory of God alone (*soli Deo gloria*).

I am therefore delighted to see this superbly cogent exposition and application of the doctrine of *solus Christus*. Stephen Wellum clearly and methodically argues for the exclusivity of Christ's identity and the sufficiency of his work (and in so doing makes an outstanding case for the penal substitutionary atonement of Christ). He also proves just how vital it is for us today to stand firm on both.

The church—indeed, the world—needs the great truths presented so well in this book. For through them we see the brilliant glory of a unique and supersufficient Savior. His is the light and glory that we happily envisage when we hold up that banner of the Reformation: *post tenebras lux* ("after darkness, light"). His is the only light that can drive away the darkness of this world. And so for his glory and for that end, we must have—and we rejoice to have!—these truths shine out today.

Michael Reeves

President and Professor of Theology, Union School of Theology, UK

Acknowledgments

What an opportunity to be a part of Zondervan's series on the five *solas*, especially in the 500th year anniversary celebration of the Reformation. To remember our forefathers in the faith, to stand on their shoulders, and to proclaim in our day what they confessed and proclaimed, namely, the glorious gospel of God's sovereign grace, is indeed a joy and pleasure. Furthermore, to have the privilege of writing on arguably the center of all the Reformation *solas—Christ alone (solus Christus)*—and why we must stand with the Reformers and confess and proclaim the Jesus of the Bible as alone the exclusive and all-sufficient Savior, is truly an honor. I want to thank Matthew Barrett, the series editor, and Ryan Pazdur and the staff at Zondervan for allowing me to be part of the team and this project.

In addition, special thanks go to Michael Wilkinson, one of my doctoral students at Southern Seminary, who helped in the editing of this work. His expertise in editing and prose made this work much better than it originally was, and I am grateful for his help, friendship, and partnership in the gospel. I also want to thank the administration and trustees of The Southern Baptist Theological Seminary, especially Drs. Albert Mohler, Randy Stinson, and Greg Wills, for investing in me as a professor and serving as a constant source of encouragement to teach, research, and write theology for the church. Michael Haykin, Fred Zaspel, and Gregg Allison, three of my colleagues at Southern, were also great resources to help me think through various aspects of historical and Roman Catholic theology. I also want to thank my colleague Bruce Ware and Southern Seminary for organizing and hosting the 5 *Solas* theological conference on the beautiful campus of Southern Seminary in September, 2015. It was a wonderful experience, and it allowed all of the contributors to the series to present papers on their respective books and to interact with each other, along with the penetrating questions of the students who attended. What a delight to spend time reflecting on and discussing the Reformation and what was central to the Reformation, namely, the triune God of sovereign grace and his glorious plan of redemption centered in Christ Jesus our Lord.

Finally, I dedicate this volume to my three brothers, Kirk, Colin, and Jonathan. Growing up in a Christian home and with parents who gladly confessed and proclaimed *Christ alone* is abundant evidence of God's grace in my life. Also having three brothers who in their own way encouraged their youngest brother to stand for the truth of God's Word, to think deeply about theology, and more importantly to glory in our Lord Jesus Christ is further proof of God's amazing grace and providence in my life. To my brothers: may *solus Christus* always be your confession, delight, and joy, and may we continue to live our lives under Christ's lordship so that "in everything *he* might have the supremacy" (Col 1:18). It is my prayer that all who read this book will not only renew their confidence and trust in the Lord of glory but also will learn anew to stand on the shoulders of the Reformers in our day and proclaim Christ alone as Lord and Savior.

Abbreviations

ANF	*Ante-Nicene Fathers*
BECNT	Baker Exegetical Commentary on the New Testament
EBC	Expositor's Bible Commentary
ESV	English Standard Version
KJV	King James Version
NASB	New American Standard Bible
NDBT	*New Dictionary of Biblical Theology*
NDT	*New Dictionary of Theology*
NICNT	New International Commentary on the New Testament
NICOT	New International Commentary on the Old Testament
NIDOTTE	*New International Dictionary of Old Testament Theology and Exegesis*
NIGTC	New International Greek Testament Commentary
NIV	New International Version
NIVAC	New International Version Application Commentary
NPNF[1]	Nicene and Post-Nicene Fathers, Series 1
NPNF[2]	Nicene and Post-Nicene Fathers, Series 2
NRSV	New Revised Standard Version
NSBT	New Studies in Biblical Theology
PNTC	Pillar New Testament Commentary
RSV	Revised Standard Version
SNTSMS	Society for New Testament Studies Monograph Series
TNTC	Tyndale New Testament Commentary
TOTC	Tyndale Old Testament Commentary
WBC	Word Biblical Commentary

Introduction

Reformation theology is often summarized by the five *solas*. Scripture alone (*sola Scriptura*) stands as the formal principle of the Reformation and the foundation of all theology. God's glory alone (*soli Deo gloria*) functions as a capstone for all Reformation theology, connecting its various parts to God's one purpose for creating this world and humanity in it. In between these two *solas*, the other three emphasize that God has chosen and acted to save us by his sovereign grace alone (*sola gratia*), through faith alone (*sola fide*), which is grounded in and through Christ alone (*solus Christus*).

If we are to learn from the Reformers, we do well to begin with these summarizing *solas*. But if we are to understand the substance of the Reformation *solas* and profit from them, we must bear in mind two points. First, all of the *solas* are interrelated and mutually dependent; you cannot have one without the others. Second, the five *solas* are just as important today as they were in the Reformation for capturing what is at the heart of the gospel. Without minimizing this mutual dependence, however, we will also need to consider that one *sola* plays a distinct part in connecting the others to bring us the full glory of God in the gospel.

Solus Christus stands at the center of the other four *solas*, connecting them into a coherent theological system by which the Reformers declared the glory of God. For this reason, we need to attend closely to what the Reformers taught about our Lord Jesus Christ. Consider the words of John Calvin:

> For how comes it that we are *carried about with so many strange doctrines* [Heb 13:9] but because the excellence of Christ is not perceived by us? For Christ alone makes all other things suddenly vanish. Hence there is nothing that Satan so much endeavours to accomplish as to bring on mists with the view of obscuring Christ, because he knows, that by this means the way is opened up for every

kind of falsehood. This, therefore, is the only means of retaining, as well as restoring pure doctrine—to place Christ before the view such as he is with all his blessings, that his excellence may be truly perceived.[1]

While the entirety of Reformation Christology lies beyond the scope of this book, we can begin to recover the Reformers' basic insights by focusing on two teachings: the *exclusive identity* of Christ and his *sufficient work*. These two aspects of Christology, while basic to the Reformers' theology, have been ridiculed and rejected by many today. And that is why, if the church is to proclaim the same Christ as the Reformers, we must understand and embrace *solus Christus* with the same clarity, conviction, urgency, and abundance of joy. To do this, we need to consider more closely why *Christ alone*[2] is at the center of the Reformation *solas* and at the heart of Christian theology.

First, Christ alone *is the linchpin of coherency for Reformation doctrine*. We come to know the person and work of Christ only by God's self-disclosure through Scripture. Yet, God speaks through the agency of human authors not simply to inform us but to save us in Christ alone. We are saved through faith alone. But the object of our saving faith is Christ alone. Our faith in Christ guards us by the power of God and his grace alone. The purpose of God's grace, however, leads to and culminates in our reconciliation and adoption through Christ alone. In the end, the ultimate goal of God in our redemption is his own glory, even as we are transformed into a creaturely *reflection* of it. And yet, the *radiance* of the glory of God is found in the person and work of Jesus Christ our Lord. The word spoken by God, the faith given by God, the grace extended by God, and the glory possessed and promised by God cannot make sense apart from the Son of God who became a man for our salvation.

Second, the Reformers placed Christ alone *at the center of their doctrine because Scripture places Christ alone at the center of God's eternal plan for his creation*. Despite the diversity of human authors, Scripture

---

1.   John Calvin, *Commentary on Philippians, Colossians, and Thessalonians* (1844–1856; repr., Grand Rapids: Baker, 1993), Col 1:12 (emphasis original).

2.   Hereafter, "*Christ alone*" (italicized) refers to the Reformation doctrine of *solus Christus*. Without italics, "Christ alone" refers to a particular characteristic, act, accomplishment, or other predicate that is true of no one but Christ.

speaks as a unified divine communicative act[3] by which God reveals himself and the whole history of redemption—from creation to new creation. And this unified word of God has one main point: the triune God of the universe in infinite wisdom and power has chosen to bring all of his purposes and plans to fulfillment in the person and work of Christ. The centrality of Christ does not diminish the persons and work of the Father and the Spirit. Scripture teaches, rather, that all the Father does centers in his Son and that the Spirit works to bear witness and bring glory to the Son. So we can agree with Michael Reeves that "[t]o be truly Trinitarian we must be constantly Christ-centered."[4]

Third, the Christ alone *of the Reformation reflects the self-witness of Christ himself.* Jesus understood that he was the key to the manifestation of God's glory and the salvation of his people. On the road to Emmaus, Jesus explained his death and bore witness to his resurrection as the Messiah by placing himself at the focal point of God's revelation: "'Did not the Messiah have to suffer these things and then enter his glory?' And beginning with Moses and all the Prophets, he explained to them what was said in all the Scriptures concerning himself" (Luke 24:26–27).[5] He confronted the religious leaders for not finding eternal life in him as the goal of humanity: "'These are the very Scriptures that testify about me, yet you refuse to come to me to have life'" (John 5:39–40). And he was remarkably clear-minded and comfortable in his role as the anointed one entrusted with the end of the world: "'The Father judges no one, but has entrusted all judgment to the Son, that all may honor the Son just as they honor the Father. Whoever does not honor the Son does not honor the Father, who sent him" (John 5:22–23). To follow Jesus as his disciples, then, the Reformers confessed that Christ alone is the person around whom all history pivots and the focus of all God's work in the world.

Fourth, the Reformers emphasized the centrality of Christ alone *because they accepted the apostolic witness to the person and work of Christ.* The opening verses of Hebrews underscore the finality and superiority of God's self-disclosure in his Son: "In the past God spoke . . . at many

---

3. This term is taken from Kevin J. Vanhoozer, "Exegesis and Hermeneutics," in *NDBT* 52–64.

4. Michael Reeves, *Rejoicing in Christ* (Downers Grove, IL: IVP Academic, 2015), 23.

5. Unless otherwise noted, all references are taken from the NIV.

times and in various ways, but in these last days he has spoken to us by his Son . . . the radiance of God's glory and the exact representation of his being . . ." (Heb 1:1–3a). Paul comforts us with the cosmic preeminence of Christ: "For in him all things were created: things in heaven and on earth, visible and invisible, whether thrones or powers or rulers or authorities; all things have been created through him and for him. He is before all things, and in him all things hold together" (Col 1:16–17). And Paul encourages our hope in Christ by declaring that God's eternal purpose and plan is "to bring unity to all things in heaven and on earth under Christ" (Eph 1:9–10). In other words, Jesus stands as *the most important figure* in God's new creation work—a work that restores and even surpasses what was lost in Eden. God brings forth a new redeemed and reconciled heaven and earth by and through Christ alone.

Fifth, beyond the other Reformation solas, Christ alone *is the linchpin of coherency for all Christian theology.* More than a century ago, Herman Bavinck wrote his magisterial *Reformed Dogmatics.* In this masterful integration of Christian teaching, Bavinck kept his eye on the key to its coherency: "The doctrine of Christ is not the starting point, but it certainly is the central point of the whole system of dogmatics. All other dogmas either prepare for it or are inferred from it. In it, as the heart of dogmatics, pulses the whole of the religious-ethical life of Christianity."[6] In the late twentieth century, J. I. Packer used the helpful analogy of a central hub that connects the spokes on a wheel. Packer helpfully explained that "Christology is the true hub round which the wheel of theology revolves, and to which its separate spokes must each be correctly anchored if the wheel is not to get bent."[7] And most recently, theologians like Michael Reeves recognize the integrative force of Christ alone. Reeves urges that "the center, the cornerstone, the jewel in the crown of Christianity is not an idea, a system or a thing; it is not even 'the gospel' as such. It is Jesus Christ."[8] In short, all of our efforts at theology ultimately rise and fall with *Christ alone.* Only a

6.   Herman Bavinck, *Sin and Salvation in Christ*, vol. 3 of *Reformed Dogmatics*, ed. John Bolt, trans. John Vriend (Grand Rapids: Baker Academic, 2006), 274.

7.   J. I. Packer, "Jesus Christ the Lord," in *The J. I. Packer Collection*, comp. Alister McGrath (Downers Grove, IL: InterVarsity Press, 1999), 151.

8.   Reeves, *Rejoicing in Christ*, 10.

4 key Doctrines flow from
Christ - Doctrine 'Christ Alone'

proper understanding of Christ can correctly shape the most distinctive convictions of Christian theology.[9]

Four quick examples will give us a better grip on the centrality of Christ to Christian theology. One of the most distinctive teachings of Christianity is the *doctrine of the Trinity.* Still, this fundamental of the Christian faith comes fully to us by the divine Son's incarnation. The church confesses the triunity of God because Scripture reveals the coming of God the Son as a man in eternal relation to the Father and the Spirit. Christ alone opens our eyes to see the Father, Son, and Spirit working distinctly yet inseparably as the one Creator-Covenant Lord. Being human, we might see the *doctrine of humanity* as intuitive, easily accessible and comprehensible on its own. But we cannot understand who we are in all of our dignity and fallenness apart from comprehending the person and work of Christ. Christ alone is the image of God, the last Adam, the beginning and end of humanity. And Christ alone is the hope of humanity. The *doctrine of salvation* brings us even closer to the center of theology because it brings the other doctrines to intersect as God's eternal plan progresses to its end. And yet again, even more clearly now, it is Christ himself, unique in his person and sufficient in his work, who makes sense of the why and how of divine-human reconciliation.

Finally, at the heart of the gospel stand the cross of Christ and the *doctrine of the atonement.* In his classic work, *The Cross of Christ*, John Stott argues that fully understanding the biblical language regarding the *death* of Christ requires correct conclusions regarding the *person* of Christ and especially making sense of the cross as penal substitution.[10] After surveying a number of options in Christology, Stott draws this crucial conclusion: "If the essence of the atonement is substitution . . . [t]he theological inference is that it is impossible to hold the historic doctrine of the cross without holding the historic doctrine of Jesus Christ as the one and only God-man and Mediator. . . . At the root of every caricature of the cross lies a distorted Christology. The person and work of Christ belong together. If he was not who the apostles say he was, then he could not have done what they say he did. The incarnation

---

9.   Packer, "Jesus Christ the Lord," 151.
10.   See John R. W. Stott, *The Cross of Christ*, 20th Anniversary Edition (Downers Grove, IL: InterVarsity Press, 2006), 149–62.

is indispensable to the atonement."[11] Also, by understanding Christ's substitutionary death, we can look through his atonement to gain still more clarity in all other doctrines: for example, the problem of human sin; the mercy and grace of God in sending his Son; the wisdom and goodness of God in his redemptive plan; God's sovereign power in overcoming evil and restoring his creation. The glory of God in all his ways depends upon Christ alone.

Simply put, *Christ alone* must connect all the doctrines of our theology because Christ alone stands as the cornerstone of all the purposes and plans of God himself. But if we misinterpret who Christ is and what he does in his life, death, and resurrection, then all other doctrines will likely suffer. Retrieving and learning from the Reformers' teaching on *solus Christus*, then, brings both sobriety and joy. Misidentifying Christ will cause confusion in the church and harm our witness in the world. However, if we rightly identify Christ in all his exclusive identity and all-sufficient work, then we can proclaim the same Christ as the Reformers with the same clarity, conviction, urgency, and abundance of joy.

Christ alone is not a slogan; it is the center of the *solas* by which the Reformers recovered the grace of God and declared the glory of God. *Christ alone* integrates the purposes and plans of God as he has revealed them in Scripture and as we represent them in theological formulation. Yet we cannot afford to pursue *Christ alone* as a mere academic interest. We must proclaim the excellencies of Christ alone "who called you out of darkness into his wonderful light" (1 Pet 2:9b). Living under the Lordship of Christ, it is our privilege to follow Paul and "proclaim [the supremacy of Christ alone], admonishing and teaching everyone with all wisdom, so that we may present everyone fully mature in Christ" (Col 1:28). For this proclamation, we want to stand with the Reformers to declare and delight in *Christ alone* to the glory of God alone.

The goal of this book is to learn from the Reformers' *solus Christus* so that we might proclaim the same Christ in our context today. Exploring the fullness and richness of this glorious Reformation doctrine is a lifelong pursuit—and well worth the effort. Our guide to understanding the basic insights of the Reformers is to focus on two

---

11. Ibid., 159. On this same point, see Robert Letham, *The Work of Christ*, Contours of Christian Theology (Downers Grove, IL: InterVarsity Press, 1993), 29.

teachings: the *exclusive identity* of Christ and his *sufficient work.* But our focus is not the Reformers themselves—it is to grasp that their teaching on *Christ alone* is worth recovering because it encapsulates the teaching of Scripture. Ultimately, we want to follow the Reformers to proclaim who Christ is and what he has done according to what Scripture says about him. So we need to spend time looking at the identity and work of Christ as they are presented in the Scriptures, and we need to take seriously the differences between the cultures and contexts of the Reformation era and our day. Theology is never constructed or communicated in a cultural vacuum. As we pursue *Christ alone* for today, we must avoid the particular pitfalls that are presented by the dominant patterns of thinking, and we must embrace the responsibility of meeting the challenges imposed by that thinking on our witness to the exclusivity and sufficiency of Christ.

Part 1 of this book establishes the exclusive identity of Christ from the storyline of Scripture. The first chapter traces the Bible's storyline according to its structures, categories, and *intratextual* dynamics to arrive at the biblical identity of Christ. The covenantal development of the biblical storyline helps us grasp who Jesus is and what he has done for us and our salvation. Chapter 2 considers the self-witness of Christ that he is God the Son incarnate. From his baptism through his life, death, and resurrection unto the inauguration of God's kingdom, Christ knew his divine-human identity and the authority given to him. He knew that he would accomplish the works of God and receive the praise of man. Chapter 3 confirms the self-witness of Christ by considering the witness of his apostles. Looking at a few key texts, it becomes clear that the apostles knew Christ as the promised God-man. Moreover, the apostles confessed this exclusivity of Christ not just because he told them but because he opened their hearts and minds to see and receive the revelation of God developed through the OT—on the Bible's own terms. Finally, chapter 4 begins the transition from a focus on Christ's person to a focus on his work by connecting them in the incarnation. The incarnation and the incarnate Son's life and death reveal who Jesus is *and* how his divine-human identity is necessary to accomplish our reconciliation.

Part 2 takes up the sufficiency of Christ in Scripture to determine the nature and necessity of his sacrifice. Chapter 5 follows the typological development of the biblical storyline to find Christ as our peerless prophet-priest-king. Through this one threefold office, Christ alone brings us into his all-sufficient revelation, mediation, and lordship for a comprehensive salvation. Chapter 6 looks more closely at the sufficiency of Christ's atonement on the cross. A brief survey of different atonement theories demonstrates that the Reformers brought a key insight into the debate: what we say about the atonement must align with who God has revealed himself to be. In the end, the sufficiency of Christ's atoning work is determined by who he is and the identity of God himself. And chapters 7 and 8 argue for penal substitution as the atonement theory that best accounts for the biblical presentation of Christ's sufficient work. Looking at Jesus's own understanding, the work required for our forgiveness, and the various perspectives on the cross in Scripture, we can conclude that Christ became our substitute to bear the penalty for our sins as an absolute necessity of God's determination to save us. And because he is God the Son incarnate, Christ's sacrifice was perfect and its effect was sufficient to accomplish all that God planned and promised. The penal substitutionary death of Christ propitiates God's wrath, redeems and reconciles a sinful people, presents them justified before God, gives Christ the victory over all God's enemies, and gives us an example for our own lives.

Part 3 concludes by looking at why the Reformers taught *Christ alone* and how intellectual shifts over the last five hundred years have created a different cultural context for us. These shifts have not changed who Christ is and what he has done for us, and they have not removed the duty and joy of knowing, praising, and proclaiming his exclusivity and sufficiency. But today's intellectual culture does present unique challenges. Chapter 9 highlights the Reformers' continuity with orthodox Christology, and chapter 10 explains their special focus on Christ's sufficiency as a reaction to Rome's sacramental theology. Chapter 11 proposes that while we must always maintain the sufficiency of Christ, we must now specifically argue for his exclusivity, something the Reformers simply assumed along with the entire Christian tradition. The reason why this is so is due to a shift in plausibility structures that determine whether people will accept something as probable or even possible. Since the Enlightenment, there has been a shift from an acceptance of orthodox Christianity to a rejection of its basic tenets that has greatly impacted our confession of *Christ alone*. Chapters 11 and 12 focus on this shift, first in the Enlightenment and second in our own postmodern era, followed by suggestions on how to proclaim faithfully an exclusive and all-sufficient Christ today.

Finally, I will offer some closing comments on how the exclusivity and sufficiency of Christ alone applies to our Christian lives. As God the Son incarnate, Christ deserves and demands our total allegiance. All we think, feel, do, and say should be given exclusively to Christ alone and governed by his Spirit as worship. And by the sufficiency of his work, Christ supplies our every need in abundant and eternal life. The new covenant accomplishments of Christ merit every spiritual blessing to strengthen us for joyful obedience in the world unto the consummation of his kingdom over the world.

From beginning to end, this book confesses with the Reformers that Jesus Christ bears the exclusive identity of God the Son incarnate and has accomplished an all-sufficient work to fulfill God's eternal plans and establish God's eternal kingdom on earth. We confess both the exclusivity and sufficiency of *Christ alone* because Scripture reveals that "[w]hat Christ has done is directly related to who he is. It is the uniqueness of his person that determines the efficacy of his work."[12] Just as the five *solas* are mutually dependent, the exclusivity and sufficiency of *Christ alone* are bound together to bring us fullness of joy in covenant with God.

May *Christ alone* fill our hearts with wonder and thanksgiving and open our mouths for praise and proclamation. And may this work encourage the church to love and follow Christ alone, especially in the tests of faith, until he comes again: "Though you have not seen him, you love him; and even though you do not see him now, you believe in him and are filled with an inexpressible and glorious joy, for you are receiving the end result of your faith, the salvation of your souls" (1 Pet 1:8–9).

---

12. Letham, *Work of Christ*, 24.

PART 1

Christ Alone: The Exclusivity of His Identity

CHAPTER 1

The Biblical Identity
of Jesus Christ

Our understanding of who Jesus is and what he does must be developed from Scripture and its entire storyline. And while the full complexity of the Bible's structure, categories, and intratextual dynamics lies beyond the scope of this volume,[1] the Bible's own terms provide us with a clear picture of Christ's identity and work: Christ alone is Lord and Savior, and therefore he alone is able to save and his work is all-sufficient.

There are four major pieces to the puzzle of Christ's identity and his accomplishments: who God is, what he requires of humans, why sin creates a problem between God and humans, and how God himself provides the solution. These four pieces fall into place as the biblical covenants develop across time to reveal Christ in the fullness of time. The covenantal storyline of Scripture unfolds both God's plan of redemption and the identity of Christ who accomplishes it. Over the next few chapters we will consider the teaching of Jesus himself and his apostles, but first we will consider how the structure and storyline of Scripture create the expectation and necessity that the Christ will bear a specific, exclusive identity. This covenantal storyline reveals both the necessity and identity of Christ and his work as the one person who (1) fulfills God's own righteousness as a man, (2) reconciles God himself with humanity, and (3) establishes God's own saving rule and reign in this world—all because, and only because, Christ alone is God the Son incarnate.

---

1. For further discussion on this point, see Peter J. Gentry and Stephen J. Wellum, *Kingdom through Covenant: A Biblical-Theological Understanding of the Covenants* (Wheaton: Crossway, 2012), 21–126.

The Necessity of Christ and His Work for Our Salvation

The structure and storyline of Scripture reveals the necessity of Christ and his work. At the heart of *solus Christus* is the confession that the salvation of humanity depends upon the person and work of Christ. *Necessity* is a tricky concept in theology. To say that Christ is necessary for salvation is true in a number of ways, some of which can mean things that are unbiblical. Our immediate task is to define *in what way* Christ is necessary.

Anselm begins his famous *Why God Became Man* with these words: "By what logic or necessity did God become man, and by his death, as we believe and profess, restore life to the world, when he could have done this through the agency of some other, angelic or human, or simply by willing it?"[2] As Anselm practices a "faith seeking understanding" by wrestling with the *why* of the incarnation and the cross, especially in light of the awful cost both were to the eternal Son, the question of necessity naturally arises. Was the incarnation and the cross merely *one* of God's chosen ways to save us, or was it the *only* way? Could the triune God, in his infinite knowledge and wisdom, have planned another way to save fallen creatures? Or were Christ and his work the only way? This is the question of necessity. Walking in the footsteps of Anselm today, John Murray also stresses the importance of Christ's necessity: "To evade [questions of necessity] is to miss something that is central in the interpretation of the redeeming work of Christ and to miss the vision of some of its essential glory. Why did God become man? Why, having become man, did he die? Why, having died, did he die the accursed death of the cross?"[3]

These questions demand some kind of explanation, not only for the sake of the church's theology in general but to warrant and establish *Christ alone* in particular. Why is Christ the unique, exclusive, and all-sufficient Savior? Scripture answers: because *he* is the *only* one who can meet our need, accomplish all of God's sovereign purposes, and save us from our sin. Christ and his work are necessary to redeem us, and apart from him there is no salvation. But what exactly is the nature of

---

2.   Anselm, *Why God Became Man*, in *Anselm of Canterbury: The Major Works*, ed. Brian Davies and G. R. Evans, Oxford World's Classics (Oxford: Oxford University Press, 1998), I:1.

3.   John Murray, *Redemption Accomplished and Applied* (Grand Rapids: Eerdmans, 1955), 11.

this necessity? Since there are a range of options, we can first reject the extremes and then focus on the remaining two possibilities.

On one end of the necessity issue, some argue that our salvation does not require the incarnation, life, death, and resurrection of Christ. In what we might call *optionalism*, God is able to forgive our sin apart from any specific Savior acting on our behalf to satisfy God's righteous demand. In the Reformation era and beyond, this view is found in Socinianism, various forms of Protestant Liberalism, and present-day religious pluralism. In all of its forms, optionalism argues that God's justice is a non-retributive, voluntary exercise of his will uncoupled from his nature. God is under no necessity to punish sin in order to forgive us. On the other extreme stands the hypothetical view of *fatalism*. Fatalism argues that God is under an external necessity to act as he does in salvation. This view removes our salvation in general and the entire Christ event in particular from the sovereign freedom of God. He is bound not by his own divine nature and character but by some standard external to God. The standard for God's actions is not God himself. Both extremes, however, err in the same way. Optionalism and fatalism both fail to understand the nature of God and the biblical presentation of his plan of salvation in Christ.

Beyond the extremes, within historic orthodox theology two options remain: *hypothetical* necessity and *consequent absolute* necessity. Throughout church history, many fine theologians have affirmed the hypothetical necessity of Christ and his work for our salvation.[4] This view argues that Christ is necessary because God in fact decreed that salvation would come through Christ as the most "fitting" means to his chosen ends. But this necessity is hypothetical because God could have chosen some other way of salvation.[5]

The other orthodox option is consequent absolute necessity, the view favored in post-Reformation theology.[6] This view argues that *consequent*

4.   Notable advocates include Augustine, Thomas Aquinas, John Calvin, and Hugo Grotius. For further discussion of the hypothetical necessity view, see Murray, *Redemption*, 9–18; Oliver D. Crisp, "Penal Non-Substitution," *Journal of Theological Studies* 59:1 (2008): 145–53.

5.   On this point, see Murray, *Redemption*, 11–12; Crisp, "Penal Non-Substitution," 145–53; Adonis Vidu, *Atonement, Law, and Justice: The Cross in Historical and Cultural Contexts* (Grand Rapids: Baker Academic, 2014), 45–132.

6.   Notable advocates include John Owen, Francis Turretin, and more recently, John Murray and Donald Macleod. See Murray, *Redemption*, 11–18; Donald Macleod, *Christ*

to God's sovereign, free, and gracious choice to save us, it was *absolutely necessary* that God save us in Christ alone. There was no Christless and crossless way of salvation after God made the decision to save sinners. Obviously, the absolute sense of necessity is stronger than the hypothetical sense. Simply put, the view of consequent absolute necessity claims that while God was not obliged to redeem sinners, once he did decide to redeem us, there is no possible world in which that redemption could be accomplished apart from the incarnation, life, death, and resurrection of God the Son.

Historic Christianity has affirmed both of these understandings of necessity, so this is not a matter of orthodoxy. Yet hypothetical necessity appears to have more fundamental problems because it seems to assume that there is nothing about God's nature that makes his forgiveness of our sins dependent upon a representative substitute, sacrifice, and covenant mediator who works on our behalf. This understanding focuses exclusively on God's sovereignty, simply positing that in such freedom God could have chosen other ways of salvation. In contrast, the consequent absolute necessity of Christ arises from the perfections of God's own nature. This view understands that the inherent holiness and justice of God are not limits on his freedom but the nature in which God acts perfectly within his freedom.

While both views of necessity are orthodox, however, which one is more biblical? This is an important question because it recognizes that some orthodox Christologies make better sense of the Bible than others. The best way to answer the question regarding the necessity of Christ is to let Scripture speak for itself, and in the next section we will trace the biblical storyline from the identity of God to the obedience he requires, to the disobedience of humanity and to God's response. Throughout this unfolding story, Scripture creates both the *expectation* and *necessity* that God would bring salvation in the person and work of Christ. This implies that we must affirm no *less* than the hypothetical necessity of Christ, and as we shall see, the Bible's own logic demands that in his unique identity and work, Christ alone is absolutely necessary given God's choice to redeem a sinful humanity. It is not that Christ and his

Crucified: Understanding the Atonement (Downers Grove, IL: IVP Academic, 2014), 194–219.

work are merely one way to save us among a number of possible options. Who Christ is and what he does is the *only* way God could redeem us.

The covenantal storyline of Scripture reveals the *necessity* of Christ and his work. And the same covenantal development also reveals the *identity* of Christ and the nature of his work. Christ is the one person who (1) fulfills God's own righteousness as a man, (2) reconciles God himself with humanity, and (3) establishes God's own saving rule and reign in this world—all because, and only because, Christ alone is God the Son incarnate.

The Covenantal Development of Christ Alone

Nearly fifty years ago, Francis Schaeffer put his finger on a serious problem that remains today. He wrote:

> I have come to the point where, when I hear the word "Jesus"— which means so much to me because of the Person of the historic Jesus and His work—I listen carefully because I have with sorrow become more afraid of the word "Jesus" than almost any other word in the modern world. The word is used as a contentless banner . . . there is no rational scriptural content by which to test it. . . .
>
> Increasingly over the past few years the word "Jesus," separated from the content of the Scriptures, has been the enemy of the Jesus of history, the Jesus who died and rose and is coming again and who is the eternal Son of God.[7]

Schaeffer was right. The name "Jesus" has become a mostly meaningless word due to its separation from the content and storyline of Scripture. Jesus is now anything we want him to be, except the Jesus of the Bible. Imposing a foreign worldview on the biblical text, as many do today, necessarily obscures God's authoritative revelation of Jesus's identity.[8] To proceed *intratextually* toward the Bible's Jesus—who is the real Jesus of history—we need to read the Bible on its own terms. We must interpret Jesus within the revealed categories, content, structure, and storyline of Scripture. And this revelational reading starts with the identity of God himself.

---

7.   Francis A. Schaeffer, *Escape from Reason* (London: InterVarsity Fellowship, 1968), 78–79.

8.   This point will be developed in more detail in chapters 11–12.

God as the Triune Creator-Covenant Lord

Starting with who God is to identify Christ might seem to be an inefficient or needless investigation when the words and life of Christ are recorded for us in the New Testament. But we must start with the identity of God to make sure that we come to the Bible on its own terms. Scripture begins with God creating the world out of nothing and continues with God relating to his creation according to his character, will, and power. Who God is, then, shapes the entire course of human history and gives unity, meaning, and significance to all of its parts.

Who, then, is the God of Scripture? In a summary way, we can say that he is the triune Creator-Covenant Lord.[9] From the opening verses of Scripture, God is presented as the uncreated, independent, self-existent, self-sufficient, all-powerful Lord who created the universe and governs it by his word (Gen 1–2; Pss 50:12–14; 93:2; Acts 17:24–25). This reality gives rise to the governing category at the core of all Christian theology: the Creator-creature distinction. God alone is God; all else is creation that depends upon God for its existence. But the transcendent lordship of God (Pss 7:17; 9:2; 21:7; 97:9; 1 Kgs 8:27; Isa 6:1; Rev 4:3) does not entail the remote and impersonal deity of deism or a God uninvolved in human history. Scripture stresses that God is transcendent *and* immanent with his creation. As Creator, God is the Covenant Lord who is fully present in this world and intimately involved with his creatures: he freely, sovereignly, and purposefully sustains and governs all things to his desired end (Ps 139:1–10; Acts 17:28; Eph 1:11; 4:6). And yet this immanent lordship does not entail panentheism, which undercuts the Creator-creature distinction of Scripture. Even though God is deeply involved with his world, he is not part of it or developing with it.

As Creator and Covenant Lord, rather, God sovereignly rules over his creation perfectly and personally.[10] He rules with perfect power, knowledge, and righteousness (Pss 9:8; 33:5; 139:1–4, 16; Isa 46:9–11;

---

9.   For an extended discussion of God as the "Covenant Lord," see John M. Frame, *The Doctrine of God* (Phillipsburg, NJ: P&R, 2002), 1–115. Cf. John S. Feinberg, *No One Like Him: The Doctrine of God*, Foundations of Evangelical Theology (Wheaton, IL: Crossway, 2001).

10.   For a discussion of God's existence and actions as a personal being, see Feinberg, *No One Like Him*, 225–31; Frame, *Doctrine of God*, 602; see also Herman Bavinck, *God and Creation*, vol. 2 of *Reformed Dogmatics*, ed. John Bolt, trans. John Vriend, 4 vols. (Grand

Acts 4:27–28; Rom 11:33–36) as the only being who is truly independent and self-sufficient. God loves, hates, commands, comforts,
punishes, rewards, destroys, and strengthens, all according to the personal, covenant relationships that he establishes with his creation. God
is never presented as some mere abstract concept or impersonal force.
Indeed, as we progress through redemptive history, God discloses himself not merely as uni-personal but as tri-personal, a being-in-relation,
a unity of three persons: Father, Son, and Spirit (e.g., Matt 28:18–20;
John 1:1–4, 14–18; 5:16–30; 17:1–5; 1 Cor 8:5–6; 2 Cor 13:14; Eph
1:3–14). In short, as the Creator-Covenant triune Lord, God acts in,
with, and through his creatures to accomplish all he desires in the way
he desires to do it.

Scripture also presents this one Creator-Covenant Lord as the Holy
One over all his creation (Gen 2:1–3; Exod 3:2–5; Lev 11:44; Isa 6:1–3;
57:15; cf. Rom 1:18–23). The common understanding for the meaning
of holiness is "set apart," but holiness conveys much more than God's
distinctness and transcendence.[11] God's holiness is particularly associated with his aseity, sovereignty, and glorious majesty.[12] As the one who
is Lord over all, he is exalted, self-sufficient, and self-determined both
metaphysically and morally. God is thus *categorically different in nature
and existence* from everything he has made. He cannot be compared
with the "gods" of the nations or be judged by human standards. God
alone is holy in himself; God alone is God. Furthermore, intimately
tied to God's holiness in the metaphysical sense is God's personal-moral
purity and perfection. He is "too pure to behold evil" and unable to
tolerate wrong (Hab 1:12–13; cf. Isa 1:4–20; 35:8). God must act with
holy justice when his people rebel against him; yet he is the God who
loves his people with a holy love (Hos 11:9), for he is the God of "covenant faithfulness" (*hesed*).

Rapids: Baker, 2004), 15–19; cf. D. A. Carson, *The Gagging of God: Christianity Confronts
Pluralism* (Grand Rapids: Zondervan, 1996), 222–38.

    11. See Willem VanGemeren, *New International Dictionary of Old Testament Theology
and Exegesis*, 3 vols. (Grand Rapids: Zondervan, 1997), 3:879; see also Feinberg, *No One Like
Him*, 339–45. For a discussion of the belief by past theologians that holiness is the most fundamental characteristic of God, see Richard A. Muller, *The Divine Essence and Attributes*, vol.
3 of *Post-Reformation Reformed Dogmatics*, 4 vols. (Grand Rapids: Baker Academic, 2003),
497–503. Even though we must demonstrate care in elevating one perfection of God, there is
a sense in which holiness defines the very nature of God.

    12. See Muller, *Divine Essence and Attributes*, 497–503.

Often divine holiness and love are set against each other, but Scripture never presents them at odds. We not only see this taught in the OT, but the NT, while maintaining God's complete holiness (see Rev 4:8), also affirms that "God is love" (1 John 4:8). It is important to note, in light of who God is, the biblical tension regarding how God will simultaneously demonstrate his holy justice and covenant love. This tension is only truly resolved in the person and work of Christ, who alone became our propitiatory sacrifice and reconciled divine justice and grace in his cross (Rom 3:21–26).[13]

This brief description of God's identity is the first crucial piece of the puzzle that grounds Christ's identity and provides the warrant for *Christ alone*. God's identity as the holy triune Creator-Covenant Lord gives a particular theistic shape to Scripture's interpretive framework.[14] And so this interpretive framework gives a particular theistic shape to the identity of Christ. To help make this point, we should consider three specific examples.

First, the *triunity of God* shapes the identity of Christ. As we will see in the next chapter, Jesus views himself as the eternal Son who even after adding to himself a human nature continues to relate to the Father and Spirit (John 1:1, 14). But it is precisely his identity *as the eternal Son* that gives the Jesus of history his exclusive identity. In fact, it is because he is the divine Son that his life and death has universal significance for all of humanity and the rest of creation. Moreover, Jesus's work cannot be understood apart from Trinitarian relations. It is the Son and not the Father or the Spirit who becomes flesh. The Father sends the Son, the Spirit attends his union with human nature, and the Son bears our sin and the Father's wrath as a man in the power of the Spirit. And yet, as God the Son, Jesus Christ lived and died in unbroken unity with the Father and Spirit because they share the same identical divine nature. Christ is not some third party acting independently of the other two divine persons. At the cross, then, we do not see three parties but only

---

13. On this point, see D. A. Carson, *The Difficult Doctrine of the Love of God* (Wheaton, IL: Crossway, 2000).

14. All other "theistic" frameworks (deism, panentheism, etc.) are incompatible with the unique biblical-theological framework of Scripture established by its specific metaphysical-moral identification of God. And so only the Bible's particular theistic framework can provide the correct identification of Christ.

two: the triune God and humanity. The cross is a demonstration of the Father's love (John 3:16) by the gift of his Son.[15]

Second, the *covenantal character* of the triune God shapes the identity of Christ. Here we are not first thinking about the biblical covenants unfolded in history, but what Reformed theologians have called the "covenant of redemption."[16] Scripture teaches that God had a plan of salvation before the foundation of the world (e.g., Ps 139:16; Isa 22:11; Eph 1:4; 3:11; 2 Tim 1:9; 1 Pet 1:20). In that plan, the divine Son, in relation to the Father and Spirit, is appointed as the mediator of his people. And the Son gladly and voluntarily accepts this appointment with its covenant stipulations and promises, which are then worked out in his incarnation, life, death, and resurrection. This eternal plan establishes Christ as mediator, defines the nature of his mediation, and assigns specific roles to each person of the Godhead. None of the triune persons are pitted against each other in the plan of redemption. All three persons equally share the same nature and act inseparably according to their mode of subsistence—as Father, as Son, and as Spirit. Finally, the covenant of redemption provides for our covenantal union with Christ as our mediator and representative substitute. The work of Christ as God the Son incarnate, then, is the specific covenantal work designed by the Father, Son, and Spirit to accomplish our eternal redemption.

Third, the *lordship* of the triune covenant God shapes the identity of Christ. As noted, Scripture begins with the declaration that God is the Creator and sovereign King of the universe. He alone is the Lord who is uncreated and self-sufficient and thus in need of nothing outside himself (Pss 50:12–14; 93:2; Acts 17:24–25). Throughout history, theologians have captured the majestic sense of God's self-sufficiency and independence with *aseity*, literally, "life from himself." But, as John Frame reminds us, we must not think of aseity merely in terms of God's self-existence. Aseity is more than a metaphysical attribute; it also applies to epistemological and ethical categories. As Frame notes, "God is not

15. On this point, see Macleod, *Christ Crucified*, 90–100; John R. W. Stott, *The Cross of Christ*, 20th Anniversary Edition (Downers Grove, IL: InterVarsity Press, 2006), 133–62.

16. See Macleod, *Christ Crucified*, 90–100; cf. David Gibson and Jonathan Gibson, eds., *From Heaven He Came and Sought Her: Definite Atonement in Historical, Biblical, Theological, and Pastoral Perspective* (Wheaton, IL: Crossway, 2013), 201–23, 401–35.

only self-existent, but also self-attesting and self-justifying. He not only exists without receiving existence from something else, but also gains his knowledge only from himself (his nature and his plan) and serves as his own criterion of truth. And his righteousness is self-justifying, based on the righteousness of his own nature and on his status as the ultimate criterion of rightness."[17] Yet in his aseity, God chooses to enter into relationships with his creatures. From the first Adam to the last Adam, the lordship of God has consequences for his covenant partners. God's lordship determines who can be a fitting covenant partner with him. To mediate the new and eternal covenant, the Christ must be one who is able to satisfy the demands of covenant life with the Covenant Lord.

With just these three examples, we see how the identity of God functions as the first major piece to the identity of Christ. We will develop this connection in more detail in the next few chapters. Here we can simply note how the particular theistic shape of the Bible's interpretive framework gives particular meaning and significance to the New Testament description of Jesus Christ as the Son of God who mediates a new and eternal covenant as the last Adam. To be this person and do these works, Christ must be identified fully with humanity and with God himself.

The Requirement of Covenantal Obedience

At the heart of God's complex relationship with humanity lies the concept of covenantal obedience. Simply put, it is the demand of God

---

17. Frame, *Doctrine of God*, 602. The Bible grounds the concept of a moral universe in the nature and character of God. In Scripture, God is the Holy One, Judge, and King. As the divine king, Yahweh is the just judge, able to enforce his judgments by his power (see Deut 32:4). Abraham's appeal binds God to absolute standards of justice—God's own standards: he is the supreme and universal judge (Gen 18:25). Today, this point is significant in light of the "new perspective on Paul." Although this view is diverse, it unites in linking "righteousness" and "justice" to "covenant faithfulness," i.e., God is righteous in that he keeps his promises to save. No doubt there is truth in this: God's faithfulness means that he will keep his word. Specifically, he will keep his promises to his people and will execute justice for them and act to save them. Yet this is a reductionistic view of God's righteousness. At its heart, it fails to see that "righteousness-justice-holiness" is tied to the nature and character of God, which entails that God's faithfulness also means that he will punish wrong. It is this latter emphasis which grounds the biblical concept of God's retributive justice, which is often dismissed as merely a Western construct. But this is incorrect. If we are rightly thinking of God's aseity vis-à-vis his moral character, then God's holiness, justice, and righteousness are tied to his nature; this is why God *must* punish sin. On the new perspective on Paul, see Stephen Westerholm, *Perspectives Old and New on Paul: The "Lutheran" Paul and His Critics* (Grand Rapids: Eerdmans, 2004).

and the joy of human beings to maintain a relationship of love and loyalty. To understand who Christ is and what he does in his new covenant ministry, we must go back to the Edenic roots of the creation covenant between God and man. We need to trace the Bible's interpretive link between the charge and curse of the first Adam to understand the coming and crucifixion of the last Adam.

The biblical storyline divides the entire human race and every person in it under two representative heads: the first Adam and the last Adam. In the beginning of time, God created the first ʿādām from the earth; in the fullness of time, God sent his Son from heaven to become the last ʿādām on the earth (Rom 5:14). God covenanted with the first Adam as the head of the human race to spread the image of God in humanity over the whole earth.[18] Adam's headship, then, had a deeper privilege than ordinary fatherhood. It also had the dignity of defining what it means to be human: a son of God and his true image bearer. Yet the first Adam would fail in his headship over humanity, thereby creating the necessity for a final Adam who would prevail in his headship over a new humanity. But if we pursue the necessity for a new Adam too quickly, we will miss an important clue to his identity.

The second major piece to the puzzle of Christ's identity is that God requires covenant obedience from humanity. This requirement flows from God's own identity and becomes apparent in his charge to the first Adam and in his curse following the rebellion of his first vice-regent. As Creator-Covenant Lord, God requires perfect loyalty and obedience as the only proper and permissible way to live in covenant with him. Moreover, the Lord created and covenanted with Adam for the purpose of bearing God's image in human dominion over creation. This dominion, therefore, must be a vice-regency. Adam was called to rule over creation under the rule of God in obedience to his commands and ways of righteousness. Yet it is precisely at this point that Adam fails and ruins the entire human race.

We can look at the two trees of Eden to see the inherent nature of this requirement for covenantal obedience. When the Creator-Covenant Lord placed Adam in the garden, he gave the man two trees in particular

---

18. See Gentry and Wellum, *Kingdom through Covenant*, 147–221, 591–652, for a defense of a creation covenant.

to guide him into the joy of covenantal obedience. The first tree in the midst of the garden held forth the conditional promise of eternal life.[19] The promise is not explicit, but it is clearly implied when God expels Adam from Eden *so that* he could not "take also from the tree of life and eat, and live forever" (Gen 3:22). The tree of life was placed before Adam as a sign of his reward for obedience under God's blessing to fill the earth with God's image. But Adam rejected this reward of the first tree by eating from the second tree. The tree of the knowledge of good and evil came with a clear prohibition against eating its fruit under penalty of death. This tree of death, then, was placed before Adam as a test of his willingness to rule under God and in obedience to his word and ways. But with ruinous effect, Adam disobeyed God in an attempt to rule without God by becoming "like God, knowing good and evil" (Gen 3:5).

This glimpse back into Eden shows us how the requirement of covenantal obedience shapes the storyline of Scripture to help present us with the identity of Christ. The historical drama of the two trees and Adam's charge and curse dramatically illustrate that covenant loyalty lies at the heart of the relationship between God and man. Where the first Adam failed, the last Adam must prevail for our salvation. More specifically, we can now say that as the last Adam, the Christ must be someone who can walk in complete covenantal obedience with the Creator-Covenant Lord to spread his glorious image over the earth.

The covenantal framework establishes the person and work of Christ in representative, legal, and substitutionary terms (Rom 5:12–21). To undo, reverse, and pay for the first Adam's sin, the last Adam will indeed be a "seed of the woman" (Gen 3:15), but this time one who will render the required covenantal obedience. By his obedience, the Christ will demonstrate what a true image bearer is supposed to be: a loving, faithful, loyal, and obedient Son of God. Yet, as we will see below, the reversal of Adam's sin and all of its disastrous effects will require more than a demonstration of true humanity; it will require a representative substitute who will pay the penalty for our sin and give us his righteousness, thereby reconciling us to God.

---

19. See G. K. Beale, *A New Testament Biblical Theology: The Unfolding of the Old Testament in the New* (Grand Rapids: Baker Academic, 2011), 29–87.

Human Sin and Divine Forgiveness

With just two of the major pieces to the puzzle of Christ's identity, we have already seen the ultimate purpose of God in his relationship with the human race. The triune Creator-Covenant Lord of the universe has determined to display his glory in the world through a humanity that bears his image by walking with God in peace and covenantal obedience. But what happens, then, when humanity rebels against God and fails to bear the image of his righteousness? Can the divine purpose still be accomplished? Must God choose between covenant peace and covenant obedience? Is covenant peace with God even possible without covenantal obedience? More to the point, can God tolerate sin? And if not, how can God forgive those who sin against him?

The storyline from Genesis 3 forward clearly demonstrates that the first Adam's sinful disobedience brought the human race into corruption and brought us under God's wrath.[20] In Genesis 1:31, "God saw all that he had made, and it was very good." In Genesis 3, Adam disobeys God (3:6) and God expels Adam and his wife from the garden (3:21–24). And by Genesis 6:5, "The Lord saw how great the wickedness of the human race had become on the earth, and that every inclination of the thoughts of the human heart was only evil all the time." Due to his disobedience, the first covenantal representative of humanity filled the earth with a corrupt image of God instead of a true image, with wickedness instead of righteousness. Looking back on these days and into the last days of history, the apostle Paul confirms the sinful Adamic nature of all humanity: "There is no one righteous, not even one . . . for all have sinned and fall short of the glory of God" (Rom 3:10, 23). In short, the first Adam's covenant disobedience turned the created order upside down. By Adamic corruption and through our own sinful acts and omissions, we worship idols of creation, not the Lord of creation (cf. Rom 1:25). We obey our sinful passions, not the Covenant Lord who has created us for a holy happiness in him and his ways. But still worse, the first Adam's sin that we inherit and imitate brings the entire human race under the divine sentence of death (Rom 6:23). We were made to

---

20. On this point, see Douglas J. Moo, *The Epistle to the Romans*, NICNT (Grand Rapids: Eerdmans, 1996), 315; cf. Gentry and Wellum, *Kingdom through Covenant*, 611–28.

know, love, and serve God for eternity. But now we live under his just condemnation as enemies of his kingdom and objects of his wrath.

Human sin, however, is only the first part of the third major piece to the puzzle of Christ's identity. We now need to consider what God's response to human sin tells us about who the person must be that will save us from the wrath of God. Standing in the tradition of the Reformers and in their recovery of the gospel of God's grace in Jesus Christ, we might not at first recognize what John Stott calls the "problem of forgiveness."[21] Considering the divine response to human corruption, it seems that God must do two things that appear to be mutually exclusive: punish and forgive sin in humanity. On the one hand, God must punish sin because that is the just, proper, and glorious response of the one who is the Creator-Covenant Lord of the universe. On the other hand, God created and covenanted with man according to his eternal, unchanging decree to glorify himself in the righteous rule of humanity over creation, not in the destruction of all humanity throughout creation.

As serious as this problem seems to be, however, the "problem of forgiveness" goes even deeper—into the nature of God himself. Since God is *a se* (self-sufficient), holy, and personal, he must punish sin; he cannot overlook it, nor can he relax the retributive demands of his justice, since to do so would be to deny himself. That is why Scripture repeatedly emphasizes that our sin and God's holiness are incompatible (e.g., Lev 18:25–28; 20:22–23; Isa 6:5; 59:1–4; Heb 12:29; 1 John 1:5). God's holiness exposes our sin, and it must ultimately be dealt with.[22] Furthermore, closely related to God's holiness is his wrath, i.e., his holy reaction to sin. Scripture speaks of the wrath of God in high-intensity language, and it is important to note that a substantial part of

---

21.   John Stott describes the problem this way: "The problem of forgiveness is constituted by the inevitable collision between divine perfection and human rebellion, between God as he is and us as we are. The obstacle to forgiveness is neither our sin alone, nor our guilt alone, but also the divine reaction in love and wrath towards guilty sinners. For, although indeed 'God is love,' yet we have to remember that his love is 'holy love,' love which yearns over sinners while at the same time refusing to condone their sin. How, then, could God express his holy love?—his love in forgiving sinners without compromising his holiness, and his holiness in judging sinners without frustrating his love? Confronted by human evil, how could God be true to himself as holy love? In Isaiah's words, how could he be simultaneously 'a righteous God and a Savior' (Is 45:21)?" (Stott, *Cross of Christ*, 90–91).

22.   See Stott, *Cross of Christ*, 124–32.

the Bible's storyline turns on God's wrath. No doubt, God is forbearing and gracious, yet he is also holy and just.[23] Where there is sin, the holy God *must* confront it and bring it to judgment, especially given the fact that sin is not first against an external order outside of God; it is against God himself. Now it is precisely this *necessity* in God to judge human sin that creates a severe *tension* in the biblical storyline and the covenantal relationship. God has promised to redeem us and be our covenant Lord who is present with us. But how, when the necessary punishment for sin is death? Ultimately, in order for God to forgive, he must first satisfy himself, which is precisely what he does in God the Son incarnate, who bears our sin for us as our substitute.

At this point, one might think that we are getting lost in the details and losing our focus on Christ's identity. But if we put together the two parts of human sin and divine forgiveness, we have the third piece to the puzzle. And we can now connect the three pieces to get still closer to the biblical presentation of Christ.

With three of the four pieces to the puzzle of Christ's identity, we can summarize our progress with three points. First, because it is God's own perfect nature that makes it impossible for him to tolerate sin, God must provide his own solution to the problem of forgiving sin. Second, because God has determined to spread his image over the earth in the covenantal fidelity of humanity, his solution must be a perfectly obedient man. Third, because of the universal corruption of sin, this last Adam cannot come from the first Adam. And finally, because God must punish covenantal disobedience, this new man of God must be able to bear our sins for our redemption.

This still incomplete interpretive framework already allows a preliminary conclusion: the Christ must somehow identify with God himself in his divine nature and lordship *and* with humanity in our nature and need for both a representative substitute and obedient covenant mediator. The last piece of the puzzle will complete the shape of the biblical storyline and allow a final conclusion regarding the identity of Christ.

God Himself Saves through His Obedient Son

Just as human sin and divine forgiveness bring tension into the

---

23. See Carson, *Difficult Doctrine of the Love of God*, 65–84.

biblical storyline, so its resolution raises the question of just *who* it is that will save humans and establish God's kingdom through his saving rule on earth. The covenantal development up to this point has sharpened the focus of our christological query. God will forgive the sins of his people by punishing a substitute for them. And God will establish his kingdom through the rule of a righteous man over the earth when none can be found on the earth. So who is able to bear the sins of others, forgive the sins of others, and rule over the world in perfect obedience to God while simultaneously establishing the rule of God himself? When the fourth major piece of our puzzle comes into place, the answer becomes clear: Christ alone as God the Son incarnate.

This point is uniquely demonstrated in the unfolding of God's plan *through* the biblical covenants. God's initial promise of redemption (Gen 3:15) is given greater definition and clarity over time. Instead of God leaving us to ourselves and swiftly bringing full judgment upon us, he acts in sovereign grace, choosing to save a people for himself and to reverse the manifold effects of sin. This choice to save is evident in the *protevangelium* (the first gospel), given immediately after the fall to reverse the disastrous effects of sin upon the world through a coming of a Redeemer, the "seed of the woman," who, though wounded himself in conflict, will destroy the works of Satan and restore goodness to this world. This promise creates the expectation that when it is finally realized, all sin and death will be defeated and the fullness of God's saving reign will come to this world as God's rightful rule is acknowledged and embraced. As God's plan unfolds, we discover *how* God will save us in Christ and why Christ's work is absolutely necessary. Let us develop this last point in three steps.

First, God's plan unfolds across time as God enters into covenant relations with Noah, Abraham, Israel, and David. By his mighty acts and words, God step by step prepares his people to anticipate the coming of the "seed of the woman," the deliverer, the Messiah. A Messiah who, when he comes, will *fulfill* all of God's promises by ushering in God's saving rule to this world.[24] This point is vital for establish-

---

24. See Gentry and Wellum, *Kingdom through Covenant*, 591–652. Cf. Graeme Goldsworthy, *According to Plan: The Unfolding Revelation of God in the Bible* (Downers Grove, IL: InterVarsity Press, 1991), and Stephen Dempster, *Dominion and Dynasty: A Biblical Theology of the Hebrew Bible* (Downers Grove, IL: InterVarsity Press, 2003).

ing the identity of the Messiah, especially the truth that this Messiah is more than a mere man; he is God the Son incarnate. On the one hand, Scripture teaches that the fulfillment of God's promises will be accomplished *through a man* as developed by various typological persons such as Adam, Noah, Moses, Israel, and David, all seen in terms of the covenants. On the other hand, Scripture also teaches that this Messiah is more than a mere man since he is *identified with God*. How so? Because in fulfilling God's promises he literally inaugurates *God's* saving rule (kingdom) and shares the very throne of God—something no mere human can do—which entails that his identity is intimately tied to the one true and living God.[25] This observation is further underscored by the next point which brings together the establishment of God's kingdom through the inauguration of the new covenant.

Second, how does God's kingdom come in its *redemptive/new creation* sense? As the OT unfolds, God's saving kingdom is revealed and comes to this world, at least in anticipatory form, through the biblical covenants and covenant mediators—Adam, Noah, Abraham and his seed centered in the nation of Israel, and most significantly through David and his sons. Yet in the OT, it is clear that all of the covenant mediators (sons) fail and do not fulfill God's promises. This is specifically evident in the Davidic kings who are "sons" to Yahweh, the representatives of Israel, and thus "little Adams," but they fail in their task. It is only when a true obedient son comes, a son whom God himself provides, that God's rule is finally and completely established and his promises are realized. This is why, in OT expectation, ultimately the arrival of God's kingdom is organically linked to the dawning of the new covenant. This is also why when one begins to read the Gospels, one is struck by the fact that the kingdom of God is so central to Jesus's life and teaching; he cannot be understood apart from it.[26] But note: in

---

25. See David F. Wells, *The Person of Christ: A Biblical and Historical Analysis of the Incarnation* (Westchester, IL: Crossway, 1984), 21–81 and Richard Bauckham, *Jesus and the God of Israel: God Crucified and Other Studies on the New Testament's Christology of Divine Identity* (Grand Rapids: Eerdmans, 2008). Some specific texts we have in mind are Pss 2, 45, 110; Isa 7:14; 9:6–7; Ezek 34; Dan 7.

26. In the Gospels, the kingdom is mentioned directly thirteen times in Mark, nine times in sayings common to Matthew and Luke, twenty-seven additional instances in Matthew, twelve additional instances in Luke, and twice in John. Even though John's Gospel does not use kingdom terminology as often, John refers to these same realities in the language of "eternal life" [see I. Howard Marshall, *New Testament Theology* (Downers Grove, IL:

biblical thought one cannot think of the inauguration of the kingdom apart from the arrival of the new covenant.

In this regard, Jeremiah 31 is probably the most famous new covenant text in the OT, even though teaching on the new covenant is not limited to it. New covenant teaching is also found in the language of "everlasting covenant" and the prophetic anticipation of the coming of the new creation, the Spirit, and God's saving work among the nations. In fact, among the post-exilic prophets there is an expectation that the new covenant will have a purpose similar to the Mosaic covenant, i.e., to bring the blessing of the Abrahamic covenant back into the present experience of Israel and the nations,[27] yet there is also an expectation of some massive differences from the old, all of which are outlined in Jeremiah 31.

What is most *new* about the new covenant is the promise of complete forgiveness of sin (Jer 31:34). In the OT, forgiveness of sin is normally granted through the sacrificial system. However, the OT believer, if spiritually perceptive, knew that this was never enough, as evidenced by the repetitive nature of the system. But now in v. 34, Jeremiah announces that sin will be "remembered no more," which certainly entails that sin finally will be dealt with in full.[28] Ultimately, especially when other texts are considered, the OT anticipates a perfect, unfettered fellowship of God's people with the Lord, a harmony restored between creation and God—a new creation and a new Jerusalem—where the dwelling of God is with men (see Ezek 37:1–23; cf. Dan 12:2; Isa 25:6–9; Rev 21:3–4). That is why it is with the arrival of the new covenant age that we also have God's saving kingdom brought to this world, which is precisely the fulfillment of the *protevangelium*.

InterVarsity Press, 2004), 498; D. A. Carson, *The Gospel According to John*, PNTC (Grand Rapids: Eerdmans, 1991), 187–90]. For John, eternal life belongs to the "age to come," which is, importantly, identified with Jesus (John 1:4; 5:26; 1 John 5:11–12) since Jesus himself is the "life" (John 11:25: 14:6). In this way, John ties eternal life to Jesus, just as the Synoptics link the kingdom with Jesus in his coming and cross work. Cf. Andreas J. Köstenberger, *John*, BECNT (Grand Rapids: Baker, 2004), 123.

27.   The "new covenant" will bring about the Abrahamic blessing in that it will benefit both Israel and the nations. See Gentry and Wellum, *Kingdom through Covenant*, 644–52.

28.   The concept of "remembering" in the OT is not simple recall (cf. Gen 8:1; 1 Sam 1:19). In Jer 31:34, for God "not to remember" means that under the terms of the new covenant a full and complete forgiveness of sin will result. See William Dumbrell, *Covenant and Creation: A Theology of the Old Testament Covenants*, 2nd ed. (Milton Keyes: Paternoster, 2002), 181–85, for a development of this point.

Third, let us now take the Bible's basic covenantal storyline and see how it identifies who Christ is and establishes *why* he is unique and necessary. If we step back for a moment and ask—*Who* is able, or what kind of person is able to fulfill all of God's promises, inaugurate his saving rule in this world, and establish all that is associated with the new covenant, including the full forgiveness of sin?—in biblical thought the answer is clear: it is *God alone* who can do it and no one else.[29]

Is this not the Old Testament message? Is this not the covenantal message? As the centuries trace the history of Israel, it becomes evident that the Lord alone must act to accomplish his promises; he must initiate in order to save; he must *unilaterally* act if there is going to be redemption at all. After all, who ultimately can achieve the forgiveness of sin other than God alone? Who can usher in the new creation, final judgment, and salvation? Certainly these great realities will never come through the previous covenant mediators because they have all, in different ways, failed. Nor will it come through Israel as a nation because her sin has brought about her exile and judgment. If there is to be salvation at all, God *himself* must come and usher in salvation and execute judgment; the arm of the Lord must be revealed (Isa 51:9; 52:10; 53:1; 59:16–17; cf. Ezek 34). Just as he once led Israel through the desert, so he must come again, bringing about a new exodus in order to bring salvation to his people (Isa 40:3–5; cf. Isa 11).

However, as the biblical covenants are established, alongside the emphasis that God *himself* must come and accomplish these great realities, the OT also stresses that the Lord will do so *through* another David, a human figure, but one who is closely identified with the LORD himself. Isaiah teaches this point. This king to come will sit on David's throne (Isa 9:7), but he will also bear the titles and names of God (Isa 9:6). This King, though another David (Isa 11:1), is also David's Lord who shares in the divine rule (Ps 110:1; cf. Matt 22:41–46). He will be the mediator of a new covenant; he will perfectly obey and act like the

---

29. See Bauckham, *Jesus and the God of Israel*, 184, who argues this point. Bauckham labels this teaching of the OT "eschatological monotheism." By this expression he stresses not only God's unique lordship, but also as sole Creator and Lord there is the expectation that "in the future when YHWH fulfills his promises to his people Israel, YHWH will also demonstrate his deity to the nations, establishing his universal kingdom, making his name known universally, becoming known to all as the God Israel has known." Cf. N. T. Wright, "Jesus," *NDT* 349.

Lord (Isa 11:1–5), yet he will suffer for our sin in order to justify many (Isa 53:11). It is through him that forgiveness will come because he is "The LORD our righteousness" (Jer 23:5–6 NASB). In this way, OT hope and expectation, which is all grounded in the coming of the Lord to save, is joined together with the coming of the Messiah, one who is fully human yet also one who bears the divine name and identity (Isa 9:6–7; Ezek 34).

It is this basic covenantal storyline which serves as the framework and background to the New Testament's presentation of Jesus and which identifies Christ and his work as utterly unique. *Who* is Jesus? According to Scripture, *he* is the one who inaugurates *God's* kingdom and new covenant age. In him, the full forgiveness of sin is achieved; in him, the eschatological Spirit is poured out, the new creation dawns, and all of God's promises are fulfilled. Yet in light of the OT teaching, *who* can do such a thing? Scripture gives only one answer: The only one who can do it is one who is both the Lord *and* the obedient Son, which is precisely how the New Testament presents Jesus.

The New Testament unambiguously teaches that this *human* Jesus is also the Lord since he alone ushers in *God's* kingdom. He is the eternal Son in relation to his Father (see Matt 11:1–15; 12:41–42; 13:16–17; Luke 7:18–22; 10:23–24; cf. John 1:1–3; 17:3), yet the one who has taken on our flesh and lived and died among us in order to win for us our salvation (John 1:14–18). In him, as fully human, the glory and radiance of God is completely expressed since he is the exact image and representation of the Father (Heb 1–3; cf. Col 1:15–17; 2:9). In him, all the biblical covenants have reached their *telos*, terminus, and fulfillment, and by his cross work, he has inaugurated the new covenant and all of its entailments. To say that he has done all of this is to identify him *as God the Son incarnate*, fully God and fully man.[30]

It is for this reason that Jesus is utterly unique and that the NT

---

30. Wells, *Person of Christ*, 38, insists on this point. He develops Christ's significance in inaugurating the kingdom and the new covenant age, which, in biblical thought, *only God can do*. He writes: "This 'age,' we have seen was supernatural, could only be established by God himself, would bring blessings and benefits which only God could give, would achieve the overthrow of sin, death, and the devil (which only God could accomplish), and was identified so closely with God himself that no human effort could bring it about and no human resistance turn it back. If Jesus saw himself as the one in whom this kind of Kingdom was being inaugurated, then such a perception is a christological claim which would be fraudulent and deceptive if Jesus was ignorant of his Godness."

presents Jesus in an entirely different category from any created thing. In fact, Scripture so identifies him with the Lord in all of his actions, character, and work that he is viewed, as David Wells reminds us, as "the agent, the instrument, and the personifier of God's sovereign, eternal, saving rule."[31] In Jesus Christ, we see all of God's plans and purposes fulfilled; we see the resolution of God to take upon himself our guilt and sin in order to reverse the horrible effects of the fall and to satisfy his own righteous requirements, to make this world right, and to inaugurate a new covenant in his blood (Rom 3:21–26; 5:1–8:39; 16:25–27; 1 Cor 15:1–34; Eph 1:7–10; Heb 8:1–13). In Jesus Christ we see the perfectly obedient Son, who is also the Lord, taking the initiative to keep his covenant-promises by taking upon himself our human flesh, veiling his glory, and winning for us our redemption (Phil 2:6–11; Heb 2:5–18; 9:11–10:18). In him we see two major OT eschatological expectations unite: he is the sovereign Lord who comes to save his people, and he is simultaneously David's greater Son (Isa 9:6–7; 11:1–16; 59:15–21; Jer 23:1–6; Ezek 34). In this way, our Lord Jesus Christ fulfills all the types and shadows of the Messiah in the OT, and he is also the eternal Son, identified with the covenant Lord and thus God—equal to the Father in every way. The biblical covenants as developed along the Bible's own storyline beautifully identify who Jesus is and provide the biblical warrant for his unique identity and work.

In fact, the primary message of the covenants is this: unless *God himself* acts to accomplish his promises, we have no salvation. After all, *who* ultimately can remedy his own divine problem of forgiveness other than *God alone*? If there is to be salvation at all, the triune God himself must save, which is precisely what he has done as a triune work, in and through the incarnate Son. The Son is absolutely necessary in his person and work to act as our new covenant representative and substitute, and apart from *him*, there is no salvation.

In order to identify Christ and his work correctly, we must place him within the Bible's covenantal storyline. Yet something else must also occur. To grasp the truth of Christ alone and to glory in *him alone*, we must also, by God's grace, come to realize our own sin and lostness

---

31. Wells, *Person of Christ*, 172. Cf. Gerald Bray, "Christology," *NDT* 137, who makes the same point.

before God. Our greatest need as humans is to be reconciled to the holy God and Judge of the universe. Our secular, postmodern culture does not understand this because of its rejection of Christian theology for alien worldview perspectives. But to understand the biblical Jesus correctly, we must also know something of our own guilt before God and why we need the kind of Redeemer Scripture presents him to be. Not until we know ourselves to be lost, under the sentence of death, and condemned before God can we begin to appreciate and rejoice in a divine-human Redeemer who meets our deepest need. Once we see ourselves as fallen rebels against the holy God of the universe, we gladly rejoice that there is such a Redeemer for human beings. Once again, Wells gets it right when he observes the priority of knowing our sinfulness: "This means that to understand Christ aright, we must also know something about our own guilt. We must know ourselves to be sinners. . . . The New Testament, after all, was not written for the curious, for historians, or even for biblical scholars, but for those, in all ages and cultures, who want to be forgiven and to know God."[32] Unless this is a reality in our lives, it should not surprise us that we, or anyone else, will be baffled by the biblical Jesus and will fail to appreciate the truth and to glory in Christ alone.

Identifying Christ Alone in Scripture

Scripture alone identifies Christ alone. Reading the Bible on its own terms—according to its own covenantal storyline, in its own categories, and in its biblical-theological framework—we discover that the Jesus of the Bible is utterly unique in his person and work, and that apart from him there is no salvation. It is in this way that the whole Bible is *Christocentric*, since the entire plan of the triune Creator-Covenant God for humanity and all of creation centers in *his* unique identity and work. In addition, as we trace out the Bible's storyline through the biblical covenants, we also discover that Scripture is also *Christotelic*. The entire plan of God moves to its conclusion in Christ. *He alone* is the *telos*, the terminus and fulfillment of God's promises and covenants. He is life and life eternal (John 17:3).

All of this provides the biblical warrant, rationale, and theological

---

32. Wells, *Person of Christ*, 175.

grounds for *Christ alone* in his exclusive identity and all-sufficient work. Scripture is clear: In Christ alone is our salvation, the hope of the future, the worship of heaven, and the adoration of his people. Christ alone is the one who fulfills God's righteousness as a man, reconciles God with humanity, establishes God's kingdom in this world, and achieves the forgiveness of sin because, and only because, *he* is utterly unique as God the Son incarnate.

CHAPTER 2

The Self-Witness of Christ:
God the Son Incarnate

The prologue to John's Gospel (John 1:1–18) identifies our Lord Jesus Christ in all of his glory, majesty, grace, and truth as the unique Son from eternity who in our time has become flesh. In so doing, it not only follows the storyline of the OT, insisting that Christ's identity can only be discerned by placing him within its categories and framework, but it also insists that Christ's identity cannot be understood unless he is viewed as *God* the Son.

By the use of the title "Word" (*logos*)—an OT word closely associated with God who is active in creation, revelation, and redemption—John unambiguously identifies Christ as *God*.[1] But John is clear in verse 1 that this Word is also God *the Son*, thus a distinct person from God (the Father): "And the Word was with [*pros*] God, and the Word was [*ēn*] God." So the Word is distinct from, yet equal with, the Father. Andreas Köstenberger and Scott Swain capture the significance of this verse for identifying Christ: "Having distinguished the Word from God, John shows what they both have in common: they are God."[2] In this crucial verse at the beginning of his Gospel, John declares that the Word shares the intrinsic nature of God and eternally exists in personal intercommunion with God.

But the prologue continues to explain that the Word, "God's own self-expression,"[3] became (*egeneto*) flesh and dwelt among us (John 1:14a). The Word is now the Word *incarnate*. The *subject* of the

---

1. See D. A. Carson, *The Gospel According to John*, PNTC (Grand Rapids: Eerdmans, 1991), 114–18.
2. Andreas J. Köstenberger and Scott R. Swain, *Father, Son, and Spirit: The Trinity and John's Gospel*, NSBT 24 (Downers Grove, IL: InterVarsity Press, 2008), 49.
3. See John M. Frame, *The Doctrine of God* (Phillipsburg, NJ: P&R, 2002), 471.

incarnation is *not* the divine nature itself, nor was it the Father or the Spirit. The acting subject of the incarnation is the Word, the Son, who united himself to a human nature for the purpose of revealing the divine glory that he shares with the Father and fulfilling his mission to obey the Father's will even to death on a cross.[4] David Wells captures well how John has connected the deity of the Word with the incarnational revelation of God: "In the Word, then, we are met by the personal and eternal God who has joined himself to our flesh. In Jesus, the permanent and final unveiling of God has taken place, and the center of this truth is coincidental with the life of this man. Jesus is the means through which and in conjunction with whom God has made known his character, his will, and his ways (see John 14:6)."[5]

This point is reinforced by the *inclusio* that concludes the prologue: "No one has ever seen God, but the one and only Son, who is himself God and is in closest relationship with the Father, has made him known" (John 1:18). Although some in the OT saw visions of God (e.g., Exod 33–34; Isa 6:5), no one ever saw God himself. John now tells us that the unique Son (*monogenēs*) from the Father is the unique God (*monogenēs theos*) at the Father's side who makes God known to humans in grace and truth.[6] John places *theos* in apposition to *monogenēs* to call Jesus Christ the "one-of-a-kind son, God [in his own right]."[7]

In this way, John, along with the entirety of Scripture, teaches the exclusive, unique identity of Christ, which is precisely the ground for *solus Christus*. In the Bible's presentation of Christ, *he* is in an entirely different category than any created thing. *Jesus alone* is identified with the Creator-Covenant Lord in all of his actions, character, and work.

---

4.   See Donald Macleod, *The Person of Christ* (Downers Grove, IL: InterVarsity Press, 1998), 185–86.

5.   David F. Wells, *The Person of Christ: A Biblical and Historical Analysis of the Incarnation* (Westchester, IL: Crossway, 1984), 69–70.

6.   For a defense of this reading of the verse, see Köstenberger and Swain, *Father, Son, and Spirit*, 78.

7.   Ibid. Historically, *monogenēs* has been translated, "only begotten" (KJV) and used to explain the Son's "eternal generation" from the Father. Today, many doubt whether *monogenēs* by itself refers to uniqueness of origin (see Carson, *John*, 111–39). Usage in the NT does demonstrate semantic overlap among *monogenēs*, *prōtotokos* ("firstborn"; see Col 1:15; Ps 89:27), and *agapētos* ("beloved"; see Mark 1:1; 9:7; 12:6; Luke 3:22; 9:35; 20:13). However, the etymology of *monogenēs* connects it to *ginomai* ("become"), not *gennaō* ("beget"). So it is best to understand *monogenēs* as "the only member of a kin or kind" (Carson, *John*, 128), and thus when applied to Jesus, it means that he is unique, a "one-of-a-kind Son" (Köstenberger and Swain, *Father, Son, and Spirit*, 76; see Macleod, *Person of Christ*, 72–73).

Furthermore, in Christ, God's plan, promises, and purposes are ful-filled, and in his work, we see the resolution of God to take upon himself our sin and guilt in order to reverse the horrible effects of the fall and to satisfy his own righteous requirements, to make this world right, and to inaugurate a new covenant in his blood. In Jesus Christ, the Word made flesh, we see the perfectly obedient Son who is also the Lord, taking the initiative to keep his covenant promises by taking on our full human nature, veiling his glory, and winning for us our redemption. In him, we find the eternal Son, one with the Father and Spirit, who is now in his incarnation our new covenant head and Mediator.

What John reinforces in his prologue—namely, that Christ is *alone* in the exclusivity of his identity and the sufficiency of his work—we will continue to confirm in this chapter by unpacking Christ's exclusive identity from his own self-witness. We want to investigate what the Word says about himself. Our argument is that Jesus understood he is both the promised man-Messiah *and* the eternal Son of the Father. Jesus knew that he had come to do his Father's will to inaugurate the promised kingdom of God and to redeem a people for that kingdom by establishing a new covenant in his blood. The Son knew that he came to do the work of God as a man. Bottom line: Jesus knew that he is both God and man.

In chapter 3 we will reinforce Christ's unique identity by turning to the apostolic witness. As the men that Jesus authorized to continue bearing witness to him, they taught exactly what Jesus taught and what the entire Bible teaches: Jesus Christ is God the Son incarnate and therefore salvation is found in him alone. The NT writings form a pattern that puts the man Jesus Christ at the center of divine revelation and redemption as God the Son who alone could come to reconcile humanity and all creation to himself (see Eph 1:7–10; Col 1:15–20).

In chapter 4, we will conclude Part 1 by linking the Bible's presenta-tion of Christ's unique identity with his work. This will not only allow us to transition to Part 2 where we will primarily discuss Christ's unique, all-sufficient work, but it will also provide further warrant for the overall argument of this book for *Christ alone*. Because of *who* Christ is and *what* he does, the church must confess that Christ alone is God the Son incarnate and that Christ alone accomplishes the works of God and man that are necessary to complete the eternal plan of salvation.

In the following sections of this chapter, then, we will consider the implicit and explicit witness of Jesus to his own identity by considering how he understood certain events in his life, his relationship to the Father, and his place in the plan and purpose of God.[8]

Taking the Word at His Word

Whom did Jesus understand himself to be? Did he view himself to be God the Son incarnate? What is the biblical evidence that Jesus self-identified as the promised Messiah-Christ, the man who would come to do the works of God himself as one who is thus in a category all by himself? Before we answer these questions, it is necessary to make an important distinction. We must distinguish between Jesus's self-consciousness and his self-identity.[9] *Self-consciousness* is a psychological term that refers to a person's inner awareness, which includes multiple aspects, such as moral and religious desires, fears, joys, and anxieties. Most acknowledge that access to a person's self-consciousness is difficult, especially historical individuals who no longer can be interviewed. If we are trying to determine Jesus's self-consciousness, we will be disappointed or deceived because it is simply not available to us.[10]

Instead, we should think in terms of Jesus's *self-identity*. We do have access to what a person thinks about himself because, barring disability or deceit, people tend to act (and in Jesus's case, speak) according to

---

8.   For a similar development of biblical Christology, see Richard Bauckham, *Jesus and the God of Israel: God Crucified and Other Studies on the New Testament's Christology of Divine Identity* (Grand Rapids: Eerdmans, 2008). Bauckham rejects the evolutionary and developmental approach to Christology in contemporary scholarship. An *evolutionary* approach represents the Enlightenment and classic liberal theology, which argued that the earliest Christology evolved by adding on new ideas and claims that were not found in the historical Jesus but later placed on his lips by the church. A *developmental* approach argues that the earliest Christology was simply the outworking of what was always there in principle. Instead, Bauckham argues for a divine identity Christology, namely that the NT authors related Jesus to the strict monotheism of the OT by including him within the divine *identity* rather than as a second, separate "divine" figure. Given the strict monotheism of Israel, to identify Jesus with the name, character, and works of Yahweh is indeed staggering and it helps explain how monotheistic Jews could identify Jesus with Yahweh and view him as God-equal with Yahweh.

9.   See Wells, *Person of Christ*, 36–37; J. D. G. Dunn, *Christology in the Making: A New Testament Inquiry into the Origins of the Doctrine of the Incarnation*, 2nd ed. (Grand Rapids: Eerdmans, 1996), 22–33.

10.   Contra Dunn, *Christology in the Making*, 22–33.

their self-identity. So we can interpret a person's words and deeds to understand that person's self-understanding of who they are. But even with self-identity, we must be careful to interpret what the person says and does within the proper context. Generally, it is doubtful that we will ever know the entire context of an event in a person's life. Apart from a clear and explicit statement, then, we usually lack certainty in our interpretation of another person's self-identity. But regarding the self-identity of Jesus, we have the context we need. Jesus's self-understanding of *who* he is and *what* his mission is, comes to us within the Bible's storyline that forms the entire interpretive framework in which Jesus understands his own identity.

The Implicit Witness of Christ

In one sense, Jesus's entire life bore witness to whom he understood himself to be. But to bring his self-identity into focus, we will consider the five most significant aspects of his earthly life: his baptism, the kingdom he inaugurated, his life and ministry, his death and resurrection, and the worship he received. As we will see, Jesus understood himself to be God the Son incarnate so clearly that even his actions implied this particular divine-human identity.

Baptism

Jesus came to the Jordan and John the Baptist with the understanding that "it is proper for us to do this to fulfill all righteousness" (Matt 3:15). And upon his baptism, "he went up out of the water. At that moment heaven was opened, and he saw the Spirit of God descending like a dove and alighting on him. And a voice from heaven said, 'This is my Son, whom I love; with him I am well pleased'" (Matt 3:16–17). Jesus knew that to have the Spirit from the Father for the sake of righteousness signaled that he was the promised Messiah and that the messianic age had dawned—an age identified with God's sovereign, saving rule (Isa 61:1–2; Luke 4:16–21; see Ezek 34; Jonah 2:9).[11] As

---

11. See R. T. France, *The Gospel of Matthew*, NICNT (Grand Rapids: Eerdmans, 2007), 121–22; D. A. Carson, *Matthew*, EBC 8 (Grand Rapids: Zondervan, 1984), 106–10; Thomas R. Schreiner, *New Testament Theology: Magnifying God in Christ* (Grand Rapids: Baker, 2008), 172–73; Max Turner, *The Holy Spirit and Spiritual Gifts: In the New Testament Church and Today* (Peabody, MA: Hendrickson, 1997), 19–30; Sinclair B. Ferguson, *The Holy Spirit*, Contours of Christian Theology (Downers Grove, IL: InterVarsity Press, 1996), 45–52.

such, to be the Spirit-anointed Messiah according to the storyline of Scripture is to be identified with God himself, who must act to fulfill the OT expectation of redemption and restoration (Isa 9:6–7).

Significantly, the Gospel accounts make the man Jesus the recipient of the divine action at his baptism and focus our attention on Jesus's understanding of the event: "*he saw* heaven being torn open and the Spirit descending *on him*" (Mark 1:10, emphasis added). Jesus joined other men in John's "baptism of repentance" (Acts 12:24) to sympathize and align himself with their plight in his ministry of reconciliation between God and man. At the same time, however, God spoke to *this* man to declare, "'You are my Son, whom I love; with you I am well pleased'" (Mark 1:11). As a combination of Psalm 2:7 and Isaiah 42:1,[12] these words confirm that Jesus heard the Father tell him directly that he is the Son-King who will bring justice and righteousness to all the nations through the sovereign and saving reign of the Creator-Covenant Lord himself.[13] This event signals a functional identity with God. But given Jesus's virginal conception (Matt 1:18–25; Luke 1:26–38), the typological significance of his status as the "beloved" (*agapētos*) Son, and his ability to inaugurate the kingdom rule of God, the baptism of Jesus also implicitly testifies to his ontological identification with God (see also Matt 11:25–27).[14]

In the event of his baptism and the affirmation of the Father, then, the NT presents Jesus with the self-understanding that he comes as the promised Davidic Son-King to fulfill God's covenantal promises that culminate in the coming of God himself to save a people for himself. As David Wells comments, "It was visibly signaled and audibly declared. And the Synoptic authors plainly wanted their readers to understand this."[15] Even at his baptism and the beginning of his earthly ministry, Jesus self-identified as God the Son incarnate, the one man anointed and able to do what only God can do.[16]

---

12. See France, *Matthew*, 123–24; Carson, *Matthew*, 106–10; Schreiner, *New Testament Theology*, 172–73.

13. See France, *Matthew*, 119–21; Carson, *Matthew*, 107–8.

14. See Carson, *Matthew*, 109–10.

15. Wells, *Person of Christ*, 39.

16. This divine-human identity is also reaffirmed at Jesus's transfiguration (Matt 17:1–8; Mark 9:2–8; Luke 9:28–36).

Life and Ministry

Not only at his baptism, but also throughout his life and ministry, Jesus understood himself to be the eternal Son in unique relation to the Father and the only man to share the authority and power of God himself. While we cannot here consider every work of Christ between his baptism and ascension, Matthew gives us a clue that much of Jesus's ministry was encapsulated in his teaching and miracles. On two occasions, Jesus "went throughout Galilee, teaching in their synagogues, proclaiming the good news of the kingdom, and healing every disease and sickness among the people" (Matt 4:23; see 9:35). As Murray Harris observes, Matthew carefully places the two verses in the narrative as an *inclusio* to bookend and characterize Jesus's ministry up to his death.[17] And we must also recognize that the NT presents the works of Jesus as qualitatively (not just quantitatively) greater than everything that has preceded him.

In short, Jesus's teaching (Matt 5–7) and healing/miracles (Matt 8–9) are set within the context of the kingdom of heaven to imply that Jesus is God the Son incarnate. Jesus's teaching ministry highlights the authority he shares with God himself. It is through his teaching (in part) that Jesus brings the kingdom of God into this world in "this present age." Jesus is not presented as a mere man—even a sinless man—who is specially endowed by the Spirit with amazing wisdom and power. The OT brings forth numerous Spirit-empowered men who performed mighty works of God (e.g., Moses, Elijah). And in the NT, the apostles are commanded "to heal every disease and sickness" (Matt 10:1) and to teach and preach (Matt 28:20). The crucial difference, however, is that none of these forerunners inaugurated God's long-awaited and promised kingdom in their own words and works. But Jesus did, placing him in a different category than any previous prophet, priest, or king. In fact, everything that the apostles would say and do later on was based solely on the authorization and power they received from Jesus (Acts 3:6; 4:10; 9:34; Matt 28:18–20). Jesus gave his own teaching on his own authority—"I say unto you"—and he viewed his miracles as evidence that in himself God's supernatural reign had arrived.

---

17. See Murray J. Harris, *Three Crucial Questions about Jesus* (Grand Rapids: Baker, 1994), 82–83.

A good example of how Jesus understood the import of his teaching comes in how he related it to the OT law. One of the most important texts in this regard is Matthew 5:17–20. Debate has surrounded how best to interpret Jesus's words, "'I have not come to abolish [the Law or the Prophets] but to fulfill them'" (Matt 5:17).[18] But the best interpretation stresses the *antithesis* between *abolish* and *fulfill* to highlight that Jesus claimed to be the prophetic end toward whom all of the teaching of the OT pointed for its ultimate significance.[19] This interpretation understands *fulfill* to have the exact same meaning as its use in Matthew 1–2 (and elsewhere in Matthew), which relies on the prophetic function of the OT. The OT anticipates the Messiah and leads us to Jesus Christ, particularly through typological persons, events, and institutions. Jesus was not abolishing the canonical authority of the OT but correctly orienting it to terminate in his own authority. D. A. Carson explains that "the OT's real and abiding authority must be understood through the person and teaching of him to whom it points and who so richly fulfills it."[20]

Implied though it may be, the christological claim here is simply staggering. Jesus understood himself to be the eschatological goal of the entire OT and the sole authoritative interpreter of its teaching. In other words, Jesus self-identified as a man who shared authority with God, the author of the Law under his covenant with Israel.

Along with his teaching, Jesus's miracles bear witness to his unique relation to the Father. In fact, the healing and nature miracles performed by Jesus display both the authority and power of God himself. Jesus's healing miracles announce the arrival of the messianic age (Luke 7:22–23; see Isa 29:18–19; 35:5–6; 61:1) and manifest the supernatural rule of God coming in and through him. Jesus exercised divine authority over nature when he calmed the stormy sea by his command (Matt 8:26). He walked on the sea, and the waters were obliged to support him (Matt 14:25, 28–30). While these acts of authority and power simply amaze in isolation, they take on crucial christological significance as the storyline of Scripture comes out of the epochs and covenants of the OT. The development of the drama of redemption reveals that the

---

18. See Carson, *Matthew*, 140–47; France, *Matthew*, 177–91.
19. See Carson, *Matthew*, 143–45; France, *Matthew*, 182–84.
20. Carson, *Matthew*, 144.

Lord alone triumphs over the stormy sea (see Pss 65:7; 107:23–31) and treads upon its waters (Job 9:8 LXX; see Ps 77:19; Isa 51:9–10).[21] And in similar manner, the NT presents many other healings and miracles and even the exorcism of demons (Matt 4:23; 9:35; 10:7–8; Luke 9:11; 10:9, 17; 11:20) as an indication of Jesus's self-identification with God in authority and power.

So based on the miracles he performed, we can say that Jesus implicitly but also quite convincingly identified himself as the Lord by doing what God alone can do.[22]

Finally, in addition to his teaching and miracles, Jesus exercised the authority and power of God himself through judgment and resurrection. Jesus understood himself to be the man appointed by his Father to exercise divine judgment (Matt 7:22–23; 16:27; 25:31–33, 41; see John 5:22–23). Scripture is clear that judgment is the work of God alone (Deut 1:17; Jer 25:31; Rom 2:3, 5–6; 14:10; 1 Pet 1:17), yet Jesus knew he came as the appointed judge of all humanity and that his verdict assigns every person to either eternal punishment or eternal life (Matt 25:46; see John 5:29; 2 Cor 5:10).[23] In relation to this judgment, Jesus understood that he had the authority and power of the resurrection. The prophetic anticipation of God's kingdom and the new covenant age contains the hope of resurrection life (Ezek 37:1–23; see Dan 12:2; Isa 25:6–9), a hope based on the singular ability of God to raise the dead to new life (1 Sam 2:6; Ezek 37). Jesus knew he had received this divine authority and power directly from the Father: "For just as the Father

---

21. As Simon Gathercole, *The Preexistent Son: Recovering the Christologies of Matthew, Mark, and Luke* (Grand Rapids: Eerdmans, 2006), 64, explains, "The reference to walking on the sea is a 'theophany' motif which is taken over from Yahweh to Jesus . . . the combination of the two passages showing Jesus's mastery of the sea (Matt 14:22–33; Mark 6:45–52) points very strongly to a close identification of him with Yahweh in the OT."

22. This understanding of the significance of Jesus's miracles is different from those who teach that Jesus did most or all of his miracles by the power of the Spirit, and as such, Jesus's miracles are not evidence of his deity. For example, see Gerald F. Hawthorne, *The Presence and the Power: The Significance of the Holy Spirit in the Life and Ministry of Jesus* (Eugene, OR: Wipf & Stock, 2003); Garrett DeWeese, "One Person, Two Natures: Two Metaphysical Models of the Incarnation," in *Jesus in Trinitarian Perspective*, ed. Fred Sanders and Klaus D. Issler (Nashville: B&H Academic, 2007), 114–53; Klaus Issler, "Jesus's Example: Prototype of the Dependent, Spirit-Filled Life," in Sanders and Issler, *Jesus in Trinitarian Perspective*, 189–225. For a critique of this view, see Wellum, *God the Son Incarnate: The Doctrine of Christ* (Wheaton, IL: Crossway, 2016), 373–444.

23. By speaking of the judgment seat of God (Rom 14:10) and the judgment seat of Christ (2 Cor 5:10) together, Paul depicts not two judgments but one, which again highlights the close identity between the Father and Son.

raises the dead and gives them life, even so the Son gives life to whom he is pleased to give it. . . . Very truly, I tell you, a time is coming and has now come when the dead will hear the voice of the Son of God and those who hear will live" (John 5:21, 25).[24] Throughout his entire life and ministry, then, from his earliest teaching and miracles to his final acts of eternal judgment and resurrection to eternal life, the man Jesus self-identified as God himself—he knew he was God the Son incarnate.

Death and Resurrection

Jesus also self-identified as God the Son incarnate in his death and resurrection. As he approached his death, Jesus did not view it as martyrdom but as central to his divinely planned messianic mission. At Caesarea Philippi, after he blessed Peter for identifying him as the Christ, Jesus explained to his disciples that he *must* (*dei*) suffer and die and in three days rise again (Matt 16:21–23). Jesus knew that he would die. As John Stott comments, "Thus the Synoptic Evangelists bear a common witness to the fact that Jesus both clearly foresaw and repeatedly foretold his coming death."[25] But Jesus did not react with fatalistic resignation, as if divine sovereignty eliminated his responsible action. Rather, Jesus embraced his death as a voluntary, obedient act according to the will of his Father that was planned before the foundation of the world (Mark 10:45; see John 10:17–18).

Jesus understood, moreover, that by his death, "everything that is written by the prophets about the Son of Man will be fulfilled" (Luke 18:31). Thinking along the epochal and covenantal development of the OT, Jesus knew that as the Son of God he would through his death bring divine judgment upon the world, depose Satan as "the ruler of this world," and install himself as king over all creation for the sake of all people (John 12:30–33). And as the Son, Jesus understood that he could accomplish these divine works that would reconcile God and man because he had authority on earth to forgive sins (Mark 2:5–12; Luke 5:20–26).

---

24. Jesus also says, "'I am the resurrection and the life'" (John 11:25). In the context of John's Gospel, D. A. Carson explains that Jesus is claiming not merely that he has the power to resurrect and give life, but that "there is neither resurrection nor eternal life outside of him" (Carson, *John*, 412), which must be understood as a claim to deity.

25. John R. W. Stott, *The Cross of Christ*, 20th Anniversary Edition (Downers Grove, IL: InterVarsity Press, 2006), 34.

Wells sums up the identifying power of Jesus's death and resurrection with a rhetorical question: "His actions, in this regard, had an implied christological significance, for who can forgive sin but God alone? (Mark 2:7/Luke 5:21)."[26]

Praise and Worship

God alone is worthy of worship because of his metaphysical-moral perfections, and he demands this worship from his creatures as the one Creator-Covenant Lord. Indeed, no other being can cross the Creator-creature divide, and God is unwilling to share his glory and worship with any created thing (Isa 42:8). In fact, to worship the creature rather than the Creator is blasphemy (see Acts 14:14–15; Rom 1:18–23; Rev 19:10) and high treason against the Covenant Lord (Deut 4:17–20; 1 Kgs 11:1–11; see John 19:15).

As a man, however, Jesus received the praise of man and never rebuked his worshipers (Matt 14:33; 21:15–16; 28:9, 17; John 20:28). A person might bow down (*proskyneō*, sometimes translated "worship") before Jesus out of deep respect. But Peter rebuked someone who bowed down to him as an apostle in a similar context (Acts 10:25–26), and the angels know that it is categorically improper to bow to anyone other than God himself (Rev 19:10; 22:8–9). Yet Jesus never rejected this kind of worship when it was given to him on earth.[27] In fact, knowing that the Father had committed divine authority to him to judge as God himself, Jesus also understood the purpose of this power: "that all may honor the Son, just as they honor the Father. Whoever does not honor the Son does not honor the Father, who sent him" (John 5:23).

So Jesus not only received the honor, praise, and worship that should be given only to God; he also demanded it because he self-identified as God the Son incarnate.

Inauguration of God's Kingdom

In the Gospels, especially the Synoptics, the life, ministry, death, and resurrection of Jesus all focus on the kingdom of God. As we have

---

26. Wells, *Person of Christ*, 41.

27. For a helpful treatment of the worship of Jesus in the early church, see Larry W. Hurtado, *Lord Jesus Christ: Devotion to Jesus in Earliest Christianity* (Grand Rapids: Eerdmans, 2003).

just seen, all that Jesus taught, all of the miracles he performed, and all of the authority and power he exercised helped to bring the kingdom of the "age to come" into "this present age." The coming of the kingdom of heaven has been the plan of God throughout all the epochs of redemptive history and the promise of God developed through all of the OT covenants. By the time this plotline reaches into the NT, we expect that this kingdom will come as *God's* kingdom that he himself initiates *through* the Davidic king. It is God who must act in power and grace to save his people, yet he will do so through a human king, thus identifying the king with Yahweh, given the divine nature of the kingdom. It is quite revealing, then, for Jesus to appear knowing these kingdom expectations and claiming to meet them all. The works Jesus accomplished were so clearly linked to the inauguration of God's kingdom that if Jesus did not think he was doing the work of God himself, he would have been morally obligated to say so. As Wells observes:

> This "age" . . . was supernatural, could only be established by God himself, would bring blessings and benefits which only God could give, would achieve the overthrow of sin, death, and the devil (which only God could accomplish), and was identified so closely with God himself that no human effort could bring it about and no human resistance turn it back. If Jesus saw himself as the one in whom this kind of Kingdom was being inaugurated, then such a perception is a Christological claim which would be fraudulent and deceptive if Jesus was ignorant of his Godness.[28]

Much of Jesus's implicit witness to his self-identity, then, depends upon this important and unavoidable deduction: if the works that Jesus performed could be accomplished only by God himself, then by performing those works, the man Jesus implied that he is God himself. This divine-human deduction should not be disregarded for its subtlety. It might seem counterintuitive, but the indirect nature of Jesus's claim to be God the Son incarnate reveals the depth of his self-identity. The reality of his deity and humanity pressed into every aspect of Jesus's life on this earth, such that every word was spoken and every work was performed with the understanding that he was fulfilling the promise

---

28. Wells, *Person of Christ*, 38.

that the Creator-Covenant Lord himself would redeem humanity and reign over his creation in perfect righteousness.

Although Jesus never said explicitly in the Gospels, "I am God the Son incarnate," his implicit witness to this self-identity is no less convincing. The clarity and weight of Jesus's self-identity comes not from his words and works alone but from their place in the interpretive framework of Scripture. Jesus knew the structure and expectations of the OT, and he knew that he was the one to accomplish these works and receive the worship that is unique to God himself. So even though he may have never used these exact words, Jesus certainly self-identified as God the Son incarnate—so much so that every significant aspect of his life and death bore witness to it.

The Explicit Witness of Christ

In addition to the implicit witness of Jesus, the NT also gives us explicit statements by Jesus regarding his unique relationship with the Father and connection with his works. More specifically, the Gospels demonstrate that Jesus self-identified as God the Son incarnate.

Use of *Abba*

In each of the Synoptics, Jesus addresses God by the Aramaic term *Abba*, which reveals how he perceived his relationship to the Father (see Matt 6:9; 11:25–26; 26:39, 42; Mark 14:36; Luke 10:21; 11:2; 22:42; 23:34, 46). As Joachim Jeremias has shown in his study of the contemporary Jewish literature, "there is *no analogy at all* in the whole of Jewish prayer for God being addressed as Abba."[29] The reason for this reticence was due to the fear that one needed to give proper deference to God's holiness and majesty. Yet Jesus, as Wells notes, "with utmost regularity, addresses God by this term of intimacy and familiarity."[30]

In this regard, it is important to note how Jesus distinguishes his use of *Abba* from that of his disciples when he teaches them to pray, "Our Father" (Matt 6:9; John 20:17). Jesus views his relation to his Father as utterly unique, but as Paul later emphasizes, we call God *Abba* as *adopted* sons of God due to the work of Christ and our relationship

---

29. Joachim Jeremias, *The Prayers of Jesus* (Philadelphia: Fortress, 1989), 57.
30. Wells, *Person of Christ*, 43.

to him (see Rom 8:15; Gal 4:6). In other words, it is only because we are united by faith to the Son that we have access to the Father by the Spirit (John 1:12; see 14:6; 17:26; Rom 8:15). As such, our use of the term is only due to our adoption in Christ, but Jesus's use of the term is due to his eternal, unique relation to his Father, which is another way of underscoring Jesus's unique sonship.

By his use of *Abba*, then, Jesus understands himself to be the unique Son in relation to the Father. The precise nature of this sonship is not explained by his use of *Abba* alone; ultimately, the nature of Jesus's sonship is revealed in the entire plotline of Scripture. But when read within the structure and storyline of Scripture, it is clear that Jesus's sonship is not merely functional but also ontological. This point is demonstrated further in Jesus's use, understanding, and application of the title "Son" to himself.

"Son of God"

Far more than a generically descriptive phrase, *Son of God* functions in Scripture as a title that discloses the identity of the one who bears it.[31] The title appears throughout the Synoptic Gospels (Matt 3:17; 11:25–27; 28:19; Mark 1:1, 11; 9:7; Luke 1:32; 3:32; 9:35) and occupies a central role in John's Gospel (3:16, 17, 35–36; 5:19–23; 6:40; 8:36; 14:13; 17:1). *Son of God* is applied to Jesus at his baptism (Mark 1:11), temptation (Luke 4:9), and transfiguration (Mark 9:7; Matt 17:5; Luke 9:35). And the title is used to address Jesus by the centurion (Mark 15:39), the high priest (Mark 14:61), and the demons (Mark 3:11; 5:7). The title *Son of God* is so central to the identity of Jesus Christ that John wrote his Gospel "that you may believe that Jesus is the Messiah, the Son of God . . ." (John 20:31).

To grasp the significance of what Jesus meant by calling himself the Son of God, it will be helpful to think again in both functional and ontological terms. First, the NT does not hesitate to emphasize a strong functional aspect to Jesus's sonship, rooted in the typological figures of the OT—Adam, Israel, and the Davidic king. Building on

---

31. For a detailed treatment of the title *Son*, see D. A. Carson, *Jesus the Son of God: A Christological Title Often Overlooked, Sometimes Misunderstood, and Currently Disputed* (Wheaton, IL: Crossway, 2012); Graeme Goldsworthy, *The Son of God and the New Creation* (Wheaton, IL: Crossway, 2015).

this pattern, Jesus is the true Son who is the Last Adam, true Israel, and David's greater Son. In addition, by virtue of *what he does*, Jesus is appointed to be Son and Lord. By becoming incarnate (John 1:1, 14) and obediently identifying with us and representing us as our covenant head and substitute, Jesus brings about our eternal redemption. As a result of this work, Jesus takes up the title *Son of God* at a particular time in history (see Rom 1:3–4; Phil 2:6–11).[32] But Jesus's incarnational sonship culminating in his representative and substitutionary death for us is only half of the story. By virtue of *who he is*, Jesus has been the Son of God from eternity. Jesus's eternal sonship provides the basis for his incarnational and redemptive sonship.

Jesus regularly addressed God directly as "Father" (e.g., Matt 11:25; Luke 23:46; John 11:41; 12:28) and referred to him as "my Father" (e.g., Matt 16:17; 26:29; Luke 22:28; John 15:8). Even by themselves, these expressions go beyond a relationship of obedience to a relationship of begottenness. As a child, before he had accomplished the works given to him by the Father, Jesus spoke of his heavenly sonship to his earthly parents: "Didn't you know I had to be in my Father's house?" (Luke 2:49). And just before his death, Jesus prayed to God on the basis of his own life as the eternal Son of God: "And now, Father, glorify me in your presence with the glory that I had with you before the world began" (John 17:5).

Jesus certainly knew that he was appointed to be the Son of God in his incarnate life. By considering how Jesus addressed and referred to God as his Father, we can say that Jesus also knew he had always been the Son of God from eternity. And by reading Jesus's own words within the plotline of Scripture that he knew he was completing, we can see deeper into Jesus's self-identification as God the Son incarnate. Two examples will suffice.

In John 5:16–30, after healing a crippled man, Jesus responds to those who criticize him for working on the Sabbath: "My Father is always at his work to this very day, and I too am working" (v. 17). In Jesus's time, the rabbis agreed that God worked on the Sabbath without becoming a Sabbath-breaker. After all, if he did not, who would uphold

---

32. See Douglas Moo, *The Epistle to the Romans*, NICNT (Grand Rapids: Eerdmans, 1996), 44–53; P. T. O'Brien, *The Epistle to the Philippians*, NIGTC (Grand Rapids: Eerdmans, 1991), 205–53.

the universe? In other words, God's working on the Sabbath is an exception to the Sabbath law. So Jesus not only calls God his own Father in intimate terms, but he also makes himself equal with God by claiming the same authority as God to work on the Sabbath. And in the following verses, Jesus will explain that the validity of his Sabbath work is based on the divine nature of all his works, the divine worship warranted by these works, and the divine aseity of the one who performs these works.

The literary structure of verses 19–23 is framed around four *gar* ("for" or "because") statements. The first *gar* statement introduces the last clause of verse 19: "So Jesus said to them, 'Very truly I tell you, the Son can do nothing by himself; he can only do what he sees his Father doing, because whatever the Father does the Son also does.'" Jesus here makes three points about his Sonship grounded in his dependence upon the Father: the Son is *not* the Father; the Son does *only* what the Father does; the Son does *all* that the Father does. The Father and the Son are distinct from one another yet perform the same works. The Son does no less and no more than the Father—they are perfectly united in their work. As Carson observes, "Jesus is not equal with God as *another* God or as a *competing* God."[33] Rather, the Father always "initiates, sends, commands, commissions, grants; the Son responds, obeys, performs his Father's will, receives authority."[34] It is *this* eternal and intimate Father-Son relationship that accounts for Jesus's authority and ability to do as the Son all that the Father does as the Father. And it is *this* Son, the promised Image-Son whose identity has been progressively unfolded through the biblical storyline, who finally comes in the person of Jesus Christ.

The second *gar* statement explains the fundamental dynamic of this unique Father-Son relationship: "For [*gar*] the Father loves the Son and shows him all he does" (v. 20). Jesus speaks here of an intimate life with the Father that far surpasses any Creator-creature covenantal relationship. The relational dynamic that moves the Father to bring the Son into all that the Father is doing is divine love. This love is eternal and infinite; the Son has shared the Father's will, desires, and power without any limits of time or capacity. And yet this love is also temporal

---

33. Carson, *John*, 250 (emphasis original); see Köstenberger and Swain, *Father, Son and Spirit*, 87–90.
34. Carson, *John*, 251.

and incarnational in that some of the works given by the Father to the Son are to be accomplished as a man on the earth in the fullness of time.

The first two *gar* statements of John 5:19–20, then, establish that Jesus understood the divine nature of his own works that are possible for God alone. The next two *gar* statements will show that Jesus knew his works would bring him the worship that is proper for God alone.

In verses 21–23, Jesus explains in particular that the Father has given the Son the divine works of resurrection from the dead and judgment upon all humanity. Resurrection and judgment are the sole prerogatives of God (see Gen 18:25; 2 Kgs 5:7; Ezek 37:13; see Rev 20:11–15). For example, even the powerful prophet Elijah did not himself raise the Zaraphath widow's son, but he prayed to the Lord as a "man of God" (1 Kgs 17:19–24). In the third *gar* statement of John 5, however, Jesus claims the authority and power of resurrection as the *Son of God*: "For just as the Father raises the dead and gives them life, even so the Son gives life to whom he is pleased to give it" (v. 21). Moreover, closely linked to the divine power of resurrection is the prerogative of divine judgment. In the NT, the resurrection prepares all humanity to stand before God for judgment and proves that those raised with Christ (see Rom 6:4; Eph 2:6; Col 3:1) will not be condemned (see Rom 8:1). The fourth *gar* statement shows us that Jesus understood that *both* resurrection and judgment were given to him *for* God-only worship: "For [*gar*] not even the Father judges anyone, but He has given all judgment to the Son, so that all will honor the Son even as they honor the Father. He who does not honor the Son does not honor the Father who sent Him" (vv. 22–23, NASB).

It is important to pause here to grasp fully the christological significance of Jesus's claim for himself. This open claim by Jesus to receive the honor due the Father is based not on ambassadorial authority under God but on ontological equality with God. As Carson concludes:

> This goes far beyond making Jesus a mere ambassador who acts in the name of the monarch who sent him, an envoy plenipotentiary whose derived authority is the equivalent of his master's. That analogue breaks down precisely here, for the honour given to an envoy is never that given to the head of a state. The Jews were right in detecting that Jesus was "making himself equal with God" (vv.

17–18). But this does not diminish God. Indeed, the glorification of the Son is precisely what glorifies the Father, just as in Philippians 2:9–11, where at the name of *Jesus* every knee bows and every tongue confesses that Jesus Christ is Lord, and all this is to the glory of God the Father. Because of the unique relation between the Father and the Son, the God who declares "I am the LORD; that is my name! I will not yield my glory to another" (Isa 42:8; see Isa 48:11) is not compromised or diminished when divine honours crown the head of the Son.[35]

Based on the connections between the four *gar* statements in John 5:19–23, then, we can summarize Jesus's self-identity as follows: *He is the Son loved eternally and infinitely by the Father such that the Father has sent his Son to do the works of God himself temporally and incarnationally, specifically exercising the authority and power of resurrection and judgment, all so that the Son will receive worship as God himself.* In other words, Jesus understood that he was God the Son incarnate come to do the works of God as a man.

Moreover, in a later *gar* statement, Jesus explains further why he is able to give resurrection life: "For as the Father has life in himself, so he has granted the Son also to have life in himself" (John 5:26). In the context of John's Gospel and the metanarrative coming out of the OT, this claim to divine aseity must refer to the Son's eternal ontology, not to a function of his incarnation. As we discussed in chapter 3, aseity is one of the fundamental attributes that highlights the Creator-creature distinction. God alone exists by his own nature and power; all creatures, including all humanity, exist as a prerogative of God. Without entering into the debate regarding the eternal generation of the Son here, we must at least agree with Carson that Jesus understood that his power of resurrection flowed from divine aseity: "It is this eternal impartation of life-in-himself to the Son that grounds his authority and power to call the dead to life by his powerful word."[36] Simply put, the man Jesus understood that, as the Son of God, he shared in the divine nature.

Jesus also speaks of his divine-human sonship in Matthew 11:25–27, this time in terms of mutual knowledge and shared sovereignty with the

---

35. Ibid., 254–55.
36. Ibid., 257.

Father. After addressing God as "Father, Lord of heaven and earth" (v. 25), Jesus thanks God for concealing the significance of his miracles from some as an act of judgment upon their sin and revealing it to others as an act of grace. But then Jesus turns the spotlight on himself as the exclusive agent of God's self-revelation: "All things have been committed to me by my Father. No one knows the Son except the Father, and no one knows the Father except the Son and those to whom the Son chooses to reveal him" (v. 27). In an explicit claim to deity, Jesus affirms two realities that are unique to the Father-Son relationship. First, Jesus's claim to mutual knowledge with the Father, as Robert Reymond argues, "lifts Jesus above the sphere of the ordinary mortal and places him in a position, not of equality merely, but of absolute reciprocity and interpenetration of knowledge with the Father."[37] This intimate and comprehensive knowledge of the Father cannot come to Jesus as a man in consequence of his incarnational Sonship and messianic mission. The finite cannot comprehend the infinite. Rather, as George Ladd has argued, "sonship precedes messiahship and is in fact the ground for the messianic mission."[38] Second, Jesus claims to share sovereignty with the Father, whereby both must take the initiative to reveal each other in order for anyone to come to a saving knowledge of God.

Simply put, Jesus's self-identity as the Son must be understood in divine terms. In B. B. Warfield's words:

> Not merely is the Son the exclusive revealer of God, but the mutual knowledge of the Father and Son is put on what seems very much a par. The Son can be known only by the Father in all that He is, as if His being were infinite and as such inscrutable to the finite intelligence; and His knowledge alone—again as if He were infinite in His attributes—is competent to compass the depths of the Father's infinite being. He who holds this relation to the Father cannot conceivably be a creature.[39]

And yet, Jesus's divine self-identity does not contradict or diminish his self-identity as the Son of God in human terms.

---

37. Reymond, *Jesus, Divine Messiah*, 207.
38. George Eldon Ladd, *A Theology of the New Testament* (Grand Rapids: Eerdmans, 1974), 167.
39. B. B. Warfield, *The Lord of Glory* (reprint, Grand Rapids: Baker, 1974), 83.

So we can now bring together the ontological and functional aspects of Jesus's self-identity: Jesus understood that he is the eternal Son of God and that he became the incarnational Son of God. Jesus knew that he has always been the Son by eternal dependence upon the Father. Jesus also knew he came to fulfill the covenantal promise of the Father to bring forth his true Image-Son and the last Adam of the human race. In short, Jesus intentionally and explicitly identified himself to be God the Son incarnate.

"Son of Man"

Jesus also testified to his identity as God the Son incarnate by his most common self-designation, the *Son of Man*. The title is used in all the Gospels, and in every case by Jesus himself.[40] In order to grasp what Jesus meant by calling himself the Son of Man, it is crucial to understand it within the storyline of Scripture and its OT background.[41]

In the OT, "son of man" is used as a synonym for humans within the context of our role in creation (see Ps 8:4; see Num 23:19; Job 25:6; Isa 51:12; 56:2; Jer 49:18, 33; 50:40; 51:43). But as the biblical metanarrative unfolds through God's covenants with man, "son of man" refers more specifically to one who is unique among humanity. In Daniel 7, the title takes on the significance of a superhuman figure who functions alongside the "Ancient of Days," God seated for judgment. In Daniel's vision, four kingdoms of man appear as four beasts that terrorize the peoples of the earth. The kingdom of God, however, ultimately triumphs and destroys all rival kingdoms. And yet, in an unexpected turn after the destruction of every kingdom of man, God gives his own kingdom and all dominion over the nations to "one like a son of man" (v. 13–14). But *this* son of man is different from all others: he comes on the "clouds of heaven" (v. 13); his reign lasts forever (v. 14); and his reign gives dominion over the whole earth to his kingdom people (vv. 18, 22, 27). So we have in this son of man who comes from heaven the promised Son-king who will bring covenantal reconciliation

---

40. The title appears thirty times in Matthew, fourteen in Mark, twenty-five in Luke, and thirteen in John. Outside the Gospels, the term is used with reference to Jesus only in Acts 7:56, Heb 2:6, and Rev 1:13 and 14:14. The title is not used at all after Jesus's death, except in Acts 7:56.

41. See Schreiner, *New Testament Theology*, 213–31; C. F. D. Moule, *The Origin of Christology* (Cambridge: Cambridge University Press, 1977), 11–22.

between God and man, restoring man's righteous vice-regent rule over God's creation. Schreiner gives us the overall significance of Daniel's vision: "Indeed, the son of man in Daniel does not grasp rule through military conquest by which he brutally rules over other human beings. He is given the kingdom of God himself, and thereby he fulfills the role for which human beings were created (Psalm 8)."[42]

So when Jesus steps into *this* storyline as the self-designated Son of Man, he makes a clear statement regarding his identity. Jesus refers to himself as the Son of Man in (1) his ministry (Mark 2:10, 28; Luke 7:34; 9:58; 19:10); (2) his suffering and resurrection (Mark 10:45; Luke 17:24–25; 22:48; 24:7; John 3:14; 6:53; 8:28; 12:23; 13:31); and (3) his future coming (Matt 10:23; 19:28; 24:30; 25:31; Mark 8:38; 13:26; 14:62; Luke 12:8–10, 40; 17:22–30; 18:8).[43] And putting these Son of Man sayings together, we can conclude that "Jesus employed a term which has specific content in the Old Testament, but in applying it to himself and his work it came to have a meaning both larger and more complex than it does in the Old Testament."[44] To become the promised Son of Man, the Son of God came from heaven through incarnation, conquered Satan, sin, and death through crucifixion and resurrection, gives victory to his people through vicarious suffering and justification, and will return to bring eternal judgment upon all his enemies and reign forever with his people in righteousness.

As the Son of Man, Jesus again self-identifies as both God and man. Jesus uses the title in his humiliation as a man to save the lost (Matt 8:20; Mark 10:45), in his divine authority to forgive sins, and in his divine power to resurrect the dead (Mark 2:10; Matt 17:9). And Jesus refers to himself as the Son of Man in his resurrected-incarnational ascension to the throne of heaven (Matt 19:28) and in his future return as the king of heaven, "coming on the clouds of heaven, with power and great glory" (Matt 24:30).

Divine Purpose and Work

Even more explicit evidence of Jesus's self-identity as God the Son incarnate comes in how he understands the purpose of his coming. On

---

42. Schreiner, *New Testament Theology*, 216.
43. See Wells, *Person of Christ*, 80; Schreiner, *New Testament Theology*, 219–21.
44. Wells, *Person of Christ*, 80.

numerous occasions, Jesus offers "I have come to" statements (or an equivalent phrase) in which he reveals the various reasons for his advent and work on the earth. Simon Gathercole has provided what is probably the best treatment of these purpose statements in *The Preexistent Son*.[45] While Gathercole reaches many conclusions and implications, we need only consider his main arguments here by looking at a few examples.

The NT gives us eight statements by Jesus that declare why he has come. In two of these purpose statements, Jesus reveals that he came to serve others and offer his life as a ransom (Matt 20:28); and to seek and save the lost (Luke 19:10). As we have just seen, Jesus's self-identification as the Son of Man within the storyline of Scripture shows that he understood himself to be both God and the man to whom God would give his own kingdom for the sake of his own people. In these two Son of Man purpose statements, Jesus specifies that he came to do the God-only work of pastoral care for God's people. According to the unfolding metanarrative of the Creator-Covenant Lord's commitment to humanity, God himself promised to seek his sheep and shepherd his flock (Ezek 34). According to Jesus's self-understanding, he came as the Son of Man to fulfill this promise. As the divine-human Lord of the earth, Jesus says that he came to gather God's own people to himself.

In the six remaining purpose statements, Jesus declares that he came to preach the good news of the kingdom in Israel (Mark 1:38); to fulfill rather than to abolish the OT (Matt 5:17); to call sinners to himself (Matt 9:13); to bring a sword and division rather than peace to the earth (Matt 10:34); to divide family members against one another (Matt 10:35); and to cast a fire onto the earth (Luke 12:49).[46] In each case (especially Luke 12:49), Jesus understands his own identity in divine terms. Jesus came and preached with divine authority that was confirmed by attendant miracles; he came as the embodied righteousness of the kingdom of heaven; and he came to purify the earth by separating a people for himself in that righteousness.

Even more than these explicit statements, however, perhaps the most significant indication of Jesus's self-identity concerning the purpose and work of God comes in his forgiveness of sins. In Mark 2, Jesus tells a

---

45. See Gathercole, *Preexistent Son*, 83–189. I am summarizing Gathercole's work in my discussion.

46. Ibid., 84.

paralytic, "Son, your sins are forgiven" (v. 5). The religious leaders who charge Jesus with blasphemy are correct that God alone can forgive sins (v. 7). So Jesus does not challenge their theological reasoning. But he does challenge their theological conclusion that Jesus is not God: "Why are you thinking these things? Which is easier: to say to this paralyzed man, 'Your sins are forgiven,' or to say, 'Get up, take your mat and walk'?" (vv. 8–9). In explaining the point of Jesus's rhetorical question, R. T. France argues that "if the 'harder' of the two options can be demonstrated, the 'easier' may be assumed also to be possible."[47] Forgiving sins is harder because only God has the requisite authority and power. But Jesus's question "is not about which is easier to *do*, but which is easier to *say*, and a *claim* to forgive sins is undoubtedly easier to make, since it cannot be falsified by external events, whereas a claim to make a paralyzed man walk will be immediately proved true or false by a success or failure which everyone can see."[48] It logically follows, then, that "Jesus's demonstrable authority to cure the disabled man is evidence that he also has authority to forgive sins."[49]

France's explication is certainly true, but there seems to be more here. Jesus has stepped into the plotline of Scripture at a point where he can fulfill the plan of God by inaugurating the kingdom of God. Everything that Jesus says and does must be interpreted within this overarching purpose and work. Healing the paralytic, then, is proof that Jesus has authority to forgive sins *as the man in whom the saving rule and reign of God himself has finally come into the world* (see Matt 8:17; see Jer 31:34; Isa 35:5–6; 53:4; 61:1). As Carson notes, "This is the authority of Emmanuel, 'God with us' (Matt 1:23), sent to 'save his people from their sins' (Matt 1:21)."[50] Even the location of Jesus's claim reinforces his self-identification as God the Son incarnate. Jesus proves that he has the divine authority to forgive sins *outside the temple.*

The plotline, the scene, and the dialogue combine to reveal that the promised forgiveness of sin and covenantal reconciliation between God and man is fulfilled in the person of Jesus. The temple,

47. France, *Matthew*, 346.
48. Ibid.
49. Ibid.
50. Carson, *Matthew*, 222.

priesthood, and sacrificial system played their typological function to set the stage for God himself to come as the man Jesus to redeem a people for himself.

"I AM"

In addition to the purpose statements in the Synoptics, John's Gospel gives us the eminent "I am" (*egō eimi*) statements by which Jesus identifies himself with the Creator-Covenant Lord of the OT. When Jesus refers to himself as "I am" without a predicate (6:20; 8:24, 28, 58; 18:6), he connects his personal identity with the covenantal identity of Yahweh. In Exodus 3, God identifies himself to Moses as the "I am" (vv. 6, 14), which becomes the unique and personal name for God in his covenant with Israel and with David. And in Isaiah 40–48, the prophet uses God's covenantal name to make the point that as the one true and living God, Yahweh is unique and incomparable by nature (41:4; 43:10, 25; 45:8, 18, 19, 22; 46:4, 9; 48:12, 17). The *I am* is in a category by himself as the eternally self-existent being who alone is sovereign, omniscient, and omnipotent in contrast to the idols and false gods. The OT reserves "I am" for Yahweh; by definition, this name cannot apply to any mere man.

So when Jesus steps into the storyline coming out of the OT and refers to himself as "I am," he is making an explicit statement regarding his identity. In John 8, for example, Jesus concludes a particular controversy with the Jews regarding his origin and identity by declaring, "'Very truly I tell you, before Abraham was born, I am'" (v. 58). At this point in the developing covenantal plotline, the Jews are clinging to their descent from Abraham, who received the covenant promise of blessing from God. Jesus explicitly refers to himself as "I am" to reveal himself to be the God of Abraham.

As another example, in John 13, Jesus begins predicting the events leading up to his death so that "'when it does happen you will believe that I am [*egō eimi*]'" (v. 19). Schreiner makes the case that Jesus uses *egō eimi* here as the unique name of God—so "I am," not "I am he" as in most translations—and notes the christological significance: "The use of 'I am' demonstrates that such predictions are not merely the prophecies of an ordinary prophet. Jesus demonstrates his deity by proclaiming what will happen before it occurs."[51] In short, the man Jesus claims to be standing before the Jews as their Creator-Covenant Lord.

Jesus also identifies with Yahweh of the OT by referring to himself as the typological fulfillment of certain OT persons, events, and institutions. These particular "I am" statements, therefore, have predicates: the bread of life (6:35); the light of the world (8:12); the gate (10:7, 9); the good shepherd (10:11, 14); the resurrection and the life (11:25); the way, the truth, and the life (14:6); and the true vine (15:1, 5). In John 6, for example, Jesus declares, "'I am the bread of life'" (vv. 35, 48) to reveal that he is greater than the manna that sustained Israel in the wilderness because he gives eternal life to the people of God as a work of God himself (vv. 51, 58). And in John 10, Jesus declares, "'I am the good shepherd'" (v. 11), in contrast to a thief or mere hired hand. By using this predicate within the plotline of Scripture, Jesus is claiming to fulfill the role of Israel's kings to shepherd the people where all of those kings failed (Ezek 34:1–9). But Jesus also identifies with Yahweh, who promised, "'I myself will search for my sheep and look after them. . . . I will bring them out from the nations . . . and I will bring them into their own land'" (Ezek 34:11–13).

In all of Jesus's "I am" sayings, then, he continues to bear witness intentionally and explicitly to his self-identification as God the Son incarnate.

Our Object of Faith

Finally, Jesus explicitly makes himself the object of saving faith and trust that is reserved for God alone. The OT affirms repeatedly that "salvation comes from the Lord" (Jonah 2:9); "Truly he is my rock and my salvation" (Ps 62:2, 6); "My salvation and my honor depend on God" (Ps 62:7). The NT certainly does not contradict this convention; but the covenant security offered to God's people does expand to include the salvation, blessings, and peace available in Jesus Christ (see John 14:1; Acts 10:43; 16:31; Rom 10:12–13). In fact, the NT signals the significance of this expansion by focusing saving faith on Jesus while referring to God as the proper object of faith on only twelve occasions

---

51. See Schreiner, *New Testament Theology*, 253.

(see John 12:44; 14:1; Acts 16:34; Rom 4:3, 5, 17, 24; Gal 3:6; 1 Thess 1:8; Titus 3:8; Heb 6:1; 1 Pet 1:21).[52]

This shift to Jesus, however, does not mean that Jesus becomes a rival object of faith. Rather than replace God as the one worthy of our trust for our salvation, Jesus reveals himself to be God in the flesh, divine yet distinct from the Father. For example, in John 14, Jesus tells his disciples, "'Do not let your hearts be troubled. You believe in God; believe also in me'" (v. 1). As Jesus has moved ever closer to the cross, he has become deeply troubled in heart (12:27) and spirit (13:21). His disciples are greatly troubled, but for entirely different reasons. They are not facing the horrors of crucifixion like Jesus and cannot understand what Jesus will experience. It is enough, however, that Jesus's disciples know that he is leaving for them to fear losing him. The disciples have set their hopes fully on Jesus as the Christ, even if they do not yet fully grasp his identity. And rather than redirect them to God, Jesus encourages them that their belief in him is belief in God.

Within the developing storyline and covenants of the OT, which Jesus knows well, he can so confidently center his disciples' faith in him only because he knows he is God the Son incarnate. The NT presents Jesus as a model of faith in his relationship as a man with God. But before we can model our faith after Jesus, the NT and Jesus himself command us to trust Jesus as the object of our faith in his coming as the God of our salvation. As the apostles testify in light of the advent of Christ, "there is no other name under heaven given to mankind by which we must be saved" (Acts 4:12; see Acts 10:43; 16:31; Rom 10:9–11; 1 Cor 1:2; 1 John 3:23; 5:13).[53]

---

52. See Harris, *Three Crucial Questions about Jesus*, 77.

53. Our conclusion that Jesus views himself as God the Son incarnate differs from N. T. Wright. Wright has turned back unwarranted skepticism among biblical scholars regarding the accuracy of the NT's presentation of Jesus, but he denies that Jesus knew he was God the Son (see N. T. Wright, *The Challenge of Jesus* [Downers Grove, IL: InterVarsity Press, 1999], 96–125; idem., *The New Testament and the People of God* [Minneapolis: Fortress, 1992]; idem, *Jesus and the Victory of God* [Minneapolis: Fortress, 1996]). Wright contends that Jesus viewed himself as carrying out the vocation of Yahweh, yet awareness of vocation is not the same thing as Jesus knowing he is God the Son. Although there is much to commend in Wright's work, his conclusion does not account for Jesus's self-identity and the entire biblical storyline. Jesus views himself as the messianic "son" *and* the eternal Son who has come to fulfill his Father's will and to redeem God's people.

Listening to Christ Alone

We have seen in the implicit and explicit words and works of Christ that he has self-identified as both divine and human from his baptism and the beginning of his earthly ministry. Taking the Word at his word has given us the convincingly clear indication that Jesus knew he came from heaven to do as a man on earth what only God can do. Every aspect of Jesus's life and death demonstrates the intentional and incarnational accomplishment of the works of God himself. By making the specific claims he made and doing the particular works he did at the precise point he came in the storyline of Scripture, Jesus made a clear and overarching point: Christ alone is God the Son incarnate.

We do well, then, to listen to Christ alone in two ways related to our concern with the *Christ alone* of the Reformation. First, we should pay attention to Christ's self-identification because as God the Son, he gives us the divinely accurate and authoritative interpretation of who he is and what he has done for us and our salvation. Disregarding or misunderstanding the words of Christ can only lead to a failure to identify who Jesus is. And as we have seen, missing the identity of Jesus will rob him of the glory he is due and keep us from the salvation, comfort, and joy that are found in him alone.

Second, we should listen to Christ alone for our confession because as God the Son incarnate, he shows us how to interpret his exclusive identity and all-sufficient work in the plotline of the Bible. The words of Christ, then, give us hermeneutical instruction from our covenantal head on how to understand the contours of his identity and work. These words are absolutely necessary to help us not just recover the truth of the Reformers' *Christ alone*, but also to remain faithful as we confess the exclusivity and sufficiency of Christ in our own context.

To continue recovering and learning to confess *Christ alone*, we can now consider the apostolic witness of the men Jesus first taught and then authorized to extend his own self-witness into the world.

CHAPTER 3

The Apostolic Witness to Christ: God the Son Incarnate

In this chapter we continue to develop *Christ alone* in his unique identity by thinking through the apostolic witness. It should not surprise us that the apostles' understanding of Jesus's identity is based on Jesus's understanding of his own identity—they learned it from him. In fact, it is Jesus's own implicit and explicit words and works as God the Son incarnate that forms the theological foundation and motivation for the apostles' witness to his exclusive identity.

Given the limitations of this work, we cannot survey every biblical text that shows what the apostles understood about who Jesus is. A number of helpful books have been written that survey the apostolic teaching,[1] so we can focus here on four key texts that provide the main apostolic witness to Christ's unique identity: Romans 1:3–4; Philippians 2:5–11; Colossians 1:15–20; Hebrews 1:1–3. For our purposes, it will be helpful to discuss these particular texts because they beautifully illustrate *how* the apostles understand the identity of Christ. Following their Lord's reading of Scripture, the apostles interpret who Jesus is by placing his words and works at the climax of the Bible's covenantal-typological storyline. More specifically, the apostles trace how the Bible presents Christ as fully divine and fully human and unites his person with his work: who Christ is determines what he does; what he does reveals who he is.

---

1. See Richard Bauckham, *Jesus and the God of Israel: God Crucified and Other Studies on the New Testament's Christology of Divine Identity* (Grand Rapids: Eerdmans, 2008); Robert Bowman Jr. and J. Ed. Komoszewski, *Putting Jesus in His Place: The Case for the Deity of Christ* (Grand Rapids: Kregel, 2007); Gordon D. Fee, *Pauline Christology: An Exegetical-Theological Study* (Peabody, MA: Hendrickson, 2007); Thomas Schreiner, *New Testament Theology: Magnifying God in Christ* (Grand Rapids: Baker Academic, 2008), 305–38, 380–430.

Too often in theological studies, biblical texts are dichotomized, and this is especially true in the study of Christ. In recent years, a number of theologians have tried to identify Jesus according to a dominant but unhelpful dichotomy between his ontology and his function. In this kind of thinking, to speak of Christ's *ontology* is to stress Christ's deity over against his humanity. "Ontological" Christology, then, is identified with classical Christology as represented by the Chalcedonian Definition, which is claimed to diminish Christ's humanity. By contrast, to speak of Christ's *function* is to stress Christ's humanity over against his deity. "Functional" Christology, then, is identified with downplaying Christ's deity and thus with various departures from orthodoxy. One of its key assumptions is that Jesus is not the eternal Son, but he only becomes the Son by virtue of his work and appointment at his resurrection.[2]

However, in erecting this dichotomy between "ontology" and "function" in Christ, a wedge is driven between the divine and human natures of Christ that often results in the depreciation or complete loss of his deity. Furthermore, this way of thinking stands in opposition to the biblical presentation of Christ. Instead of separating Jesus's ontology and function, Scripture holds them together to bear witness to both Jesus's deity and humanity. Jesus's two natures are complementary and necessary to understand his identity, which in turn provides the biblical rationale for *Christ alone*.

The NT's refusal to pit Jesus's ontology over against his function is grounded in the Bible's storyline.[3] As noted in chapter 1, because the storyline moves from the OT to the NT, Christ's identity is first understood in terms of OT messianic expectation that unites the eschatological hope of the Lord's coming to save his people with the coming

---

2.   For a current discussion of this dichotomy, see Myk Habets, *The Anointed Son: A Trinitarian Spirit Christology* (Eugene, OR: Pickwick, 2010), 10–52. "Ontological" Christology is often identified with Chalcedonian orthodoxy while "Functional" Christology is identified with various departures from orthodoxy. For example, in regard to the latter, see James Dunn and Oscar Cullmann who argue that Jesus was appointed to sonship and lordship by virtue of his work and that he was not the Son or Lord prior to his resurrection (James D. G. Dunn, *Christology in the Making* [Philadelphia: Westminster, 1980]; Oscar Cullmann, *The Christology of the New Testament* [London: SCM, 1959], 3–4).

3.   See Bauckham, *Jesus and the God of Israel*, 31. Bauckham nicely demonstrates that the category of *divine identity* better explains NT Christology than the categories of *ontology* and *function*.

of the Davidic king. In the NT, we discover who this Messiah is: the eternal Word made flesh (John 1:1–3, 14), the one who has come to save his people from their sins as the "son of David" (Matt 1:1, 21). The OT, then, anticipates and promises the Messiah; the NT announces his arrival and identifies him as the Lord who is the great King.

Thus, the overall pattern of biblical Christology does not pit Christ's ontology (*who he is*) and function (*what he does*) against each other; instead, it unites them to reveal his exclusive identity: the divine Son who has become man in order to act on our behalf to save us from our sin and to do what no mere man could. For this reason the NT does not see the divine works performed by the man Jesus as a problem. Jesus's works, rather, are the key to understanding his true and full identity. For the apostles, Jesus's actions do not speak louder than his words, but Jesus's works do combine with his words in the context of certain kingdom promises and expectations to say something astounding about Jesus: he is the divine Son, the Creator-Covenant Lord come as a man to redeem humanity and restore the divine rule over all creation—that which *God alone* can do is accomplished by *Christ alone*.

By placing Jesus within the Bible's unfolding covenantal storyline, the apostolic witness follows a basic, unified pattern that stresses a two-fold truth regarding Jesus's sonship. *First, Jesus is Son and Lord because he is the eternal Son, the second person of the one, triune Covenant Lord.* This truth underscores the uniqueness of Jesus as the divine Son in relation to his Father and the Spirit. Ultimately, this truth grounds the Son's deity and provides the seedbed for Trinitarian formulation. Furthermore, this truth is also presented in terms of the storyline of the OT, which identifies Jesus with Yahweh as the one true and living creator God, the God of Israel, who alone must save. *Second, Jesus is Son and Lord because he becomes or is appointed as Son and Lord due to his incarnation, life, death, and resurrection.* This truth accents the reality and necessity of the incarnation and what Jesus achieves as the *incarnate* Son. Furthermore, it also picks up the storyline of the OT. As promised in the garden (Gen 3:15), typologically developed through the biblical covenants, and epitomized in the coming of the Davidic king (e.g., Isa 7:14; 9:6–7; 11; 42, 49, 53, 61; Ezek 34), redemption must come through a man. In his humanity, then, the divine Son fulfills the role of previous *sons* (e.g., Adam, Israel, David). As a man, Christ alone inaugurates God's long-awaited kingdom and the new covenant age. Yet the same storyline reveals that this last Adam, true Israel, and great Davidic king is able to do this work of an obedient covenant son because he has always been God the Son.

This two-fold truth of Jesus's sonship forms the basic pattern of NT Christology, grounding both the identity and necessity of Christ in God's eternal plan of redemption. A complete treatment of the theological implications of Jesus's sonship lies beyond our reach. For our purposes here, however, we can consider four key texts that provide the main apostolic witness to Christ's unique identity: Romans 1:1–4; Philippians 2:5–11; Colossians 1:15–20; Hebrews 1:1–3. These texts function together to provide the biblical-theological warrant for *Christ alone*.

Romans 1:1–4

[1] Paul, a servant of Christ Jesus, called to be an apostle and set apart for the gospel of God—[2] the gospel he promised beforehand through his prophets in the Holy Scriptures [3] regarding his Son, who as to his earthly life was a descendant of David, [4] and who through the Spirit of holiness was appointed the Son of God in power by his resurrection from the dead: Jesus Christ our Lord.

Romans 1:1–4 is a significant christological text. Some scholars argue that it is proof that Paul's Christology was adoptionistic; that is, Jesus was not the eternal Son but rather he *became* the Son at his resurrection. Opponents argue that since the participle *horisthentos* (the aorist passive of the verb, *horizō*) in verse 4 means "to appoint," then we should interpret from this passage that Jesus was *appointed* the Son at his resurrection. This interpretation, then, denies that Jesus was the Son prior to this event. James Dunn, for example, argues this view by linking Romans 1:1–4 with Acts 13:32–33 and its use of Psalm 2. Appealing to Psalm 2:7—"I will proclaim the LORD's decree: He said to me, 'You are my son; today I have become your father'"—Dunn argues that "today" teaches that Jesus's divine sonship should be viewed "principally as a role and status he had entered upon, been appointed to, at his resurrection."[4] And as such, Jesus's sonship was something he gained and did not always have.

Conversely, Robert Reymond, resisting any hint of adoptionism, translates the participle *horisthentos* as "was marked out" or "was designated."[5] Reymond also understands "the spirit of holiness" in verse 4 as a reference to Christ's divine nature. Taking these together, then, Reymond argues that the resurrection did not begin a new role or state for Jesus, i.e., transitioning him from the state of "humiliation" to the state of "exaltation." The resurrection, rather, simply marked out Jesus as the Son "in accordance with what he is on his divine side (that is, 'according to the spirit of holiness')."[6]

A third option, however, makes better sense of the text and accords with the NT pattern of Jesus's two-fold, divine and human sonship. We can summarize this view in three points.

First, Romans 1:1–4 teaches the Son's preexistence, which establishes his deity. By placing the phrase, "concerning or regarding his Son" (*peri tou huiou autou*) before the first of two participial clauses of verses 3 and 4, Paul underscores the Son's preexistence. No doubt the reference to Jesus as the "Son" recalls Israel's status as God's son (Exod 4:4).[7] But the title *Son* works at two levels: it designates Jesus as the historical Son who is the honored antitype of previous *sons*, but also as the eternal Son who has always shared the honor of deity with the Father. Recognizing both of these truths in this text, Thomas Schreiner explains: "The one who existed eternally as the Son was appointed the Son of God in power as the Son of David. . . . In other words, the Son reigned with the Father from all eternity, but as a result of his incarnation and atoning work he was appointed to be the Son of God as one who was now both God and

---

4.   Dunn, *Christology in the Making*, 36.

5.   R. L. Reymond, *Jesus, Divine Messiah: The New and Old Testament Witness* (Fearn: Mentor, 2003), 378–79.

6.   Ibid., 382. Reymond also argues two further points, which are difficult to sustain. First, "flesh," *sarx*, in v. 3 is a reference to Christ's human nature that is contrasted in v. 4 with "according to the spirit of holiness," which he understands as a reference to Jesus's divine nature (see 376–81). Second, he rejects vv. 3–4 as teaching "successive stages" in the life of Christ or inserting a contrast between what Jesus was *before* and what he was *after* his resurrection. Thus, the relation between the two participial phrases of vv. 3–4 is one of climax, not contrast, so that at the resurrection Jesus was not appointed as Son but displayed his sonship or demonstrated it in accordance with his divine nature (see 381–84).

7.   See J. D. G. Dunn, *Romans 1–8*, WBC 38A (Dallas: Word, 1988), 11–12.

man."[8] The apostle Paul, then, uses the pre-participial placement of the phrase, "concerning his Son," to affirm that this Son who *became* the seed of David and who was *appointed* God's Son in power *was already the Son* before these events.[9]

Second, it is best to render the participle, *horisthentos* (v. 4) as "appointed" or "designated" instead of "declared" or "marked out."[10] The emphasis of the verse is on the *appointment* of the Son *as Son* by God the Father because of the work of Christ. This does *not* entail a merely functional Christology. As Douglas Moo reminds us, "We must remember that the Son is the subject of the entire statement in verses 3–4: It is the *Son* who is appointed Son. The tautologous nature of this statement reveals that being appointed Son has to do *not* with a change of essence—as if a person or human messiah becomes Son of God for the first time—but with a change in status or function."[11] This point is tied to OT typological structures rooted in the enthronement of the Davidic king. As the Davidic Son and Messiah, God the Son incarnate comes as the Lord and as the antitype of the sons of the OT. And by his work, the Messianic age has dawned.

The work of Christ is performed "in power" such that it "appoints" him as Son, not in terms of his nature but in terms of his mediatorial role as the God-man. By virtue of his entire cross work, a new order is inaugurated in which the Son incarnate attains a new, exalted status as a man—he is appointed Son of God. Jesus, then, is Son from eternity and now Son in power. In him, the two eschatological strands of the OT come together: It is Yahweh who saves in and through his king (Isa 9:6–7; Ezek 34). As Moo explains, "The transition from v. 3 to v. 4, then, is not a transition from a human messiah to a divine Son of God (adoptionism) but from the Son as Messiah to the Son as both Messiah *and* powerful, reigning Lord."[12]

---

8. Thomas R. Schreiner, *Romans*, BECNT (Grand Rapids: Baker, 1998), 38–39.

9. See Schreiner, *New Testament Theology*, 38–39; Douglas Moo, *The Epistle to the Romans*, NICNT (Grand Rapids: Eerdmans, 1996), 46–47; Fee, *Pauline Christology*, 240–44.

10. See Moo, *Romans*, 47–48; Schreiner, *Romans*, 42.

11. Moo, *Romans*, 48 (emphasis original).

12. Ibid., 49. This understanding is further grounded in the fact that there is probably an allusion to Ps 2:7 in this verse: "You are my Son; today I have begotten you." In the NT, Psalm 2 is quoted a number of times and in quite diverse ways (see Acts 4:25–26; 13:33; Heb 1:5; 5:5; Rev 2:7; 12:5; 19:15). For example, Reymond argues, consistent with his interpretation

Third, this interpretation of the text is confirmed by the antithetical parallel between "according to the Spirit of holiness" and "according to the flesh." Some suggest that the flesh-spirit contrast is between Jesus's human and divine natures.[13] Others argue that "spirit of holiness" is a reference to Christ's obedient, consecrated spirit that he manifested throughout his earthly life.[14] A better suggestion, however, does justice to Paul's overall redemptive-historical framework: the contrast between flesh and spirit refers to a contrast between eras or ages in redemptive history. In this understanding, the old era is represented by Adam and dominated by sin, death, and the *flesh*; the new era is represented by Christ and characterized by salvation, life, and the *Spirit*.[15]

As applied to Christ, then, the eternal Son has now come and taken up our humanity to move redemptive history from the old age into the new. In his earthly life, his life in the realm of the flesh, Christ is the promised Messiah come into the end of the old age. And by his powerful work epitomized in the resurrection, Christ has brought with him the Spirit of the new age. Moo gives us a clear summary of this point: "In Christ the 'new era' of redemptive history has begun, and in this new stage of God's plan Jesus reigns as Son of God, powerfully active to bring salvation to all who believe (see 1:16)."[16] So the contrast is not between the two *natures* of Christ or his human nature and his consecrated spirit, but between the two *states* of Christ—between his state of humiliation and exaltation. While Jesus was on earth, "he

---

of Rom 1:1–4 and along with many in the early church, that Ps 2:7 in its OT context does not apply to the Davidic king but rather should be understood as a direct reference to Christ (Reymond, *Jesus, Divine Messiah*, 77–81). In this way, it is an address of the Father to the Son in eternity past, which for many in the early church was used as one of the proof-texts for the doctrine of the eternal generation of the Son. However, this interpretation is not necessary. A better view is to read Ps 2 typologically. In its immediate context, it is difficult *not* to read Ps 2 as a reference to the Davidic king. As each Davidic king was enthroned, so this psalm pointed forward to the day when the Messiah would usher in God's kingdom and all that it entails by his triumphant cross work and resurrection, exalting and seating him at God's right hand and giving him the name above every name. In this way, as Schreiner notes, the new dimension that results by virtue of Jesus's work "was not his sonship but his heavenly installation as God's Son by virtue of his Davidic sonship" (Schreiner, *Romans*, 39).

13. See Moo, *Romans*, 49.

14. See Reymond, *Jesus, Divine Messiah*, 378–81.

15. See Moo, *Romans*, 49–50; Schreiner, *Romans*, 43–45; Herman Ridderbos, *Paul: An Outline of His Theology* (Grand Rapids: Eerdmans, 1975), 64–68. The use of "flesh" in Paul is diverse but predominately tied to the old age associated with Adam, sin, and death, which is contrasted with the "Spirit" who is associated with Christ.

16. Moo, *Romans*, 50.

was the Messiah and the Son of God, but his death and resurrection inaugurated a stage of his messianic existence that was not formerly his. Now he reigns in heaven as Lord and Christ."[17] It is in this sense that Christ's resurrection constitutes him the messianic Son of God with power, "Jesus Christ our Lord" (1:4).

Romans 1:1–4 is a beautiful illustration of the two-fold truth of biblical Christology that stresses the deity and humanity of our Lord and rightly establishes *Christ alone*. Jesus is Son and Lord because he is the *eternal* Son and because of his work as the *incarnate* Son. The kind of Redeemer we need—one who can undo the work of Adam, accomplish our forgiveness, and usher in God's kingdom and the new creation—must be God the Son incarnate.

Philippians 2:5–11

[5] In your relationships with one another, have the same mindset as Christ Jesus: [6] Who, being in very nature God, did not consider equality with God something to be used to his own advantage; [7] rather, he made himself nothing by taking the very nature of a servant, being made in human likeness. [8] And being found in appearance as a man, he humbled himself by becoming obedient to death—even death on a cross! [9] Therefore God exalted him to the highest place and gave him the name that is above every name, [10] that at the name of Jesus every knee should bow, in heaven and on earth and under the earth, [11] and every tongue acknowledge that Jesus Christ is Lord, to the glory of God the Father.

This text has been at the center of heated christological discussions for a variety of reasons. In theological studies, it has served as an important proof-text for the "kenotic theory," a phrase taken from the Greek verb, *kenoō* (v. 7), that means "to empty." In the nineteenth century, a number of theologians advocated a view of the incarnation in which the Son gave up or "emptied" himself of some of his divine attributes in taking on our human nature.[18]

---

17. Schreiner, *Romans*, 42–43.
18. On kenoticism, see Oliver D. Crisp, *Divinity and Humanity* (Cambridge: Cambridge University Press, 2007), 122–39; Donald Macleod, *The Person of Christ* (Downers Grove, IL: InterVarsity Press, 1998), 205–12.

In biblical studies, a couple of important discussions have surrounded this text. First, much has been written on whether this text is a pre-Pauline hymn or original to Paul. Regardless of how one resolves this debate, most acknowledge that minimally we must accept it as representing Paul's own view and as such interpret it accordingly.[19] Second and more recently, some, like James Dunn, have proposed that the text is dependent upon an Adam-Christ contrast.[20] If so, then the text is simply contrasting the first Adam, who was in the image of God but tried to become like God, with the second Adam, who existed in the image of God but never strove to be equal with God. The text refers only to the human Jesus and his exaltation to an *earthly* position of glory; it does not refer to the preexistent divine Son who humbles himself by taking up our humanity.[21] The arguments against this view, however, are strong and the traditional view is better grounded.[22] Moreover, the traditional interpretation again accounts better for the text and accords with the NT pattern of Jesus's two-fold, divine and human sonship.

First, the structure of the text gives us guidelines for its interpretation. The text is broken into two parts, verses 6–8 and 9–11. In each section, two verbs describe Jesus's humbling himself in taking our human nature (i.e., the state of humiliation) and the Father's exalting him because of Jesus's victorious work (i.e., the state of exaltation).[23] The thought of the text, then, moves from the preexistent Son to his humiliation that results in his exaltation as the Son in a *new* role due to his obedience to the Father. The text is not describing how the Son gained equality with God but how, being equal with God, he still effected our salvation by a humiliating incarnation and willing submission to the Father on our behalf.

Second, the preexistence and deity of the Son is stressed by the phrase "who, though he was in the form of God" (*hos en morphē theou huparchōn*).[24] There has been much debate on the precise meaning of

19. See P. T. O'Brien, *Commentary on Philippians*, NIGTC (Grand Rapids: Eerdmans, 1991), 188–202.

20. See e.g. Dunn, *Christology in the Making*, 114–21.

21. See ibid., esp. 119.

22. See N. T. Wright, *The Climax of the Covenant: Christ and the Law in Pauline Theology* (Minneapolis: Fortress, 1992), 56–98; O'Brien, *Philippians*, 196–98; Fee, *Pauline Christology*, 375–93.

23. See O'Brien, *Philippians*, 205–32; Schreiner, *New Testament Theology*, 324.

24. O'Brien rightly observes that the relative pronoun *hos* links and identifies the

"form of God." And it is true that whatever is said of "form" (*morphē*) in verse 6 must also apply in verse 7 where the same word is used. But in recent years, P. T. O'Brien's treatment of the term is most helpful.[25] After surveying the use of *morphē*, O'Brien concludes that it refers to that "form which truly and fully expresses the being which underlies it."[26]

As applied to Christ, then, the Son has always existed in the "form of God" (*morphē theou*), which is another way of affirming the full deity and equality of the Son with the Father.[27] This text assumes and provides a contrast between two forms of existence and appearance of the Son: the majesty and glory he had from eternity as he shared in the divine glory as God the Son and what he became by taking the "form of a servant/slave" (*morphēn doulou*) (verse 7). The Son who was and remains eternally and fully divine has become fully and truly human as God the Son incarnate.[28] Macleod captures the heart of this contrast:

> The subject of the *kenōsis*, therefore (the one who "emptied himself"), is one who had glory with the Father before the world began (Jn. 17:5). . . . He possessed all the majesty of deity, performed all its functions and enjoyed all its prerogatives. He was adored by his Father and worshipped by the angels. He was invulnerable to pain, frustration, and embarrassment. He existed in unclouded serenity. His supremacy was total, his satisfaction complete, his blessedness perfect. Such a condition was not something he had secured by effort. It was the way things were, and had always been; and there was no reason why they should change. But change they did, and they changed because of the second element involved in the *kenōsis*:

---

historical Jesus with this Son who existed prior to the incarnation (O'Brien, *Philippians*, 206).

25. See ibid., 205–11.

26. Ibid., 210. This conclusion is indebted to R. P. Martin, who focused on the use of "form" (*morphē*) in the LXX. See R. P. Martin, *Carmen Christi* (Cambridge: Cambridge University Press, 1967), 99–120. Martin discovered that: (1) *morphē* denoted the appearance or form of something by which we describe it; (2) *morphē* and *eikōn* ("image") are used interchangeably; and (3) *eikōn* and *doxa* ("glory") are also equivalent terms. Taken together, this entails that *morphē* belongs to a group of words that describes God not as he is in himself but as he is to an observer. *Morphē*, then, does not describe God's nature *per se*, but it assumes the nature and it is a term that truly and fully expresses the nature that underlies it.

27. O'Brien, *Philippians*, 211.

28. See Bauckham, *Jesus and the God of Israel*, 41–42.

Christ did not insist on his rights . . . he did not regard being equal with God as a *harpagmos*.[29]

Third, it is best to translate the difficult phrase, *ouch harpagmon hēgēsato to einai isa theō* as "he did not think equality with God something to be used for his own advantage."[30] The issue is not whether Jesus gains equality with God or whether he retains it. The text is clear: the Son exists in the "form of God" and thus shares "equality with God" (v. 6).[31] Instead, the issue is one of Jesus's *attitude* in regard to his divine status.[32] As Schreiner points out, "Paul *assumes* that Jesus is equal with God. The verse does not teach that Jesus quit trying to attain equality with God. Rather, Paul emphasizes that Jesus did not take advantage of or exploit the equality with God that he already possessed."[33] In other words, the grasping or advantage-taking does not have equality with God as its goal; rather, it begins from that equality.[34] The emphasis of the text, then, is on the attitude of the preexistent Son who already is fully God. The Son did not regard equality with God as excusing him from the task of redemptive suffering and death; his equality with God uniquely qualified him for that vocation.

Fourth, in terms of the controversial phrase in verse 7, "but he emptied himself," we should understand it as a metaphorical expression that refers not to the subtraction or reduction of divine attributes but to the addition of a human nature. A clear and strong contrast is introduced by the voluntary act of the preexistent Son that ultimately takes him to the cross. But what is the precise meaning of the verb *ekenōsen*? Should it be translated "to empty" (NRSV) or "made himself nothing" (NIV, ESV)? What does this voluntary act consist of?

Before going further, it is important to note what the text does *not* say. Contrary to the extreme kenotic views, there is no hint that the Son emptied himself of his divine attributes or of the "form of God." Such views cannot claim this text as evidence for their position. The verb

---

29. Macleod, *Person of Christ*, 213–14.
30. Bauckham, *Jesus and the God of Israel*, 41.
31. For the argument that to exist in the "form of God" is parallel to being "equal with God," see Schreiner, *New Testament Theology*, 325; O'Brien, *Philippians*, 216; Wright, *Climax of the Covenant*, 72, 75, 80–83.
32. See Bauckham, *Jesus and the God of Israel*, 41.
33. Schreiner, *New Testament Theology*, 325 (emphasis original).
34. O'Brien, *Philippians*, 216.

should be understood in an idiomatic way—"to give up one's rights"—
and thus metaphorically (hence the translation of the NIV, ESV). But
even more clearly, the nature of the *kenōsis* is explained by two participial phrases that describe the manner in which the Son "emptied"
himself: (1) by "taking the form of a servant" (*morphēn doulou labōn*),
and (2) by "being made in human likeness" (*en homoiōmati anthrōpōn
genomenos*).[35]

Thus, the context itself interprets the "emptying" as equivalent
to "humbling himself" and *taking on* a lowly status and position by
becoming human and by choosing to die on a cross for us (v. 8). The
nature of the incarnation does not involve the subtraction or reduction
of the Son's deity but the addition of a human nature. The stress, then,
is not on exchanging the "form of God" for the "form of a servant
(slave)," but on the Son *manifesting* the "form of God" *in* the "form of
a servant." The text says nothing about Christ's "emptying" as the giving up of divine attributes; rather, it consists in the adding to himself a
complete human nature and in that human nature willingly undergoing
the agony of death for our salvation. As Macleod rightly concludes, "It
is what Christ *assumes* that humbles and impoverishes him: hence the
justice of Augustine's comment that he emptied himself 'not by changing His own divinity but by assuming our changeableness.'"[36]

Space forbids a more detailed reflection on the nature of the Son's
self-humbling, yet something more needs to be said regarding his state
of humiliation. Macleod notes that verses 7–9 stress three movements
in the Son's humiliation. First, it began with his taking the form of
a servant/slave (*morphēn doulou*) (v. 7): "He became a slave, without
rights: a non-person, who could not turn to those crucifying him and
say, 'Do you not know who I am?'"[37] In other words, the eternal Son,
who had all the rights of deity, became a nobody and willingly submit-
ted to his Father's will for us. Second, the incarnation involved the Son's
taking on our human likeness (*homoiōma*) and being found in human
form (*kai schēmati heurtheis hōs anthrōpos*) (vv. 6–7), which entails that
he became all that we as humans are, except without sin (see Rom 8:3).

---

35. See ibid., 218–23.
36. Macleod, *Person of Christ*, 216; cf. Augustine of Hippo, *On the Trinity*, trans.
Edmund Hill (Brooklyn, NY: New City, 1991), 7.5.
37. Ibid.

Just as strongly as this text stresses the full deity of Christ, it also, along with the entire NT, emphasizes the full humanity of Christ. One cannot think of Jesus's unique identity apart from him being fully God and fully man. Third, the emptying of Christ terminated not in his incarnation but in his obedient death on a cross (v. 8). Having fully identified himself with us in his incarnation, Christ willingly humbled himself in a final, climatic act of obedience—death on a cross! Apart from the emptying and humbling of Christ, there would be no salvation for us. But the emptied Christ, i.e., God the Son incarnate on a cross, bears our sins, satisfies divine wrath and justice, and secures our eternal redemption. Christ is Yahweh in the flesh who works and saves in a way that temporarily hides his glory. In this sense, then, we can say that *kenōsis* involved an obscuring of the divine glory of Christ, what many have rightly labeled *krypsis* ("hiddenness"), but without the loss of his deity.[38]

Of course, this is not the end of the story. Even though the glory of the Son in the incarnation and the cross is hidden by his flesh, that hiddenness is only our perception of it. God the Son did not become less than God. As he clothed himself in our human nature, he also bore our sins in that very nature. And in that act of obedience, he turned his great moment of vulnerability into the moment of greatest victory over sin, death, and the evil one.

Fifth and finally, verses 9–11 conclude where the passage began, with the Son exalted in the heavens. Only now every knee will bow, not just in heaven but also on the earth; and every tongue will confess not that God but that Jesus Christ is Lord in his "state of exaltation." In verses 6–8, Christ is the subject of the verbs and participles, and attention has been focused upon his self-humbling and obedience as the eternal Son taking to himself a human nature. Then in verse 9, the emphasis shifts to the Father's decisive action to exalt the Son *as a result of his work*.[39] It is precisely because of Jesus's obedience that

---

38. See Crisp, *Divinity and Humanity*, 118–53.
39. *Kenōsis* involved a real renunciation, but not of his deity. This is best seen in the temptation accounts, when Satan tells the incarnate Son to turn stones into bread, which assumes he can do so. And later, Jesus in fact exercises this kind of power in feeding the 5,000 in the wilderness and in other miraculous acts. Macleod points out the difference between the two incidents. "In the first, Jesus was tempted to use his power for himself. In the second, he used it for others" (Macleod, *Person of Christ*, 220). This distinction helps explain the self-humbling of the Son in the incarnation. Even though Jesus is able to exercise all of his divine

the Father now vindicates him by exalting him to the highest position, the heavenly throne of God.[40] The Father bestows on Christ the name above all names, which is his own name, Yahweh (Phil 2:9–11; see Isa 45:22–23). And with *this* name comes universal lordship and the worship of all creation. There is simply no way to do justice to these final verses, let alone the entire section, without affirming the full deity and humanity of the Son. Moreover, Paul's application of Isaiah 45:20–25 to Jesus—a text that refers exclusively to Yahweh—is part of a pattern whereby OT texts concerning Yahweh are translated "Lord" in the NT and repeatedly applied to Christ.[41]

Consistent with the NT pattern, then, Philippians 2:5–11 accords with the two-fold truth of Jesus's divine and human natures and identifies him as God the Son incarnate.

Colossians 1:15–20

[15] The Son is the image of the invisible God, the firstborn over all creation. [16] For in him all things were created: things in heaven and on earth, visible and invisible, whether thrones or powers or rulers or authorities; all things have been created through him and for him. [17] He is before all things, and in him all things hold together. [18] And he is the head of the body, the church; he is the beginning and the firstborn from among the dead, so that in everything he might have the supremacy. [19] For God was pleased to have all his fullness dwell in him, [20] and through him to reconcile to himself all things, whether things on earth or things in heaven, by making peace through his blood, shed on the cross.

It is an understatement to say that this text is "one of the Christological

---

prerogatives, he chose not to unless the Father allowed. As our Redeemer, Jesus chose to live his life so that he never acted for his own interest but always for ours.

40. See O'Brien, *Philippians*, 233–34.

41. In its OT context, Isa 45:20–25 engages in a polemic against idolatry, insisting that the God of Israel is the only true God. The allusion to this text in Phil 2:10–11 is impossible to miss. By the use of this text, Paul not only confesses that there is only one true God, but also that Jesus, the crucified and resurrected one, is the Lord—not in the sense that he is the same person as the Father, but that he shares in the divine rule and thus is equal to the Father in every way. As Schreiner concludes, "Clearly, Paul teaches that Jesus shares in the same divine nature as Yahweh himself, but Paul does this without denying monotheism or the distinctions between the Father and the Son" (Schreiner, *New Testament Theology*, 326–27).

high points of the New Testament."[42] Similar to Philippians 2:6–11, many have argued that it is an early Christian hymn that Paul adopted. Regardless of whether this is so, we must at least affirm that Paul has incorporated it into his letter and then interpret it as his own view. The text is divided into two main stanzas (vv. 15–17 and 18b–20) with a transitional stanza between the two (vv. 17–18a).[43] In the first main and transitional stanzas, Jesus is presented as Lord/deity because he is the eternal Son, the agent of creation, and the sustainer of the universe. In the second main stanza, Jesus is presented as becoming Lord due to his work as Redeemer. In both these ways, the lordship of Christ is presented in both creation and redemption. It will help to consider this text in three steps.

Step 1. The full deity of the Son is clearly taught in the first main stanza (vv. 15–16). Three affirmations ground this assertion.

First, the Son is described as "the image of the invisible God" (*eikōn tou theou tou aoratou*), which strongly suggests that he possesses the very nature of God. "Image" carries the sense of "something that looks like, or represents, something else."[44] As in 2 Corinthians 4:4, the stress is on the Son as the perfect revelation of God. "No one has ever seen God," writes John, but "the one and only Son, who is himself God and is in closest relationship with the Father, has made him known" (John 1:18). Paul here makes the same point by stressing that the Son, from eternity, has perfectly reflected the Father, and now in his incarnation reveals the invisible God just as perfectly. Only a divine Son can justify such an assertion.

Moreover, the use of "image" (*eikōn*) also suggests an echo back to the creation of humanity. In Genesis 1, humans are created as God's image bearers, designed to represent him in the world. However, we are not to think that we are the original image. Rather, the Son is the original image in accordance with which humans were created: he is the archetype and we are the ectype.[45] This is why God the Son, who was the perfect image of God, "is not only the pattern of our creation but in

---

42. Douglas J. Moo, *The Letters to the Colossians and to Philemon*, PNTC (Grand Rapids: Eerdmans, 2008), 107; N. T. Wright, *Colossians and Philemon*, TNTC (Grand Rapids: Eerdmans, 1986), 64.

43. See Moo, *Colossians and Philemon*, 114–16.

44. Ibid., 117.

45. See ibid., 118–19; see also Schreiner, *New Testament Theology*, 327.

becoming human has now taken on the role of the last Adam."[46] In this sense, as N. T. Wright notes, Jesus has from eternity "held the same relation to the Father that humanity, from its creation, had been intended to bear."[47] Humanity was designed to be a finite representation of God's self-expression within his world and to rule over creation under God's lordship. But sadly, in the first Adam, we failed. However, in Jesus, the one who has eternally borne the Father's image perfectly and completely now takes up our humanity in order to fulfill the purposes that God had marked out both for himself and for us (see Heb 2:5–18). As God the Son incarnate, then, Jesus Christ has also taken up the role marked out for humanity.

Second, the Son is "the firstborn of all creation" (*prōtotokos pasēs ktiseōs*). Since the Arian controversy in the fourth century, much debate has centered on the meaning of this phrase. At first glance it might suggest, as Arius proposed, that Jesus is the first creature in time and thus a created being. However, in the Nicene Creed, the church rejected this understanding and instead affirmed, along with Scripture, that Christ is the "firstborn" in terms of rank and authority.[48] The background to understanding the meaning of "firstborn" is the OT. There the term is closely linked to the right of the primogeniture. Israel is God's "firstborn" son (Exod 4:22), which entails their ruling the world for God. And the Davidic king also receives this title: "I will appoint him to be my firstborn, the most exalted of the kings of the earth" (Ps 89:27).

As Schreiner points out, in the case of David, he "was not the first Israelite king. That privilege belonged to Saul. Nor was David the oldest in the family; in fact, he was the youngest. Designating him as the 'firstborn' signals his sovereignty, and this is confirmed by Hebrew parallelism. The word 'firstborn' is elucidated by the phrase 'the highest of the kings of the earth.'"[49] In this way, "firstborn" has the connotation of "supreme over," which is precisely its meaning in Colossians 1:15.[50] And this interpretation is confirmed by verse 16—"for [*hoti*] by him all things were created"—which not only explains the fact that the Son

---

46. Wright, *Colossians and Philemon*, 70.
47. Ibid.
48. "Firstborn" (*prōtotokos*) can convey both the idea of priority in time *and* rank. Context determines its use.
49. Schreiner, *New Testament Theology*, 327.
50. See Moo, *Colossians and Philemon*, 119–20; O'Brien, *Colossians, Philemon*, 44–45.

existed before creation and is the agent of creation, but also that he is supreme over creation *because* he is its creator.

Third, v. 16 contains a third affirmation that further solidifies the deity of the Son. Not only is the divine work of creation attributed to the Son, but the extent of the Son's supremacy is also highlighted in his relation to creation: all things were created "*in* him, *through* him, and *for* him." All things were created "*in* him" (*en autō*) in the sense that all of God's creative work was "in terms of" or "in reference to" Christ,[51] which links the Son to the Father in the closest of terms and makes creation entirely dependent upon the Son. All things were created "*through* him" (*di' autou*) and "*for* him" (*eis auton*) in the sense that all things begin and end with Christ. The Son stands at the beginning as the *agent* of creation and at the end as the *goal* of creation.[52] The thought of this verse moves from the past (the Son is the agent of creation), to the present (the world owes its allegiance to the Son), and then to the future (the Son whose sovereignty will become universal). Again, we would be hard pressed to find stronger affirmations of the Son's deity.

Step 2. The intervening stanza (vv. 17–18a) continues to underscore the *deity* of the Son as it transitions to the glorious work of the *incarnate* Son. The opening line, "And he is before all things," looks back to verses 15–16 with its focus on the Son's relationship to creation, while the last line, "and he is the head of the body, the church," introduces a focus on Christ's redemptive work that is developed in verses 18b–20. The middle line, "and in him all things hold together," looks both directions, uniting the twofold presentation of NT Christology: Jesus is Son and Lord because of who he is *and* by virtue of what he does. In particular, verse 17 teaches the Son's preexistence and supremacy over the entire universe as its Creator *and* providential Lord. In other words, apart from the Son's continuous sustaining activity, prior to his

---

51. For a discussion of the preposition *en*, see Moo, *Colossians and Philemon*, 120–21; O'Brien, *Colossians, Philemon*, 45–46. Both Moo and O'Brien argue that the preposition in this case should be taken in the sense of sphere, "in him all things were created," not in the instrumental sense, "by him all things were created."

52. Murray Harris rightly notes that in v. 16, the verb "to create" is first used in the aorist passive (*ektisthē*) and then in the perfect tense (*ektistai*) (Murray J. Harris, *Three Crucial Questions about Jesus* [Grand Rapids: Baker, 1994], 80–81). This is more than stylistic. It probably underscores the emphasis that creation not only came to exist by the Son but that it now continues to exist by him (see Moo, *Colossians and Philemon*, 124).

incarnation *and* as the incarnate Son, the universe would disintegrate.[53] Even in the state of humiliation, the NT attributes to Jesus of Nazareth divine cosmic functions that underscore his identity as God the Son incarnate, thus making most kenotic views impossible.

Step 3. Turning to the second main stanza (vv. 18b–20), we see Jesus's work accented as God the Son *incarnate*. The same sovereign Creator and providential Lord is also head over his people, the church. Moreover, the Creator-Covenant Lord accomplishes this great work of reconciliation by his crucifixion and resurrection. As Schreiner explains, "Jesus rules over death because he was the first to conquer death."[54] In this way, he is the founder of a new humanity by his incarnation, death, and resurrection, so that "in everything he might have the supremacy" (v. 18). Thus, by his resurrection (which is tied to his entire work) Christ inaugurates a new order; "he is the beginning [*archē*]" and becomes the founder of a new humanity as "the firstborn from among the dead" (v. 18).[55] In Christ and his work, the resurrection age has burst forth and he has set the pattern for all those who have fallen asleep: he is the "firstfruits" who guarantees our future resurrection (1 Cor 15:20, 23). Thus, the lordship that is Christ's by right of his divine nature has now become his by right of his incarnational work, due to his inauguration of the new creation via his entire cross work for us.[56]

But Paul is not finished. In verse 19, he again stresses Jesus's deity as God the Son: "For God was pleased to have all his fullness dwell in him."[57] In other words, the Son is the place where God in all of his fullness was pleased to take up his residence and display his glory. As Moo notes, "In typical New Testament emphasis, Christ replaces the temple as the 'place' where God now dwells."[58] And O'Brien rightly adds, "All the attributes and activities of God—his spirit, word, wisdom and glory—are perfectly displayed in Christ."[59] This is not a temporary dwelling, either, as Colossians makes clear. In Colossians 2:9, the verb

---

53. The verb used, *sunestēken*, is in the perfect tense. Moo notes how "the use of the perfect tense suggests a stative idea: the universe owes its continuing coherence to Christ" (Moo, *Colossians and Philemon*, 125).

54. Schreiner, *New Testament Theology*, 328.

55. See ibid; Moo, *Colossians and Philemon*, 128–29.

56. See N. T. Wright, *Colossians and Philemon*, 73–75.

57. See O'Brien, *Colossians and Philemon*, 52; Moo, *Colossians and Philemon*, 130–33.

58. Moo, *Colossians and Philemon*, 133.

59. O'Brien, *Colossians and Philemon*, 53.

"dwells" or "lives" (*katoikeō*) is not only in the present tense, but the adverb, "in bodily form" (*sōmatikōs*) is separated from the verb, which Harris suggests entails two distinct affirmations: "that the entire fullness of the Godhead dwells in Christ eternally and that this fullness now permanently resides in Christ in bodily form."[60] Thus, what is true of God the Son prior to the incarnation is also true of him post-incarnation: the entire fullness of deity (nature and attributes) resides in him.

It is hard to find a higher Christology than this. In the man Jesus, the revelation and reign of God has dawned in order to accomplish God's re-creative and redemptive work. There is no sphere of existence over which he is not sovereign and supreme.[61] No wonder that all people are summoned to submit to him in trust, love, worship, and obedience.

Hebrews 1:1–4

[1] In the past God spoke to our ancestors through the prophets at many times and in various ways, [2] but in these last days he has spoken to us by his Son, whom he appointed heir of all things, and through whom also he made the universe. [3] The Son is the radiance of God's glory and the exact representation of his being, sustaining all things by his powerful word. After he had provided purification for sins, he sat down at the right hand of the Majesty in heaven. [4] So he became as much superior to the angels as the name he has inherited is superior to theirs.

The entire book of Hebrews is centered in Christology. From the opening verses to the close of the book, the main subject matter of the letter is the majesty, supremacy, and glory of the Son, our Lord Jesus Christ. Additionally, in Hebrews the basic pattern of NT Christology continues: Jesus is Son and Lord because of who he has always been (1:2–3) *and* by his work of taking on our humanity and fulfilling the role of Adam (2:5–18), David (1:4–14), and the High Priest (4:14–10:39), thus securing our redemption and inaugurating the promised "age to come." Hebrews places alongside one another the unqualified

---

60. Harris, *Three Questions about Jesus*, 66; see O'Brien, *Colossians and Philemon*, 110–14.
61. Wright, *Colossians and Philemon*, 79.

affirmation of the Son's deity (e.g., 1:2–3, 4–14) *and* his humanity. Jesus is from the tribe of Judah (7:14), he was vulnerable to temptation (but not to sin) as we are (4:15), he learned obedience as we do, and even though he was the Son (5:8), he still had to be made "perfect through what he suffered" (2:10).

It is crucial to note why Hebrews requires both the divinity and humanity of Christ. It is only as God the Son incarnate that the Son is able to inaugurate the promised age associated with the coming of Yahweh and Messiah, undo the work of Adam, and most importantly, fulfill the role of the great High Priest by perfectly representing us and accomplishing for us a full and effective atonement for sin (Heb 7–10). Even though Hebrews does not explain how the eternal Son became human, the author is vitally concerned to stress the full deity and humanity of the Son in order for us to have an all-sufficient Lord and Savior. For the Son's sacrifice on the cross to be efficacious, the Redeemer had to be both divine and human. That is why, as Wells insists, for the author an affirmation of Jesus's full humanity as well as sinlessness "was not an incidental matter (4:15; 7:26); it was the sine qua non for the Son's sacrificial mission. His pure humanity was as much necessitated by his pretemporal appointment as was his full divinity, for each was indispensable to his saving work."[62]

Hebrews establishes these truths in its opening sentence. Unlike other NT letters, the author dispenses with the usual greetings and lays out his thesis in a single, complex sentence, built around the main statement, "God . . . has spoken." As the author looks across the panorama of redemptive history, he speaks both of the "continuity" and "discontinuity" of God's work centered in the Son. He highlights the glorious identity of our Lord, an identity that he will develop throughout the remainder of the book. In so doing he intertwines the two complementary truths of NT Christology by stressing that Jesus is God the Son incarnate. We can consider this text in two steps.

Step 1. Through a series of three contrasts, the author asserts that God has spoken finally and definitively in these "last days" in his Son. The first contrast focuses on the eras of God's speaking: "long ago" versus "in these last days" (vv. 1–2). Along with the entire NT, the author

---

62. Wells, *Person of Christ*, 54–55.

divides redemptive history into two successive ages and views the Son as the one who inaugurates the "last days," i.e., God's sovereign rule and reign.[63] Implicit (if not explicit) in this affirmation is the identification of Jesus with Yahweh.[64]

The second contrast stresses the qualitative superiority of God speaking in the Son. "Long ago," God spoke "at many times and in various ways," but now, in the Son, God's speech is complete. This is not to say that the OT prophetic revelation was inferior (i.e., not fully authoritative); rather, the point is that the previous revelation was deliberately incomplete, fragmentary, and anticipatory.

This point is reinforced by the third contrast between the agents of revelation: "through the prophets" versus "by his Son," or better, "in the Son [en huiō]" (vv. 1–2).[65] By this contrast, the author presents the Son as more than a prophet; he is in a qualitatively different category. Once again, this is not to downplay the authority of the OT prophets; rather, the point is that the previous revelation was incomplete and intended by God to point beyond itself to its fulfillment in the Son. That is why the Son is greater: he is the one about whom the prophets spoke. Even more, the Son is the one in whom all of God's revelation and redemptive purposes culminate (see Eph 1:9–10). The OT prophets, priests, and kings all point forward and anticipate the final prophet, priest, and king; the sacrifices and ceremonies of the old covenant point forward to what has now come in Christ and the inauguration of a new covenant era foretold by the OT.

Step 2. The author identifies the Son as God incarnate to substantiate his claims that God speaking in the Son is far greater than anything that has preceded him and that the Son is precisely whom the OT prophets spoke of, longed for, and anticipated (vv. 2b–4). In fact, the author gives us five crucial identity statements.

First, the Son is described as the appointed "heir of all things" (v. 2b). It is best to understand this appointment similar to Romans 1:3–4 and in light of such OT texts as Psalm 2, especially given the fact that Psalm 2:7 is quoted in verse 5 as the basis for the argument that Christ

---

63. See William L. Lane, *Hebrews 1–8*, WBC 47A (Dallas, TX: Word, 1991), 10–12.

64. See Wells, *Person of Christ*, 21–66; Bauckham, *Jesus and the God of Israel*, 233–41.

65. See Lane, *Hebrews 1–8*, 11; George H. Guthrie, *Hebrews*, NIVAC (Grand Rapids: Zondervan, 1998), 46–47.

is better than angels.[66] Some early church fathers understood Psalm 2:7–8 to refer to the Son's appointment in eternity past, or what was called the eternal generation of the Son.[67] However, it is better to interpret Psalm 2 as a reference to the Davidic king, a type and pattern of the one to come. That is why the entire NT applies Psalm 2 to Jesus in terms of his appointment as the antitype of David (Heb 1:2, 5, 8–9, 13; 5:5; see Acts 13:33; Rom 1:3–4), who by virtue of his incarnation, death, and resurrection is now installed to God's right hand as the messianic king.[68] However, even though Jesus's appointment to be the "heir of all things" (v. 2b) is directly tied to his incarnation and saving work as a man, the author makes it clear that we must not think that the Son is merely another David (1:5; 5:5) or Adam (2:5–9) or Moses (3:1–6) or priest (5:1–10). He is also God the Son from eternity and thus identified as divine.

Second, the Son is now described as the agent of creation (v. 2b): "through whom also he made the universe." This description is consistent with other NT texts that attribute the *divine* work of creation to the Son, thus teaching his deity (John 1:1–3; Col 1:15–17). Moreover, it also speaks of the roles of the Father and Son in creation; it is *through* the Son that the world is made. God's work in creation is ultimately a triune work.

Third, the Son's full deity is further underscored in verse 3a: "He is the radiance of God's glory and the exact representation of his being." Two statements appear in synonymous parallelism to describe the Son's inherent divinity: "the radiance (*apaugasma*) of God's glory" and "the exact representation (*charaktēr*) of his being (*hypostaseōs*)." Taken together, these statements make one clear point: we cannot understand the identity of Jesus apart from affirming that he is God the Son and thus fully God.[69] In fact, this language so strongly affirms the full

---

66. See Lane, *Hebrews 1–8*, 12; Guthrie, *Hebrews*, 47; Schreiner, *New Testament Theology*, 380–81.

67. See Reymond, *Jesus, Divine Messiah*, 77–81.

68. See Schreiner, *New Testament Theology*, 380–81.

69. The terms *apaugasma* and *charaktēr* are found only here in the NT. The term *apaugasma* is best translated "radiance" or "effulgence," and not "reflection" (see Lane, *Hebrews 1–8*, 12–13). The emphasis is that the Son is the one who makes visible the very glory of God, something that only God can do (see John 1:14–18). As in John, so here in Hebrews the stress is on this point: as a result of the incarnation, the Son of the Father from all eternity now makes visible to us the Father's glory. The latter term, *charaktēr*, continues this same thought.

deity of the Son that in church history, as Wells reminds us, the Arians refused to recognize the authenticity of Hebrews on the basis of this text alone.[70]

Fourth, the Son is presented in verse 3b as the Lord of providence (similar to Col 1:15–17): "sustaining all things by his powerful word." In speaking of the Son upholding (*pherōn*) the universe, the concept expressed is dynamic, not static. The verb implies the idea of carrying something from one place to another,[71] such that the entire created order comes to exist, is sustained, and is carried to its appointed end by the Son. Attributing these cosmic functions to the Son describes his deity in unambiguous terms, identifying the incarnate one as God himself.

Fifth and finally, after stressing the *deity* of the Son, the author returns to his work as the *incarnate* one. The Son is now presented as the only Redeemer of humans, presupposing that he has taken on our humanity and accomplished a work for us as our great High Priest—a work that no human (or angel) could achieve. In this way, the Son is presented as the all-sufficient Redeemer: "After he had provided purification for sins, he sat down at the right hand of the Majesty in heaven" (v. 3). The use of the aorist participle, "having made" (*poiēsamenos*), underscores the once-for-all-time nature of the Son's purification for our sins.[72] While the Son ceaselessly radiates the glory of God and exactly corresponds to the divine nature, and while he continuously upholds the universe, he has now finished his glorious work for us as our High Priest. Furthermore, the Son's lordship is also stressed by the use of Psalm 110 in verse 3—a Psalm used extensively in Hebrews (see 1:13; 5:6; 6:20; 7:1–8:13). Significantly, the Son is identified with the heavenly throne of God and thus included in the unique identity of

---

Originally, the term denoted an instrument used for engraving and, later, the impression made by such an instrument. Used in this sense, the word "thus speaks of the features of an object or person by which we are able to recognize it for what it is" (Guthrie, *Hebrews*, 48). In the case of coins, for example, the term was used to speak of the exact reproduction of the image on the stamp (Macleod, *Person of Christ*, 80). In this context, then, as this word is applied to the Son, the author is asserting in the strongest of terms that what the Son represents perfectly is the very nature of God.

70. See Wells, *Person of Christ*, 53. The Arians denied the eternal preexistence and deity of the Son.

71. Hughes, *Hebrews*, 45–46.

72. See Lane, *Hebrews 1–8*, 15.

Yahweh as further proof of his deity.[73] Jesus is able to fulfill all of the divine-human roles and accomplish all of the divine-human work for us precisely because he is God the Son incarnate.

Accepting the Apostles of Christ Alone

The apostolic witness to Christ teaches the exclusivity of his identity and the sufficiency of his work. Grounded in the Bible's storyline and framework, Jesus is presented as the divine Son and the eternal *imago Dei* who, by taking on our humanity, is now the incarnational *imago Dei* and the man who fulfills all of God's covenant promises as his true Son-King and the last Adam. Ultimately, it is this understanding that establishes *Christ alone* and the *necessity* of his person and work. Because he alone is God the Son incarnate, Christ alone can accomplish the work that no one else can do. He restores us to our image-bearing role by virtue of who he is as the incarnate Son, our great and glorious mediator and new covenant head, and by his sin-bearing death and powerful resurrection.

The apostolic word is clear: in and through *Christ alone* salvation is found and all of God's promises are fulfilled; conversely, apart from him there is no salvation but only condemnation. One's relationship to the Jesus of the Bible, then, is a matter of life and death. It is for this reason that accepting the apostolic word is crucial in our daily lives. Given *who* Jesus is, receiving the apostolic instruction means that we must come to Christ alone by faith alone in complete trust, love, devotion, and obedience. The Jesus of the Bible not only demands it but he deserves it!

---

73. See Bauckham, *Jesus and the God of Israel*, 21–23, 233–53.

CHAPTER 4

From Incarnation to Atonement: An Exclusive Identity for an All-Sufficient Work

In the last two chapters we focused on Christ's exclusive identity by thinking through Jesus's own self-identity as God the Son incarnate before turning to the apostolic witness which confessed the same truth. In this chapter, we begin to transition from the exclusive identity of Christ to the sufficiency of his work by looking at the relationship between the two, namely *who* Christ is determines *what* he does; *what* he does reveals *who* he is. Let us begin to think about this crucial interrelationship which grounds *Christ alone* by turning to Anselm's famous question.

Why Did God the Son Become Man?

In the eleventh century, Anselm of Canterbury asked, "Why did God become man?"[1] The answer to the question is significant, to say the least. To answer it takes us to the heart of Christian theology and what J. I. Packer labels "the supreme mystery with which the gospel confronts us."[2] Of all the glorious truths of Christian theology, there is none more excellent and central than the truth that Jesus of Nazareth was "God made man—that the second person of the Godhead became the 'second man' (1 Cor 15:47), determining human destiny, the second

---

1. See Anselm's classic work, *Why God Became Man*, in *Anselm of Canterbury: The Major Works*, ed. Brian Davies and Gillian R. Evans (Oxford: Oxford University Press, 2008).
2. J. I. Packer, *Knowing God*, 20th Anniversary Edition (Downers Grove, IL: InterVarsity Press, 1993), 53.

representative head of the race, and that he took humanity without loss of deity, so that Jesus of Nazareth was as truly and fully divine as he was human."[3] It is a glorious truth *that* God the Son became incarnate. But here we are asking *why*. God does all things by his plan and purpose. So why the incarnation?

Turning to Scripture, the immediate answer is that the incarnation took place *for our salvation*. The angel told Joseph of the primary reason for the coming of Christ: "[Mary] will give birth to a son, and you are to give him the name Jesus, because he will save his people from their sins" (Matt 1:21). Picking up the new covenant promise of Jeremiah 31:34, the angel announced that the incarnation of God's Son is for the ultimate purpose of atonement, thus underscoring the biblical truth that there is an inseparable bond between *who* Christ is and *what* he does. In the incarnation, Christ identifies with us; the eternal Son becomes *like us*, yet he does so to act *for us*. Solidarity is not enough, as vital as it is, since "solidarity is not itself atonement, only its prerequisite."[4] Christ must identify *with us* in order to die *for us* as our new covenant representative and substitute.

Scripture goes even further to underscore both Christ's exclusive identity and all-sufficient work. Apart from the incarnation of a *specific* person and *his* atonement, we have no salvation. But why? Why did God the Son have to become man? Why was it *necessary*? And, furthermore, what kind of *necessity* was it? Was it necessary merely because of God's decree alone, or is there a deeper necessity tied to the very nature of God and the problem of sin?

In chapter 1 we suggested that the consequent absolute necessity of Christ was better than mere hypothetical necessity. The entire Bible teaches that Christ is unique because of *who* he is as the divine Son who has now become flesh (John 1:1, 14). Yet, Christ's incarnation is not an end in itself; it is a means to the end of fulfilling his mission—to do his Father's will, to accomplish God's eternal plan, and to do what was absolutely necessary to redeem us. No doubt there are many aspects to God's glorious plan: the inauguration of the kingdom, the dawning of the new creation, and the defeat of God's enemies. But at the center of

---

3.   Ibid. *J.I Packer Knowing God*

4.   Donald Macleod, *Christ Crucified: Understanding the Atonement* (Downers Grove, IL: IVP Academic, 2014), 80.

the eternal plan is the goal of restoring humanity to our image-bearing role, bringing us into a new and better covenant relationship with our Creator-Covenant Lord, and to do so by atonement that results in the forgiveness of our sin.

But why is the forgiveness of sin the focal point of God's redemptive plan? As the storyline of Scripture reveals, our greatest problem as fallen creatures/image bearers is our fractured relationship with God due to sin. Sin results in many disastrous effects, all of which are remedied by Christ and his cross. Yet, first and foremost the consequence of sin is God's judicial sentence against us and our state of condemnation before him (Rom 6:23; see 8:1; Eph 2:1–3). And given *who* God is in all of his triune self-sufficiency, holiness, justice, and moral purity, when God and human sin collide, the *tension* is unbearable. As Job rightly asks, "How can mere mortals prove their innocence before God?" (Job 9:2). Or, when Isaiah stands before the Lord seated on his throne, high and lifted up, he cries, "Woe to me! ... I am ruined. For I am a man of unclean lips, and I live among a people of unclean lips, and my eyes have seen the King, the LORD Almighty" (Isa 6:5). Simply put, it is no small matter for the triune Creator-Covenant Lord to choose to forgive the sins of his creatures. As the moral standard of the universe, God cannot simply deny himself; forgiveness of our sin ultimately requires that *God himself* must satisfy his own righteous demand against us, which is precisely what he has done for us in Christ and him alone.

We will consider it in more detail below, but at the beginning it will help to summarize in six points the biblical rationale for the necessity of Christ's incarnation and atonement: (1) as the offended party, the triune Covenant Lord necessarily demands just satisfaction from us for our sin against him; (2) yet in grace, God chooses to forgive us, not by overlooking but by punishing sin in humanity;[5] (3) the divine Father and Son agree that the Son will become a man and take the punishment for our sin; (4) the Son comes into the human race by incarnation, thus qualifying himself to become the last Adam and our glorious Mediator and Savior; (5) Christ offers to God an incarnational obedience and sacrificial death on our behalf as our covenantal representative substitute;

---

5. See John Stott, *The Cross of Christ*, 20th Anniversary Edition (Downers Grove, IL: InterVarsity Press, 2006), 89–162.

(6) the life, death, and resurrection of God the Son incarnate satisfies God's own righteous demands. From these summary points, then, it becomes clear that the incarnation and atonement of the eternal Son are absolutely necessary.

This truth is what Scripture teaches and Christian theology rightly confesses.[6] Christ's incarnation and atonement are not only interrelated, but they are inseparable. And so both the exclusive identity and the all-sufficient work of Christ are necessary for our salvation.[7] *Who* Christ is enables the kind of work he does, and *what* he must do requires who he is.[8] The church must confess *Christ alone*, both because he is unlike anyone else and also because he does what no one else can do.

In this chapter, we will explore and discuss this interconnection between the identity and work of Christ by looking at Hebrews 2:5–18. An exhaustive examination of this identity-economy connection deserves a full-length treatment, but for our purposes we can simply consider how Hebrews 2 answers Anselm's question long before he asked it. The author of Hebrews unpacks the reason for Christ's coming by encapsulating the Bible's entire storyline and explicating the inseparable bond between Christ's incarnation and his atonement.

The Biblical Rationale for Incarnation and Atonement

The entire book of Hebrews focuses on the majesty, supremacy, and glory of the Son, our Lord Jesus Christ. By expounding multiple OT texts and by a series of contrasts with various OT figures, the author encourages a group of predominantly Jewish Christians with the truth that Jesus has come as the Lord in the flesh to fulfill all of his promises and covenantal expectations. Structurally, Hebrews 1:1–4 serves as the thesis for the book: the Son is better, greater, and superior to everyone because in him God has finally and definitely spoken and the Son has finished his cross-work of "purification for sins" and sat down "at the

---

6. See Calvin, *Institutes*, 2.12.3, for the inseparable bond between Christ's incarnation and the atonement.

7. See the helpful discussion in Geerhardus Vos, *Christology*, vol. 3 of *Reformed Dogmatics*, trans. and ed. Richard B. Gaffin Jr. (Bellingham, WA: Lexham, 2014), 21–27; Herman Bavinck, *Sin and Salvation in Christ*, vol. 3 of *Reformed Dogmatics*, trans. John Vriend and ed. John Bolt (Grand Rapids: Baker, 2006), 364–77.

8. See Robert Letham, *The Work of Christ* (Downers Grove, IL: InterVarsity Press, 1993), 24–32.

right hand of the Majesty in heaven" (Heb 1:3b). In Christ's glorious person and work, he is presented as the unique and exclusive Lord and Savior—the final and perfect self-disclosure of God, our great high priest and conquering king.[9]

From these opening verses, the author, through a series of comparisons and contrasts, unpacks his thesis. Before he discusses such OT figures as Moses, Joshua, and the high priests and sets Christ's new covenant work over against the old covenant priests and sacrifices, he begins by arguing Christ's superiority over angels in two steps.

First, Jesus is greater than angels because of *who* he is as the divine Son become incarnate, having ushered in God's rule and reign. This Son has fulfilled all of God's promises, especially those associated with David and the Davidic covenant (Heb 1:5–14; see the author's use of Pss 2, 45, 110). The Son has a name/title greater than any angel (vv. 4–5), he is identified with the Lord and receives the worship of angels (v. 6), he has an absolute and unchanging existence as the universe's Creator and Lord (vv. 10–12), and he shares the eternal, righteous rule and reign of God (vv. 7–9, 13). Angels, on the other hand, are simply creatures and ministering servants (vv. 7, 14); they are not in the same transcendent category as the Son. Christ bears a truly exclusive identity in that no one is like him and no one can ever be like him.

Second, after a stern warning (2:1–4), the argument continues but shifts focus to the work of Christ. The author now explains that the Son is superior to angels because he has come to do the work that no angel could ever do. By taking on our humanity, the Son becomes the representative man of Psalm 8—the last Adam—who is now able to undo the first Adam's failure by his own obedient life and death. And in so doing, the incarnate Son ushers in the "world to come"—the new creation—bringing all things into subjection under his reign. In this short section, the author beautifully unpacks the Bible's storyline and demonstrates the inseparable bond between Christ's incarnation and atonement. In fact, he gives reasons why God the Son had to become a man, and argues that unless the Son had taken on our humanity, he could not have undone the first Adam's failure and redeemed us from sin, guilt, and corruption. Christ's incarnation and atonement, then, are

9.   See Thomas R. Schreiner, *Commentary on Hebrews* (Nashville: B&H, 2015), 51–62.

both necessary for our salvation. Apart from *who* Jesus is and *what* he does, God's purposes for creation cannot be fulfilled, we cannot enjoy covenant reconciliation with God in true sonship, and our enemies will not be defeated. All because our sin would remain unforgiven.

In Hebrews 2:5–18, the author then further develops his argument for the necessity and inseparability of Christ's incarnation and atonement according to a four-part rationale.

First, God the Son becomes man to fulfill God's original intention for humanity (Heb 2:5–9). The author demonstrates this point by an appeal to Psalm 8. In its OT context, Psalm 8 celebrates the majesty of God as the Creator and the exalted position humans have in creation. As one reads the psalm, he is challenged to look back to God's original design of creation and remember that God created man in his image and bestowed on him glory and honor by giving him the right to exercise dominion over the world as his vice-regents (Gen 1–2).[10] In fact, in transitioning from the quotation of Psalm 8:4–6 to Jesus, Hebrews stresses the honor and glory of humanity by emphasizing how God intended that all things be subjected to Adam and, by extension, to the entire human race: "Now in putting everything in subjection to him, he left nothing outside his control" (v. 8b). However, as we know from Genesis 3, human beings, in covenantal relation to Adam, failed in this task, and as a result, we are now under God's judgment. Hebrews makes this exact point: "Yet at present we do not see everything subject to them" (v. 8c), which is certainly an understatement. When we look at the world, we know that God's original design for the human race has been frustrated; we do not rule as God intended us to rule. Instead of putting the earth under our feet as God's kingly stewards, we are eventually put under the earth as God's rebellious image bearers.

Thankfully, this is not the end of the story. Just as Psalm 8 challenges us to look back to Genesis 1–2, it also challenges us, in anticipation, to look forward to God's restoration of the human race. Given its position

---

10. *Anthrōpos* ("man") in verse 6—"What is mankind that you are mindful of them, a son of man that you care for him?"—is a collective noun referring to humanity. Some interpret "son of man" as a direct reference to Christ. But given its OT context and synonymous parallelism, "son of man" is best viewed as a reference to Adam and the human race. However, in the storyline of Scripture Adam serves as a type, and the one who fulfills Adam's role is ultimately Christ. See P. T. O'Brien, *The Letter to the Hebrews*, PNTC (Grand Rapids: Eerdmans, 2010), 95–96.

in the OT, especially in light of God's *protevangelium* promise (Gen 3:15) and the unfolding development of his promises through the biblical covenants, Psalm 8 speaks prophetically. David looks forward to a day when God will restore humans to his original intention for us, a restoration that will take place through another man—one who comes from the human race and identifies with us, who acts on our behalf like Adam of old, but who, instead of failure via disobedience, gives us victory via obedience (see Rom 5:12–21). In him, the world to come arrives with all that is entailed by the dawning of the new creation.

This is precisely how Hebrews 2:9 applies Psalm 8 to Christ: "But we do see Jesus, who was made lower than the angels for a little while, now crowned with glory and honor because he suffered death, so that by the grace of God he might taste death for everyone." Jesus is presented as the antitype of Adam, the representative human being who experienced humiliation not merely due to his incarnation, but supremely in his death. Yet in light of that work, he has also experienced exaltation by which he won the victory for us. He succeeded where the rest of the human race failed. As Thomas Schreiner nicely states, "In that sense, [Jesus] is the true human being, the only one who has genuinely lived the kind of life that humans were intended to live under God."[11]

In the *man* Christ Jesus, then, the rule promised to humans has now been restored for us, and *this* is why God the Son *had* to become a man. Apart from the Son's identification with us by assuming our human nature, our Lord could not properly represent us and restore us. But by becoming man, our Lord became perfectly qualified to act as our covenant representative and to render obedience for us *as a man* in order to restore what Adam had lost in his disobedience. In these few verses, the entire story of Scripture is told. In Christ, we are now being restored to our position of glory and honor as God's image bearers, by the one who in his deity is the perfect image of God, yet now in his humanity restores us to our image-bearing role and thus makes us truly human again.

Second, and building on the first point, God the Son became a man to bring many sons to glory (see Heb 2:10–13). In the context of Hebrews

---

11. Thomas R. Schreiner, *New Testament Theology: Magnifying God in Christ* (Grand Rapids: Baker Academic, 2008), 382.

2, the word "glory" is not a reference to heaven; rather, it is a term from Psalm 8 referring to God's intention to restore us to what he originally created us to be. The imagery identifies Jesus with Yahweh who led Israel out of Egypt in the first exodus to make them into a people for his own possession and purposes. Jesus has now brought about the new exodus through his death and resurrection. As the "founder [*archēgon*] of their salvation" (Heb 2:10 ESV)—a word that conveys the idea of leader/forerunner and founder/victor—Jesus is now leading a people out of slavery to sin and death (vv. 14–15) and into the covenant life and representative reign under God that he has planned from the beginning.[12] Jesus is presented as the first man of the new creation. He is the trailblazer and the champion who has won the victory for new humanity by opening up new territory through his redemptive work.

This new exodus and the glory of a new humanity, then, depend upon the Son's suffering, which *requires* his incarnation, thus linking Christ's unique identity and work. To bring many sons to glory, "it was fitting that he [God] . . . should make the founder of their salvation perfect through suffering" (Heb 2:10). As Peter O'Brien rightly observes, the idea that the suffering of the Son "was fitting" corresponds to the fact that to help the offspring of Abraham, the Son "had to be" made like them in every respect (v. 17).[13] In other words, unless the Son took upon himself our humanity *and* suffered for us, there would be no suffering to help humanity, no fulfillment of God's promises for humanity, and no return to the planned glory of humanity. In the context of the first-century world where crucifixion was despised by the Gentiles as a public form of execution for the worst of criminals, or by the Jews who viewed a crucified person as under God's curse, the author stresses that Jesus's suffering and death was not a failed end to the incarnation but the precise purpose of the incarnation, all of which fulfills the triune Creator–Covenant Lord's plan to perfect a new humanity to rule over his good creation. Jesus's identification with us in his incarnation is only the first step to achieving our eternal redemption. Our redemption requires incarnational identification *and* atonement. Christ's identification and solidarity *with us* is a prerequisite to atonement, not atonement

---

12. See O'Brien, *Hebrews*, 103–8.
13. See ibid., 102–3.

itself. Both are necessary, and apart from Christ's incarnation and atonement there is no eternal redemption for God's people.

Moreover, this point is further reinforced by the author's statement that Jesus himself was made "perfect through what he suffered," or better, "through sufferings" (*dia pathēmatōn*) (Heb 2:10). The precise meaning of "perfection" (*teleiōsai*) in Hebrews remains a matter of much debate.[14] In the present context, however, it is best to understand *perfection* vocationally. As O'Brien argues, "Christ's being perfected is a vocational process by which he is made complete or fully equipped for his office."[15] In addition, "through what he suffered" is not synonymous with "suffered death" (v. 9), but it "designates the sufferings *through which* Christ had to pass."[16] And this entails the entire experience of suffering associated with and leading up to Christ's death.[17] In other words, in order for Christ to accomplish his work and to fulfill his office of Redeemer for us, he had to become one with us, and his entire incarnate experience qualified him to become our "merciful and faithful high priest" (v. 17).

Finally, this incarnate identification and suffering was necessary for "bringing many sons and daughters to glory" (Heb 2:10). God's fitting action of perfecting the Son by the incarnation and his suffering serves as the basis for a community of sons and daughters who are beginning to be restored to the very purpose of their creation. Both the Son as sanctifier and the sons who are sanctified are all of one origin (*ex henos pantes*, v. 11). And that is why "Jesus is not ashamed to call them brothers and sisters" (v. 11b). In other words, through the incarnation the Son came to share in the source and suffering of our human nature. And this incarnate identification and suffering was the only way to bring a ruined humanity into the glory of a new humanity.

What is important to observe is that without this action, there would be no salvation for God's people or the fulfillment of God's redemptive plan. Christ alone, because of *who* he is and *what* he does, is the only one who can accomplish God's saving purposes. No angel and no

---

14. See O'Brien, 107–8. For a detailed discussion of "perfection" in Hebrews, see David G. Peterson, *Hebrews and Perfection: An Examination of the Concept of Perfection in the "Epistle to the Hebrews,"* SNTSMS 47 (Cambridge: Cambridge University Press, 1982).

15. O'Brien, *Hebrews*, 107.

16. Ibid.

17. See ibid.; Peterson, *Hebrews and Perfection*, 69.

mere human can bring about this salvation work. Only the Son who becomes incarnate is able to meet our need and do the work that we could not do. As F. F. Bruce explains, "Since those who are sanctified to God through His death are sons and daughters of God, the Son of God is not ashamed to acknowledge them as His brothers—not only as those whose nature He took upon Himself, but those whose trials He endured, for whose sins He made atonement, that they might follow Him to glory on the path of salvation which He Himself cut."[18]

Third, God the Son became a man to destroy the power of death and the Devil (see Heb 2:14–16). The author of Hebrews directly connects the incarnation with the destruction of all that holds the new humanity back from its divinely planned and promised glory: "Since the children have flesh and blood, he too shared in their humanity so that by his death he might break the power of him who holds the power of death— that is, the devil—and free those who all their lives were held in slavery by their fear of death" (vv. 14–15). In short, the destruction of our slave-master and our deliverance from the cage of fear requires that, like us, the Son would come to "share in flesh and blood."

At this point, although the author emphasizes a strong *Christus Victor* theme, one must exercise caution in thinking that Christ's entire work can be subsumed under this category. In the Bible's storyline, it is important to remember the tight connection between sin, death, and judgment (see Gen 2–3). Today, as we will discuss in chapters 8–9, it is common to argue that the central *means* of the cross is *Christus Victor* and not penal substitution. Yet as important as *Christus Victor* is in Scripture for grasping the expansive glory of Christ's work, we must not so quickly and decidedly move to this entailment of the atonement that we miss its center.[19]

According to Scripture, death is not normal to God's original creation; rather, it is the result of human sin (Gen 2:17) and God's judicial sentence and penalty for our disobedience (see Rom 6:23). As a result of our sin and death, God, in judgment against his rebellious vice-regents,

---

18.   F. F. Bruce, *The Epistle to the Hebrews*, NICNT (Grand Rapids: Eerdmans, 1964), 45.

19.   On the distinction between viewing the atonement in terms of *outcome* and *means* (or its internal mechanism), see Jeremy R. Treat, *The Crucified King: Atonement and Kingdom in Biblical and Systematic Theology* (Grand Rapids: Zondervan, 2014), 45–50, 174–226.

gave us over to the power of Satan (see 2 Cor 4:4; Eph 2:1–3; Col 1:13). Created to rule over God's creation as his image bearers, we now cower in fear before God as those who are spiritually dead, which ultimately shows itself in our physical death and Satan's power over us. Our only hope, then, is found in a deliverer, a "pioneer" (Heb 2:10) who goes before us and defeats our enemies. But in order to defeat our enemies, our deliverer and champion must deal with the problem of sin and death by sharing, suffering, and dying in our humanity.

As the author of Hebrews unpacks the glory of Christ's work, it almost sounds like an oxymoron. Through death, Jesus destroys death! How can that be? Usually death is viewed as defeat and not victory. But thankfully, our covenant mediator's death is the means of his victory over death. Because of who he is and what he does, Jesus's death defeats death. Death is only our enemy because we are sinners before God. But in obeying for us as our representative and dying for us as our penal substitute—the just for the unjust—Christ removes the sting of death. This is why the grave could not hold our Lord: his death paid for sin in full, leaving no cause for death such that resurrection necessarily followed.[20] This is why Jesus can triumphantly proclaim as the crucified and risen Lord, "Do not be afraid. I am the First and the Last. I am the Living One; I was dead, and now look, I am alive for ever and ever! And I hold the keys of death and Hades" (Rev 1:17b–18). In fact, that is why we who are united to Christ can confidently proclaim, "Where, O death, is your victory? Where, O death, is your sting? The sting of death is sin, and the power of sin is the law. But thanks be to God! He gives us the victory through our Lord Jesus Christ" (1 Cor 15:55–57). O'Brien captures the point of these verses by explaining, "Only through his incarnation and death could the Son effect God's ultimate purpose for these members of his family—a purpose that is described in terms of their being glorified (v. 10), sanctified (v. 11), liberated (v. 15), and purified from sins (v. 17)."[21]

Why, then, did God the Son become man? The incarnation was the necessary means by which the eternal Son became our all-sufficient

---

20. It is important to note that I am treating the cross and resurrection as inseparable events in Christ's *one* work. The cross *and* resurrection are necessary for our justification but necessary in distinct (though inseparable) ways.

21. O'Brien, *Hebrews*, 113.

Redeemer and Lord. Jesus is able to redeem humanity precisely because he came to share in our common human nature. It is not angels he helps, or better, "takes hold of" (*epilambanomai*), since he does not identify with or take on the nature of an angel. Rather, the Son identifies with the offspring of Abraham, his people, and leads them to glory in a new exodus of victory and triumph.[22] By his incarnation and atonement, the Son becomes our victor who wins the battle, and apart from him there is no salvation. Our plight is so desperate due to sin that it requires nothing less than the enfleshment of God's own unique Son. But even more: our plight is so desperate that it not only requires the Son to become a man, but it also requires that he act in that same humanity as our covenant representative in life and in death. The only way we can be restored to the glory of a new humanity and brought back into full covenant relationship with God is through Christ and him alone.

Fourth, God the Son became a man to become a merciful and faithful high priest (see Heb 2:17–18). The mention of Jesus as our high priest serves a twofold function. First, it introduces the readers to one of the major themes of Hebrews which the author will develop in greater detail (4:14–5:10; 7:1–10:25), a point I will return to below in more detail in chapters 5–8. Hebrews, like no other NT book, presents Christ as our great high priest. More importantly for our current interest, its description of Jesus as our great high priest serves as the capstone on the argument for the purpose and necessity of the incarnation. The author begins by stressing both the mandatory and the comprehensive nature of the incarnation: "Therefore [*hothen*, "for this reason"] he had [*ōpheilen*] to be made like [*homoiōthēnai*] his brothers in every respect [*kata panta*]" (Heb 2:17a ESV). In other words, to become incarnate according to the plan of God, the Son could not take on a partial or pseudo human nature. The Son was under obligation (*ōpheilen*) by the Father to take on a human nature (*homoiōthēnai*) that exactly corresponds to every aspect of our human nature (*kanta panta*), except for sin.[23]

Why this necessity? Two reasons are given in two purpose clauses, clauses that are linked to the entire argument of the author starting in verse 5: God the Son had to become man, (1) "in order that he

---

22. On the exodus theme, see ibid., 116–18.
23. See ibid., 118–22.

might become a merciful and faithful high priest in service to God"; and (2) "to make propitiation for (*hilaskesthai*) the sins (*tas hamartias*) of the people" (Heb 2:17b).[24] Or, to state it in the language of the early church, the Son had to become flesh because "he could not redeem what he did not assume." Representation requires identification.[25] If the Son did not become one with us in every way, he could not redeem us in every way. Only by the Son's becoming man could he become our perfect high priest; in light of the previous verses, only through the incarnation could he function as the obedient Son, reversing the effects of sin and death, defeating the power of the evil one, and bringing many sons to glory. The incarnation, then, is essential to the Son's entire work to fulfill the Father's plan—a plan before the foundation of the world— and to win for us our salvation as our covenant mediator and head.[26]

Given how the author has developed his argument within the Bible's storyline, is it any surprise that he presents Jesus as greater than angels—indeed, greater than any created thing? In the case of angels, they cannot represent us, nor can they act as our penal substitute. No angel is sufficient to stand in our place, to satisfy God's own righteous demands, and to turn away God's wrath by the bearing of our sin. Only Jesus can satisfy God's own righteous requirements because he is one with the Lord as God the Son; only Christ alone can do this for us because he is truly a man and can represent us. Identification requires representation, and in all these ways our Lord is perfectly suited to meet our every need and to save us completely (Heb 7:25).

But as Hebrews 2:18 also reminds us, Jesus, our all-sufficient Lord and Redeemer, is also our helper: "Because he himself suffered when he was tempted, he is able to help those who are being tempted." The

---

24. There is considerable debate over how the verb *hilaskesthai* with the object "sins" should be understood. Does it mean: (1) "to make expiation for" (RSV); (2) "to make atonement for" (NIV); (3) "to make propitiation for" (ESV)? In context, it refers to expiation, but expiation is only through propitiation. See Macleod, *Christ Crucified*, 101–50.

25. John of Damascus represents this view: "For the whole Christ assumed the whole me that he might grant salvation to the whole me, for what is unassumable is incurable" (cited in Bavinck, *Sin and Salvation in Christ*, 297). Also see Gregory of Nazianzus, who states in response to Apollinarianism, "What he has not assumed he has not healed" (Epistle 101, 'To Cledonius the Priest against the Apollinarians" in http://www.newadvent.org/fathers/3103a.htm).

26. In Hebrews, this point is developed in the type-antitype high priestly relationship (Heb 5:1–10; 7:1–10:25). In Heb 5:1, a summary of the priestly office is given, which Jesus perfectly fulfills, which we will discuss in chapter 8.

author draws special attention to the fact that Jesus himself suffered and that this suffering perfectly qualifies him to help us when we are tempted—help in finally putting away our sin and giving us strength. In this way, Jesus, in his humanity, serves as an example and source of strength for us in our time of need. He knows what it means to be fully tempted; he also knows what it means to overcome by dependence on his Father and reliance on the Spirit. When Christians feel alone, facing trials and struggles too difficult to share, we know there is one who understands and is able to help. Donald Macleod captures these truths well when he writes:

> Above all, he shared with us the misery of our human condition: human existence as determined by the fall. He knew poverty, homelessness, contempt, loneliness, rejection, death in its cruelest form, and, at last, the loss of all sense of the presence of God. He lived amid squalor, violence and injustice. He heard the cursing, the blasphemy and the threats. He was tormented by the needs of the widow, the orphan and the leper. He felt for the tax-collector. He feared for his people. He wept for the world.[27]

The truth of Christ's identification with us in all of these ways is also important for our grasp of *Christ alone*. In Christ, we find a Lord and Savior who knows exactly what we are going through. In the Word made flesh (John 1:14), Jesus is able to know our temptations and struggles. He knows them not merely in terms of his omniscience, but now *by experience* (Heb 2:17–18; 4:14–15). When we pray to him, we find one who understands and sympathizes with us. Even though he "has ascended into heaven" (Heb 4:14) and is now seated at the Father's right hand as the victorious King and Lord, he has not forgotten our experience of living in this poor, fallen world. Hebrews 4:15 uses a double negative to stress that Jesus is able to empathize with us: "For we do not have a high priest who is unable to empathize with our weaknesses, but we have one who has been tempted in every way, just as we are—yet he did not sin." This empathy extends beyond the mere sharing of feelings of compassion to include Jesus's ability to help us. All of this is only possible because of the incarnation. As Macleod

---

27. Macleod, *Christ Crucified*, 80.

beautifully writes, "[Jesus] lived not in sublime detachment or in ascetic isolation, but 'with us, as the fellow-man of all men,' crowded, busy, harassed, stressed and molested. No large estate gave him space, no financial capital guaranteed his daily bread, no personal staff protected him from interruptions and no power or influence protected him from injustice. He saved us from alongside us."[28]

However, it is crucial to remember that in Christ's identification with us, our Lord not only understands and sympathizes with us, but in his powerful and all-sufficient work he also thankfully saves us. Christ *with us* is a precious truth, but it is never enough. We need also a trail-blazer, champion, and Savior who can act *for us* to defeat our enemies and especially pay for our sin. Our great Savior was faithful to the end, bearing our sin and drinking the cup of God's own wrath in our place. He acted on our behalf as our covenant representative and substitute, and his work as our mediator won the victory for us so that, in him, we are now the righteousness of God (2 Cor 5:21).

With this four-part rationale from Hebrews 2:5–18 in place, we can now summarize the purpose and necessity of the Son's incarnation, and why there is an inseparable bond between Christ's incarnation and atonement. The Son was obligated by the Father to take on a genuine and full human nature because a complete incarnation was the only way that the Son could: (1) rule as God's obedient vice-regent over creation; (2) bring many disobedient sons into the glory of his own obedient vice-regency through sufferings that fit him for the vocation; (3) suffer the death penalty on behalf of the disobedient, releasing them from fear of death under divine judgment; (4) and represent sinners before God as reconciled to him through the forgiveness of their sins.

Concluding Reflection

Why is it necessary for the church to confess and proclaim Christ alone? Because only Christ alone in his person *and* work can do what is necessary to redeem us. Apart from him, there is no salvation. The triune God's eternal plan required the Son to assume our human nature. The only way that Adam's human role could be restored is by the true,

---

28. Donald Macleod, *The Person of Christ*, Contours of Christian Theology (Downers Grove, IL: InterVarsity Press, 1998), 180.

obedient Son acting as our representative and substitute, defeating the power of sin, death, and the devil and becoming our merciful and faithful high priest. Hebrews 2, then, encapsulates the entire biblical storyline and explicates the biblical rationale for the necessity of Christ's incarnation and atonement.

As Scripture makes clear, Christ *with us* is not enough; our Lord must also act *for us*. This is especially evident in Christ's role as our great high priest. The incarnation makes it possible for the divine Son to become our great high priest and new covenant head. But we also need our great high priest to make atonement for our sin, for "without the shedding of blood there is no forgiveness" (Heb 9:22; see Lev 17:11). If the incarnation was enough, then our salvation would only require Bethlehem and not Gethsemane, Calvary, or the empty tomb. But Bethlehem is not enough. As Macleod reminds us:

> In reality, the incarnation was but the prelude to the atonement, an absolutely indispensable prelude because only *this* man, in our place, could expiate sin and propitiate God. But his enfleshment was not itself propitiation. He became flesh only in order to give his life as a ransom, and there could be no *"Tetelestai!"* till that life was given. He could make peace only by the blood of his cross. The union of the two natures, divine and human, in the person of Christ was indeed intimate beyond our imagining, but though it was a personal (*hypostatic*) union it was not a reconciling union. The critical relationship, so far as the atonement is concerned, is not that between the two natures in the one person of Christ, but the personal relationship between the Father and the Son, incarnate as the last Adam and bearing the world's sin. It is by his obedience, not by the constitution of his person, that the many are put right with God (Rom 5:19); and that obedience must reach its climax in the cross.[29]

In part 2 we will develop this point by turning from a primary focus on Christ's exclusive and unique identity to his all-sufficient work. Ultimately both incarnation and atonement are needed, and needed in more than a hypothetical sense. When Christ and his work are rooted

---

29. Macleod, *Christ Crucified*, 141–42.

in the Bible's storyline, and ultimately our sin is seen in proper relationship to the triune Creator-Covenant Lord, we begin to realize that *the only way* for God to forgive sinners is *through Christ alone*. In every possible world where sinners stand before the self-sufficient, holy, and triune God, the only way to save us is by Christ alone. We need a divine Redeemer who can represent us as he satisfies his own demand against sin. And so it was *absolutely necessary* for the eternal Son to become flesh—"him who had no sin to be sin for us, so that in him we might become the righteousness of God" (2 Cor 5:21).

PART 2

Christ Alone: The Sufficiency of His Work

The Threefold Office of Christ Alone: Our Prophet, Priest, King

We have now looked carefully at the biblical presentation of Christ's identity. We began by attending to the basic terms by which Scripture identifies Christ to us, and by listening to Christ and accepting the witness of his apostles. In this we have seen how Scripture progressively reveals the unique identity of Christ. Now, in this chapter, we will begin to consider how Scripture uses *covenantal-typological development* to declare not just the *exclusivity* of Christ but also his *sufficiency* as God the Son incarnate.

In particular, this chapter will discuss the sufficiency of Christ as our prophet, priest, and king—a biblical truth which was developed by John Calvin and the heirs of the Reformation.[1] As with his person, the work of Christ becomes more precise across the biblical covenants. And within the developing covenantal context, the Bible brings many

---

1. Viewing Christ's work in terms of his threefold office (*munus triplex*)—prophet, priest, and king—goes back to the early church. For example, Eusebius of Caesarea identifies Jesus as "the only High Priest of all, the only King of every creature, and the Father's only High Prophet of prophets" (*Historia ecclesiastica* 1:3:8). However, in the Reformation this way of viewing Christ's work was uniquely developed by Calvin and his theological heirs (see Calvin, *Institutes*, 2.15; Francis Turretin, *Institutes of Elenctic Theology*, trans. George Musgrave Giger and ed. James T. Dennison Jr., 3 vols. [Phillipsburg, NJ: P&R, 1994], 2:391–499). For more contemporary treatments of Christ's threefold office in Reformed theology, see Geerhardus Vos, *Christology*, vol. 3 of *Reformed Dogmatics*, trans. and ed. Richard B. Gaffin Jr. (Bellingham, WA: Lexham Press, 2014), 85–182; Herman Bavinck, *Sin and Salvation in Christ*, vol. 3 of *Reformed Dogmatics*, trans. John Vriend and ed. John Bolt (Grand Rapids: Baker, 2006), 323–482; Robert Letham, *The Work of Christ*, Contours of Christian Theology (Downers Grove, IL: InterVarsity Press, 1993); Robert A. Peterson, *Calvin and the Atonement* (Fearn, Ross-shire, UK: Mentor, 1999), 45–60; Michael S. Horton, *Lord and Servant: A Covenant Christology* (Louisville: Westminster John Knox, 2005), 208–70; Jeremy R. Treat, *The Crucified King* (Grand Rapids: Zondervan, 2014), 149–73.

OT types to their fulfillment in Christ and what he accomplishes for the salvation of God's people. As we have seen, the fulfillment of OT types helps identify who Christ is. But to continue standing with the Reformers in confessing *Christ alone*, we need to read the Bible on its own terms to understand all that Christ has done as the final prophet-priest-king. We can gain a deeper understanding of the entirety of Christ's mediatorial work by tracing these particular types from the OT and the old covenant to the NT and the new covenant in Christ.

A Threefold Office for an All-Sufficient Work

For our purposes, we can focus on three reasons why it helps to consider the sufficiency of Christ's work in terms of his threefold office of prophet-priest-king.

First, the threefold office of Christ comes from the covenantal-typological development of the biblical storyline to demonstrate how Christ functions as our covenantal mediator and why his work is superior. In a significant sense, all typology begins with the first Adam.[2] And as the storyline progresses through the biblical covenants, the prototypical roles of prophet, priest, and king first seen in Adam separate and develop through later individuals (e.g., Moses, Aaron and the Levites, David and his sons).[3] Ultimately, however, all three roles unite again in

---

2. And this underscores the necessity of Christ as both the center of the biblical plotline and the end of God's plan for humanity. As Doug Moo rightly reminds us from Rom 5:12–21: "All people . . . stand in relationship to one of two men, whose actions determine the eternal destiny of all who belong to them" (Douglas J. Moo, *The Epistle to the Romans*, NICNT [Grand Rapids: Eerdmans, 1996], 315). Either we stand condemned by God "in Adam" or we stand reconciled to God "in Christ."

3. It is not difficult to see in Adam the prototypical role of prophet and king. For example, in Gen 2:16–17, God speaks to Adam and calls him to obedience. Adam, then, was responsible to speak God's word to Eve and his progeny, thus functioning as a prophet. Additionally, as God's image bearer, Adam (and Eve with him) is given dominion over the earth (Gen 1:28), put in Eden to nurture and protect it, and to put everything under his feet by extending the geographical borders of Eden until it covered the whole earth (see Ps 8). God's goal in creation, then, was to magnify his glory throughout the earth by means of his faithful image bearers, inhabiting the world and putting all things under their feet, in obedience to him (see Peter J. Gentry and Stephen J. Wellum, *Kingdom through Covenant: A Biblical-Theological Understanding of the Covenants* (Wheaton, IL: Crossway, 2012), 177–221, 611–28; see also G. K. Beale, *The Temple and the Church's Mission*, NSBT 17 [Downers Grove, IL: InterVarsity Press, 2004]). Adam's role as the prototypical priest is disputed. John Owen, for example, argued that priests only emerge post-fall due to sin's entrance into the world (see John Owen, *The Priesthood of Christ: Its Necessity and Nature* [Fearn, Ross-shire, UK: Christian Focus, 2010], 39–73). Certainly, the predominant role of priests is to deal with sin (see Heb 5:1). However, a strong case can be made for Adam functioning as a priest before the

Christ who is the final and better prophet, priest, and king.[4] In this way, our Lord Jesus Christ brings to completion God's original intention for humanity in his incarnation and work (Heb 2:5–18). Jesus serves as the last and better Adam. He obeys where Adam disobeyed and by his representative life and substitutionary death wins for us our redemption and becomes the head of the new creation and a new humanity (Rom 5:12–21; 1 Cor 15:12–58). As the head of the new creation and new humanity, he restores all that was lost in Adam, and by the Spirit, he remakes us to be what God created us to be in the first place, namely image bearers who rule over the creation in relationship to him (2 Cor 5:17; Eph 2:1–22; see Rev 21–22).

Second, the threefold office of Christ shows us the comprehensive nature of both sin's corruption and Christ's salvation. In short, the sin of the first Adam has affected every aspect of humanity, which affects every aspect of our relationship with our triune Creator-Covenant Lord. Christ's threefold work demonstrates how sin ruined our knowledge of God (prophet), the righteousness of our desires and deeds (priest), and our submission and obedience to the Lord (king). But to the praise of God's glorious grace, the manifold work of Christ also demonstrates how he is the finality of God's revelation, the one who accomplishes our justification, and brings God's rule and reign to this world.

Third, the threefold office of Christ summarizes and integrates the rich and far-reaching biblical data on all that Christ has done to fulfill God's plans and purposes. When dealing with any doctrine, but particularly with Christology as the center of all doctrine, there is always the danger of reductionism.[5] Considering Christ as prophet, priest, and king allows us to highlight the essentials of what he has accomplished *and* integrate the major aspects of his work, all on the Bible's own terms. As we will

---

fall, and that Eden ought to be viewed as a garden-temple sanctuary (G. K. Beale, *The Temple and the Church's Mission*, and Rikki E. Watts, "The New Exodus/New Creational Restoration of the Image of God: A Biblical-Theological Perspective on Salvation," in *What Does It Mean to Be Saved? Broadening Evangelical Horizons of Salvation*, ed. John G. Stackhouse Jr. [Grand Rapids: Baker, 2002], 15–41).

4.   In typological relations, we can speak of the superiority of Christ's person and work in terms of *a fortiori* development through the biblical covenants, i.e., "lesser to greater" as the typological patterns reach their fulfillment in Christ and the inauguration of the new covenant (see Gentry and Wellum, *Kingdom through Covenant*, 106–8).

5.   On this point, see Joel B. Green and Mark D. Baker, *Recovering the Scandal of the Cross: Atonement in New Testament and Contemporary Contexts*, 2nd ed. (Downers Grove, IL: IVP Academic, 2011), 17–51; cf. Treat, *Crucified King*, 174–92.

see, there is a primacy to Christ's priestly work given the central problem of sin. But even then, the priestly work of Christ cannot be separated from or be fully comprehended without his work as prophet and king.

As we unpack the threefold office of Christ, we can expect to see that *who* Christ is and *what* he does places our Lord in a category all by himself. Set within this covenantal framework, Scripture presents our Lord as the unique and all-sufficient Savior precisely because he is God the Son incarnate who is our great prophet, priest, and king. In Christ alone, we see the resolution of God to take our sin and guilt, satisfy his own righteous requirements, reverse the horrible effects of the fall and make this world right, and inaugurate a new covenant in his blood. In the sections below, we will discuss how each aspect of Christ's work is revealed in Scripture and is sufficient for our salvation.

The Prophetic Work of Christ

To understand Christ's prophetic work, we will first focus on the covenantal-typological development of the prophet along the storyline of Scripture by asking two questions: What is the basic function of the prophet? Why is a prophet necessary? We can then comprehend the sufficiency of Christ's prophetic work by considering how he fulfills the function and need of a prophet for our salvation.

Revelation for Salvation

What is the basic function of a prophet?[6] In Scripture, the prophet is a "man of God" who speaks God's word to the people. Since God is the source and standard of truth, his people need to hear a word from him. But this is no generic truth about life or general wisdom for living in the world. The prophet brings covenant instruction from the Creator-Covenant Lord to his covenant people. The words of the prophet, then, function to guide God's people in his ways to live in the world under his covenant blessings and ultimately for the glory of his name.

As the prototypical prophet, Adam brought the word of the Covenant Lord to his first family that was to fill the earth (Gen 2:16–17). Under

---

6.   For a helpful treatment of the biblical concept of a prophet, especially in the OT, see Edward J. Young, *My Servants the Prophets* (Grand Rapids: Eerdmans, 1952); Vos, *Christology*, 92; see also John M. Frame, *The Doctrine of the Word of God* (Phillipsburg, NJ: P&R, 2010), 87–100.

God's blessing for them to be fruitful and multiply and to fill and rule over all creation, Adam was to lead his wife and train his offspring to work and keep the garden of God's presence in righteousness so that humanity would cover the earth with God's image (cf. Gen 1:26–30; cf. Ps 8). Adam was to keep his family from disobeying the Lord under penalty of death. This covenant word was given by God for his people. Similarly, Moses gathered the nation of Israel under the covenant word of God at Mt. Sinai (Exod 19–24). Moses gave the people the way of the Lord for life and blessing and warned them against abandoning the Lord for idols under penalty of death by exile (Deut 27–30). And even throughout Israel's history of idolatry, God showed he is slow to anger and abounding in steadfast love by sending a series of prophets with warnings and encouragement to turn back his people to the covenant ways of the Lord.

Why is a prophet and a prophetic word necessary? The biblical presentation gives us at least two reasons. First, we need a prophet because as finite creatures we do not know objective, universal truth in a warranted way apart from God's revelation, both in nature and primarily in Scripture. Even before the fall, it was necessary for God to speak to Adam in Eden and to reveal truth to him.[7] God never intended for Adam or the entire human race to know truth apart from his Word-revelation, whether in creation (general revelation) or in divine speech (special revelation).

This point must be emphasized in today's context of pluralism and postmodernism. The current intellectual conditions insist that objective truth does not exist, or that if it does we have no access to it anyway. All we have are our differing contextual perspectives. This leaves us in skepticism about the possibility of knowing the truth, even truth revealed by God. From a Christian worldview, however, truth is possible because it is grounded in the triune God who not only plans and knows all things but also creates a world according to that plan and speaks the universe into existence and speaks to us in words.[8] As a result of

---

7.   Prior to the fall, both general and special revelation were bound together; it is only due to sin that they are temporarily separated (see Cornelius Van Til, "Nature and Scripture," in *Thy Word Is Still Truth: Essential Writings on the Doctrine of Scripture from the Reformation to Today*, ed. Peter A. Lillback and Richard B. Gaffin Jr. [Phillipsburg, NJ: P&R, 2013], 921–31).

8.   For example, Francis Schaeffer emphasized the need for the triune God's existence

his divine speech, both in creation and Scripture, it is possible to know objective truth without ourselves being omniscient because our finite knowledge is a subset of his exhaustive knowledge.[9] A prophet, then, is necessary because as finite creatures, humans are dependent upon divine speech.

Moreover, we need a prophet because the corruption of Adamic sin renders all humanity spiritually blind and bent on distorting the truth and rejecting God's Word (Rom 1:18ff; Eph 4:1–4; 2 Cor 4:4). Scripture pictures sinful humanity as groping in the dark and yet deliberately suppressing God's clear and authoritative revelation. In our sin, we readily believe lies over the truth because we refuse to fear God in our thinking but reject the source and standard of truth (Ps 14:1; Prov 1:7). We need a prophet to speak God's Word to us, then, because we are finite and fallen.[10] We cannot live by bread alone but must live by every word that proceeds from the mouth of God (Matt 4:4).

The Sufficiency of Christ's Revelation

Under the old covenant with Israel, Moses spoke for God, promising that one day the Covenant Lord would raise up from and for his people another prophet like Moses (Deut 18:15–19). This new Moses would again bring the covenant word of truth for a blessed life that brings glory to the name of the Lord. And even though a number of prophets came and went, including the mighty Elijah and the prolific Isaiah, none of them fulfilled God's promise. This new Moses would finally come in Christ alone (see Acts 3:22–26).[11] Yet while Christ is a new Moses, he

---

and his speech for truth to exist (see *The God Who Is There*; *Escape from Reason*; and *He Is There and He Is Not Silent*, in Francis A. Schaeffer, *A Christian View of Philosophy and Culture*, vol. 1 of *The Complete Works of Francis A. Schaeffer* [Westchester, IL: Crossway, 1982], 5–352).

9.   See D. A. Carson, *The Gagging of God: Christianity Confronts Pluralism* (Grand Rapids: Zondervan, 1996), 93–191; Kevin J. Vanhoozer, *Is There a Meaning in This Text? The Bible, The Reader, and the Morality of Literary Knowledge* (Grand Rapids: Zondervan, 1998), 198–366; Michael S. Horton, *Covenant and Eschatology: The Divine Drama* (Louisville: Westminster John Knox, 2002), 123–219.

10.   Although we are finite and sinful, we can know the truth because God has spoken to us in a Word-revelation bound up with the Son, and the Son has sent the Spirit to remove the noetic effects of sin and renew our minds, enabling us to respond to God's covenant word (see Vanhoozer, *Is There a Meaning in This Text?*, 367–452).

11.   Some insist that this text is only a prediction of the continued existence of the institution of prophecy or the succession of prophets, not a prediction of an eschatological messianic prophet (for example, see Daniel I. Block, "My Servant David: Ancient Israel's Vision of the

is also the final prophet who is superior to Moses. Christ comes not only with the word of God but also as the Word of God himself (John 1:1). And although God spoke to his people through many different prophets in many different ways, he has now spoken his full and final covenant word by God the Son incarnate (see John 1:14–18; Heb 1:1–3a).[12]

How does Christ fulfill the function of prophet and provide the prophetic word we need for our salvation? We can see the sufficiency of Christ's prophetic work at three points. First, Jesus is both the end of all prophets and prophetic words and he is the source of all divine revelation. Scripture presents Christ, especially in the Gospels, as a prophet, but not merely or even primarily as a prophet.[13] In fact, often those who call Jesus a prophet know very little about him (see Matt 16:14; Luke 7:16; 9:8; John 4:19; 9:17). Nevertheless, the testimony of Scripture is that Jesus is a prophet, indeed *the* prophet that Moses anticipated (Acts 3:22–24; 7:37). Why this seeming ambiguity in reference to Christ's prophetic work? Although Jesus is the prophet whom Moses predicted, *he is also far greater and as such transcends all prophets before him.* Jesus, then, is not merely a prophet since he is the one about whom the prophecies in the OT were made (e.g., Luke 24:24–27, 44–47; John 5:45–47; 1 Pet 1:10–12). Moreover, Jesus is the source of revelation from God. All of the OT prophets indicated their ambassadorial authority with "Thus says the Lord." But Jesus speaks with divine authority: "But I tell you" (Matt 5:22). The word of the Lord *came to* the OT prophets. As the final prophet, Jesus speaks the word of the Lord on his own authority as the one who perfectly reveals the Father to us (John 1:14, 18; 14:9).

Second, Jesus is the prophet *par excellence* in bringing God's word to man because he is the Son *incarnate.* Scripture demonstrates in many

---

Messiah," in *Israel's Messiah in the Bible and the Dead Sea Scrolls*, ed. Richard S. Hess and M. Daniel Carroll [Grand Rapids: Baker, 2003], 29). Although it is probably correct to take "prophet" in a collective sense, this does not rule out a messianic sense to the prophecy. This is especially the case given that Moses and the prophets function typologically. Typology functions in terms of installments of types who ultimately culminate in the anti-type. Just as many of the Messianic predictions are generic in nature and then terminate specifically in the Messiah (e.g., Gen 3:15; 49:8–12), this is also the case here. Also, we must realize that none of the prophets who followed Moses were able to match him (see Deut 34:10–12; Num. 12:6–8). This creates an expectation of not only a prophetic line, but also *the* prophet like Moses to come.

12. On this point, see Turretin, *Institutes of Elenctic Theology*, 2:402–3.
13. On this point, see Letham, *Work of Christ*, 91–95.

ways that Christ as prophet is in a category all his own. Here we can focus on two texts in particular that connect the identity of Christ and his superiority as the prophet of our salvation: John 1:1–18 and Hebrews 1:1–3. In the prologue to John's Gospel, Jesus is presented as the "Word" (*logos*) (John 1:1–18), which already identifies Christ as more than a prophet. The meaning of *logos* is found in the OT, where "word of God" is associated with creation (Gen 1:3ff; Pss 33:6; 147:15–18), revelation (Gen 3:8; 12:1; 15:1; Pss 119:9, 25, 28, 65), redemption (Isa 55:1; see Pss 29:3ff; 107:20), and is ultimately identified with God himself (Ps 119:89). John Frame argues that "God's word . . . is his self expression,"[14] and that "Where God is, his word is, and vice versa."[15] By identifying Christ as the eternal *logos* (John 1:1) now become flesh (John 1:14), John affirms that in Christ we have "God's ultimate self-disclosure."[16] This emphasis reaches its climax in the conclusion to John's prologue: "No one has ever seen God, but the one and only Son, who is himself God and is in closest relationship with the Father, has made him known" (John 1:18). Although some in the OT saw visions of God (e.g., Exod 33–34; Isa 6:5), no one actually saw God himself before the incarnation of Christ. John tells us that the unique Son (*monogenēs*) from the Father is the unique God (*monogenēs theos*) at the Father's side who makes God known to humans in grace and truth.[17] No mere prophet could bear this identity and credentials, but only God the Son incarnate. Christ's prophetic ministry is categorically different from all other prophecy because Christ himself speaks as the source and standard of divine revelation.

Or consider the beginning of Hebrews, which even more explicitly uses Christ's Sonship to make the case for his superiority as prophet. As we saw in chapter 6, Hebrews 1:1–3 presents a series of contrasts to show that God has spoken finally and definitively in these "last days" in his Son. "In the past" God spoke "at many times and in various ways" through the prophets. But now God's speaking is complete in the

---

14. John M. Frame, *The Doctrine of God* (Phillipsburg, NJ: P&R, 2002), 471.

15. Ibid., 472.

16. D. A. Carson, *The Gospel According to John*, PNTC (Grand Rapids: Eerdmans, 1991), 116.

17. See Andreas J. Köstenberger, *A Theology of John's Gospel and Letters: The Word, the Christ, the Son of God*, Biblical Theology of the New Testament (Grand Rapids: Zondervan, 2009), 336–54.

Son. This is not to say that the OT prophetic revelation was inferior in the sense of not fully authoritative. Rather, the previous revelation was deliberately and necessarily incomplete, fragmentary, and anticipatory, precisely because it came "by the prophets" and not yet by the Son, or better, "in the Son" (*en huiō*).[18] The prophetic ministry of Christ is both quantitatively and qualitatively different from previous revelation because he is the one about whom the prophets spoke. Even more, the Son is the one in whom all of God's revelation and redemptive purposes culminate (see Eph 1:9–10).[19]

Third, the prophetic work of Christ continues from the throne of heaven through the apostles and the Scriptures. It is important to note that Christ's prophetic ministry was not merely limited to our Lord's time on earth.[20] Prior to his incarnation and during Christ's time on earth, the revelation of God was mediated through the Son (1 Pet 1:10–12), and after his ascension he continues to mediate knowledge of the triune God to us by the apostolic teaching in the Scriptures. In appointing and preparing the apostles, our Lord made careful provision for the continuation of his prophetic ministry after his departure. His apostles would write new covenant instruction that paralleled old covenant writings (see Matt 10:1ff; Mark 3:13–19; Luke 6:12–16).[21] The apostles function as a special group of Jesus's disciples whose authority is unique.[22] They were eyewitnesses of the resurrection and called to build the church upon the basis of their teaching and authority (Acts 2:42; Eph 2:17). Yet their teaching and authority are a Spirit-empowered

---

18. See Peter T. O'Brien, *The Letter to the Hebrews*, PNTC (Grand Rapids: Eerdmans, 2010), 44–51.

19. This same emphasis is found in Heb 3:1–6 (see O'Brien, *Hebrews*, 126–38). Here Jesus is deliberately contrasted with Moses. The OT repeatedly says that God did not speak as directly with anyone else as he did with Moses (see Num 12:6–8). This is why Deut 18:15–18 is significant; the great prophet to come must be like Moses but greater, which is precisely how the author of Hebrews presents Christ.

20. See Letham, *The Work of Christ*, 95–102; Vos, *Christology*, 92–94; Peterson, *Calvin and the Atonement*, 47–51.

21. See Frame, *Doctrine of the Word of God*, 105–39; Michael J. Kruger, *Canon Revisited: Establishing the Origins and Authority of the New Testament Books* (Wheaton, IL: Crossway, 2012), 27–194.

22. There were three prominent characteristics of an "apostle of Jesus Christ." First, they were called and appointed by Christ himself. Second, they were associated with Jesus's ministry from the beginning; the only exception was Paul. Third, they were eyewitnesses of the resurrection.

extension of Christ's own teaching and authority.[23] These altogether human apostles wrote Scripture, yet Scripture is most fundamentally the communicative action of the triune God.[24]

The locus and sufficiency of Christ's prophetic-covenantal word, then, is Scripture. As Robert Letham instructs us:

> The doctrine of Scripture is an inherent part of the gospel, not an additional extra tacked on to supplement the redemptive actions of Christ. The Bible does not compete with Christ. It is complementary. In entrusting ourselves to the Saviour, we believe, trust and obey his word to us, given by the Holy Spirit through the mouths of prophets and apostles. Christ himself is the great, chief and final prophet, not only declaring to us the works and ways of God but also embodying in himself the truth of God, since he is the truth, the creator and sustainer of all that is. Thus the word of the Spirit to us, as found in the Old and New Testaments, is Christ's own word to us.[25]

The ongoing prophetic ministry of Christ stretches from the first years he spent with his disciples, through the writings of the apostles of Christ, and into the contemporary work of the Spirit of Christ who illuminates the church for reading the Scriptures.[26]

So Christ's prophetic work is sufficient to bring us the covenant instruction we need for salvation. But our salvation requires more than covenantal instruction; it requires covenantal mediation. In fact, at the heart of Christ's word to us is the call to repentance and faith in him as our covenant mediator. Our human problem is more than mere ignorance; what we also need is a Savior who can pay for our sin, remove our guilt and defilement, and bring us into a right relationship with our holy and righteous Creator-Covenant Lord.

The Priestly Work of Christ

Most agree with John Murray that our Lord's work is presented

---

23. See Vos, *Christology*, 92–94.
24. See Kevin J. Vanhoozer, *First Theology: God, Scripture and Hermeneutics* (Downers Grove, IL: InterVarsity Press, 2002), 159–203.
25. Letham, *Work of Christ*, 102.
26. See Frame, *Doctrine of the Word of God*, 87–100, 129–39.

in Scripture as a priestly work: "The atonement must more broadly be subsumed under the Mediatorial work of Christ, and more specifically under the priestly office. But there is one Mediator, and Christ alone was called a High Priest after the order of Melchizedek."[27] But what exactly is the biblical concept of priest, and what is his work that Christ fulfills and executes?[28]

As with Christ's prophetic ministry, we can understand his priestly work by first focusing on the covenantal-typological development of the priest along the storyline of Scripture. And we will ask the same two kinds of questions: What is the basic function of the priest? Why is a priest necessary? We can then comprehend the sufficiency of Christ's priestly work by considering how he fulfills the function and need of a priest for our salvation.

Mediation for Salvation

What is the basic function of a priest? Hebrews 5:1 is a helpful summary: "Every high priest is selected from among the people and is appointed to represent the people in matters related to God, to offer gifts and sacrifices for sins." Already from this NT summary of the OT system, we can highlight three central aspects of the priesthood: a priest is selected by God, represents a particular people before God, and offers sacrifices to God.

In Israel, the office of priest was reserved for Aaron and his direct descendants from the tribe of Levi (Exod 29:9, 44; Num 3:10; 18:1–7), but even certain Levites were excluded by physical defects (Lev 21:16–23). The priest was a carefully chosen individual who came from among the covenant people of Israel. Moreover, this select group was chosen to represent a particular people before God, namely, all those under the old covenant. This select representation is vividly displayed in the special clothing required of the OT high priest.[29] For example, the priest's breastplate contained twelve gems with the twelve tribes of Israel engraved on them to show that the priest represented those

---

27. John Murray, "The Atonement," in *Collected Writings of John Murray, Volume 2: Lectures in Systematic Theology* (Carlisle, PA: Banner of Truth, 1977), 148.

28. See the helpful discussion in Vos, *Christology*, 94–95, and Calvin, *Institutes*, 2.15.6.

29. Carol Meyers rightly notes that the "priestly office and priestly garb are inextricably related" (Carol Meyers, *Exodus* [New York: Cambridge University Press, 2005], 240).

in covenant with Yahweh (see Exod 28:17–21).[30] Hugh Martin makes it clear that "priesthood rests on personal relation."[31] The OT priests "acted for individuals; and besides such action, they had no priestly action whatsoever, no official duty to discharge. . . . Indefiniteness, generality, vagueness, unlimitedness, universality, are ideas with which no theory of their office can possibly cohere."[32]

With a select group representing God's covenant people to him, we come to the central function of the priesthood: "to offer gifts and sacrifices for sins" (Heb 5:1). The author of Hebrews here describes the function of priests as representative mediators between a sinful people and their holy God. And this mediation means that at the heart of priestly work lies expiation, i.e., the covering of our sin and propitiation, i.e., in covering our sin, God's holy wrath against sin is satisfied.[33] By considering four parts of this particular mediatorial function in its OT, old covenant context, we will prepare the way to understanding the priesthood of Christ in the NT under the new covenant.

First, OT priests mediated between one God and one people in one place. OT priests performed their work in a particular place (tabernacle, temple) and for a particular people (Num 3:7–8). Nowhere in the OT did the priest make atonement for all the nations or function as a universal mediator. The covenantal blessings of atonement are only provided for those within the covenant community.[34]

Second, OT priests always applied the atoning blood of sacrifice to the altar on behalf of those they represented. In other words, there was no separation between the provision of atonement and its application

---

30. See Letham, *Work of Christ*, 106.

31. Hugh Martin, *The Atonement: In Its Relations to the Covenant, the Priesthood, the Intercession of Our Lord* (Edinburgh: James Gemmell, 1882), 58.

32. Ibid., 65.

33. Some have argued that "gifts" merely refers to peace and cereal offerings, while "sacrifices" refers to animal sacrifices. However, O'Brien notes that "the terms are probably being used synonymously, even as a fixed phrase for sacrifices generally. . . . Thus, the prepositional phrase, *for sins*, qualifies the whole, not simply the latter term" (O'Brien, *Hebrews*, 190). The heart of the priest's work dealt with the people's sins before God. This is not to say that the priest did not serve in other capacities, since the priest also had a prophetic function as evidenced by the Urim and the Thummim (Exod 28:30; Lev 18:8). The priests were also teachers of the covenant (Lev 10:10–11; Deut 33:10; see 2 Chron 35:3; Ezek 22:26; Hag 2:11–13; Mal 2:5–9) and instructed God's people regarding holiness (see Lev 11–15) (see Gordon Wenham, *The Book of Leviticus*, NICOT [Grand Rapids: Eerdmans, 1979], 159).

34. See David Williams, *The Office of Christ and Its Expression in the Church* (Lewiston: Mellen, 1997), 14.

to the people.[35] In fact, application of the atonement to the altar had a two-fold effect: it propitiated God and made the people acceptable to God, effecting a real change in the very dwelling place of God.[36] For example, on the Day of Atonement the high priest atoned for the people and applied the blood to the altar in order to cleanse the people *and* the sanctuary from any defilement before God (Lev 16:15–19). No OT priest offered a sacrifice without simultaneously applying its blood to the altar to allow God to dwell with his people under the terms of the old covenant.

Third, OT priests provided a relatively efficacious mediation between God and Israel. The sacrifices had a real effect on the relationship between God and his old covenant people. But God never intended the sacrificial system to effect ultimate atonement and eternal salvation. Old covenant priests and sacrifices functioned as types/shadows of a greater priest and a perfect sacrifice to come (Heb 10:1–18). The OT sacrificial system did provide a means of divine forgiveness, but that forgiveness was typological and therefore temporary.[37]

Fourth, OT priests guarded the temple of God's presence to maintain the purity and holiness of Israel.[38] The priestly duty included a defensive posture toward anyone who attempted to enter God's house in a non-prescribed way (Num 3:5–10; see 18:1–7; 25:1–9; Exod 32:19–20). This too was part of the design of the priesthood: to mediate God's presence to the people, to protect the people from God's wrath, and to take revenge upon the enemies of God, beginning within the house of Israel.

Why is priestly mediation necessary for our salvation? In short, the biblical presentation of priests has everything to do with the reality of sin, morality, justice, guilt, the need for justification before God, and ultimately the question of whether we live in a moral universe. But for our purposes, we can focus on three main points: we have sinned

---

35. Geerhardus Vos notes the intertwined nature of the provision and application of the atonement (Geerhardus Vos, *Biblical Theology* [Carlisle, PA: Banner of Truth, 1975], 164).

36. See Richard Nelson, *Raising Up a Faithful Priest* (Louisville: Westminster John Knox, 1993), 76–78.

37. On this point, see Vos, *Christology*, 88–91, 94–95.

38. See Richard Gamble, *The Whole Counsel of God, Volume 1: God's Mighty Acts in the Old Testament* (Phillipsburg, NJ: P&R, 2009), 444–45; Nelson, *Raising Up a Faithful Priest*, 25–31; Beale, *Temple and the Church's Mission*, 66–121.

against the holy and just Creator-Covenant Lord; his forgiveness of our sins requires the death of a representative substitute who bears our sins; the Lord has promised to provide such a mediator for us.

First, we have rebelled against God who by his own nature must punish our sin. From Genesis 3 on, Scripture teaches that there is something desperately wrong with the human race which will require more than a bandage to fix. Due to Adam's disobedience as our covenant representative, sin entered the world, and sin, at its heart, is willful rebellion against God. The covenant Lord we have sinned against is holy, righteous, and just. God rightly demands from Adam and his image bearers complete obedience, but Adam and the entire human race have not been faithful.

Given that God is personal and that *he is* the standard of righteousness, he cannot deny himself by overlooking our sin. We know with David: "If you, Lord, kept a record of sins, Lord, who could stand?" (Ps 130:3). Our holy Creator-Covenant God diagnoses our condition and concludes we are guilty, condemned, and both unable and unwilling to save ourselves (Rom 3:23; 6:23; 8:7–8; Eph 2:1–3). Apart from God's own sovereign, gracious initiative to solve our problem, our prognosis is fatal. We must die physically and spiritually in the fire of eternal judgment.

Second, God can only forgive our sins if he punishes a representative substitute who bears our sins. What is needed to save us? We certainly need more than knowledge or a power encounter. To destroy death, to reverse the effects of sin, and most importantly, to make us right before the triune covenant Lord, we need a *priest*—a representative figure who will stand between God and ourselves—indeed, a priest who acts as our substitute. We need such a person who can stand legally and representatively in our place, obey perfectly, and bear our individual sin and guilt by propitiating God's wrath and thus bring about our justification before God.

Why is this so? As we saw in chapter 1, there is a "problem of forgiveness,"[39] that is, the collision course between God and sin. God cannot simply forgive our sin apart from its full satisfaction. Since God

---

39. See John R. W. Stott, *The Cross of Christ*, 20th Anniversary Edition (Downers Grove, IL: InterVarsity Press, 2006), 89–111.

is the moral standard of the universe, in forgiving our sin he cannot relax the retributive demands of *his* justice. Ultimately to do so would be a denial of his own will and moral character. Sin is not merely against an external order outside of God; it is against God himself. This is why the problem of forgiveness is an *intrinsic* moral problem for God. How, then, can God save us and satisfy himself simultaneously? How can God who is righteous forgive sinners and be both "just and the justifier" (Rom 3:25–26)? How can he forgive in his love and grace and yet remain holy and just?

Third, the only way is for God himself to provide this mediator for our forgiveness. In Scripture, this is uniquely tied to the priest. In the OT, priests served as mediators for the people, but only typologically as they prophetically anticipated the coming of our Lord Jesus Christ, who perfectly meets our need in his person and work. As *God the Son*, *God's* own righteous demand is perfectly satisfied; as the *incarnate* Son, our Lord acts *with* and *for us* as our mediator. In Christ alone, our great and glorious high priest, *God* himself has kept his promise to save, and in Christ alone he has done a work that neither we nor any OT priest could ever do.[40] In the end, Christ as our great high priest is absolutely necessary for our salvation.

The Sufficiency of Christ's Mediation

The central aspects of the OT priesthood have shown us that God's people need a mediator. But the OT sacrificial system has also shown us that God designed it as a means of *relative* forgiveness that was both *typological* and *temporary*. The function of priests in the biblical storyline develops from Adam's prototypical priesthood of service in God's garden-temple to the offering of sacrifices in God's Jerusalem temple. The fulfillment of this representative mediation, however, would finally come in the person and work of Christ (Heb 8–10). Yet as with his prophetic work, Christ comes as a qualitatively different priest because he mediates between God and man first within himself as the divine incarnate Son.

The NT is clear that Christ not only *fulfills* the OT priests and

---

40. On this point, see Turretin, *Institutes of Elenctic Theology*, 2:417–26; Vos, *Christology*, 21–30, 95; Bavinck, *Sin and Salvation in Christ*, 361–68, 393–406.

their mediation, but he also *transcends* that work by inaugurating a new and better priesthood. We can look again to Hebrews for a better understanding of the typological fulfillment-transcendence of Christ as the mediator of our salvation.[41]

The book of Hebrews argues that Christ is greater than the OT priests and *fulfills* their ministry of mediation by making five points of contrast. In particular, these points demonstrate the supremacy of Christ in the perfection of his person and work.

(1) The OT priests were selected by God based on physical descent and a lack of physical defects. Christ is called and appointed to fulfill the office of priest based on his inherent divine Sonship and his perfect obedience as a man (see Heb 5:5–10).

(2) The OT priests represented Israel before God based on the Lord's determination to gather a people to himself from among the nations of the old humanity. Christ represents a new humanity created in himself as God the Son incarnate (Heb 2:5–18).

(3) The OT priests offered the blood of bulls and goats as sacrifices that effected a temporary covenant with God but could never take away the sins of humanity (see Heb 5:1; 8:3; 10:1–4). Christ offers himself as the perfect sacrifice that atones for all the sins of his people, once for all and forever (see Heb 7:25–27; 9:12; 10:15–18). As such, Christ "is able to save completely those who come to God through him" (7:25).

(4) The OT priests applied the blood of animals to an earthly altar for a temporary and typological atonement. Christ applies his own precious blood to bring the new humanity in himself into the presence of God himself, securing an eternal redemption (see Heb 9:11–15). As William Lane notes, the introductory clause in Hebrews 9:15—"For this reason" (*kai dia touto*)—establishes a strong causal relationship between the achievement of Christ's priestly work (vv. 11–14) and the effects of that work in his new covenant people (v. 15).[42] In

---

41. Like no other NT book, Hebrews presents Christ as our great high priest. Some scholars have argued that Hebrews imposes this concept of priest on Jesus since in the Gospels Jesus never claimed this office for himself. For a response to this charge, see Letham, *Work of Christ*, 110–12.

42. William Lane, *Hebrews 9–13*, WBC 47B (Dallas: Word, 1991), 241.

other words, Jesus's priestly work achieves and applies new covenant realities to all those in the covenant.

(5) The OT priests provided a unified but imperfect work of covenantal mediation due to their own sin and death. Christ provides a unified and perfect work of covenantal mediation—a perfection of work established by the perfection of his person and eternal life as God the Son incarnate—in both provision and intercession. In regard to provision, his cross work is perfect. In terms of intercession, our Lord, as priest, effectively prays for his people *before* the cross (Luke 22:31–32; John 17:6–26) and *after* his ascension (7:24–25; Rom 8:32–34; 1 John 2:1–2), guaranteeing that *all* the new covenant blessings are ours in him. Hebrews 7:23–28 makes this point. Because of *who* he is, in his cross work, he becomes our permanent priest who secures a better covenant (see Heb 8–10) and saves us completely. As Lane comments, "The perfection and eternity of the salvation he mediates is guaranteed by the unassailable character of his priesthood. . . . The direct result of his intercessory activity is the sustaining of the people and the securing of all that is necessary to the eschatological salvation. . . ."[43]

In addition to fulfillment, Hebrews argues that Christ is greater than the OT priests in that he *transcends* the entire Levitical order. In fact, Christ establishes a *new* order of priest that requires a *new* covenant (Heb 7:11). In biblical thought, priest and covenant are intertwined, hence the reason why a change in priesthood *must* result in a change in covenants (Heb 7:11–12; 8; cf. Luke 22:20; 1 Cor 11:25). Yet Scripture is clear that the new covenant is far better since it results in an eternal salvation (Heb 7–10). In fact, Scripture gives many reasons why the new covenant in Christ is better than the old covenant with Israel under Moses. But here we will focus on the central concern of the new

---

43. Lane, *Hebrews 9–13*, 189–90. For a discussion as to the nature of this intercession, see O'Brien, *Hebrews*, 275–78. O'Brien argues that given Christ's definitive sacrifice, his intercession is more in terms of the application of the benefits of his sacrifice than in providing the basis for the forgiveness of sins (which has already been achieved). He concludes, "Whatever precise form the ascended Lord's intercessions for his people take, we may assume that they cover anything and everything that would prevent us from receiving the final salvation he has won for us at the cross" (Ibid., 278). This again underscores the fact that Christ's priestly work involves both provision and application to those he represents and further highlights its superiority to the old order.

covenant that is responsible for these better implications and greater realities.[44]

First and foremost, the new covenant brings *the full forgiveness of sin*. In the OT, forgiveness of sin is normally granted through the priest and the sacrificial system; however, the OT believer, if spiritually perceptive, knew that this was not enough, as evidenced by the repetitive nature of the system and the lack of proper representation and substitution in the sacrifice. But in the new covenant, God will "remember their sins no more" (Jer 31:34). The concept of remembering is not simple recall (see Gen 8:1; 1 Sam 1:19). In the context of Jeremiah 31:34, for God not to remember means that no action will need to be taken in the new age against sin. In the end, to be under the terms of the new covenant entails that the covenant member experiences a full and complete forgiveness of sin.[45] By considering other new covenant texts, it becomes clear that Jeremiah anticipates a perfect, unfettered fellowship of God's people with the Lord, a harmony restored between creation and God—a new creation and a new Jerusalem—where the dwelling of God is with men and they will be his covenant people (see Ezek 37:1–23; Dan 12:2; Isa 25:6–9; Rev 21:3–4). Indeed, with the new covenant in Christ we have the long-awaited fulfillment of the *protevangelium* from the first covenant with creation.

The high priesthood of Christ, then, transcends all other priestly work because he accomplishes a different order of mediation. It is true that Christ fulfills the typological mediation and atonement under the old covenant system in that these things pointed to his final and better work. But here, the typological increase is both quantitative and qualitative. The OT type of priestly work was not the sacrifice of a good man for the forgiveness of certain types of sin. The old covenant priests offered the blood of animals on behalf of human sinners as a temporary means so that the holy covenant Lord could dwell with Israel without destroying her in judgment—what Hebrews 9:13 ESV calls, "the purification of the flesh." As the high priest of the new covenant, however, Christ bears all of our sin and dies our death to bring us into full and

---

44. For a more developed answer to this question, see Gentry and Wellum, *Kingdom through Covenant*, 644–52.
45. See William J. Dumbrell, *Covenant and Creation: A Theology of the Old Testament Covenants* (Carlisle, UK: Paternoster, 1984), 181–85.

eternal reconciliation with our Covenant Lord. In Christ alone, we have a full, effective, and complete salvation unlike the types/shadows of the old.[46] And the flipside is also true: apart from Christ and his priestly work, there is no salvation for us. The only way that the holy, just, triune Creator-Covenant Lord can redeem us is through the priestly work of God the Son incarnate. In Christ, we have a high priest who meets our need (see Heb 7:26–28)—an all-sufficient Savior.

The Kingly Work of Christ

Finally, we discover the glorious kingly work of Christ in its typological development by repeating the same two questions we asked of prophet and priest: What is the basic function of the king in the biblical storyline? Why is a king necessary? We can then come to the sufficiency of Christ's kingly work by considering how he fulfills the function and need of a king for our salvation.

Lordship for Our Salvation

What is the basic function of a king? A king in Scripture is tied to our image-bearing role of ruling over the world (Gen 1:26–31; Ps 8). This first begins in Adam's prototypical lordship as the image-son, and then after the fall, it is picked up through the biblical covenants in other covenant mediators.[47] In the OT, the ultimate expression of kingship is found in David and his sons, who are to bring God's rule and reign to this world, and to put everything under their feet (cf. 2 Sam 7:18–21; Pss 2; 8; 72). Yet in the OT, starting with Adam and continuing through the Davidic kings, there is sin and failure, which ultimately leads to the prophetic anticipation of the coming of a greater David—one who is human but also identified with the Lord. Indeed, one who will perfectly bring God's rule and reign to this world and restore us to our role as God's vice-regents (see e.g., Isa 7:14; 9:6–7; 11:1–16; 42:1–9; 49:1–7; 52:13–53:12; Ezek 34:1–24).

Why is the lordship of a king necessary for our salvation? In Scripture, the human problem is portrayed in multiple ways. It is a universal problem due to Adam's sin and our individual choices (Rom 3:9–12, 23).

---

46. See William Lane, *Hebrews 1–8*, WBC 47A (Dallas: Word, 1991), 200–211.
47. On this point, see Gentry and Wellum, *Kingdom through Covenant*, 181–209.

Before God, our sin results in a verdict of condemnation (Rom 5:12, 15–19; 8:1); it leaves us defiled (Isa 6:3–5); it results in spiritual and physical death (Gen 2:18; 5:5; Rom 6:23); and, ultimately, it leave us helpless and powerless. Under sin's power, we cannot save ourselves; it is only by God's sovereign grace and provision that we can be saved. Ephesians 2:1–3 summarizes our pitiful state: we are dead in our transgressions and sins, under the power of the world, the flesh, and the devil, and ultimately under God's wrath.

We need a Victor to defeat our enemies—sin, death, and Satan—and to restore us to our image-bearing role. As noted above, in the OT, this Victor is portrayed through various leaders (e.g., Moses, Joshua, the Judges), but it is uniquely tied to the Davidic king (2 Sam 7; Pss 2; 72; Isa 11). However, as redemptive history unfolds, not only do David and Solomon fail—all the kings fail. But in their failure they also prophetically anticipate the true King who will not fail.[48] In Christ, the prophetic anticipation is now fulfilled in his coming, his perfect obedience, and his triumphant defeat of our enemies in his cross and resurrection (Eph 1:20–22; Col 2:14–15; Heb 2:14–15). All of this reminds us that outside of Christ's work as our king, we have no hope. We are corrupted from within, unable to save ourselves, and under the power of sin, death, and Satan. But Jesus the King has come and done a work that only *he* can do. In Christ alone is found the solution to our corruption, defilement, powerlessness, and helpless state.

The Sufficiency of Christ's Lordship

Christ's lordship means he rules in the church and over the whole world. First, Christ rules in our lives by his transforming power and grace. By means of his coming and the work he accomplished, he subdues us, pours out the Spirit to remake us and transform us from within. As a result, Christ exercises his lordship over us individually and in the church. As he subdues us and remakes us, we are patterned after his new humanity. Second, Christ also reigns in the world. Jesus is not merely a local ruler over the church; he is also the King over the entire world. In his first coming, he comes as a King to destroy sin, death, and the devil,

---

48. On this point, see Mark Jones, *Knowing Christ* (Carlisle, PA: Banner of Truth, 2015), 226.

and in his return, he will execute justice and usher in the consummated state. In Jesus's resurrection, he is raised to the Father's right hand and invested with full authority over the entire cosmos. Jesus, by his kingly and mediatorial work, is the appointed Son of God with power and exalted to supremacy (see Rom 1:3–4; Eph 1:18–22; Phil 2:9–11; Col 1:15–20). Abraham Kuyper captures this wonderful and glorious truth well in his famous statement, "There is not a square inch in the whole domain of our human existence over which Christ, who is Sovereign over all, does not cry: 'Mine!'"[49]

More specifically, we better grasp the sufficiency and supremacy of Christ's lordship by looking at two redemptive events central to Christ's *one* saving work. Although we must exercise extreme caution in artificially dividing up the redemptive events in Christ's life since they are all part of *one* saving work, it is helpful to identify the cross with Christ's work as *priest*-king, and the resurrection, ascension, and Pentecost with Christ's work as *king*-priest. In this way, our minds can better grasp the *unity* of Christ's work in all of its necessary and complementary parts.[50]

Our Lord Jesus not only performed his saving work as our prophet-priest but also as our king. Christ's kingship is most commonly associated with his resurrection, ascension, and the pouring out of the Spirit at Pentecost—what is rightly called his state of exaltation.[51] But, of course, it is vital that we do not divorce Christ's exaltation from his state of humiliation, that is, his life and death. Both states are necessary to achieve our salvation, and both are achieved by the same person. All of the events in Christ's life are organically linked and constitute the *one* work of our great Redeemer, the Lord of glory, on our behalf as his new

---

49. Abraham Kuyper, "Sphere Sovereignty," in *A Centennial Reader*, ed. James D. Bratt (Grand Rapids: Eerdmans, 1998), 488.

50. On this point, see Turretin, *Institutes of Elenctic Theology*, 2:405. Turretin argues that Christ's priesthood is distinguished from his kingship "formally." "Although the kingly and sacerdotal offices in Christ unite amicably to the same common end (to wit, the salvation of men), still they are distinguished by peculiar functions." In making this point, Turretin is following Calvin, *Institutes*, 2.16.13, who speaks of Christ's death dealing with our sin, and his resurrection as restoring us to life. Calvin rightly notes: "Let us remember that whenever mention is made of his death alone, we are to understand at the same time what belongs to his resurrection. Also, the same synecdoche applies to the word 'resurrection': whenever it is mentioned separately from death, we are to understand it as including what has to do especially with his death."

51. For a discussion of the distinction between Christ's state of humiliation and exaltation, see Vos, *Christology*, 183–241; Bavinck, *Sin and Salvation in Christ*, 323–482; Horton, *Lord and Servant*, 208–70.

covenant people. In that light, we will develop Christ's kingly work in two steps. First, how is Christ's kingship presented in the NT and why is it important? Second, how do the saving events associated with Christ's kingship further establish the sufficiency of Christ's work?

How is Christ's Kingship-Lordship presented in the NT? Chapter 3 explained that unlike some biblical scholarship, Scripture never separates Jesus's ontology and function. By placing our Lord in the Bible's storyline and framework, Christ is first identified with Yahweh (and thus he is *God* the Son) who comes to save his people. Yet Christ is also the Davidic king who becomes son by his incarnation and work, centered in his life, death, and resurrection. In this way, Christ's Kingship-Lordship unites two complementary truths: Christ *is* Son, Lord, and King because of *who* he is from eternity *and* because of *what* he does in his incarnation, life, death, and resurrection. The first truth stresses that Christ is the divine Son in relation to his Father and the Spirit, while the second truth accents the necessity of our Lord's incarnation and work as the *man* Christ Jesus. In the NT, more emphasis is placed on the second truth, given the Son's coming to fulfill the roles of the previous *sons* (e.g., Adam, Israel, David) by inaugurating *God's* long-awaited kingdom. Yet both truths are taught in the NT and we cannot understand *who* Christ is and *what* he does apart from this unified presentation.

The Resurrection

It is not an overstatement to say that the bodily resurrection of Christ is central to Christ's saving work and thus the gospel itself.[52] For example, think of Paul's statement in 1 Corinthians 15: "For what I received I passed on to you as of first importance: that Christ died for our sins according to the Scriptures, that he was buried, that he was raised on the third day according to the Scriptures" (vv. 3–4). Paul further explains that "if Christ has not been raised, our preaching is useless and so is your faith. . . . And if Christ has not been raised, your faith is futile; you are still in your sins. Then those also who have fallen asleep in Christ are lost. If only for this life we have hope in Christ, we

---

52. For a helpful discussion of the importance of the resurrection, see N. T. Wright, *The Resurrection of the Son of God* (Minneapolis: Fortress, 2003).

are of all people most to be pitied" (vv. 14, 17–19). Paul is clear that apart from Christ's bodily resurrection, there is no gospel.

Why? After all, prior to Christ's resurrection there are rare occurrences of other resurrections in Scripture. No doubt, in light of Christ's resurrection, it is probably best to view these previous resurrections more as resuscitations since there is no evidence that those who were raised remained permanently alive. In the case of Lazarus, for example, our Lord raised him from the dead, but we presume that he died again and now awaits the final resurrection. So what makes *Christ's* resurrection so unique and singular in importance?

The answer is not merely because it demonstrates the historical fact of the resurrection—as significant as that is—since the Bible knows of other resurrections. Instead, the answer is found in *whose* resurrection it is, namely, the resurrection of Jesus the Lord. When *his* resurrection is placed in the Bible's storyline, it is not only viewed as a fact of history but also as *the* resurrection of all resurrections, literally the beginning of the new creation order. In fact, Christ's resurrection is evidence that his work to save his people from their sins (Matt 1:21) has been achieved. It is literally the beginning of an entire new order! Why? Because in paying for our sin, Christ destroyed the power of death such that death could not hold him (1 Cor 15:55–57; Col 2:13–15; Heb 2:5–18; cf. Rev 1:17–18).

This is why *Christ's* resurrection inaugurates the new creation (2 Cor 5:17), and it is the firstfruits of more to come (1 Cor 15:20)![53] Because of Christ's resurrection, salvation has been accomplished, although we await its consummated end, and Christ's resurrection body now is the pattern of what we shall be (1 Cor 15:42–44). Also, Christ's resurrection not only demonstrates that salvation is accomplished but also confirms that God's future judgment is sure. Paul makes this point clear at Athens, where he proclaims that Christ's resurrection not only ushers in salvation but also judgment (Acts 17:31). The holy and righteous Creator of the universe will not let sin go unpunished forever. Instead, the triune God speaks in Christ with certainty to this poor, lost world: judgment is coming, the books are going to be balanced, and this will

---

53. See Richard B. Gaffin Jr. *Resurrection and Redemption: A Study in Paul's Soteriology* (Phillipsburg, NJ: P&R, 1987).

be accomplished by the crucified and risen Lord of Glory, our great and glorious King.

Moreover, Scripture teaches that many glorious benefits of Christ's resurrection are applied to his people. Christ's resurrection ensures our regeneration by the Spirit (Rom 6:1–23; Eph 1:19–20; Col 3:1; 1 Pet 1:3). It serves as the ground for our justification before God (Rom 4:25; see Eph 2:6; Phil 2:8–9). And it guarantees our future glorification as we are conformed to Christ and patterned after his glorified human nature (1 Cor 6:14; 15:12–58; 2 Cor 4:14). In Scripture, then, Christ's resurrection is central to his work as our victorious king. The entirety of Christian theology depends on it—not merely the fact of the resurrection, but the truth of what it signifies: our Lord's work is sufficient as the only Savior, Redeemer, Judge, and King.

The Ascension and Pentecost

To grasp Christ's work as our King, we must also include his glorious Ascension and his sovereign pouring out of the Spirit at Pentecost. Christ's work is not complete unless we include these unique, singular redemptive events, which unfortunately are often neglected in the discussion.

First, consider the *fact* that Christ's ascension is taught in Acts 1:6–11 and alluded to in many places in the NT (see Luke 24:50–53; Eph 1:20; 4:8–10; Phil 2:9–11; 1 Tim 3:16; Heb 1:3; 4:14; 9:24). The ascension establishes that Christ has personally departed to the Father's right hand, and that in the future he will return again visibly and publicly (Matt 25:29–31; Acts 1:11). More significantly, however, the ascension speaks of Christ's present sovereign rule over the world as King and Lord (Matt 28:18; Eph 1:20–22; 1 Cor 15:27; 1 Pet 3:22). Furthermore, when the ascension is linked to Christ's priestly ministry, we have the confidence that our Lord is accessible to all who invoke him (Heb 4:14), as he continues to intercede for us as our priest-king (Rom 8:34; Heb 7:25), to help us anywhere in the world (Heb 4:16; 7:25; 13:6–8), and to equip the church for works of service by the Spirit (Eph 4:8–12).

Second, the giving of the Spirit at Pentecost demonstrates that Christ is King because he has inaugurated the long-awaited new covenant age.

In his work, the new creation has come and now awaits its fullness at Christ's return. In the OT there are about a hundred explicit references to the "Spirit (*ruach*) of God," starting from Genesis 1:2 and throughout.[54] None of these references demand that we think of the "Spirit of God" as the third person of the Godhead (except possibly Isa 63:7–14). The Spirit's distinct "person" vis-à-vis the Father and the Son only becomes clear in the NT with the coming of the Son. Since then it is no longer possible to think of the "Spirit of God" merely as the "power" or "manifest presence" of God. Instead, the Spirit must be viewed as a divine "person" in relation to the Father and Son, and an equal colleague in the plan of salvation, albeit with a different role and function. Nevertheless, although the OT prophets did not explicitly speak of the third person of the Trinity, they did anticipate a future day when *God's* Spirit would be poured out upon the coming King/Son in the establishment of the new covenant age.[55]

Specifically, the prophets predict that when the Messiah/King comes—David's greater Son—*he* will have the Spirit in full measure, far greater than any anointed leader of the past (Isa 11:1–5; 42:1–8; 61:1–3; see Luke 4:17–21; Matt 12:28). In the OT, leaders (primarily prophets, priests, and kings) were anointed by the Spirit (e.g., 1 Sam 16:13–14). But all of them failed in their representative task before the Lord. As the prophets announce, however, the Messiah/King will have the Spirit in full measure to perfectly obey God's will and bring with him an entirely new age—literally the "age to come" associated with the dawning of the new creation.

In the NT, this prophetic anticipation is precisely what is stressed in the Son-Spirit relationship. From conception and throughout the entirety of Christ's life and ministry, the Spirit is present (Luke 1:31, 35; 2:47; 4:16–21; John 1:33–34; Mark 1:10; Matt 4:3, 6; Rom 1:4; 1 Tim 3:16; 1 Pet 3:18; 1 Cor 15:45; 2 Cor 3:17–18). As Max Turner

54. Max Turner, "Holy Spirit," in *NDBT* 551–58; see David F. Wells, *God the Evangelist* (Grand Rapids: Eerdmans, 1987), 1–4; Gordon D. Fee, *Paul, the Spirit, and the People of God* (Peabody, MA: Hendrickson, 1996), 9–15; Sinclair B. Ferguson, *The Holy Spirit* (Downers Grove, IL: InterVarsity Press, 1996), 15–33; J. I. Packer, *Keep in Step with the Spirit* (Old Tappan, NJ: Revell, 1984), 55–63.

55. On these points, see Anthony A. Hoekema, *The Bible and the Future* (Grand Rapids: Eerdmans, 1979), 55–67; see also Geerhardus Vos, "The Eschatological Aspect of the Pauline Conception of the Spirit," in *Redemptive History and Biblical Interpretation*, ed. Richard B. Gaffin Jr. (Phillipsburg, NJ: P&R, 1980), 91–125.

reminds us, this portrait of Jesus and the Spirit functions primarily "to confirm to readers that Jesus is indeed the Messiah anticipated by the OT."[56] The eschatological era predicted in the OT has finally dawned in the Son with the Spirit. Moreover, Jesus himself reminds us in John 13–16 that the primary significance of the Spirit's coming is announced in programmatic terms: "When the Advocate comes, whom I will send to you from the Father—the Spirit of truth who goes out from the Father—he will testify about me. And you also must testify, for you have been with me from the beginning" (John 15:26–27). In other words, the Spirit is with Christ to bear witness to him in a very specific way. As Sinclair Ferguson reminds us, "From womb to tomb to throne, the Spirit was the constant companion of the Son."[57] In relation to Christ, then, a crucial work of the Spirit is to bear witness to Christ and bring people to saving faith in him.

In addition to the Messiah having the Spirit in full measure, the entire new covenant, Messianic age will be characterized by the Spirit. And that Messiah's people will have the Spirit as well (Isa 32:15–17; 44:3–4; 59:20–21; Ezek 36:25–27; 37:14; 39:29; Joel 2:28–32; Zech 12:10; see Jer 31:29–34). OT prophets often presented the time of the Lord's visitation of his people in terms of the anticipated new covenant, "as the time when the Spirit will be poured out upon men and women, young and old, without the distinctions implicit in the essentially tribal nature of the old covenant."[58] In Acts 2, for example, Peter quotes from the prophet Joel as proof that the work of Jesus, the Messiah, is complete and has resulted in the coming of the promised Spirit. As D. A. Carson reminds us, "When in Acts the prophetic Spirit falls upon the church, mediating God's presence, enabling believers to speak with tongues and to perform deeds of power, forging the early links among Jewish, Samaritan, and Gentile believers, and gently nudging the church into an expanding vision of Gentile mission, this is understood to be nothing other than what God himself had promised in Scripture."[59]

It is for this reason that it is best to interpret Pentecost as a unique, redemptive-historical event, rooted and grounded in OT prophetic

56. Turner, "Holy Spirit," 552.
57. Ferguson, *Holy Spirit*, 37.
58. Carson, *Gagging of God*, 265.
59. Ibid.

expectation, and a public demonstration that Jesus is both Messiah and Lord/King (Acts 2:36). Pentecost, then, is not a secondary event to Christ's work; instead it is central to it, particularly associated with Christ's kingly office. In fact, Pentecost is the *culmination* of Christ's earthly work (see John 7:39) by which he has inaugurated the new covenant age, thus giving the Spirit to all Christians so that they may not only come to know him, but also be gifted and empowered for service.[60] In other words, it is because Christ's work as our priest-king is complete and sufficient that the Spirit is poured out at Pentecost. Apart from Christ and his work, there would be no Pentecost. All OT hopes and promises would remain unfulfilled.

But precisely because Christ is triumphant in his work as our king-priest, the promised future age has now arrived, full of its benefits, awaiting only its final consummation. In the NT, especially in Paul, the Holy Spirit "is the *arrabōn*, the deposit and hence the guarantee, of the promised inheritance awaiting us in the consummation."[61] By the reception of the Spirit, we now become participants in the new mode of existence associated with the new creation, even though we still await the fullness of the Spirit's work. This "already-not yet" sense to the Spirit's work in us is borne out in five ways in the NT. First, the Spirit testifies to our "sonship" (Gal 4:4–5; Rom 8:14–27). The Spirit bears witness that we are children of God now, even though we still await our full rights associated with sonship. Second, the role of the Spirit is that of "firstfruits" (*aparchē*—1 Cor 15:20, 23; Rom 8:23), which speaks both of what we now have yet await in the future. Third, the Spirit is our "pledge" or "deposit" (*arrabōn*—2 Cor 1:22; 5:5; Eph 1:14) guaranteeing our future inheritance. Fourth, the Spirit is God's "seal" of ownership given to us thus signifying that we are forever God's treasured possession (2 Cor 1:22; Eph 4:30; 1:13). Fifth, the Spirit is related to the resurrection of our bodies (Rom 1:3–4; 8:11; 1 Cor 15:42–44). Not only is the Spirit said to be active in Christ's resurrection, but ours as well, which signifies that our bodies shall be raised from the dead, just as Christ's body was raised from the dead so that we will share in the glorious existence of the final, consummated state.

---

60. For a more detailed treatment of this data, see Christopher J. H. Wright, *Knowing the Holy Spirit through the Old Testament* (Downers Grove, IL: InterVarsity Press, 2006).

61. Carson, *Gagging of God*, 265–66.

Moreover, the Spirit of Christ is currently at work in believers to break the power of sin and progressively conform us to the image of Christ. By his Spirit, Christ preserves us through temptations and sufferings, and he disciplines and rewards our obedient submission to him. In the church, Christ is her head, and as the head of the church, he rules and governs his people. No pope, pastor, or church board is the head of the church; it is only King Jesus. He visibly manifests his rule by instituting a government in the church, who govern under him. Jesus authorizes the leaders to carry out church discipline by exercising the keys of the kingdom, to preach, and to practice the ordinances or sacraments, but it is under his sovereign rule that the church functions. In the world, Christ is the sovereign king and, in the future, he will return in power. All humans owe their allegiance to King Jesus, and if they do not acknowledge him in this life, they will come under his judgment in the next. In the end, all kings, rulers, and peoples will submit to his rule either in salvation or under his eternal judgment. This is our confidence as we live our lives and wait expectantly for his return. Thus, to speak of Christ's work as king in the full biblical sense is glorious, and it reminds us why Christ is truly *alone* and incomparable in his unique and all-sufficient person and work.

Resting in Christ Alone

Why must the church confess Christ alone? The threefold office of Christ has helped uncover the Bible's answer to this question. Given *who* Christ is and *what* he has done, *he* is the only one who deserves our trust, love, and obedience as our Lord and Savior.

What a glorious Savior he is! Once again consider Christ in his entire identity, life, and work. In his birth, he is the divine Son and Lord who chooses to become our Mediator in obedience to his Father's will. In his life, as the incarnate Son, he is still the sovereign King who willingly and gladly chooses to die for us. In his death, he does not die as a victim or martyr but as one who is fully in control, choosing to die for us. By his death, he pays for our sin, destroys death, and defeats Satan by putting him under his feet in triumph. In his resurrection, which is inseparable from his life and death, the Father by the Spirit exalts the Son and inaugurates the glorious new covenant age of the new creation. From that posture of authority, the glorified and exalted Son pours out the Spirit, once again proof that he is Lord and Messiah/King. From that same posture of authority, the exalted and ascended Lord rules over his people, governs history, and will return in power to consummate all that he has begun in his first coming.

Truly, in Christ alone all our needs are met completely and perfectly. Our need for truth is found in him as the final prophet and revelation of God. Our need for a righteous standing before God is achieved by him as our priestly representative, substitute, and new covenant head. Our need to have our rebel hearts subdued, our enemies defeated, and the new creation inaugurated and ultimately consummated is accomplished by him alone as our conquering king. Christ's threefold office brings into focus the glory of his person and his saving work, and it helps us understand the Reformation confession, *Christ alone.*

CHAPTER 6

The Cross-Work of Christ in Historical Perspective

Why do we affirm *solus Christus* with the Reformers? Our thesis is this: we affirm *Christ alone* because of his exclusive identity and all-sufficient work as our Lord and Savior. In the last chapter, we saw this truth emphasized in terms of Christ's work viewed through his threefold office as our new covenant head and mediator. John Calvin developed the biblical categories of prophet, priest, and king, unpacking Christ and his work on the Bible's own terms. Understanding Christ's work this way reveals why in *Christ alone* we have the fullness of God's promises and purposes. As the Word-incarnate, Christ discloses the final and complete revelation of God. As our great high priest, Christ wins the full forgiveness of sins by his perfect sacrifice. And as our King, Christ inaugurates God's kingdom in this world by his incarnation, cross, resurrection, and ascension. To view Christ's identity and work in this comprehensive way avoids reductionism and speaks of a glorious work that only the incarnate Son can do, thus explicating the biblical and theological rationale for *Christ alone*.

In this chapter, we continue to think about Christ's unique and all-sufficient work. Our Lord's work is integrated, unified, and comprehensive. Yet central to Christ's work is the forgiveness of our sin before God (Matt 1:21; 1 Cor 15:3–4). Although it is difficult to prioritize one aspect of our Lord's work, Scripture acknowledges the centrality of Christ's priestly office and his sacrificial death for us.

We have already demonstrated the priestly priority or centrality of Christ's work from the Bible's storyline, especially in Christ acting as our new covenant head. There are many implications and outcomes of our Lord's inaugurating the kingdom through the new covenant, but ultimately Christ's mediation is about the forgiveness of sin by his sacrificial death. As we saw in Hebrews 2, the very rationale for the incarnation was to undo the disastrous role of Adam and defeat the power of death and Satan *by becoming our great high priest*, but it is only through his death that our Lord defeats sin, death, and the devil. Over a century ago, Hugh Martin captured this point well: "It is not enough to maintain that Christ's Priesthood is a real and veritable office; it must be regarded and set forth as pre-eminently *the* office—the foundation office—which Christ as a Redeemer executes."[1]

In thinking about *Christ alone* and his sufficient work, it is vital to go further by focusing specifically on the nature of the cross. Given its centrality, we cannot leave the cross unexplained. And yet the history of the church's confession reveals a variety of interpretations which demand further reflection and adjudication. In the Reformation era, the dominant interpretation of the cross in regard to its central *means* was penal substitution, which provided strong warrant for the Reformers' cry of *Christ alone*.

In the next three chapters, we will defend the Reformation view as still the best way of understanding the *means* or "internal mechanism" of the cross and of grounding *Christ alone*.[2] Given the vastness of the subject, we will make this argument in two steps. First, in this chapter we will set in context the Reformation's affirmation of penal substitution by outlining the basic parameters of atonement theology in historical theology. Then, in chapters 7–8 we will offer a defense of penal substitution as the view that best accounts for the biblical data regarding the *means* of atonement, thus further reflecting on *why* the cross is absolutely necessary for our salvation. Our aim is to add warrant for *Christ alone* as our exclusive and sufficient Lord and Savior.

Atonement Theologies in Historical Theology

A common claim is that the church has no official confession or theology of the cross. Unlike the ecumenical confessions of Nicaea and

---

1.   Hugh Martin, *The Atonement: In Its Relations to the Covenant, the Priesthood, the Intercession of our Lord* (Edinburgh: James Gemmell, 1882), 53. Martin does not deny that Christ also fulfills the role of prophet and king; nevertheless, he argues for the priority of Christ's priestly work because of our sin (see ibid., 54).

2.   For a description of "means" and "internal mechanism," see Jeremy R. Treat, *The Crucified King* (Grand Rapids: Zondervan, 2014), 45–50, 225n123.

Chalcedon that established orthodox Trinitarian and christological doctrine, the cross has been understood in a variety of ways. And since we have no ecumenical statement regarding the cross, we cannot claim that our view is orthodox in a way that others are not. Although true, this reading of church history is reductionistic since, as Donald Macleod points out, the assumption that there is no unity in our understanding of the cross is misleading for a couple of reasons.

First, despite no ecumenical council on the atonement, "there has been agreement on the core elements of this doctrine down the Christian centuries and across all traditions."[3] For example, all Christians have agreed that "we owe our salvation to the death of Christ; that that death was an oblation and a sacrifice; and that this sacrifice was piacular, atoning for sin, making peace with God and securing forgiveness."[4] Second, the early church did not convene a council to settle the doctrine because the basic understanding of the cross was taken for granted. No doubt, theologians emphasized different points in describing the nature of the cross, but "they were absolutely clear that the redemptive power of Christ lay precisely in his death, the one great sacrifice for the sin of the world."[5]

This is *not* to say that we cannot find diverse theologies of the cross proposed in history. But it is to say that throughout history there has been more agreement than not on the NT emphasis that the cross was a sacrifice for our sins before God. Yet, admittedly, the conceptual clarity of the doctrine was not always taught as in later theology.[6] As with most

---

3. Donald Macleod, *Christ Crucified: Understanding the Atonement* (Downers Grove, IL: InterVarsity Press, 2014), 73.

4. Ibid.

5. Ibid., 75. Macleod illustrates his point by appealing to the work of Athanasius, Augustine, Anselm, and Aquinas as all affirming that Christ's death was an objective work, a sacrifice on our behalf for our sins before God. The precise way the cross was explained differed but the tradition was united in affirming that Christ died as a sacrifice for our sin (see ibid., 73–75).

6. H. D. McDonald, *The Atonement of the Death of Christ: In Faith, Revelation, and History* (Grand Rapids: Baker, 1985), 136–37, makes a similar assessment. In acknowledging that the patristic fathers were not always clear on the precise nature of the cross, McDonald makes this important observation: "Perhaps these Greek fathers do tend to focus on the incarnate life of Christ and do not give enough regard to the atoning significance of his death. And perhaps, too, they do not stress sufficiently the relation of that death to the forgiveness of sins, leaving the impression that the whole purpose and effect of Christ's work was to assure to man immortal life. These two facts, however, they saw clearly: namely, that only by a Christ authentically of the nature of God can a divine salvation be available to man; and that the idea of the solidarity of the race is a necessary postulate of any right view of the atonement."

doctrines, clarity and precision regarding the atonement came over time and in light of various theological debates. Specifically, the boundaries and content of atonement theology became especially clear during the Reformation and post-Reformation eras.[7]

We can think through the development of atonement theology by walking through the eras of historical theology and observing how the Reformation era brought greater clarity and precision to our theologizing about the cross.

The Patristic Era

Although no formal church council addressed atonement theology, we must not conclude that the church did not have a doctrine of the atonement. From its inception, the church affirmed that Christ's death was a sacrifice for sin before God.[8] She emphasized that by Jesus's coming and work he had brought about a new and restored relationship between our triune God and humanity. No doubt the church also appealed to the cross as an example of how we ought to live in the face of persecution; however, she did not teach an exemplary view of the atonement as the *central* achievement of the cross. Instead, the church connected our Lord's death to our salvation by emphasizing three interlocking themes: recapitulation, ransom-victory, and substitution—themes that developed later into more robust atonement theologies.

---

7.   See Harold O. J. Brown, *Heresies: The Image of Christ in the Mirror of Heresy and Orthodoxy from the Apostles to the Present* (Garden City, NY: Doubleday, 1984); Steve Jeffery, Mike Ovey, and Andrew Sach, *Pierced for Our Transgressions: Rediscovering the Glory of Penal Substitution* (Nottingham, UK: Inter-Varsity Press, 2007), 161–204.

8.   On this point, see McDonald, *The Atonement of the Death of Christ*, 115–62. McDonald offers two examples. First, Clement of Rome called Christ the "High Priest" (St. Clement, *The First Epistle of Clement to the Corinthians* 36 [*ANF* 1:15]) and noted that his blood is "precious in the sight of God" that was "shed for our salvation" (ibid., 7 [*ANF* 1:7]). Believers are to "reverence the Lord Jesus Christ, whose blood was given for us" (ibid., 21 [*ANF* 1:11]). It was "on account of the love he bore us, Jesus Christ our Lord, gave His blood for us by the will of God; His flesh for our flesh, and His soul for our souls" (ibid., 49 [*ANF* 1:18]). Second, in his seven letters Ignatius the bishop of Antioch viewed Christ's death, blood, and passion as necessary for our salvation. By his incarnation, Christ has united God and human beings; and by his presence in the world he has brought truth and illumination to humanity and the hope of our full restoration in perfection at the last day. The cross is the ground upon which all of this is secured. Ignatius speaks of the cross as "a stumbling-block to those who do not believe, but to us salvation and eternal life" (Ignatius, *Epistle to the Ephesians* 18 [*ANF* 1:57]). However, while he is clear that Christ's death secured our salvation, Ignatius did not formulate an understanding of these exact relationships.

The Cross as Recapitulation

Recapitulation[9] was one way of explaining the cross in the patristic era, a view often associated with Irenaeus, and to a lesser extent with Athanasius.[10] This view interpreted Christ's redemptive work primarily in terms of his identification with humanity through the incarnation. But recapitulation also stressed the real identity of the race in Adam, and thus gave support to the unity of humanity in judgment, which helped lead to the substitutionary satisfaction view. It is called "recapitulation" because it emphasizes the need for the divine Son to become a man and live our life and die our death for us in order to undo Adam's disobedience.

Additionally, recapitulation sees Adam as the representative of the human race who by his disobedience brought sin into the world. This original disobedience had a twofold effect: the corruption of our nature and the deprivation of Godlikeness. Given the nature of sin and the need to undo what Adam did, our only hope is found in God himself graciously acting to redeem us through Christ. Yet in order to save us, Christ could not be merely human; he had to be fully human and divine—he had to be God the Son incarnate. In order to restore humanity by destroying sin and death, God must save us in Christ, the last Adam, who is also the Lord.[11] Also, our redemption requires not just

---

9.   "Recapitulation" is from *anakephalaiōsis* (Greek) and *recapitulation* (Latin) (see Eph 1:10). The term conveys the idea of "having passed through every stage of life, restoring to all communion with God" (see Irenaeus, *Against Heresies* 3.18.7 [*ANF* 1:448]).

10.   See Irenaeus, *Against Heresies* (*ANF* 1:315–567); Athanasius, *Four Discourses against the Arians* (*ANF* 4:303–447) and *On the Incarnation* (*ANF* 4:36–67); see also Gregg R. Allison, *Historical Theology: An Introduction to Christian Doctrine* (Grand Rapids: Zondervan, 2011), 389–95.

11.   See Irenaeus, *Against Heresies*, 3.19.1 [*ANF* 1:449]. Athanasius argues that for our sake, it was necessary for the Son to become incarnate because only in a body could he reveal God's love that would bring about our restoration to incorruptible and immortal life (see Athanasius, *On the Incarnation of the Word*, trans. and ed. Penelope Lawson [New York: Macmillan, 1946], 1.1, 1.4). However, by taking a body like ours, he was also liable to corruption and death. And yet Christ "surrendered His body to death instead of all, and offered it to the Father. This He did out of sheer love for us, so that in His death all might die, and the law of death thereby be abolished because, having fulfilled in His body that for which it was appointed, it was thereafter voided of its power for men" (ibid., 2.8). In this way, Christ became "in dying a sufficient exchange for all" (ibid., 2.9). Moreover, "For the solidarity of mankind is such that, by virtue of the Word's indwelling in a single body, the corruption which goes with death has lost its power over all" (ibid., 2.9). By Christ's taking a body subject to death, his death has a vital and necessary place in the scheme of man's redemption. Athanasius states: "The end of His earthly life and the nature of His bodily death [is] the centre of our faith" (ibid., 4.19). Man by his sinful disobedience involved himself "in a debt that must be

the incarnation of the Son but also his representational, substitutionary, and sacrificial death for us. This is why Christ must come as the last Adam in willing obedience to his Father. He must undo Adam's disobedience and die for us in order to destroy the power of sin and death.[12] In Christ's life *and* death, what was lost in Adam is now recovered.[13]

In the recapitulation view, what is central to the cross? Irenaeus (and Athanasius to a lesser extent) did not explain *how* the cross atones for our sin as later Reformation theology would. Yet this view thinks of the cross in representational and substitutionary terms. For example, Athanasius writes about the incarnate Word that he offered "the sacrifice on behalf of all, surrendering His own temple [body] to death in place of all, to settle man's account with death and free him from the primal transgression."[14] In fact, Athanasius raised the question of *why* the cross is necessary. His answer is instructional: If "any honest Christian wants to know why He suffered death on the cross and not in some other way, we answer thus: in no other way was it expedient for us, indeed the Lord offered for our sakes the one death that was supremely good. He had come to bear the curse that lay on us; and how could He 'become a curse' otherwise than by accepting the accursed death? And that death is the cross, for it is written, 'Cursed is everyone that hangeth on a tree.'"[15] Athanasius understood the necessity of the cross, then, in terms of Christ bearing our curse in order to defeat the power of sin and death.[16] He further explained, "The death which is ascribed to him [the incarnate Word] may be a redemption of the sin of men and an abolition of death."[17] "Formerly the world guilty, was under judgment from the Law; but now the Word has taken on Himself the judgment, and

---

paid" (ibid., 4.20). And to meet that debt, "death there had to be, and death for all, so that the due of all might be paid" (ibid., 4.20).

12. See Irenaeus, *Against Heresies* 5.1.

13. See ibid., 3.18.7; see also 3.18.1; 3.18.7; 3.21.10.

14. Athanasius, *On the Incarnation* 4.20.

15. Ibid., 4.25.

16. Athanasius states: "Since then the Word, being the Image of the Father and immortal, took the form of the servant, and as a man underwent for us death in His flesh, that thereby He might offer Himself for us through death to the Father (*Four Discourses against the Arians* 1.41 [*NPNF²* 4:330]). Athanasius continues: "When then He [Christ] is said to hunger and weep and weary, and to cry Eloi, Eloi, which are our human affections, He receives them from us and offers to the Father, interceding for us, that in Him they may be annulled" (ibid., 4.6 [*NPNF²* 4:435]).

17. Ibid., 1:45 (*NPNF²* 4:332).

having suffered in the body for all, has bestowed salvation to all."[18] J. K. Mozley's assessment of Athanasius is on target: "There is more than a hint of substitution when he does deal with the death of Christ."[19]

The Cross as Ransom and Victory

Christus Victor was another way of viewing the cross, a view often associated with the ransom theory to Satan. In this view, the primary object of Christ's death is the power of sin, death, and Satan. By the cross, the divine Son released us from our captivity to Satan by paying our ransom price. Over time, this view became elaborate and speculative and focused more on Christ freeing us from our bondage to Satan than satisfying our sin before God. Yet it still viewed the cross as objective and substitutionary since Christ stood in our place. And it is important to note that the victory of Christ is necessary because it is our sin that first placed us in bondage—sin that Scripture describes in terms of rebellion against God and his just punishment.

In establishing biblical warrant, *Christus Victor* appealed to the abundant NT teaching that Christ's death achieved our redemption (which conveyed the notion of ransom price) and defeated the power of Satan (Mark 10:45; Luke 4:18; Col 2:13–15; Heb 2:14–16). This theme is dominant in Scripture, from the *protevangelium* of Genesis 3:15, through Christ's defeat of the powers in his life and ministry, to the crushing of Satan's head on the cross (Rom 16:20; Rev 12:1–12). So it is not surprising that *Christus Victor* gained traction. Unfortunately, over time this view took on a life of its own as it developed in ways that went beyond the biblical data. At first, theologians were content merely to declare the conquest of the devil in Christ's death. Irenaeus and Athanasius made passing allusion to what Christ accomplished in this regard by his coming, life, and death. But neither of them went any further. Athanasius, for example, was content to state the fact that "the death which is ascribed to him [the incarnate Word] may be a redemption of the sin of men and a abolition of death"[20] without speculating as to how the cross is connected with sin's remission or how it relates to the human liberation from demonic evils.

---

18. Ibid., 1:60 (*NPNF*[2] 4:341).
19. J. K. Mozley, *Doctrine of Atonement* (London: Duckworth, 1915), 107.
20. Athanasius, *Four Discourses against the Arians* 1.45 (*NPNF*[2] 4:332).

Over time, however, it was eventually asked to whom Christ pays the ransom price. And many argued that Satan was the payee. Origen moved in this direction and introduced analogies that later writers expanded.[21] He argued that God had given Satan a certain amount of authority due to the fall. In order to ransom us, God himself came into the world in his Son, and the Father handed Jesus over to Satan. Satan fell into the trap, thinking that he had Christ in his grasp, but he miscalculated the ransom bargain. Because Christ's deity was concealed by his humanity, he was enabled to overpower Satan and rise from the dead, thus destroying "him who had the power of death" (Heb 2:14). By the cross, then, God frees us from Satan's power and now subjects Satan to death and condemnation. After Origen, the view received even more embellishment by Gregory of Nyssa and others. Although the view emphasized much biblical truth, it veered in unbiblical directions, something later theologians sought to remedy.[22]

Even within the patristic era, however, not everyone endorsed the ransom view. For example, Cyril of Alexandria and John of Damascus rejected it. They retained the idea of ransom, and accepted the idea that the devil had dominion over human beings and that Christ's work secured that release. But they denied that any payment was paid to Satan.[23] These early theologians argued that the ransom view finds no direct confirmation in Scripture, mistakes Satan for God as the one who requires a payment (thus giving Satan more power than he has), and completely neglects the demands of God's justice with respect to sin. Nowhere does Scripture say that we as sinners owe anything to Satan; but Scripture repeatedly affirms that God requires of us a payment for

---

21.   For example, see *Against Celsus*, in *ANF* 4:395–669. Yet even for Origen, the ransom theory is only one aspect of his view of the cross since he also stressed Christ as our vicarious substitute (e.g., *Homilies in John* 28.19.165).

22.   For example, whereas Origen conceives of the devil miscalculating the ransom bargain, Gregory of Nyssa sees him "tricked" into miscalculation by God. Gregory justifies the ransom transaction in terms of a slave-master image (see Gregory of Nyssa, *The Great Catechism* 22 [*NPNF*[2] 5:492]). In Gregory's view, the devil justly bargained for a ransom for the release of his slaves, and God justly entered the bargain. The devil, thinking that the Son of God was weakened in his state of humiliation, that his authority would easily be usurped and that he would become subject to his power, demanded a ransom. But hidden from him was Christ's divine nature, which when he took it as ransom was too overpowering for him to hold. Gregory pictures Satan as a fish caught by the bait of Christ's humanity and left hanging on the hook of his divinity (see Gregory of Nyssa, *Great Catechism*, 22–24 [*NPNF*[2] 5:492–94]).

23.   For his criticism of the ransom view, see John of Damascus, *Exposition of the Orthodox Faith*, 3.18, 27 (*NPNF*[2] 9:67, 72).

our sins. The strength of the ransom view is that it emphasizes the objective, sacrificial nature of Christ's death and that apart from the cross we have no salvation.

The Cross as Penal Substitution

Penal substitution is also a truth emphasized in the patristic era. For starters, substitution is part of the recapitulation and ransom views, but in *penal* substitution, the accent is placed on Christ's death paying our debt in our place before God. It is *this* emphasis that Anselm later develops in the satisfaction view and the Reformers teach in penal substitution. At this point in church history, the *why* and *how* of the cross still require further clarification, yet what develops later is in continuity with the embryonic insights of the early church.

Eusebius of Caesarea contended that the heart of Christ's "sacrifice" is penal substitution.[24] Despite his identification with the ransom theory, Origen also stressed the propitiatory nature of Christ's death. Origen's theology is complex since it emphasizes that Satan and God are both objects of the cross.[25] Athanasius, who views the cross in terms of recapitulation, also contends that it pays our debt that we owed God.[26] And Chrysostom taught that men "ought to be punished; God did not punish them; they were to perish: God gave his Son in their stead."[27] The same emphasis is found in Tertullian and Augustine who thought of Christ's death as a priestly sacrifice and offering for sin.[28] Specifically, Augustine spoke of Christ's death as a sacrifice for sin: "We came to death through sin; [Christ came to it] through righteousness; and, therefore, as our death is the punishment of sin, so his death was made a sacrifice for sin."[29] Moreover, Augustine is clear that Christ's death brought about our redemption: "Christ, though guiltless, took our punishment, that he might cancel our guilt, and do away with our

---

24.   Eusebius of Caesarea, *The Proof of the Gospel*, trans. W. J. Ferrar (New York: Macmillan, 1920), 10.1, 54–62.

25.   See Origen, *Homiliae Numeros*, homily 24. Propitiation is the crucial word. It emphasizes the Godward focus of the cross. For a full discussion of propitiation, see Leon Morris, *The Apostolic Preaching of the Cross*, 3rd ed. (Grand Rapids: Eerdmans, 1965), 144–213.

26.   See Athanasius, *On the Incarnation* 20 (*NPNF*² 4:343).

27.   John Chrysostom, *Homilies on 1 Timothy* (*NPNF*¹ 13:431).

28.   See Tertullian, *Flight in Persecution* 12 (*ANF* 4:123). See Augustine, *The City of God* 10.20 (*NPNF*¹ 2:193); idem, *The Trinity* 4.14.19 (*NPNF*¹ 3:79).

29.   Augustine, *The Trinity* 4.12.15 (*NPNF*¹ 3:77).

punishment. . . . Confess that he died, and you may also confess that he, without taking our sin, took its punishment."[30] Augustine views the cross in terms of its multiple benefits—Satan is defeated, eternal life is won, God's love for us is demonstrated—yet it is also substitutionary at its core. Gregg Allison captures Augustine's view: "[F]or Augustine, Christ's atoning death rescued sinful human beings by liberating them from Satan, removing the divine wrath, reconciling humanity to God, demonstrating the love of God, and providing escape from death. In short, it cured the fallen world of its many miseries."[31]

One of the earliest examples of penal substitution is found in Diognetus. The author and recipient of the letter are unknown, and it dates from the latter half of the second century. In chapter 8, the author unpacks briefly the nature of human sin, and then on the heels of this discussion he turns in chapter 9 to the nature of the cross:

> When our wickedness had reached its height, and it had been clearly shown that its "reward," punishment and death, was impending over us God manifested his kindness and power. . . . He himself took on him the burden of our iniquities, he gave his own Son, as a ransom for us, the holy One for the transgressors, the blameless One for the wicked, the righteous One for the unrighteous, the incorruptible One for the corruptible, the immortal One for them that are mortal. For what other thing was capable of covering our sins than his righteousness? By what other one was it possible that we, the wicked and ungodly, could be justified, than by the only Son of God? O sweet exchange! O unsearchable operation! O benefits surpassing all expectation! That the wickedness of many should be hid in a single righteous One, and that the righteousness of One should justify many transgressors![32]

This ancient text gives us the basic view of penal substitution. Sin is viewed as a transgression resulting in unrighteousness and divine judgment. But Christ, the righteous and just one, has taken our place, paid for our sin, and justified us before God. Apart from Christ and his cross,

---

30. Augustine, *Against Faustus the Manichaean* 14:4, 7 (*NPNF*[1] 4:208–9).
31. Allison, *Historical Theology*, 394–95.
32. Diognetus 9.2–5 (*ANF* 1:28).

we remain in our sin and under God's righteous condemnation; but in Christ, due to his work, ungodly people are declared just and righteous.

In the patristic era, we find the church fathers teaching three different aspects of the cross. These aspects often overlap and join together, demonstrating that they are fundamentally complementary, yet more clarity is needed to explain the *nature* of the cross and *how* it achieves the forgiveness of our sin. As atonement theology developed in the medieval and Reformation eras, the *how* and *why* of the cross became more precise. Specifically, the ransom theory faded into the background and the main points of recapitulation, victory, and penal substitution took center stage.

The Medieval Era

For a number of reasons, Anselm of Canterbury's *Why God Became Man* is one of the most significant theological treatments of the atonement in the medieval era.[33] First, it was largely responsible for the church's moving away from the ransom theory to the satisfaction view of the cross. Second, it was a major attempt to give a rational and theological account of the atonement by reflecting on the necessity of the cross. Third, it was a development of the earlier views that brought more precision to the proper object of the cross, namely God himself.

Anselm's view is often criticized for being too influenced by his cultural background.[34] As the story goes, the transition from the patristic era to the medieval-feudal era brought a strong emphasis on legal relationships by elevating the concept of *honor* into an entire framework that required exact satisfaction to restore a person's dishonored name. By interpreting the cross within this feudal-legal(istic) framework, Anselm argued that Christ provided the exact payment or satisfaction for our sin. Although there is truth in this critique, it is a mistake to think that Anselm's view is *merely* indebted to feudalism. Anselm did not view sin as only a wrong done against an abstract principle or arbitrary law. Anselm spoke of sin as dishonoring God to emphasize the fact that God

---

33. Anselm, *Why God Became Man*, in *Anselm of Canterbury: The Major Works*, ed. Brian Davies and G. R. Evans, Oxford World's Classics (Oxford: Oxford University Press, 1998), 260–356.

34. For example, see Joel B. Green and Mark D. Baker, *Recovering the Scandal of the Cross: Atonement in New Testament and Contemporary Contexts*, 2nd ed. (Downers Grove, IL: InterVarsity Press, 2011), 151–61.

is an infinitely great and perfect person—an important biblical truth. Later the Reformers will strengthen Anselm's view by stressing God's aseity, holiness, justice, and righteousness. What is more significant to grasp is not Anselm's feudalism but the central role the doctrine of God plays, a crucial point also vital to the Reformation view of penal substitution.[35]

The following five points capture Anselm's overall argument. First, Anselm's treatise is written in the form of a dialogue between himself and Boso, a supposed disciple, who raises difficulties regarding the concept of atonement and problems inherent with the ransom theory. Anselm sets out to provide a rational and theological account of the cross. Second, in Book 1, Anselm argues against the ransom view by demonstrating that: (1) the only necessity for Christ's death is due to Christ's willingness to endure the cross for our redemption; and (2) humans *and* Satan belong to God. As such, it is not Satan who must be satisfied but God.[36]

Third, in contrast to the ransom view, Anselm develops the idea that the atonement is first and foremost a satisfaction made to God. Anselm argues that there is a need for satisfaction because sin dishonors God's name in the rejection of his majestic glory by the image bearers that God created to rule under his sovereign authority. Anselm writes, "[E]veryone who sins is under an obligation to repay to God the honour which he has violently taken from him, and this is the satisfaction which every sinner is obliged to give to God."[37] Why can't God overlook the dishonor done to him and freely forgive humans without the demand for satisfaction? Anselm answers: Because of who God is as the moral ruler of the universe. For God to forgive without satisfaction would compromise his character and nothing could be "more intolerable in the universal order than that a creature should take away honour from the creator and not repay what he takes away,"[38] In fact, if God were to forgive arbitrarily without satisfaction, God would annul the moral order through which he has expressed himself

35. On this point, see Adonis Vidu, *Atonement, Law, and Justice: The Cross in Historical and Cultural Contexts* (Grand Rapids: Baker, 2014).
36. Anselm, *Why God Became Man*, 1.7 (272–74).
37. Ibid., 1.11 (283).
38. Ibid., 1.13 (286).

in the world, and he would cease to be the most perfect being. Also, the sin in which humans are involved is *our* sin. We are responsible for not rendering to God the honor due to him and for our inability to do so.[39] We have failed to satisfy the conditions of our existence, and have brought dishonor to God. But God, the most perfect being, cannot allow this dishonor to go unpunished; it is fitting that he restores the original creation to its balance and harmony.

Fourth, God's righteous character demands either punishment or satisfaction for every sin.[40] If God chooses punishment, he is vindicated but his purpose for humans in creation is ultimately frustrated. Thankfully, God has chosen the more difficult way of satisfaction. But in choosing satisfaction, there is a major problem: humans must pay the debt of satisfaction, and yet we cannot because we have caused the dishonor and whatever we do in honoring God is only what we already owe. Besides, even if present debts could be paid, this would not compensate for past ones. Our human condition is this: "I have nothing to give him [God] in recompense for sin."[41]

Fifth, Anselm argues in Book 2 that Jesus alone can save us because of who he is and what he does for us. Since our sin and debt before God is infinite, only God can pay it; but since we owe it, we must pay it: "No one is capable of bringing about the recompense by which mankind may be saved except someone who is God. . . . But the obligation rests with man, and no one else, to make the payment . . . [o]therwise mankind is not making recompense."[42] The only solution to this dilemma is for the God-man to satisfy divine honor by paying for human sin. Thus, in order to redeem us, God the Son must become man in order to pay our debt *as God* in his life and death *as man* in which he fulfills the obligation we owe (i.e., fully honoring the Father). We come to benefit from the Son's obedient life and death because in Christ's voluntary self-sacrifice, he wins an *excess* of honor or reward—not for himself since he is sinless and perfect—but for sinners like ourselves.[43] God's mercy allows Christ's reward to be given

39. See ibid., 1.24 (309–12).
40. See ibid., 1.15 (288–89).
41. Ibid., 1.20 (304).
42. Ibid., 2.6 (319–20).
43. See ibid., 2.10 (325–28); 2.19 (352–54).

to sinners to provide satisfaction for their sins, and thus redemption is a gift to all who receive the Son.[44]

The main biblical-theological strength of Anselm's argument is twofold: it integrates the incarnation with the atonement and it locates the cross's necessity in the nature of God. These points together provide greater precision in our understanding of the nature of the atonement, its proper object, its necessity, and why Christ alone is Lord and Savior. Anselm clearly sees the centrality of God in the purpose of the cross and the problem of forgiveness, namely how God can remain true to himself and simultaneously forgive our sin. In these areas he is on solid ground.[45]

Anselm's argument, however, has at least four weaknesses. First, Anselm overemphasizes God's honor instead of accentuating God's holiness and justice. In so doing, Anselm does not stress fully that Christ underwent vicarious punishment to meet the demands of God's holiness and, as an expression of God's holiness in relation to sin, his wrath. This would entail Anselm connecting the cross's necessity more directly to God who is the moral standard of the universe. Second, Anselm says too little about God's love.[46] God necessarily upholds his honor and the ends for which he created humans, but the dominating idea in Anselm is that God cannot endure the shame of failure. In its full biblical proportion, however, Scripture declares the priority of God's love and grace as the reason he takes the initiative to save us.

Third, Anselm does not fully explain how Christ atones for sin. Anselm explains how Christ satisfies divine honor, but what about sin? Is there still something we must do for our salvation? True, Anselm will say in the words of God the Father, "Take my only-begotten Son," and in the words of Christ, "Take me and redeem yourself,"[47] but this is not really explained. In fact, for all of Anselm's emphasis on Christ satisfying God's honor and demand, he also implies that the satisfaction offered by Christ merely puts us in a position where we can imitate him; and by imitating him we satisfy God for ourselves.[48] There appears to be an

---

44. See ibid., 2.20 (354).

45. On this point, see Herman Bavinck, *Sin and Salvation in Christ*, vol. 3 of *Reformed Dogmatics*, ed. John Bolt, trans. John Vriend (Grand Rapids: Baker Academic, 2006), 344.

46. See McDonald, *Atonement of the Death of Christ*, 171–72.

47. Anselm, *Why God Became Man*, 2:20 (p. 354).

48. On this point, see McDonald, *Atonement of the Death of Christ*, 169; Macleod, *Christ*

inconsistency in Anselm's explanation of how Christ atones for our sin and our response to it.

Fourth, for all of Anselm's stress on the incarnation, he fails to "connect" Christ with his people with a robust doctrine of union with Christ.[49] He fails to place Christ's work within its biblical, covenantal context, and thus he loses the sense of covenant representation and substitution. He does not "connect" the life *and* death of Christ as the obedient incarnate Son to his people, and thus does not stress the vicarious obedience of Christ for us as the only basis for our justification before God. In other words, by neglecting Christ's obedience as our new covenant head, Anselm loses the biblical rationale that explains how Christ's righteousness becomes ours, how his death fully satisfies God's righteous demands, and how we benefit from his entire work. It is *this* point, namely the relationship between Christ's cross and its application to us, which the Reformers will address in their grasp of our covenantal union in Christ.

In fact, Timothy George argues that the real issue in the Reformation was not "the reality and efficacy of the atoning work of Christ on the cross, but rather how that achievement was to be appropriated."[50] Was it by faith formed by love, or by faith alone? Was Christ's work appropriated by believing the gospel promises or through the sacraments of the church? One of the reasons why this was at dispute in the Reformation was partly due to Anselm's silence on *how* Christ's cross is appropriated by us.

Into this silence, Thomas Aquinas (1224–1274) spoke. As Gwenfair Walters notes, Aquinas made more explicit the relationship between Christ's cross and our appropriation of it via the sacraments as mediated by the church.[51] As Aquinas makes clear:

Crucified, 175. Anselm asks: "On whom is it more appropriate for him to bestow the reward and recompense for his death than on those for whose salvation, as the logic of truth teaches us, he made himself a man, and for whom, as we have said, he set an example, by his death, of dying for the sake of righteousness? For they will be imitators of him in vain, if they are not to be sharers in his reward" (*Why God Became Man*, 2:19 [p. 353]).

49.   See, McDonald, *Atonement of the Death of Christ*, 172–73.

50.   Timothy George, "The Atonement in Martin Luther's Theology," in *The Glory of the Atonement*, ed. Charles E. Hill and Frank A. James III (Downers Grove, IL: InterVarsity Press, 2004), 263.

51.   See Gwenfair M. Walters, "The Atonement in Medieval Theology," in Hill and James, *Glory of the Atonement*, 239–62.

Christ's Passion is the sufficient cause of man's salvation. But it does not follow that the sacraments are not also necessary for that purpose: because they obtain their effect through the power of Christ's Passion; and Christ's Passion is, so to say, applied to man through the sacraments according to the Apostle Paul (Rom vi. 3): *All we who are baptized in Christ Jesus, are baptized into His death.*[52]

As this developed in medieval theology, the sacraments were *necessary* for salvation because it was through them that Christ's atonement was applied to us and we are made righteous. By baptism, Christ's work is applied to us by infusing grace into us that cleanses us from original sin, regenerates us, and incorporates us into the church. The grace that is communicated through the sacraments is infused so that our very nature is transformed, and by this infusion, we are enabled to cooperate with God to merit eternal life. In addition, by this application of Christ's work we are delivered from eternal punishment and from guilt. But subsequent sins after our baptism also demand satisfaction, which is paid for either in purgatory or "through the power of the keys exercised in the sacrament of penance."[53] Penance became one of the most important ways Christ's cross was applied to us in our daily lives, given the necessity of additional satisfaction to be made by Christians due to ongoing sin. As Walters concludes, "While Anselm most likely did not intend such a large role to be played by human beings in activating and completing the work of atonement, his emphasis on the idea of satisfaction was certainly echoed in the piety of the late Middle Ages."[54]

In this context, the Reformation took place. The Reformers rejected Rome's sacramental theology, namely, her understanding of the mediatorial role of the church and the church's authority to infuse grace by the sacraments *ex opere operato* ("by the work worked") regardless of whether faith is present in the recipient. On the basis of *Christ alone* the ground of our justification is secure, both in terms of its accomplishment and application to us by the Spirit. By faith alone in the gospel promises, Christ's all-sufficient work is applied to us by the Spirit. As important as the sacraments are as means of grace, they do not infuse

---

52. Thomas Aquinas, *Summa Theologica*, 5 vols., Christian Classics (Notre Dame, IN: Ava Maria, 1981), pt. 3, Q. 61, Art. 1 (4:2347).

53. Walters, "The Atonement in Medieval Theology," 249.

54. Ibid., 252.

grace into us. They are God's promises to us and our bearing witness that our justification before God is accomplished by *Christ alone*, and that by faith alone in Christ we stand justified before God clothed in Christ's righteousness. In solidarity with his people, Christ alone has accomplished and secured everything necessary and sufficient for our salvation.

The Reformation Era

The Reformers continued the Trinitarian and christological thought of the patristic and medieval eras.[55] In the doctrine of the atonement, the Reformers (e.g., Martin Luther, John Calvin, and Ulrich Zwingli) held to the basic insights of Anselm's satisfaction theory, especially in making the doctrine of God central to the cross and keeping the cross as a requirement for the forgiveness of sin.[56] Yet the Reformers *and* the post-Reformation Reformed theologians also corrected Anselm's view. By theologizing about Christ's death in more biblical categories, they achieved greater clarity in regard to the nature of the cross.[57]

The Reformers and their heirs, for example, viewed sin primarily as a violation of God's holy and righteous character. This focus entailed a proper sense of retributive justice tied to God's moral nature. Because sin offends God, and because God is holy and just, God *must* punish sin unless there is full satisfaction for it. But humanity cannot atone for its own sin given its divine object. Only Christ, God the Son incarnate, can stand in our place and act as our substitute by bearing our sin, paying the penalty for it, and removing its condemnation.

Martin Luther captures the Reformation view of the cross in this way:

55. See Richard A. Muller, *Post-Reformation Reformed Dogmatics: The Rise and Development of Reformed Orthodoxy, ca. 1520 to ca. 1725*, 2nd ed., 4 vols. (Grand Rapids: Baker, 2003), volumes 3 and 4.

56. In the Reformers, necessity was first hypothetical, and then in Reformed orthodoxy it was more consistently worked out in terms of absolute necessity in theologians such as Francis Turretin and John Owen. On this point, see John Murray, *Redemption Accomplished and Applied* (Grand Rapids: Eerdmans, 1955), 9–18; Oliver Crisp, "Penal Non-Substitution," *Journal of Theological Studies* 59:1 (2008): 140–53; Francis Turretin, *Institutes of Elenctic Theology*, ed. and trans. James T. Dennison Jr. and George Musgrave Giger, 3 vols. (Phillipsburg, NJ: P&R, 1994), 2:418.

57. Macleod unpacks the continuity and discontinuity with Anselm in *Christ Crucified*, 171–93.

Because an eternal, unchangeable sentence of condemnation has passed upon sin—for God cannot and will not regard sin with favor, but his wrath abides upon it eternally and irrevocably—redemption was not possible with a ransom of such precious worth as to atone for sin, to assume the guilt, pay the price of wrath and thus abolish sin. This no creature was able to do. There was no remedy except for God's only Son to step into our distress and himself become man, to take upon himself the load of awful and eternal wrath and make his own body and blood a sacrifice for sin. And so he did, out of the immeasurably great mercy and love towards us, giving himself up and bearing the sentence of unending wrath and death.[58]

Expressing a similar understanding, John Calvin specifically uses *satisfaction language* to convey the outcome of Christ *propitiating the Father's wrath*: "No one can descend into himself and seriously consider what he is without feeling God's wrath and hostility toward him. Accordingly, he must seek ways and means to appease God—and this demands a satisfaction. No common assurance is required, for God's wrath and curse always lie upon sinners until they are absolved of guilt."[59] Moreover, it is only in *Christ alone* that our guilt can be absolved. Calvin explains that because our Lord has acted in our place, "we have in his death the complete fulfillment of salvation, for through it we are reconciled to God, his righteous judgment is satisfied, the curse is removed, and the penalty paid in full."[60]

Furthermore, in contrast to Anselm, the Reformers expounded the atonement in more robust biblical categories. For example, Calvin places Christ's work within its proper covenantal context and unpacks his threefold office of prophet, priest, and king. Similar to the recapitulation theme of the early church, Calvin also speaks of the cross's achievement by tracing the Adam-last Adam typological relationship with a particular focus on Christ's active and passive obedience as our covenant head. In addition, Calvin discusses the cross in *Christus Victor*

---

58. Martin Luther, "Epistle Sermon: Twenty-fourth Sunday after Trinity," cited in John Nicholas Lenker, ed., *The Precious and Sacred Writings of Martin Luther* (Minneapolis: Luther Press, 1909), 9:43–45.

59. Calvin, *Institutes*, 2.16.1.

60. Ibid., 2.16.13.

terms while simultaneously speaking of the achievement of Christ's work in the biblical categories of covenant, sacrifice, reconciliation, redemption, and justice.[61] In short, the Reformers improved on Anselm by interpreting the cross on the Bible's own terms. In addition, the Reformers set against Rome's sacramental theology of merit the necessary and sufficient work of Christ directly applied to us through faith wrought by the Spirit—a work of the Spirit secured by the Son's work of atonement.

Reformation Atonement: Penal Substitution

Although there are nuanced differences between the Reformers and their heirs, the overall Reformation view of the atonement is penal substitution.[62]

Penal refers to the sorry state of the human race in Adam in which we stand under God's judgment and the penalty of death. This one word picks up a central feature of the Bible's storyline: as the covenant head and representative of the human race, Adam disobeyed God, and his sin then became our sin by nature, imputation, and choice. All humanity is in Adam and therefore under the power and penalty of sin—namely spiritual and physical death (Rom 3:23; 6:23; see Eph 2:1–4). As a

---

61. See Robert A. Peterson, *Calvin and the Atonement* (Fearn, Ross-shire, UK: Mentor, 1999).

62. Gustav Aulén argued that Luther's view of the cross was *Christus Victor* and not penal substitution (Gustav Aulén, *Christus Victor: An Historical Study of the Three Main Types of the Idea of the Atonement*, trans. A. G. Herbert [London: SPCK, 1965]). But this view cannot be sustained. There are diverse elements in Luther's view, but at the center of the cross for Luther is penal substitution. For example, on Gal 3:13 Luther writes, "Thus the whole emphasis is on the phrase 'for us.' For Christ is innocent so far as His own Person is concerned; and therefore He should not have been hanged from the tree. But because, according to the Law, every thief should have been hanged, therefore, according to the Law of Moses, Christ Himself should have been hanged; for he bore the person of a sinner and a thief—and not of one but of all sinners and thieves. For we are sinners and thieves, and therefore we are worthy of death and eternal damnation. But Christ took all our sins upon Himself, and for them He died on the cross. Therefore it was appropriate for Him to become a thief and, as Isaiah says (53:12), to be 'numbered with the transgressors.' . . . He is not acting in His own Person now. Now he is not the Son of God, born of the Virgin. But he is a sinner, who has and bears the sin of Paul, the former blasphemer, persecutor, and assaulter; of Peter, who denied Christ; of David, who was an adulterer and a murderer. . . . In short, He has and bears all the sins of all men in His body—not in the sense that He has committed them, but in the sense that He took these sins, committed by us, upon His own body, in order to make satisfaction for them with His own blood" (Martin Luther, *Luther's Works*, 55 vols. [St. Louis: Concordia, 1955–86], 26:277).

result, we are alienated from the triune covenant God who created us to know and love him; we are under his verdict of condemnation; and because he is personal, holy, and righteous, he stands opposed to us in his wrath.

Substitution refers to the person and work of our Lord Jesus Christ who acts on our behalf in his death on the cross. This term also picks up the Bible's storyline to speak of the triune God of sovereign grace choosing to redeem a people instead of leaving us in our sin and depravity and under his judgment. God redeems us by triune initiative and agency and in the provision of our substitute. As our new covenant head, Christ represented us in his life and in his death as the greater Adam who willingly and gladly obeyed the Father in perfection and by the power of the Spirit. In death in particular, Christ stood in our place, took God's demand for our righteousness upon himself, and paid our debt by receiving the penalty we deserved. The result of Christ's substitutionary work for us is that by our faith union in Christ, God the Father declares us just, forgiven of every sin in full, and he frees us from the power of sin and the tyranny of Satan, who once held the verdict of death and condemnation over our heads (2 Cor 5:21; see 1 Pet 3:18; Gal 3:13; Heb 9:28; Rom 8:32).

In other words, for the Reformers to say that the cross is penal substitution is another way of proclaiming the gospel of God's sovereign grace. Penal substitution is not merely an atonement theory; it is also shorthand for speaking of the triune God in all of his holiness, righteousness, and justice. Furthermore, it conveys the truth that the human race is in a pitiful state; it is a guilty, depraved, helpless sinner under the sentence of death. Penal substitution also reminds us of our glorious Savior—the Substitute—whose cross work accomplished everything for us. In our place, he bears the penalty we deserve, and by doing so, he saves us completely as our great priest-king. Lastly, penal substitution places God at the center of our salvation. It reminds us that the triune God of grace planned our great redemption from eternity and then achieved it on the stage of human history, acting in power and grace to provide, achieve, and accomplish our salvation by the Father's initiative, in and through the Son, and by the Spirit.

A Key Reformation Insight: Atonement Debates are Doctrine-of-God Debates

Probably the key theological insight the Reformers and their heirs gave to the church was their clarity regarding the God-law relationship and the corresponding God-sin relationship.[63] Anselm's insight of making the doctrine of God central to understanding the cross, and the cross as necessary for our forgiveness, is developed with more precision. In fact, this insight is key to why penal substitution is the best way to capture what is central to Christ's atoning work.

God's centrality is captured best in the doctrine of divine aseity, i.e., God's independence and complete personal self-sufficiency. The Reformers rightly saw that from the opening verses of Scripture, God is presented as the personal-triune, uncreated, independent, self-sufficient Lord who created the universe and governs it by his word (Gen 1–2; Pss 50:12–14; 93:2; Acts 17:24–25). This is why the governing category of all Christian theology is the Creator-creature distinction: God alone is God, and all else depends upon him for its existence. Also, as the triune Creator-Covenant Lord, God rules over his creation perfectly and personally. He rules with perfect power, knowledge, and righteousness (Pss 9:8; 33:5; 139:1–4, 16; Isa 46:9–11; Acts 4:27–28; Rom 121:33–36). In this rule, God loves, hates, commands, comforts, punishes, and rewards, all according to the personal covenant relationships that he establishes with his creation.

In Scripture, God is never presented as an abstract concept or impersonal force.[64] For example, Calvin argues that the law is the perfect expression of God's character because it is tied to his very nature.[65] This insight was developed in the post-Reformation theologians. In their argument against the Socinian view that retributive justice is merely a voluntary exercise of divine justice as a result of creation, the Reformation and its heirs argued that the justice of God "is not a quality

---

63. On this point, see Vidu, *Atonement, Law, and Justice*, 92–97; cf. Bavinck, *Sin and Salvation in Christ*, 345.

64. On this point, it is important to speak of the heirs of the Reformation. As Vidu points out, the Reformers link God's law to God's own nature, but they do not always do so consistently (Vidu, *Atonement, Law, and Justice*, 94). Yet in the later Reformed tradition, especially in theologians such as Francis Turretin and John Owen, the seminal insight of the Reformers regarding the relationship of God and law is more consistently worked out and applied (see Muller, *Post-Reformation Reformed Dogmatics*, 3:476–97).

65. See Calvin, *Institutes*, 2.7; 3.23.2.

or accident in him, but his very nature, essential to him."[66] This entails that God is not merely the adjudicator of laws external to him. Instead, the triune God, who is holy love, *is the law* and as such, the moral standard of the universe, who always acts consistently with who he is. God is righteous and just, and as such he always acts in perfect justice and goodness. In relation to sin, this is why, given God's aseity, a *mustness* or *necessity* results in the collision of our sin before him. Given who God is, he *cannot* tolerate wickedness (Hab 1:12–13; see Isa 1:4–20; 35:8). He *must* act with holy justice when his people rebel against him; yet he is also the God who loves his people with a holy love (Hos 11:9), for he is the God of "covenant faithfulness" (*hesed*). In Scripture, divine holiness and love are never set against each other, but there is an awful *tension* in the Bible's storyline of how God will simultaneously demonstrate his holy justice and covenant love. Ultimately, this tension, rooted in the God-sin relationship, is only resolved in Christ and his work when God himself in his Son takes on our human nature, willingly and gladly represents us as our covenant head, and dies for us as our substitute to satisfy God's own righteous requirements and secure our justification (see Rom 3:21–26).

It is this tension between God in all of his glorious self-sufficiency and human sin—between divine holiness-justice and covenant love—that the Reformers and their heirs developed in greater precision. This is not to say that this was a new insight; instead, what began in Anselm was developed further by the Reformation. Since God is the law, he *cannot* forgive our sin without satisfying his own holy and righteous demand. For God to forgive sin apart from the punishment of our sin or its full satisfaction is impossible. God cannot overlook our sin nor can he relax the retributive demands of his justice because he cannot deny himself. The God of the Bible is *a se*: self-existent, self-attesting, *and self-justifying*, which entails that *he must* punish sin because our sin is against *him*. Sin is not foremost against an external, impersonal order outside of God; it is against *him*, the triune-personal God of holy love, righteousness, and justice.

---

66. Muller, *Post-Reformation Reformed Dogmatics*, 3:481 (citing Leigh, *Treatise*, II.xii, 92 margin).

The Reformation's emphasis on the God-law relationship is foundational to grasping penal substitution. Among all the diverse atonement theologies, penal substitution is the view that best captures the God-centered nature of the cross and the divine problem of forgiveness. Other views make the object of the cross to be sin (e.g., forms of the recapitulation view), or Satan (e.g., ransom theory), or they view the cross solely as victory over the powers (e.g., forms of *Christus Victor*). These theories emphasize many biblical truths, but they downplay this central point. By contrast, penal substitution believes the ultimate object of the cross is God himself. Our triune God desires to forgive us, but he cannot deny himself. God himself must satisfy himself, and the only way he can do so is in Christ Jesus our Lord. By grasping this central truth, the Reformers provide the theological grounding to the gospel of God's sovereign grace and why Christ alone saves.

The Reformers rightly understood from Scripture that sinners can offer God nothing. We only deserve the penalty of our sin, eternal death. Yet God, prompted solely by grace and love, planned our salvation in his eternal wisdom. As Donald Macleod writes, "The triune God resolve[d] to save the world, and to accept the good offices of a Mediator who shall act for mankind as their representative and suffer for them as their substitute: so accommodating is the divine will, and so predisposed to forgive our transgressions."[67] Yet in choosing to redeem us, God cannot deny himself. For us, salvation cost nothing, but for God, *he* must save us alone. God will provide the perfect substitute, and given the problem of forgiveness, that substitute must be God himself. In God's eternal plan, the divine Son becomes our mediator: he takes our place and bears our penalty. Nothing more needs to be added to his work; it is necessary and sufficient for our salvation. In his death, as our new covenant head, no debt is left unpaid. We only need to receive what he has done by *faith alone* in *Christ alone*.

A Spectrum of Reaction to Penal Substitution

After the Reformation, a theological spectrum emerges in relation to penal substitution. First, the view of penal substitution continues in Protestant, evangelical theology as the best way to grasp what is central

67. Macleod, *Christ Crucified*, 177.

to the cross. Within this view, various debates occur such as the extent of the atonement, but the basic view remains unchanged.[68]

Second, penal substitution is rejected in non-orthodox circles. In the post-Reformation era, this is best illustrated by Socinianism. In the Enlightenment, classical liberal theology continues the Socinian critique, and this theological path continues today in a variety of postmodern, liberal theologies, all of which embrace pluralism and deny Christ's unique identity and work. These theologies, at their heart, are different theologies distinct from historic Christianity, so our disagreement with them is at the worldview level.[69] However, what unites this second path of diverse theologies is their denial of the central theological insight of the Reformation, namely that the triune, self-sufficient God *cannot* forgive our sin without satisfaction of his own righteous moral demand. Instead, these views unite in rejecting penal substitution as *unnecessary* because God can forgive without payment for our sins; *unjust* because Christ, as the innocent person, suffers while the guilty are set free; and *unloving* because it conveys the notion that God delights in innocent suffering which also fosters passivity in the face of evil.

Third, penal substitution is revised among some who are committed to orthodox, Christian theology. In the post-Reformation era, this is best illustrated by the governmental view of the cross which attempted to offer a *via media* between Socinianism and penal substitution. Usually advocates of this third path attempt to recover an earlier view of the atonement, such as recapitulation or *Christus Victor*, or they combine various views, but they unite in denying that penal substitution is the *means* by which our sins are forgiven.[70] But, similar to the second

---

68. For example, on the extent of the atonement see David Gibson and Jonathan Gibson, eds., *From Heaven He Came and Sought Her: Definite Atonement in Historical, Biblical, Theological, and Pastoral Perspective* (Wheaton, IL: Crossway, 2013). For some expositions of penal substitution, see Bavinck, *Sin and Salvation in Christ*; Geerhardus Vos, *Christology*, vol. 3 of *Reformed Dogmatics*, trans. and ed. Richard B. Gaffin Jr. (Bellingham, WA: Lexham, 2014); John Stott, *The Cross of Christ* (Downers Grove, IL: InterVarsity Press, 1984); Robert Letham, *The Work of Christ*, Contours of Christian Theology (Downers Grove, IL: InterVarsity Press, 1993); Charles E. Hill and Frank A. James III, eds., *The Glory of the Atonement: Biblical, Theological, and Practical Perspectives* (Downers Grove, IL: InterVarsity Press, 2004); Steve Jeffery, Mike Ovey, and Andrew Sach, *Pierced for Our Transgressions: Recovering the Glory of Penal Substitution* (Nottingham, UK: Inter-Varsity Press, 2007); J. I. Packer and Mark Dever, *In My Place Condemned He Stood* (Wheaton, IL: Crossway, 2007).

69. See J. Gresham Machen, *Christianity and Liberalism* (1923; repr., Grand Rapids: Eerdmans, 1981).

70. For example, this point is strongly emphasized in Darrin W. Snyder Belousek,

path, what unites the diverse perspectives of the third way is the denial, or at least revision, of the central theological insight of the Reformation: God *cannot* forgive sin without the complete satisfaction of his own righteous moral demand. In other words, the atoning work of Christ as our penal substitute is *absolutely necessary* for the forgiveness of our sins and our justification before God. It is this theological point which the third path, like the second, rejects or revises, but, unlike the second path, it does so within the confines of historic orthodox theology. With this spectrum in mind, let us now describe the two main alternatives to penal substitution.

The Socinian-Classical Liberal-Postmodern View

Socinianism represents the non-orthodox rejection of penal substitution, which in a variety of ways, and broadly conceived, continues today within the liberal theological tradition.[71] Faustus Socinus (1539–1604), founder of the movement, not only rejected penal substitution but also the authority of Scripture, the doctrines of original sin, divine foreknowledge, the deity of Christ, and correspondingly the triune nature of God. In contrast to historic Christianity, Socinianism is a different theology. Yet, in its understanding of the God-law relationship, it represents a stream of thought that continues in our present day.

What is the Socinian view of the God-law-sin relationship? Similar to earlier forms of divine voluntarism, which view God's choices solely in terms of what he wills,[72] Socinianism views the law as an expression of God's will and *not* as an expression of his will *tied to his nature*.

Atonement, Justice, and Peace: The Message of the Cross and the Mission of the Church (Grand Rapids: Eerdmans, 2012). For some evangelical revisions of the atonement, see James Beilby and Paul R. Eddy, eds., *The Nature of the Atonement: Four Views* (Downers Grove, IL: InterVarsity Press, 2006); Joel B. Green and Mark D. Baker, *Recovering the Scandal of the Cross: Atonement in New Testament and Contemporary Contexts*, 2nd ed. (Downers Grove, IL: InterVarsity Press, 2011); Steve Chalke and Alan Mann, *The Lost Message of Jesus* (Grand Rapids: Zondervan, 2003); Scot McKnight, *A Community Called Atonement* (Nashville: Abingdon, 2007); Colin E. Gunton, *The Actuality of Atonement: A Study of Metaphor, Rationality, and the Christian Tradition* (London: T&T Clark, 1988); Hans Boersma, *Violence, Hospitality, and the Cross: Reappropriating the Atonement Tradition* (Grand Rapids: Baker Academic, 2004).

71. For a helpful discussion of Socinianism, see Bavinck, *Sin and Salvation in Christ*, 347–51.

72. See Vidu, *Atonement, Law, and Justice*, 79–88.

Thus, God may choose to exercise divine retributive justice if he so desires, but he is under no obligation tied to his nature to punish sin. For this reason, Socinians argued that God can forgive sin without atonement. For Socinianism there is no "problem of forgiveness," and as such, Christ's death is *not necessary* for our justification before God. Richard Muller captures this point: "The Socinian argument was that God's punitive justice was the result of the free will of God, much like the creation of the world. Just as God was free to will or not will the existence of the world, so is he free to will or not will the enactment of justice and the punishment of sin."[73] Of course, if the Socinian view is true, then the need for Christ's unique and exclusive atonement is undercut. As Muller rightly explains: "By extension and intent, the argument undermined the satisfaction theory of atonement: if the Socinian view were correct, salvation could be grounded in something other than a satisfaction of the divine justice."[74]

What was the Socinian view of the atonement? For the most part, it was the example or moral influence view, which had its roots in the thought of Peter Abelard (1079–1142), but with some additions from their non-orthodox theology.[75] Given the Socinian view that God's mercy is more fundamental than God's justice, and given that God's justice is not grounded in his nature, Christ's death is not necessary to satisfy divine justice. Instead, Christ's death, because he is the model man, becomes merely an example for us. Allison states it this way: the cross for Socinianism "is not about a substitutionary death undertaken by the Son of God. Rather, it is the supreme example of a righteous man and is intended to lead others to embrace forgiveness."[76] The cross becomes the highest declaration of God's love and mercy, and the true

---

73. Muller, *Post-Reformation Reformed Dogmatics*, 3:491.
74. Ibid.
75. See Allison, *Historical Theology*, 397–98. Abelard is unlike the Socinians in maintaining historic, orthodox Trinitarianism and Christology. Also, although Abelard primarily emphasized that the atonement was principally a demonstration of the love of God to excite God's love in us, Abelard does not stop at this point, as is common with the moral influence position. He also links redemption with the death of Christ and his shed blood. He rejects a ransom paid to Satan since it is properly paid to God, which seems to imply a Godward focus to his view of the cross. On these points, Abelard's view is unlike the Socinian and later theology of classical liberalism.
76. Ibid., 402.

significance of Christ lies not in his sacrificial death but in his exemplary, obedient, moral life.

Unfortunately the Socinian view is not an aberration on the theological scene; it has come to dominate much of theological liberalism. In classical liberal theology and current postmodern-pluralistic thought, the basic theology of Socinianism continues, albeit with different emphases.[77] But at its heart, liberal theology separates the law of God from the nature of God; it makes the exercise of divine justice a voluntary exercise of God's will; it stresses the priority of divine love; and it argues that God does *not* demand full payment for our sin. In nonorthodox theology, Christ is only quantitatively greater than others, and so such theology has lost any sense that it is Christ alone who saves. Today, in light of postmodernism, liberalism veers toward full-blown pluralism, thus undercutting further the ground for Christ's unique identity and work.[78]

In the end, Socinian theology and its current manifestations represent a theology antithetical to historic Christianity. At its heart, it has a different view of God—his triune nature, holiness, justice, righteousness, and love—and correspondingly, a different view of sin, salvation, and Christ. Their entire viewpoint fails to do justice to the Bible's own storyline and teaching, and as such, in whatever current form it is packaged, it must be rejected *in toto* as a false gospel.

The Governmental View: A *Via Media*?

The governmental view of the atonement offers a *via media*, or middle way, between the Reformation view of penal substitution and Socinianism. Historically, the view is identified with James Arminius, Hugo Grotius, John Miley, and the Arminian tradition in Protestant theology.[79] It is a *via media* because unlike the Socinians, it affirms

---

77. In the classical liberal tradition, for example, see Friedrich Schleiermacher and Albrecht Ritschl. For these examples, see MacDonald, *Atonement of the Death of Christ*, 208–15; Allison, *Historical Theology*, 405–10. For a discussion of postmodern-pluralistic thought, see Kevin J. Vanhoozer, "The Atonement in Postmodernity," in Hill and James, *Glory of the Atonement*, 367–404.

78. See D. A. Carson, *The Gagging of God: Christianity Confronts Pluralism* (Grand Rapids: Zondervan, 1996).

79. There is some debate on whether Hugo Grotius held to the governmental view (see Garry Williams, "A Critical Exposition of Hugo Grotius' Doctrine of the Atonement in *De Satisfactione Christi*" (D. Phil. Thesis, Oxford University, 1999).

historic Christian beliefs and the necessity of Christ's cross for our salvation. Yet it contends that the cross is only hypothetically necessary for our salvation. With many in church history, it affirms that although there were other ways God could have redeemed fallen humanity apart from Christ's death, nevertheless the atoning work of Christ was the most fitting way, and, in God's plan, it is the actual way that God has chosen to redeem us.[80] Contrary to Socinianism, then, and in agreement with orthodoxy, Christ alone is Savior, and apart from his work applied to us, there is no salvation.

However, in affirming the hypothetical necessity of the cross, the governmental view breaks with the central theological insight of the Reformation, namely, that God *cannot* forgive sin without the full payment of our sin by Christ as our penal substitute. John Miley, a proponent of the view, gives us the underlying theological reason for this departure. Miley denies that God's justice *necessitates* the full payment of our sin. Miley acknowledges that God's punishment of sin is just, "but not in itself an obligation. The intrinsic evil of sin renders its penal retribution just, but not a requirement of judicial rectitude."[81] God, as the moral governor, can choose to relax the requirements of divine retributive justice without requiring full satisfaction, thus forgiving sinners by his mercy alone. Divine forgiveness does *not* demand a penal substitute to pay fully for our sin. And so this view rejects penal substitution.

But some questions arise. How can God relax the requirements of divine retributive justice and still remain just? If God can forgive on the basis of his mercy, then why Christ's death? Why not adopt the Socinian view that the cross is not necessary for our salvation? Two important points are needed to make sense of the view and to demonstrate why it is a *via media*.

First, as Oliver Crisp makes clear, to understand the governmental view correctly, one must grasp that it decouples divine rectoral justice from divine retributive justice for the purposes of satisfaction. Crisp explains this important point:

---

80. See Oliver Crisp, "Penal Non-Substitution," *Journal of Theological Studies* 59:1 (2008): 140–53.

81. John Miley, *Systematic Theology*, 2 vols. (1893; repr., Peabody, MA: Hendrickson, 1989), 2:162.

In this context, *rectoral justice* is that aspect of divine justice whereby God rightly governs the cosmos in accordance with his moral law. *Retributive justice* is that aspect of divine justice whereby God's wrath is meted out to those creatures who transgress the divine law, who remain the objects of divine wrath and are not the objects of divine mercy. Whereas the former must be satisfied in some sense, there may be a relaxation of the requirements of divine retributive justice so that Christ may act in a manner consistent with rectoral justice . . . but without acting so as to satisfy divine retribution as a penal substitute. . . . In short, for advocates of the [governmental view], rectoral justice *must* be satisfied, whereas retributive justice *may* be satisfied. God may waive the satisfaction of retributive justice and remain perfectly just in so acting because this aspect of God's distributive justice may be relaxed. The same cannot be said of rectoral justice, which is dependent on the divine moral law, and therefore may not be relaxed without vitiating God's just and moral rule of the created order.[82]

Why is this distinction important for the Governmental view? Because it helps explain why Christ's death is *necessary* in satisfying rectoral justice but not retributive justice. Since God is the moral governor, it is incumbent upon him to govern the world justly and morally. God's law is for the good order of society, and that ordering of society is secured only as the moral law is upheld. Contrary to Socinian theology, if God does not satisfy rectoral justice and simply shows mercy by forgiving sinful people, he undermines himself as the governor and does not act in the best interests of the governed.[83] Christ's death, then, is necessary to satisfy rectoral justice; to underscore the terrible nature of sin; and to emphasize that the law must be respected.

How are we forgiven and justified before God? We are forgiven by Christ's satisfying divine rectoral justice for us and by our availing ourselves of his work by faith and repentance. However, in contrast to penal substitution, Christ did *not* bear the exact penalty of divine retributive justice for us. Our guilt cannot be transferred to him and furthermore,

---

82. Crisp, "Penal Non-Substitution," 148–49.
83. Grotius called this the "common good—the conservation and example of order" (cited in McDonald, *Atonement of the Death of Christ*, 204).

this was unnecessary because God relaxed the retributive demand of the law. As such, Christ did not have to obey the law fully for me or pay the full penalty of my sin. Instead, Christ offered a suitable equivalent act of atonement which upheld God's moral governance and revealed the serious nature of human sin. Objectively, Christ's death upheld the moral governance of the universe while relaxing the demand for my sin to be fully punished. Subjectively, the punishment inflicted on Christ is *exemplary* in that it reveals God's hatred of sin and motivates persons to repent of their sins.

Second, to discern how the governmental view functions as a *via media*, we need to ask the crucial question: How can God relax the requirements of divine retributive justice and still remain just? The answer is this: the governmental view does *not* view the law as an expression of God's will *and* nature; instead, it views the law as an expression of God's will and thus "outside" of him. Because the law is not grounded in God's nature, he is free to relax its demand for retributive justice. So, unlike later Reformed theology which contends that God *cannot* forgive sin without its full payment and satisfaction, the governmental view argues that God is free to will or not will the enactment of justice and the punishment of sin.

By this understanding, the governmental theory argues that Christ's death is only hypothetically necessary and not absolutely necessary. In penal substitution, since God is the law, if God chooses to save us (which he has graciously chosen to do), he *cannot* forgive our sins without his righteous demand being fully satisfied. Christ's death is not merely one of the means God selected to redeem us; it is the *only* way. Given the God-law-sin relationship, the sacrificial death of Christ as our penal substitute is absolutely necessary for our justification before God. God himself *had* to satisfy his own righteous demand in order to forgive us; God will not and cannot deny *himself*. Yet we also needed a human representative to stand in our place, to obey the full demands of God's law, and to bear our penalty for us. In short, we need the only Savior who alone can meet our need: God the Son incarnate.

However, it is this *absolute* necessity of penal substitution that the governmental view rejects. By making rectoral justice more fundamental to God's nature than retributive justice,[84] and by decoupling the moral law from God's nature, the governmental view "dismissed the atonement of Christ as an exact payment of the penalty demanded by the [retributive] justice of God and expressed in his law. Christ suffered and died, not as a satisfaction for the exact penalty, but as a token of God's concern to uphold his moral law."[85]

How should we assess the governmental view? Positively, it does explain, contra the Socinians and the entire liberal theological tradition, why the cross is necessary. And so it provides a theological rationale for *Christ alone*. God cannot simply forgive without a suitably equivalent act of atonement. Christ's death is necessary as God's chosen means to satisfy the demands of God's rectoral justice, thus enabling God to govern the world justly and morally. No doubt, the necessity assumed in the view is of the hypothetical variety, but given God's choice to save, the cross is God's ordained, fitting means to satisfy rectoral justice and allow for the relaxation of retributive justice's demand.

Negatively, however, it has one central problem which leads to further problems. At its heart, there is an inadequate view of God. The governmental view thinks of the moral law as an expression of God's will and thus "outside" of him. The law is *not* as an expression of both his will *and* nature. Because the law is not grounded in his very nature, God can relax the demands of retributive justice and forgive sin without its full payment and satisfaction. But as we have argued in chapter 1, this view is not biblical.

As we work through the Bible's storyline, our Creator-Covenant Lord does not merely adjudicate the law as might a human judge. Rather, God *is* the law. The moral law does not function "outside" of God; rather God is the law, and as such, he is the universal, objective standard of justice. The Bible does not decouple the law from God. God *must* punish our sin because he *cannot* relax his righteous demand. God *cannot* arbitrarily forgive, nor can he forgive without the full payment for sin. God *must* satisfy *himself* in order to justify the ungodly. And he can only do so in one way: in Christ alone. Christ alone is able to meet our need because he is the perfect Savior. Apart from *this* Jesus and his

---

84. See Crisp, "Penal Non-Substitution," 149.
85. Allison, *Historical Theology*, 404.

work as our representative and covenant head, obeying for us in his life, dying for us in his death, and perfectly satisfying God's own righteous requirements, there is no justification before God. Our only hope for salvation is in Christ alone, by grace alone, through faith alone.

This decoupling of God's law from God's nature results in at least three further problems. First, as Robert Letham argues, the governmental view severs "the connection between sin and punishment,"[86] which explains why it denies the need for Christ to act as our penal substitute for the satisfaction of divine justice. Oliver Crisp demurs from Letham on this point, arguing that he overlooks the decoupling of rectoral justice from retributive justice.[87] Yet Letham assumes the main point, namely that divine justice is rooted in the very nature of God. Ultimately, sin is against God, who by his very nature is holy, just, and righteous. Sin against *him* entails that *he* cannot relax his own righteous demands. Sin *must* be punished, and satisfaction *must* be achieved if God is going to forgive. Furthermore, Scripture speaks of Christ *bearing* our sins on the cross, of the Father laying on Christ the iniquity of us all, of Christ dying specifically for our sins, and of Christ being the propitiation of our sins. This data is hard to reconcile with a governmental view.

Second, the governmental view thinks of Christ's death as *exemplary* in that it communicates God's hatred of sin and motivates persons to repent of sins and reform their lives.[88] Yet even though exemplary punishments are not uncommon in life, they are immoral to their core. Macleod captures the point this way:

> No authority has the right to use a human being as an instrument of social policy; or, to put it crudely, to impose deterrent sentences *pour encourager les autres*. Such a policy smacks of the worst atrocities. . . . God did not enact Calvary to make an example of his Son, nor was Christ's death merely a warning about what happens to sinners. It was suffering of what sin deserved, and the primary purpose of that suffering was not revelation, but redemption. What the cross *does* comes before what the cross *says*. Only by redeeming

---

86. Letham, *Work of Christ*, 168.
87. Crisp, "Penal Non-Substitution," 160.
88. The cross is exemplary in Scripture (e.g., Phil 2:5–11), yet not merely so, or not in terms of its centrality.

(at such a price) does it show the seriousness with which God takes sin. Were it not that it redeems, it would be dumb.[89]

Third, the governmental view does not view Christ's life and death as fully satisfying the retributive justice of the Father, since the guilt of sin is abolished by the graciousness of God in relaxing its punishment. No doubt Christ dies as a sacrifice to satisfy rectoral justice, but he does not die in *my* place and bear *my* sin; the penalty of sin is left unsatisfied. Obviously, this is only a problem if one assumes that the Reformation linkage between God-law-sin is correct. But assuming that it is correct, we are left with a huge problem, both theologically and experientially.

According to the governmental view, Christ's death does not give us the full satisfaction of God's justice. Sin is left unpaid. And so an offended God, not to mention the sinner's heart and conscience, are never satisfied. From this, as Donald Macleod points out, some versions of Arminian theology denied the need for the active *and* passive obedience of Christ. Because God had relaxed his law, he no longer required "legal obedience," "that is, compliance with the whole moral law."[90] Instead, as Macleod states, "he now required only 'evangelical obedience'; in other words, faith and repentance," which meant that "the righteousness of Christ had to be supplemented by something of our own. Justification was no longer *through* faith (*per fidem*); it was *on account of* faith (*propter fidem*)."[91] As Macleod explains, this may look like a distinction with no practical difference, but this is not the case. Ultimately what this subtle shift entails is an undermining of *Christ alone*. Instead of placing our faith in Christ alone, who in his perfect obedience fully satisfies God's righteous demand, our focus shifts to Christ *and* our faith as a condition for our justification. Yet our faith and repentance are never enough. Our only hope in life and in death is that Jesus paid it all and by faith union, we are complete in him.

Macleod drives this point home by recounting the dying words of J. Gresham Machen, the founder of Westminster Theological Seminary. As Machen lay dying in a North Dakota hospital in December 1936,

---

89. Macleod, *Christ Crucified*, 201.
90. Ibid., 180.
91. Ibid., 180–81.

he wrote to his young colleague, John Murray, these words: "I am so thankful for the active obedience of Christ. No hope without it."[92] Why is this so? Because unless Christ Jesus our Lord fulfills *all* righteousness, obeys God's righteous demands perfectly, and fully satisfies God's righteous demand in paying for my sin, my sin before God is not fully atoned. Consequently, I do not have a righteous standing before the Judge of the universe. The governmental view is simply not enough.

Current Debate on the Atonement

In recent days, especially within some segments of evangelical theology, the *via media* approach of the governmental view has been embraced in its understanding of the God-law-sin relationship.[93] Along with this embrace has come increased attacks on penal substitution and a number of attempts to revise it. This revision has gone in a number of directions.[94] Some try to recapture earlier atonement theologies in church history with a focus on recapitulation, vicarious repentance, and so on, and then argue that penal substitution is not required for explaining the central *means* of the atonement.[95] Others attempt to rehabilitate some form of *Christus Victor*, not merely as a crucial entailment of the cross but as the sole explanation of the cross's "internal mechanism."[96] Others try to propose a combination of views, arguing

---

92. Ibid., 181.

93. This is not to say that a large number of evangelicals continue to embrace penal substitution as the central way of understanding the nature of the cross. In recent days there have been helpful expositions of penal substitution within a larger biblical theology. For example, see Henri Blocher, *"Agnus Victor:* The Atonement as Victory and Vicarious Punishment," in *What Does It Mean to Be Saved? Broadening Evangelical Horizons of Salvation*, ed. John G. Stackhouse Jr. (Grand Rapids: Baker, 2002), 67–91, and Jeremy R. Treat, *The Crucified King: Atonement and Kingdom in Biblical and Systematic Theology* (Grand Rapids: Zondervan, 2014).

94. For example, Belousek, *Atonement, Justice, and Peace*; Green and Baker, *Recovering the Scandal of the Cross*; Chalke and Mann, *The Lost Message of Jesus*; McKnight, *A Community Called Atonement*; J. Denny Weaver, *The Nonviolent Atonement* (Grand Rapids: Eerdmans, 2001); Brad Jersak and Michael Hardin, eds., *Stricken by God? Nonviolent Identification and the Victory of Christ* (Grand Rapids: Eerdmans, 2007); S. Mark Heim, *Saved by Sacrifice: A Theology of the Cross* (Grand Rapids: Eerdmans, 2006).

95. See Boersma, *Violence, Hospitality, and the Cross.* John McLeod Campbell (1800–72) is the main proponent of the vicarious repentance view (see John McLeod Campbell, *The Nature of the Atonement*, 2nd ed. [1897; repr., Edinburgh: Handsel, 1996]).

96. See Gregory A. Boyd, *"Christus Victor* View," in Beilby and Eddy, *Nature of the Atonement*, 23–49.

for a multi-perspectival approach, incorporating substitution but not *penal* substitution.[97]

But whatever form it takes, and as creative as these views are, what unites these "newer" views of the cross is the dismissal or revision of the Reformation's central theological insight: God *cannot* forgive sin without the complete satisfaction of his own holy, righteous, and moral demand. In revising the Reformation's central insight, "newer" views cannot ultimately explain *why* Jesus had to die and the central *means* of atonement. In atonement debates, many points need to be considered, but if we neglect *this* central point, we will simply talk past each other. One of the reasons why penal substitution reached its full expression in the Reformation was due to its God-centered focus. Building on the past, the Reformers grasped with clarity the truth that the triune-personal, glorious God of Scripture is central to everything, including the cross. In fact, the grounding to the *solas* is found in the centrality of God. Why *sola Scriptura*? Because God alone is the source and standard of truth. Why *sola Deo Gloria*? Because God alone deserves and demands all of our worship, adoration, and praise. Why *sola gratia, sola fide,* and *solus Christus*? Because it is only by God's sovereign grace that our empty hands of faith receive the Savior who meets our every need in his life, death, and resurrection.

The Reformers were not wrong to argue that penal substitution is central to our understanding of the *why* and *how* of the cross. No doubt, the Bible's presentation of the cross is rich and multifaceted. Biblical language and imagery presents the cross as a beautiful gem which can be looked at from many angles. Yet, the explanation of the cross's central means is that Christ Jesus has come as our mediator and new covenant head to offer himself as our great high priest before God on behalf of sin. Our greatest problem is our sin before God, and our only solution is Christ alone. Penal substitution best accounts for the God-law-sin relationship in Scripture, why Christ had to die, and why Christ alone saves. In the end, all other atonement theologies, although they emphasize many biblical truths, downplay or miss *the* central theological point of the Reformers and thus the central *means* of the cross.

---

97. Joel B. Green, "Kaleidoscopic View," in Beilby and Eddy, *Nature of the Atonement,* 157–85.

In the next two chapters, we will provide a brief biblical defense of penal substitution and explain why it best captures *all* the biblical data, more acutely explains the *absolute necessity* of the cross, and provides the best foundation to *Christ alone*.

CHAPTER 7

The Cross of Our All-Sufficient Savior: Penal Substitution, Part 1

The work of our Lord Jesus Christ is unique and incomparable, and central to it is his death. In the previous chapter, we gained historical perspective on the church's theologizing about the cross. We concluded there was legitimate development in our understanding of the atonement in church history, and that this growth reached greater theological clarity and precision in the Reformation and post-Reformation era.

Penal substitution is the view which best captured the Reformation view of the cross. In thinking of the cross in this way, the Reformers and their heirs were *not* reducing the diversity of the biblical presentation merely to one concept. Instead, they were attempting to capture what was central to the *why* and *what* of the cross. Central to their view of penal substitution was increased clarity on the God-law-sin relationship, which previous eras had noted but which the Reformation developed in greater theological precision.

In chapters 7–8, we move from historical theology to biblical-theological formulation. We will offer a brief defense of penal substitution as the *theology* of atonement which best accounts for *all* of the biblical data *and* why the cross is absolutely necessary for our salvation. In so doing, we will provide further warrant for Christ's unique and all-sufficient work and why *he* alone is Lord and Savior.

Why is penal substitution the best way to capture the central *means* of the cross?[1] We will answer this question in four points. In this

---

1. As noted in chapter 6, to speak of the cross's *central* means is to speak of its "internal mechanism," i.e., the *biblical-theological* explanation for *why* the cross is necessary and what

chapter, we will argue that penal substitution best accounts, first for the biblical "facts" regarding the cross *and* secondly, how the divine problem of forgiveness is resolved. In chapter 8, our third point will discuss two crucial texts (Rom 3:21–26; Heb 9:15–28) which offer a clear explanation for *why* the cross is *necessary* in light of the problem of forgiveness. Then fourthly, we will briefly sketch *all* of the Bible's diverse language of the cross and argue, in the words of Roger Nicole, that penal substitution "is the vital center of the atonement, the linchpin without which everything else loses its foundation."[2]

Explaining the "Facts" of the Cross

To speak about the "facts" of the cross, we are *not* thinking of "facts" devoid of interpretation or understood apart from an overall interpretive framework. Properly understood, Scripture is God's interpretation of his mighty acts through human authors which authoritatively gives us the meaning and significance of the events in question. Theologizing about God's mighty acts, including the cross, must occur within the Bible's storyline, content, and framework. Instead, to speak about the "facts" of the cross is to ask the following question: How does Scripture present the cross that demands theological reflection?[3] Our contention is this: as the NT unpacks the "facts" of the cross, it is penal substitution which best accounts for them in their entirety. Specifically, how Scripture presents (1) the centrality of the cross to Christ's work, and (2) Jesus's own understanding of his death, is best explained by the theology of penal substitution.

The Centrality of the Cross

At the center of the NT, indeed all of Scripture, is the atoning work of Christ. In making this statement, one must avoid reductionism. After all, as emphasized in chapter 5, Christ's *one* work is that of our great prophet, priest, and king, which certainly includes within

---

is its central achievement. On this point, see D. A. Carson, "Atonement in Romans 3:21–26" in *The Glory of the Atonement: Biblical, Historical, and Practical Perspectives*, eds., Charles E. Hill and Frank A. James III (Downers Grove, IL: InterVarsity Press, 2004), 138.

2.   Roger Nicole, "Postscript on Penal Substitution," in Hill and James, *Glory of the Atonement*, 451.

3.   For this use of "fact," see Donald Macleod, *Christ Crucified: Understanding the Atonement* (Downers Grove, IL: InterVarsity, 2014), 15–16.

it many aspects. Theological formulation must account for *all* of the biblical data without diminishing any of it. But with that said, it is not reductionistic to claim that Scripture *accents* Christ's death as the basis of our salvation, and it is this "fact" which requires *theological* explanation. Scripture does not teach that Christ's death is merely due to a psychological or historical necessity; rather, it is demanded by God's righteousness to fulfill God's eternal plan of redemption, and very few atonement theologies can adequately account for this fact.

Years ago, Emil Brunner captured this point well. In stressing that Christianity cannot be understood apart from Christ's cross, he writes about the Reformation's emphasis on the cross: "The Cross is the sign of the Christian faith, of the Christian church, of the revelation of God in Jesus Christ. . . . The whole struggle of the Reformation for the *sola fide*, the *sola deo gloria*, was simply the struggle for the right interpretation of the Cross. He who understands the Cross aright—this is the opinion of the Reformers—understands the Bible, he understands Jesus Christ."[4] What Brunner observes is precisely what the NT teaches. One cannot read the NT without observing the fact that the cross is central to the entire Scriptural presentation of Christ's work and *the* place where our salvation is achieved.

Think, for example, about the lopsided treatment of Christ's life in the Gospels. The Gospels are not mere biographies since little is said about Jesus's birth, childhood, or teenage years. Instead, their primary focus is on the three years of Jesus's life and ministry, and even here, they focus mostly on the last week. Martin Kähler's famous aphorism about the Gospels is true—they are "passion narratives with extended introductions."[5] The Gospels are deliberately written to stress the centrality of Christ's death for understanding his identity and work. Apart from the cross, we cannot grasp *him* and the entire rationale for his coming.

But it is not only the Gospels that stress the centrality of Christ's cross; so do the apostles. Consider Peter's first gospel message on Pentecost. When we compare the thinking of Peter in Matthew 16 to

---

4.   Emil Brunner, *The Mediator*, trans. Olive Wyon (1927; repr., Philadelphia: Westminster, 1947), 435.

5.   Martin Kähler, *The So-Called Historical Jesus and the Historic, Biblical Christ* (Philadelphia: Fortress, 1964), 80n11.

Acts 2, there is quite a change. In Matthew 16, Peter cannot conceive of Christ dying, yet at Pentecost, in light of the cross and resurrection, he now views Christ's death as central to God's eternal, foreordained plan (Acts 2:23; cf. Rev 13:8). Or think of Paul's teaching in 1 Corinthians 1–2. Paul states: "For the message of the cross is foolishness to those who are perishing, but to us who are being saved it is the power of God" (1:18). He continues, "When I came to you, I did not come with eloquence or human wisdom as I proclaimed to you the testimony about God. For I resolved to know nothing while I was with you except Jesus Christ and him crucified" (2:1–2). Herman Bavinck captures well the centrality of Christ's cross for the apostles:

> From the beginning, therefore, it was a fixed given in the message of the apostles that Christ had died, was buried, and was raised according to the Scriptures (1 Cor 15:3). They saw the death of Christ as a great crime on the part of the Jews who thereby sought to destroy and exterminate him. But God frustrated their efforts, raised him from the dead, and made him Lord and Christ, Ruler and Savior (Acts 2:22–36; 3:13–15; 5:30–31). And not only that, but that death was itself a constituent of the work of the Messiah, determined beforehand in God's counsel (Acts 2:23; 3:18; 4:28). This Christ who died and was raised, therefore, is the only name given under heaven by which we must be saved (Acts 4:12).[6]

It is precisely *this* emphasis on the cross's centrality that requires theological reflection, especially given the first century view of the cross.[7] For the Romans, crucifixion was reserved for slaves, aliens, and barbarians. Cicero in one of his speeches condemned it as "a most cruel and disgusting punishment. . . . To bind a Roman citizen is a crime, to flog him is an abomination, to kill him is almost an act of murder: to crucify him is—What? There is no fitting word that can possibly describe so horrible a deed."[8] For Jews, the crucifixion was abhorrent, but for a different reason. The Jewish people made no distinction

---

6.   Herman Bavinck, *Sin and Salvation in Christ*, vol. 3 of *Reformed Dogmatics*, ed. John Bolt, trans. John Vriend (Grand Rapids: Baker Academic, 2006), 387.

7.   See John R. W. Stott, *The Cross of Christ*, 20th Anniversary Edition (Downers Grove, IL: InterVarsity, 2006), 23–31; see also Martin Hengel, *Crucifixion*, trans. John Bowden (Minneapolis: Fortress, 1977).

8.   Cited in Stott, *Cross of Christ*, 30.

between a "tree" and a "cross," between a hanging and a crucifixion. They automatically applied to crucified criminals the awful statement of the law: "Anyone who is hung on a pole is under God's curse" (Deut 21:23; cf. Gal 3:13). The thought of a crucified Messiah was unthinkable. As Trypho the Jew put it to Justin Martyr: "I am exceedingly incredulous on this point."[9]

Why, then, does Scripture fixate on *and* glory in the cross? The Scriptural answer is this: As awful as the cross is, *Jesus's* cross is the ground of our salvation. In fact, the cross is *necessary* in God's eternal plan to achieve our redemption, and apart from it, there is no salvation. Any atonement theology that cannot explain *this* fact is out of step with the biblical teaching. As we turn to more "facts," our contention is that penal substitution best accounts for the *centrality* and *necessity* of the cross for God's redemptive plan; indeed, it is *absolutely necessary.*

Jesus's Self-Understanding of the Cross

How did Jesus understand his own death? Did he think it was *central* to his ministry *and* necessary to fulfill his Father's will and thus God's eternal plan? The answer is yes. From beginning to end, Jesus viewed his death as central to his entire work. For Jesus, the cross was no afterthought; instead it was central to his relationship with his Father, the inauguration of God's kingdom, and the establishment of the new covenant. Five areas in Christ's life and teaching will help us warrant this observation and help us see our Lord's perspective on how he views his work as the obedient Son come to do his Father's will.

1. Jesus's Death as the Fulfillment of God's Plan

From the beginning of his ministry, Jesus knew he was the Messiah who had to die to fulfill his Father's will.[10] From his use of the title "Son

---

9. Justin Martyr, *Dialogue with Trypho* 89 (*ANF* 1:244).

10. Luke offers a brief glimpse into Jesus's thinking at the temple when he is twelve. Jesus speaks of his intimate relationship with the Father and, in the words of John Stott, "an inward compulsion to occupy himself with his Father's affairs. He knew he had a mission. His Father had sent him into the world for a purpose. This mission he must perform; this purpose he must fulfill" (Stott, *Cross of Christ*, 31). What is the mission? As the Gospels unfold it becomes clear, but Matthew, for example, frames Jesus's entire mission by the new covenant promise which the angel announces to Joseph, "She will give birth to a son, and you are to give him the name Jesus, *because he will save his people from their sins*" (Matt 1:21, emphasis added).

of Man" (from Daniel 7), which he assigned to himself with specific intent; to the application of Isaiah 61 to himself (Luke 4:21); to the prediction that the bridegroom would be "taken away" (*apairō*) from his disciples (Mark 2:20)—an allusion to Isaiah 53:8 (a description of the Suffering Servant who "by oppression and judgment ... was *taken away*," speaking of his violent death); to the comparison of himself with Jonah (Matt 12:40) and to the serpent in the wilderness (John 3:14)—"all of this proves that Jesus was certain from the beginning that suffering and death would describe the end of his life."[11] As Bavinck notes, "Prophecy, especially the prophecy of Isaiah (ch. 53), was always present to his mind (Luke 4:21; 18:31; 22:37; 24:26, 46) and instructed him concerning his departure."[12]

This truth is especially evident at Caesarea Philippi, where Peter rightly confesses that Jesus is the Messiah *and* Jesus then instructs his disciples about the nature of his Messianic work. Jesus insists that precisely because he is *the* Messiah he *must* (*dei*) suffer, die, and be raised on the third day—a fact he reiterated on three separate occasions (Mark 8:31–32; see 9:31; 10:32–34). At this point in Jesus's ministry, the apostles did not get it. They had no problem thinking of the Messiah in prophetic and kingly terms, but they could not conceive of him as a Suffering Servant who *must* die. They did not yet grasp that the Son's incarnation was not an end in itself; rather, it was a means to the end of fulfilling God's eternal plan centered in his cross. From this data, Bavinck correctly concludes that Jesus's understanding of his death is "not because he was morally obligated to die or could only remain faithful to his calling that way . . . but because it was so determined in God's counsel and predicted in Scripture (Matt 16:21; 26:54; Luke 22:22; 24:26, 44–46; John 3:14; 7:30; 8:20; 10:18; 11:7–15; 12:23; 13:1; 17:1; 20:9; 1 Pet 1:20).[13] Jesus reinforces this truth after his resurrection when he reminds his disciples about what he taught them before

---

11. Bavinck, *Sin and Salvation in Christ*, 387. On this point, see Macleod, *Christ Crucified*, 19.

12. Bavinck, *Sin and Salvation in Christ*, 387; see Stott, *Cross of Christ*, 31–38.

13. Bavinck, *Sin and Salvation in Christ*, 387. Bavinck's references in John's Gospel are significant. Jesus links his death to the "hour," which is tied to the Father's eternal plan. See D. A. Carson, *The Gospel According to John*, PNTC (Grand Rapids: Eerdmans, 1991), 171, 437, 553–54; Stott, *Cross of Christ*, 34–35.

his death: that his death and resurrection were central to God's plan and thus the fulfillment of Scripture (Luke 24:25–27, 44–47).

In addition, the transfiguration also reminds us how central Christ's death is to his mission, the inauguration of the kingdom, and the dawning of the entire new covenant era. On the mountain, we are told that our Lord received further confirmation of his Father's love (Mark 9:7) and that he met with Moses and Elijah. What did they discuss? Luke tells us: "They spoke about his departure [*exodos*], which he was about to bring to fulfillment at Jerusalem" (Luke 9:31). Why is thinking about Christ's death as his *exodos* significant? Because this language sets Christ's cross in the larger context of God's divine plan by suggesting that it is the antitypical fulfillment of the exodus, the OT's great act of redemption. Christ's impending death, then, is not the death of a mere sufferer, martyr, or victim. Jesus dies as the Messiah, the Son of God incarnate, who as the Passover Lamb and the conquering priest-king fulfills God's plan and accomplishes a new exodus in his blood.

2. The Last Supper: Jesus's Death as the Inauguration of the New Covenant

The time frame from the Last Supper to Christ's burial only lasts around twenty-four hours, but the recounting of these events is extremely detailed in the Gospels. This is a reminder that the Gospel writers viewed this time period, culminating in Christ's death, as central to Jesus's work. What is Jesus's perception of his death at the Last Supper? Two points require emphasis.

First, given the Passover context of the meal, Jesus views his upcoming death as a *sacrifice*, not only as the antitypical fulfillment of the sacrificial system but also of the Passover lamb (John 1:29; 1 Cor 5:7). Also, the sacrificial nature of Jesus's death is reinforced by his words: "This is my body given *for you*; do this in remembrance of me" and "This cup is the new covenant in my blood, which is poured out *for you*" (Luke 22:19–20, emphasis added).[14] New meaning is given to the Passover, which reveals how Jesus views the import of his upcoming death, namely, as a priestly sacrifice, in obedience to his Father's

---

14. See Macleod, *Christ Crucified*, 23–27; Stott, *Cross of Christ*, 69–74.

will, and thus fulfilling the typological significance of the sacrificial Passover lamb.

In addition, the Passover context also underscores the *penal substitutionary* nature of Jesus's understanding of his cross. It is insufficient to interpret the Passover and the subsequent event of the exodus as merely an act of power or deliverance.[15] As David Peterson has argued, not only is the first Passover associated with "the offering of animal blood as a substitute for human life" and thus "*deliverance from divine judgement*," but also that a "substitutionary blood sacrifice is linked with the deliverance that constituted Israel as God's distinct and holy people."[16] Also, what is unique about the tenth plague linked to the Passover is that it teaches both deliverance *and* payment for sin. Part of the significance of the Passover is God's judgment upon Israel *and* Egypt. In Exodus 7–14, God's wrath is consistently directed against the Egyptians and Israel is delivered from the plagues by God's merciful provision. In the tenth plague, however, "Israel is only delivered by obedience to the Lord's command and by the fulfillment of this sacrificial ritual."[17] The only way Israel's firstborn can be delivered is through the shed blood of the lamb applied to the doorposts. Peterson rightly concludes: "The Passover is more than a demonstration of God's love. The blood averts the judgement of God (12:12–13) and this deliverance initiates the whole process by which God brings the Israelites out of Egypt and enables them to function as his chosen people (12:50–13:16)."[18]

As God's redemptive plan unfolds through the biblical covenants, the Passover is also linked to elements of the sacrificial system, and most importantly, the suffering servant of Isaiah 53. From the perspective of Jesus and the NT authors, Isaiah 53 is probably the most important text in the prophetic literature for interpreting the cross, and it serves as the backdrop to Jesus's ransom sayings in the Gospels. In Isaiah 53, the Servant not only suffers undeservedly because of human sin, but he

---

15. See Joel B. Green and Mark D. Baker, *Recovering the Scandal of the Cross: Atonement in New Testament and Contemporary Contexts*, 2nd ed. (Downers Grove, IL: IVP Academic, 2011), 54–63.

16. David Peterson, "Atonement in the Old Testament," in *Where Wrath and Mercy Meet: Proclaiming the Atonement Today*, ed. David Peterson (Carlisle, UK: Paternoster, 2001), 4; see Leon Morris, *The Atonement: Its Meaning and Significance* (Downers Grove, IL: InterVarsity Press, 1983), 88–105; Stott, *Cross of Christ*, 139–49.

17. Peterson, "Atonement in the Old Testament," 4.

18. Ibid.

also suffers in the people's place as a substitute, the righteous for the unrighteous (see 1 Pet 2:24–25). As John Oswalt demonstrates, Isaiah 53, in its context, points to the Servant as both the means of salvation anticipated in chapters 49–52, and the one who achieves the salvation that the people are invited to participate in, in chapters 53–55.[19] Also, in context, Isaiah teaches that even though the exile was a temporary punishment for sin, it did not automatically restore the people to fellowship with God. Something more was needed because of the seriousness of their situation under the curse of God. Only the affliction of the Servant could make them whole, and only by his bruises could they be healed (53:5)—language that echoes the sacrificial system and the previous Passover celebration. Only by the suffering of the Righteous One, in the place of those who ought to have suffered, is salvation accomplished. And note: the suffering of the Righteous One is *not* divorced from the will of the Lord as Isaiah 53:10–12 reminds us. As Peterson rightly observes:

> Since the Lord was prepared to regard him as "an offering for sin," extraordinary benefits flow for his "offspring" and for the Servant himself. His "offspring" shall be "made righteous," because the Righteous One, God's Servant, "shall bear their iniquities." The benefit for the Servant is that "he shall see his offspring and shall prolong his days." He will also be allotted "a portion with the great" and shall "divide the spoil with the strong" (53:12; cf. 52:13). Although it is disputed, the most obvious reading of this section is that the Servant will be resurrected from death to see the fruit of his suffering. He was "numbered with the transgressors," but it was not because he was a rebel himself. Indeed, by "bearing the sin of many" he was actually "interceding" for them, that is, intervening on their behalf to rescue and redeem them (cf. 59:16).[20]

To understand correctly what Jesus is saying in his application of the Passover to himself, *all* of this OT background material is crucial. Jesus views his death as sacrificial and substitutionary in light of the exodus, Passover, sacrificial system, and Isaiah 53.

---

19. See John Oswalt, *Isaiah 40–66* (Grand Rapids: Eerdmans, 1998), 377, 385; see also J. Alec Motyer, *Isaiah*, TOTC (Downers Grove, IL: InterVarsity Press, 1999), 331–47.
20. Peterson, "Atonement in the Old Testament," 22.

Second, Jesus views the purpose of his death as a priestly sacrifice that inaugurates the promised *new covenant* in his blood (Luke 22:20). As discussed in chapter 1, the OT anticipation of the new covenant is significant. At the heart of the OT promise of the new covenant is the complete forgiveness of sins (Jer 31:34; see Matt 1:21), and the forgiveness of sins takes place only through priestly, sacrificial action. In fact, in biblical thought, the concept of "priest" and "covenant" are inseparable, which is the argument of Hebrews 7:11 where the parenthesis helps us understand the relationship between the priesthood and the covenant—"for on the basis of it [the Levitical priesthood] the law [old covenant] was given to the people." Here the author contends that the old covenant is grounded in the Levitical priesthood. That is why, given this relationship, the author argues in verse 12 that the OT, in announcing the coming of a *new* Priest (Ps 110; see Heb 7) also anticipates the arrival of a *new* covenant (Jer 31:31–34; see Heb 7–8) *because* a change in priesthood requires a change of covenant.[21]

Why? Because at the heart of the covenant relationship is the reality that God dwells with his people. But given the biblical portrayal of God as personal, holy, and just, how can *he* dwell with a *sinful* people? How can Yahweh live among his people without destroying them by the flame of his holiness? These questions are faced and answered in Exodus 32–34. In the golden calf event and the reinstitution of the covenant, the answer is this: God can be our covenant God only by the provision of the priesthood, tabernacle, and entire sacrificial system (see Lev 17:11). God can only establish his covenant, given our sin, by the blood of the covenant, the provision of his grace (Exod. 24:6–8). And that provision of grace, as the Bible's entire storyline teaches, is found in our Lord Jesus Christ, our new covenant head and mediator, the obedient Son who fulfills the covenant's demands and pays our ransom price.

Once again, this background material is crucial in order to grasp the staggering claim Jesus makes that in him and his cross, *he* is fulfilling the Passover. For Jesus to say that the Passover cup is now his blood, which inaugurates the new covenant, is to claim that his death is a priestly, substitutionary sacrifice on our behalf, which results in God's

---

21. See Peter T. O'Brien, *The Letter to the Hebrews*, PNTC (Grand Rapids: Eerdmans, 2010), 258.

"remember[ing] their sins no more" (Jer 31:34), i.e., the full payment of our sins before God.[22] Stott rightly asks and then concludes: "Is it possible to exaggerate the staggering nature of this claim? Here is Jesus's view of his death. It is the divinely appointed sacrifice by which the new covenant with its promise of forgiveness will be ratified. He is going to die in order to bring his people into a new covenant relationship with God."[23] Any theology of atonement must account for these facts, especially Jesus's own understanding of his death in these terms.

3. Gethsemane: A Foretaste of Jesus's Death as Bearing Divine Wrath for Us

How do we explain Gethsemane? Jesus knows that the cross is before him, but it horrifies him. In one sense, Jesus's prayer to his Father reveals that he wants nothing to do with the cross. Everything in him shrinks from it—Jesus is "troubled" (*adēmonein*), "deeply distressed" (*ekthambeisthai*), and "overwhelmed with sorrow (*perilypos*) to the point of death" (Mark 14:33–34)—all words that describe someone under unimaginable stress.[24] As Macleod notes, it is not only the specific words that describe the agony of the moment, but it is the entire narrative itself: "The whole account resonates the acutest torment and anguish."[25] As Jesus throws himself prostrate before his Father and his disciples sleep, he is physically exhausted, so much so that an angel must come to strengthen him (Luke 22:43; see Heb 5:7).

What explains Gethsemane? Throughout human history, as Stott notes, there have been many martyrs who have faced horrible deaths in courage and resoluteness. Even Christian martyrs have faced their certain death in joy and eagerness.[26] But what is going on here? Scripture answers this question by linking Jesus's anguish with the nature of the Father's "cup" he must drink. In the OT, the cup is linked with the pouring out of God's wrath, his judicial sentence against human sin (Ps

---

22. For the concept of "remembering" in the OT, see William Dumbrell, *Covenant and Creation: A Theology of the Old Testament Covenants*, 2nd ed. (Milton Keyes: Paternoster, 2002), 181–85.

23. Stott, *Cross of Christ*, 72.

24. See Donald Macleod, *The Person of Christ* (Downers Grove, IL: InterVarsity Press, 1998), 173; B. B. Warfield, "The Emotional Life of Our Lord," in *The Person and Work of Christ*, ed. Samuel G. Craig (Philadelphia: P&R, 1980), 129–37.

25. Macleod, *Person of Christ*, 173.

26. See Stott, *Cross of Christ*, 75–80.

75:8; Jer 25:15–29; Ezek 23:32–34; see Rev 14:10; 16:1–21; 18:6), and Jesus knows this. In this light, our Lord is not so much afraid of crucifixion itself; instead he recoils as the sinless Son from what he will experience in bearing our sin and alienation from his Father. He knows that as the incarnate Son and our new covenant head, he is acting in our place, bearing our sin, and experiencing the full weight of the Father's wrath for us. The divine, beloved Son, who from eternity has shared perfect fellowship with the Father (and Spirit), and the Father, who has always loved the Son (along with the Spirit), will experience something in their personal relations that has never been experienced before. This is why Jesus cries, "Father, if you are willing, take this cup from me; yet not my will, but yours be done" (Luke 22:42).

But given who Jesus is, why is his prayer not answered? Jesus's desire is clear: he wants the Father's will to be different. As Macleod notes, "For a moment he stands with the millions of his people who have found God's will almost unendurable, shrunk from the work given them to do, shuddered at the prospect of the race set before them and prayed that God would change his mind."[27] But the Father's will is no. Why? Some kind of explanation must be given.

The only answer that accounts for this data is that there is *no other way* for the triune God to save us except in *this* way. As Stott notes, "Although in theory 'everything is possible' to God, as Jesus himself affirmed in Gethsemane (Mark 14:36), yet this was not possible. God's purpose of love was to save sinners, and to save them righteously; but this would be impossible without the sin-bearing death of the Savior. So how could he pray to be saved from 'this hour' of death? 'No,' he had said, he would not, since 'it was for this very reason I came to this hour' (John 12:27)."[28] Gethsemane, then, reminds us that our Lord's solidarity with us in our suffering is not enough. Jesus's agony in Gethsemane is utterly unique and singular, never seen before or since. There is no other way to explain it other than within the biblical storyline of God's promise of redemption that necessarily finds its fulfillment in the cross. Gethsemane presents us with the Lord Jesus who acts as our new covenant mediator for us.

---

27. Macleod, *Christ Crucified*, 29.
28. Stott, *Cross of Christ*, 79.

In Gethsemane, Jesus aligns his human will to his Father's will and submits *in his humanity* to the Father as our representative and substitute. Just as our Lord embraced his messianic mission at his baptism identifying with us, just as he resisted the temptation in the wilderness to pursue his messianic mission apart from the cross, once again, he willingly and gladly chooses to do his Father's will to redeem us. "Son though he was, he learned obedience from what he suffered and, once made perfect, he became the source of eternal salvation for all who obey him" (Heb 5:8–9). Although Jesus knew what was ahead of him, he chose to become sin for us so that we could become the righteousness of God (2 Cor 5:21); he chose the Father's will rather than his own to save his people from their sins (Matt 1:21).

This is the best explanation of Gethsemane—an explanation which views Christ alone as Lord and Savior *and* simultaneously reveals that the cross is not merely one option among many in God's plan; it is the only way. Yet as significant as Gethsemane is, it is still not the cross; it is the prelude to it. Jesus's identification with us, even his complete submission to the Father, is not enough to redeem us. The obedient Son must still die in our place as the Father's judicial sentence is executed on him, which alone is the basis for our justification.

4. The Trial: The Priest-King Who Chooses to Be Declared Guilty for Us

What does Christ's trial teach us about the nature of the cross and Jesus's understanding of it? Two points require emphasis. First, as unjust as the trial was, it is crucial to observe, as Calvin did, that it took place in the context of a judicial sentence rendered by governmental authorities established by God (Rom 13:1).[29] Given that God's sovereign plan includes all things (Eph 1:11), this event was part of his plan to redeem us. The trial before the authorities places the cross in a judicial context. Macleod rightly notes: "[Jesus] was not murdered by an assassin or lynched by a mob or killed in an accident. He was convicted by a judge, after due process, and judicially executed."[30] Yet more needs to be said, given that the trial and execution were unjust.

---

29. Calvin, *Institutes*, 2.16.5; see Macleod, *Christ Crucified*, 31–32.
30. Macleod, *Christ Crucified*, 32.

Second, we must remember *who* was on trial and that Jesus, the sinless one, deliberately chose to be declared guilty. As the trial unfolds, the Gospels present it as totally unjust. Not only was the trial unlawfully convened, but it was hurried through without the proper hearing of the evidence. Jesus was not allowed to state his case, and no condemning evidence was given. Simply put, the trial was unjust and a sad example of human injustice. But it is also crucial to observe that anyone who knows Jesus also knows that these charges had to be false. Why? Because of *who* Jesus is. Jesus is the long-awaited Messiah, the sinless and spotless beloved Son of the Father. He alone lived a life of perfect obedience; no person could ever charge him with wrongdoing. Yet, in light of this fact the Gospel accounts teach that the incarnate Son chose to be found guilty even though he was repeatedly declared to be innocent.

In fact, in Luke's account Jesus's innocence and lack of guilt is repeatedly taught: first by the governing authorities, Pilate (23:4, 13–14, 20–22) and Herod (23:15); then by the thief on the cross (23:39–40); and finally by the centurion at the foot of the cross (23:47). Yet, Luke having repeatedly stressed Jesus's declared innocence also repeatedly demonstrates that Jesus, the innocent one, is treated *as if he were guilty* (23:16, 22, 25). The only explanation, given Jesus's identity and chosen behavior at the trial, is that *he* chose to be found guilty. Nothing in the Gospel accounts present Jesus as a victim or martyr unable to respond to the injustice of the situation; instead, our Lord—God the Son incarnate—chose to be found guilty. Wicked men, inspired by Satan himself, were intent on destroying Jesus, but the triune God was also sovereignly at work, overruling their evil and in their immoral actions bringing about the salvation of God's people according to his eternal plan.

This explanation is the only one that accounts for the data and makes sense of *why* Jesus died. As Jesus makes clear in John 10:18: "No one takes it [my life] from me, but I lay it down of my own accord. I have authority to lay it down and authority to take it up again. This command I received from my Father." But at the trial, Jesus, as King and Lord, chose to remain silent and not to defend himself, as he acted as our representative head. Jesus chose to identify with us so completely that he allowed himself to be reckoned as a sinner and treated as one, not only by human authorities but ultimately by his Father in order to act as our representative and substitute (2 Cor 5:21; 1 Pet 3:18).

5. The Cross and the Cry: God the Son Incarnate Offering Himself as Our Sacrifice

Each Gospel describes the cross in detail, and every point is significant in explaining its meaning, even the points that highlight the irony at work. From the political charge that Jesus was a rival king to Caesar (Mark 15:26), to the assumption that he was a Messianic pretender (John 19:7), readers notice the irony in the narrative. Jesus, the crucified one, is indeed the Messiah, the King of the Jews—indeed, the Lord over all. Jesus is not dying as a helpless victim. Jesus is the divine Son who has chosen to die, chosen to be declared guilty although innocent, and chosen to obey his Father's will to save his people from their sins (Matt 1:21). Furthermore, by dying, Jesus has inaugurated a new covenant and a new creation that alone conquers sin, death, and our enemies. Despite appearances, the Gospels unite in proclaiming the cross as a place of victory, especially viewed in light of the resurrection that publicly attests to this fact.

But why *death* on a cross? Normally, victory and conquest are not won by death. In fact, in Scripture death is the penalty of sin (Gen 2:18; Rom 6:23), and a death on a cross/tree is viewed as a curse (Deut 27:26; Gal 3:13). The cross can only be a place of victory if it first pays for human sin, which is precisely what the Gospels teach. As Isaiah 53:12 is brought to mind (Luke 22:37), Christ is portrayed as the Suffering Servant who wins our victory by identifying *with* us to die *for* us by becoming our penal substitute (Gal 3:13).

The climatic conditions that surround the cross confirm this fact. Darkness is present over the whole land for three hours. Something momentous is occurring; God is clearly at work. In the OT, the Day of the Lord, which often spoke of God's judgment of sin, is characterized by darkness (Joel 2:2; Amos 8:9), but there is probably more. The OT also speaks of darkness in terms of sorrow (Amos 8:10), and given the action of the Father in the Son, both truths are present. In Christ, sin is being judged and condemned in his flesh (Rom 8:3), and the triune God is being affected, which is evident in Jesus's cry of dereliction—a cry like no other ever heard—"My God, my God, why have you forsaken me?" (Matt 27:46; Mark 15:34; see Ps 22).[31]

Jesus speaks from the cross a number of times—for example, for the people's forgiveness (Luke 23:34), to the thief (Luke 23:43), and to his mother (John 19:26–27)—but *this* cry is the most profound and revealing of what is occurring. Initially, what is striking about it is Jesus's form of address: *Eloi* (Aramaic, Mark 15:34) or *Eli* (Hebrew, Matt 27:46)—"My God"—and not *Abba*, or Father. This is the only time, even on the cross, when Jesus does not invoke God as "Father." Even in Gethsemane, Jesus holds fast to "Father" (Mark 14:36), but this cry is different; it reveals the solemnity of what is occurring. No doubt Jesus's sense of forsakenness is not long, but for this moment it was utterly real.

How do we explain the cross and the cry? No trite answer will do. Jesus, God the Son incarnate, the sovereign King, the universe's creator and continual sustainer (John 1:1–3; Col 1:15–17; Heb 1:3), hangs on a cross. Jesus, the Son, who from eternity knew indescribable and glorious face-to-face communion with his Father (John 1:1, 18; see 17:3) and the Spirit, and who shared with them the same divine nature, cries as the one who is now forsaken. We cannot conclude that Jesus is a victim of his circumstances; Jesus is sovereign *and* even more, he knows that it is the Father who has delivered him up (Rom 8:32). It is the Father's wrath that is being poured out; he is now bearing the cup he pled to be removed in Gethsemane, and it is this fact alone that explains his cry. In the words of Scripture, he bore in his body our sin and condemned it in his flesh (1 Pet 2:24; Rom 8:3).

Yet even in Jesus's cry, there is still faith and trust—"Eloi," *my* God. As Jesus in that moment cries to his Father, he knows he is perfectly innocent and righteous, yet he is now experiencing what he does not deserve. He feels the full weight of the Father's wrath on him before victory is achieved in his triumphant cry, "It is finished" (John 19:30) and the temple veil is torn in two, thus signifying his completed work (Matt 27:51; Mark 15:38; Luke 23:45). As Jesus pays the ransom price needed to redeem us, he commits his spirit into the hands of his Father, as he deliberately dies, and with normal personal relations restored

---

31.   John Stott discusses various ways the cry has been interpreted other than dereliction, but argues against them. See Stott, *Cross of Christ*, 31, 80–86.

between the Father and Son—"Father, into your hands I commit my spirit" (Luke 23:46).

In saying that the Son bears the Father's wrath for us, we must never forget that the unity of the triune persons remains unbroken. Macleod rightly notes: "Even while the Father is angry with the Mediator, the Son is still the beloved and still fully involved in all the external acts (the *opera ad extra*) of the Trinity."[32] The unity of the divine persons in the same identical nature does not entail that the Father (or the Spirit) suffered on the cross—they clearly did not—yet we cannot think of the Son's suffering apart from the Father and the Spirit. The Son's suffering, then, is not external to the Father and the Spirit, although it is his own. At Calvary, in and through the mediatorial work of Christ, we see the triune God at work. This is why *Christ's* cross is the demonstration of the *Father's* love for us (John 3:16). On the cross, the triune God is at work. The Son's cry is his own but it also reverberates in all of the divine persons, which underscores the awful cost of our salvation and the *necessity* of Christ's cross to redeem.

Preliminary Reflections on Explaining the "Facts" of the Cross

What theology of the cross best accounts for these "facts"? To answer this question fully, more biblical data must be given, which we will do below and in the next chapter. However, at this point, it may be helpful to pause and reflect on the "facts" given so far. We agree with the Reformation and its heirs that penal substitution best accounts for the data given. While other views make sense of some of the "facts," it is only penal substitution that fully explains *why* the cross is central and necessary to God's glorious plan of redemption and Jesus's own understanding of his death, and *how*, as the holy and sinless Son incarnate, *he* dies so that we may become the righteousness of God (2 Cor 5:21). How so? Let us offer three truths entailed by these "facts" which, in a preliminary way, begin to answer why a penal substitutionary view of the cross best accounts for this data.

First, these "facts" teach us that our Lord Jesus Christ suffered the *penalty* due to sin. In biblical thought, it is not enough to say that Christ

---

32. Macleod, *Christ Crucified*, 50.

suffered, which is certainly true; we must also say that Jesus's suffering was *penal* in nature due to human sin *before* God. Macleod captures this point:

> [I]n terms of the biblical world-view the penal nature of his [Christ's] suffering is also a fact. Christ died, and as far as the human species is concerned, death is penal. The clearest statement of this is in Romans 6:23, "the wages of sin is death", but it is a recurring theme, indeed an axiom, throughout Scripture. When God first revealed his will to the human race and warned Adam and Eve not to eat the fruit of the tree of the knowledge of good and evil, he issued a clear warning: "when you eat from it, you will certainly die" (Gen. 2:17). This is the background to Paul's treatment of the parallel between the first Adam and the Last Adam in Romans 5:12–21. Death entered the world through sin (v. 12); the many died through the trespass of the one (v. 15); death reigned by the trespass of one man (v. 17); and sin reigned in death (v. 21).[33]

This is why Scripture teaches that Christ's cross is the undoing of Adam's sin. By our Lord's representing us as our covenant head, he pays for our sin by his death and bears sin's curse before his Father—not for himself but for us.

Second, these facts remind us that Jesus did not deserve to die; instead he died *for* us as our *covenant representative* and *substitute*.[34] Scripture teaches that Christ *is* God the Son incarnate, the mediator and great high priest of the new covenant, who is perfectly sinless, just, and righteous. Although he was tempted like us, he did not sin, nor could he sin (Heb 4:15; cf. 2 Cor 5:21).[35] Why, then, is *he* on the cross? Add this fact: the *Lord* Jesus willingly and deliberately chose to die, not as evidence of his weakness but as a demonstration of his sovereign will to fulfill God's plan. The cross is not an afterthought in God's plan; it

---

33. Ibid., 59.

34. On the use of the prepositions *anti*, *hyper*, *peri*, and *dia*, see Leon Morris, *The Apostolic Preaching of the Cross*, 3rd ed. (Grand Rapids: Eerdmans, 1965), 23, 34, 62–63, 172, 204–6, 288; Murray J. Harris, *Prepositions and Theology in the Greek New Testament* (Grand Rapids: Zondervan, 2012), 49–56, 69–82, 179–83, 207–17.

35. On the impeccability of Christ, see my *God the Son Incarnate* (Wheaton, IL: Crossway, 2016), 459–65.

is at the forefront of it and central to how the triune God intends to redeem us.

Third, these facts underscore the truth that, given that Jesus is God the Son incarnate, in eternal relation to the Father and Spirit, the object of the cross is not primarily sin, death, or Satan, *but God himself.* This point is stressed by thinking of the Father's involvement in the cross. Why does the Father permit his beloved Son to hang on a tree? Is the Father not sovereign? Does he not know what is occurring? Texts such as Isaiah 53:10, John 3:16, Romans 8:32, and Jesus's prayer in Gethsemane and his cry from the cross, all teach that the Father deliberately sacrificed his Son for us. Do we dismiss these facts as mere examples of the Bible's outdated worldview, or even worse, as an example of divine child abuse?[36]

Emphatically NO! Such conclusions reject the teaching of Scripture and *distort the Bible's own presentation of Christ and his cross.* As Macleod notes, the Bible teaches that throughout his entire life, "Jesus enjoyed the love, protection and encouragement of his heavenly Father. . . . An abused and damaged child he was not."[37] In addition, on the cross, Jesus was not a child but a mature adult. He was the sovereign Lord and King, able to make his own choices and take responsibility for them (see John 15:13; 18:11; Phil 2:8). Our Lord was no helpless victim on the cross; *he* was the Lord of Glory dying to fulfill God's plan and to secure our redemption. And as a result of Christ's obedient death for us, "the allegedly 'abusive' Father exalts him to the highest place, commands every knee to bow and orders the entire universe to confess him Lord of all (Phil 2:9–11)."[38]

Yet the Father's involvement in the cross *and* the fact that it is the divine Son who is there still require an explanation. How is the Father justified in what *he* did at Calvary? What gave him the right to sacrifice his own Son? Two points require emphasis. First, Scripture presents the action of God the Father as a priest offering the sacrifice of his

36. For example, see Steve Chalke and Alan Mann, *The Lost Message of Jesus* (Grand Rapids: Zondervan, 2003), 182; Joanne Carlson Brown and Rebecca Parker, "For God So Loved the World," in *Christianity, Patriarchy and Abuse*, ed. Joanne Carlson Brown and Carole R. Bohn (New York: Pilgrim, 1989), 2–3, 23.

37. Macleod, *Christ Crucified*, 63.

38. Ibid., 64.

only Son, as a demonstration of his love, justice, and righteousness.[39] Second, given the Trinitarian personal relations, the act of the Father also involves the active involvement of the Son and the Spirit, who together, and according to their mode of personal relations, act as the *one* God to redeem us.

What this points to, then, is that Christ's sacrifice was not offered to man. Instead, Christ's death was offered foremost *to God* (Heb 9:14) since *God himself* pays our price by satisfying *his own demand*. Or, as Macleod states it: in Christ's death "God covers our sins from himself; in propitiation, God appeases himself; in reconciliation, God makes peace with himself; . . . in redemption, God himself meets the cost of liberating moral and spiritual debtors; and he pays it to himself, because it is to himself the debt is owed."[40]

In other words, at the cross, the triune God is acting to save us. In the outworking of God's eternal plan, the Father demonstrates *his* love by giving us his Son and allowing the sword of justice to fall upon him. The Son, in glad and willing obedience to his Father's will, chooses to become our new covenant head in his incarnation, life, and entire cross-work for us. In his incarnation, our Lord becomes perfectly qualified to represent us and to act as our substitute. As the Son incarnate, *he* stands in our place bearing the penalty we deserve, which is *his* own righteous demand against us. Jesus is not a third party dragged in reluctantly to represent us. *He*, along with the Father and Spirit, is the offended party; *he* has the right to demand satisfaction from us. But in grace, the divine incarnate Son, Jesus Christ our Lord, renders perfect human obedience that satisfies his own divine righteous requirements against us in our place.

Penal substitution is the theology of atonement that best makes sense of these three truths. Jesus, the divine Son, by the initiative of the Father, bears our sin and in our place perfectly satisfies God's own righteous requirements against us. Our most fundamental problem is our sin *before* God, and ultimately it is only the triune God himself who can meet his own demand. Praise God he has gloriously done so in the provision of Jesus Christ our Lord.

---

39. See ibid., 64–72, and Macleod's argument for the priestly act of the Father at the cross.

40. Ibid., 235.

But some object to this view of the cross. They say it is incoherent to think of God as the object of the cross, or the cross as a transaction between the triune persons. For example, Joel Green and Mark Baker portray penal substitution as "one member of the Trinity punishing another member of the Trinity,"[41] which leads "to picture a God who has a vindictive character, who finds it much easier to punish than to forgive."[42] This caricature of penal substitution is problematic for multiple reasons, not least a failure to grasp basic Trinitarian theology such as the relations and inseparable operations of the divine persons. Yet, more specifically, it also seems to dismiss, or at least not take seriously, the crucial theological insight of the Reformation: the cross, at its heart, is the triune God satisfying his *own* righteous demand for us in Christ. This central *theological* point, if missed, will fail not only to grasp the *why* of the cross, but also its *necessity*. As we turn from the "facts" of the cross, let us now turn to this central *theological* point, namely, the divine problem of forgiveness, which is best accounted for by the *theology* of penal substitution.

Explaining the Problem of Forgiveness in Relation to the Cross

Why the cross? *Why* is the Son's incarnation, life, death, and resurrection *necessary* to fulfill God's eternal plan and to accomplish our salvation? The answers to these questions take us to the heart of all theologizing about the cross *and* separates penal substitution from its alternatives. One cannot make sense of the biblical presentation of Christ's identity and cross without viewing the proper object of the cross *as God himself.* No doubt, Christ's cross covers our sin, defeats death, destroys the work of Satan, cleanses us and restores us, but it achieves all of these glorious things because it first meets God's own demand against us.

This crucial theological point, which centers on a proper grasp of the God-law-sin relationship, was not only central to the Reformers and their heirs; it is also a biblical truth. From Genesis to Revelation, God is never presented as an abstract, impersonal force. Instead, he is

---

41. Green and Baker, *Recovering the Scandal of the Cross*, 174.
42. Ibid.

the triune God of holy love, the moral standard of the universe, who always acts consistently with who he is in perfect justice, righteousness, and goodness. In relation to sin, this is why, given God's moral aseity, a *necessity* results in the collision of our sin before him; God *cannot* tolerate wrong (Hab 1:12–13; cf. Isa 1:4–20; 35:8). He *must* act with holy justice when his people rebel against him; yet he is also the God who loves his people with a holy love (Hos 11:9). In Scripture, although divine holiness and love are never pitted against each other, a legitimate *tension* is created in how God will simultaneously demonstrate his holy justice and covenant love. This tension, rooted in the God-law-sin relationship, is only resolved in Christ and his cross. It is this tension between the holy God and human sin, between divine holiness-justice and covenant love, which is at the heart of answering the question: *Why Christ's cross?* Since God is the law, he *cannot* forgive our sin without satisfying his own holy and righteous demand. God *cannot* pass on our sin nor relax the retributive demands of his justice because God *cannot* deny himself. Sin is not against an impersonal order outside of God; it is against *him*. In fact, for the triune God to pardon sinners without the full satisfaction of his own moral character is to question whether *he* is the ultimate objective moral standard of the universe.[43]

Penal substitution is the only view that fully captures the God-centered nature of the cross and the problem of forgiveness. Unlike other views that make sin or Satan the object of the cross and miss this central *theological* point, penal substitution views the true object of the cross as God himself. No doubt, the triune God is the one who initiates our salvation. In love, God chooses to save us, but in order to save us he *cannot* deny himself. So the triune God, prompted solely by grace and love, chose to redeem us, and in a way consistent with himself. In Christ, our salvation costs us nothing, but for God, *he* bears it all. God in Christ became our penal substitute who took our place and died our death. In the drama of the cross, we do not see three actors but two: God and ourselves. Not, as John Stott emphasizes,

God as he is in himself (the Father), but God nevertheless, God

---

43. On this point, see Francis Turretin, *Institutes of Elenctic Theology*, trans. George Musgrave Giger and ed. James T. Dennison Jr., 3 vols. (Phillipsburg, NJ: P&R, 1994), 2:417–26.

made-man-in-Christ (the Son). Hence the importance of those New Testament passages which speak of the death of Christ as the death of God's Son. . . . For in giving his Son he was giving himself. This being so, it is the Judge himself who in holy love assumed the role of the innocent victim, for in and through the person of his Son he himself bore the penalty which he himself inflicted.[44]

In choosing to save us without denying himself, God through Christ substituted himself for us. Divine love triumphed over divine wrath by divine self-sacrifice. The cross was an act simultaneously of punishment and amnesty, severity and grace, justice and mercy. And given Christ's divine-human identity, *his* work is enough; no debt is left unpaid, and we receive *him* through faith alone, by grace alone, to God's glory alone.

Viewed in this light, the standard objections to penal substitution dissipate. As Stott contends:

There is nothing even remotely immoral here, since the substitute for the law-breakers is none other than the divine Lawmaker himself. There is no mechanical transaction either, since the self-sacrifice of love is the most personal of all actions. And what is achieved through the cross is no merely external change of legal status, since those who see God's love there, and are united to Christ by his Spirit, become radically transformed in outlook and character.[45]

Furthermore, it is precisely at this point that we discover the true *scandal* of the cross. Penal substitution not only affirms that God himself in Christ substituted himself for us but also affirms the cross's *absolute necessity*—there is no other way by which God's holy love and justice could be satisfied and rebellious humans redeemed. And is this not what sinful humanity stumbles over—what we find scandalous? As we stand before the cross, "we begin to gain a clear view both of God and of ourselves, especially in relation to each other."[46] We begin to realize that outside Christ's cross, hell is the only alternative. Our proud hearts rebel since they cannot bear to acknowledge either the seriousness of our sin and guilt or our utter helplessness before God.

---

44. Stott, *Cross of Christ*, 158.
45. Ibid.
46. Ibid., 160.

However, this central theological insight is what is neglected or, even worse, outright denied in other atonement theologies. For example, Green and Baker think of penal substitution in a purely mechanistic, impersonal way. As they discuss Charles Hodge, the famous nineteenth-century Princetonian theologian and a strong proponent of penal substitution, they give the impression that they do not accept a view of God who must be true to his own holy character and thus judge sin. With Hodge in mind they write: "Within his penal substitution model, God's ability to love and relate to humans is circumscribed by something outside of God—that is, an abstract concept of justice instructs God as to how God must behave."[47] They state further: "It could be said that Hodge presents God who wants to be in relationship with us but is forced to deal with a problem of legal bookkeeping that blocks that relationship. The solution is having God the Father punish God the Son."[48] They intensify this criticism by appealing to Robin Collins who wants to ridicule the substitutionary view by trying to insert it into the story of the prodigal son. Quoting Collins, they write: "When the son returns and recognizes the error of his ways, Collins has the Father respond, 'I cannot simply forgive you . . . it would be against the moral order of the entire universe. . . . Such is the severity of my justice that reconciliation will not be made unless the penalty is utterly paid. My wrath—my avenging justice—must be placated.'"[49] And remarkably, they think that it is instructive that Jesus pronounces forgiveness to the paralytic in Mark 2 "without reference to the sacrifice of any animal and without reference to his own, still-future death (Mark 2:1–12)."[50]

What Green and Baker sever (i.e., the God-law-sin personal relationship), others like Darrin Belousek completely render asunder. Today it is common to assert that the "biblical" concept of justice differs from the Western, classical concept of retributive justice that, as the story goes, distorted the Reformation's thinking about justification and the cross as penal substitution. In some versions of this "new" understanding, Jesus does not pay for our sin since God can forgive without payment for sin. In fact, Belousek insists that our human sense that justice requires

47. Green and Baker, *Recovering the Scandal of the Cross*, 174.
48. Ibid.
49. Ibid.
50. Ibid., 242.

satisfaction, sin demands punishment, and ultimately that God must make all things right, is a result of sin![51] For him, the "scandal" of the cross is that it

> reveals a God who is free to remain faithful and true and just—should all others prove false, should all else go wrong, even if the very "law of the universe" goes unsatisfied. . . . The scandal of the cross is thus the scandal of divine freedom and integrity, that God is who God is and will be who God will be—faithful and true and just—irrespective of human failings, rational formulas, and legal requirements.[52]

What are we to make of these statements? Can God simply forgive sin without atonement? In what sense is the cross *necessary* for our salvation? And what is the relationship between sin, punishment, law, and God? No theologian who affirms penal substitution, let alone Scripture, detaches the law from God, as Green and Baker seem to do and as Belousek does. On the contrary, Scripture teaches that God's law mirrors God's nature and is therefore inextricably related to his personal, moral, and holy character. That is why forgiveness is an *internal* or *intrinsic* problem for God. In order to forgive us, God cannot deny himself; he cannot arbitrarily forgive without a full payment, or atonement for sin. The Bible does not view the relation of sin, punishment, law, and God in a mechanistic manner but in terms of *personal* relationships.

But the "new" view does not think of the relationship between God-law-sin this way. No doubt people vary on how they conceive this relationship, yet Garry Williams contends that those who reject penal substitution affirm some form of "moral naturalism"; that is, "God has created the world in such a way that sin has its punishment as a natural consequence."[53] But this consequence occurs without any judicial act on the part of God after the sin has been committed, hence the dismissal of Christ having to be our penal substitute. "For sin to receive its punishment, God has to do nothing other than sustain the existence of the

---

51. See Darrin W. Snyder Belousek, *Atonement, Justice, and Peace: The Message of the Cross and the Mission of the Church* (Grand Rapids: Eerdmans, 2012), 389–93.

52. Ibid., 394.

53. Garry Williams, "The Cross and the Punishment of Sin," in Peterson, *Where Wrath and Mercy Meet*, 95–96.

world which he has created."[54] If this is so, what is striking about this view is that it is not the advocates of penal substitution who reduce the atonement to an impersonal mechanism, but the very critics themselves.

More to the point, moral naturalism contradicts Scripture for two reasons. First, separating the God-law-sin relationship *and* conceiving of justice in non-retributive ways ultimately undermines God's moral aseity and his divine nature as the basis for a moral universe. If God is not the perfect standard of goodness and justice, the ground for objective morality is undercut. Thankfully, the triune covenant God is not arbitrary; he does not forgive by a wave of hand; and in this fallen, cruel, unjust world, there is a higher court than man in all our corruption and sin. The triune God is the standard of righteousness, and as the true, objective, universal standard, *he* will not deny himself and let sin go unpunished. No doubt, *we* are forbidden to repay evil with evil, not because retribution is inherently wrong but because God is the Judge and *he* will make all things right in the end (Rom 12:19). As the covenant and sovereign God, *he* is faithful to his promises. *He* guarantees that sin and evil will be forever destroyed and perfect goodness established. Thankfully, as Macleod reminds us, "Whatever can be said in favour of a non-retributive deity who reacts to sin and crime with otiose indifference and takes no action beyond telling the abused victims to turn the other cheek, this is not the God of the Hebrew-Christian scriptures."[55] God, the Judge of the universe, will always do what is right (Gen 18:25)!

Second, given that the relationship between God-law-sin and punishment arises in the personal relation between God and the creature, it is now possible, if God chooses, to redeem us. But if God chooses to forgive our sin, he must do so *only* as the holy and righteous God. This entails that if God chooses to save, he *must* also satisfy his own righteous requirements, which he has gloriously done in the giving of his own Son. The cross then becomes *absolutely necessary* to redeem us; apart from it there is no holy and just forgiveness of our sins. In union with his people, our Lord, the *divine* Son willingly becomes our mediator to stand in our place and meet *God's* own demand against us. In his

---

54. Ibid., 96.
55. Macleod, *Christ Crucified*, 93.

eternal counsel, the triune God planned our redemption and enacted and secured it on the stage of human history. In Christ alone, *he*, as the divine Son incarnate, perfectly, finally, and completely met our need.

CHAPTER 8

The Cross of Our Glorious Redeemer: Penal Substitution, Part 2

Why is penal substitution the view which best captures what is *central* to Christ's cross-work as our all-sufficient Savior? In the previous chapter, we began a four-part argument by giving the first two points: penal substitution best accounts for the biblical "facts" about the cross *and* it best explains how the divine problem of forgiveness is resolved. In this chapter, we turn to our last two points: penal substitution best accounts for *why* the cross is *necessary* in light of the problem of forgiveness *and* it unites and explains better *all* of the Bible's language of the cross. Let us now turn to these last points as we further warrant *Christ alone* in his all-sufficient work.

Explaining the Necessity of the Cross

Today, the idea that Christ's cross is absolutely necessary for our salvation is widely rejected. But such an objection can only be sustained if the God-law-sin relationship is not what Scripture says it is. Given *who* the triune covenant Lord is and the nature of human sin, there is only one way God can redeem us—by *Christ alone*. One cannot account for how the cross is a demonstration of the *Father's* love in the death of Christ apart from its necessity. One cannot hear the Son's cry in Gethsemane and at Calvary without realizing that to reverse the effects of sin and death and to meet God's own demand, it is *this* Savior and *this* cross that are *absolutely necessary*. Furthermore, one cannot account for how Christ's cross is the demonstration of God's justice apart from rightly thinking about the God-law-sin and forgiveness relationship.

221

This point is poignantly made in two crucial texts: Romans 3:21–26 and Hebrews 9:15–28, which offer the clearest explanation for *why* the cross is *necessary*.

Romans 3:21–26

In a number of places, Scripture explains the *why* of the cross, but none more explicitly than here. Martin Luther scribbled in the margin of his Bible that these verses were "the chief point, and the very central place of the Epistle, and of the whole Bible."[1] Dr. Martyn Lloyd-Jones concurs with Luther when he comments on these verses, "It is no exaggeration to say of this section that it is one of the greatest and most important sections in the whole of Scripture."[2] Why is this text so important? Many answers could be given, but our singular focus is this: verses 25–26 gives us the *why* of the cross which is explained in terms of God's justice-righteousness and the problem of forgiveness, thus underscoring the central *theological* point of penal substitution. We will offer three observations about the text with our primary focus on verses 25–26.

First, it is crucial to place Romans 3:21–26 in the larger context of Paul's argument.[3] Starting in 1:18–3:20, Paul establishes that apart from the cross, all humans are under divine wrath, are guilty, and stand condemned before God.[4] Following the Bible's storyline, Paul establishes that God's wrath is revealed from heaven against all people (Jew and Gentile), ultimately due to Adam's disobedience as our covenant representative (Rom 5:12–21). As God's image bearers, although we clearly know God from creation, we suppress the truth, turn from him, and stand under his judgment. No doubt for the Jew there is a greater accountability due to the gift of covenantal privilege and special revelation, but all people, from general revelation, know God and his

---

1.   Cited in Douglas J. Moo, *The Epistle to the Romans*, NICNT (Grand Rapids: Eerdmans, 1996), 242.

2.   D. Martyn Lloyd-Jones, *Romans: Atonement and Justification—An Exposition of Chapters 3.20–4.25* (Grand Rapids: Zondervan, 1970), 31.

3.   On Rom 3:21–26, see D. A. Carson, "Atonement in Romans 3:21–26: God Presented Him as a Propitiation," in *The Glory of the Atonement: Biblical, Historical and Practical Perspectives*, ed. Charles E. Hill and Frank A. James III (Downers Grove, IL: InterVarsity Press, 2004), 119–39.

4.   On God's wrath in the OT and NT, see Leon Morris, *The Apostolic Preaching of the Cross*, 3rd ed. (Grand Rapids: Eerdmans, 1965), 147–54, 179–84.

judicial sentence against them (1:24–32). With a litany of OT texts, Paul concludes in 3:9–20 that apart from God's gracious initiative to redeem, all people stand guilty and condemned before the Judge of all the earth.

Second, in Romans 3:21, Paul now shifts to the good news centered in God's grace, initiative, and provision of Christ and his cross. The text highlights the redemptive historical shift that has now occurred in Christ's coming ("But now . . .")—a shift which introduces a crucial contrast between the old and new covenants, and a shift that explains *why* the cross is necessary in our justification before God.[5] In Christ's cross, the righteousness of God (*dikaiosunē theou*), i.e., God's justifying activity,[6] is now revealed, a righteousness rooted in his covenant promises and which results in our declaration of *justification* before him for all who believe in Christ.[7]

Third, the revelation of the righteousness of God in Christ is the fulfillment of the OT (v. 21) *and* is necessary to demonstrate that God is truly just (vv. 25–26), given the fact that God has forgiven people's sins under the old covenant without a full payment for those sins. As Paul transitions from the revelation of God's wrath (1:18–3:20) to the revelation of the righteousness of God (3:21), he stresses that God's righteousness is "apart from the law" [old covenant], though that the same law-covenant and prophets testify to it. Under the old covenant, God entered into relationship with his people, and through the Levitical priesthood and sacrificial system, God granted forgiveness to them as they believed God's promises (Gen 15:6; see Rom 4). Yet Scripture is clear: God never intended the old covenant to ultimately redeem us. Built within the old covenant were God-given limitations—for example, no adequate substitute, the repetitious nature of the system

---

5.   See Carson, "Atonement in Romans 3:21–26," 121–23; Thomas R. Schreiner, *Romans*, BECNT (Grand Rapids: Baker, 1998), 178–81.

6.   On the debate surrounding the "righteousness of God," especially in light of the New Perspective on Paul, see Moo, *Romans*, 79–89, 222. Moo argues that the "righteousness of God" is best understood as "the justifying activity of God." From God's side, this includes his active, miraculous intervention to vindicate and deliver his people in fulfillment of his covenant promises (see Mic 7:9; Isa 46:13; 50:5–8), i.e., his saving work and activity. From the human side, to those who receive God's "righteousness," it also includes the aspect of *gift* or *status* of acquittal acquired by the person declared just.

7.   On this point, see Moo, *Romans*, 79–89, 227–30; Carson, "Atonement in Romans 3:21–26," 124–25; Colin G. Kruse, *Paul's Letter to the Romans*, PNTC (Grand Rapids: Eerdmans, 2012), 182–85.

which revealed its inability to fully forgive sin, and no provision for high-handed sins.[8] But, in a whole host of ways the law-covenant and the prophets anticipated and predicted the dawning of a new covenant, a greater priest, and a better sacrifice. In this way, the OT revealed that the righteousness of God was to come "apart from the law," but that the law-covenant also anticipated a final and complete salvation that has *now* come in Christ and his cross.[9]

However, given the fact that the OT covenants did not fully pay for sins, how could God declare OT believers justified if sin remained unpunished (e.g., Gen 15:6; Ps 32:1–2)? Within the OT, this was not a minor problem. How can God declare ungodly people just before *him*, if God's righteous, holy demand was not fully satisfied? In fact, it is due to *this* problem that Paul explains *why* the cross is necessary. Why does the Father publicly set forth his Son as a propitiatory (*hilastērion*) sacrifice?[10] How is the cross *the* demonstration of God's righteousness and why was it *necessary* for Christ to die? The reason is this: "Because in his forbearance he [God] had left the sins committed beforehand unpunished" (v. 25b).[11] In other words, under the OT covenants, people were forgiven of their sins, but in truth, those covenants did not fully pay for sin. Douglas Moo explains: "This does not mean that God failed to punish or that he 'overlooked' sins committed before Christ; nor does it mean that God did not really 'forgive' sins under the Old Covenant. Paul's meaning is rather that God 'postponed' the full penalty due sins in the Old Covenant, allowing sinners to stand before him without their having provided an adequate 'satisfaction' of the demands of his holy justice (cf. Heb 10:4)."[12]

Why is this a problem for God? For atonement theologies other

---

8.   See Bruce K. Waltke, "Atonement in Psalm 51: My Sacrifice, O God, Is a Broken Spirit," in Hill and James, *Glory of the Atonement*, 57–58.

9.   See Carson, "Atonement in Romans 3:21–26," 122–25.

10.   On the debate regarding *hilastērion*, see Carson, "Atonement in Romans 3:21–26," 129–35; Kruse, *Romans*, 188–91; Morris, *Apostolic Preaching of the Cross*, 144–213.

11.   John Ziesler and Stephen Travis argue that "passing over" (*paresis*) refers to God's forgiveness, *not* his forbearance or postponing the full requirement for the payment of our sin. Given this interpretation, there is no tension between God's righteous demand against sin and his "passing over" our sins. But as Carson argues, *paresis* does *not* mean "forgiveness" but "postponement," which warrants the traditional view that there is a tension between God's righteous demand against us and his declaration of justification in the OT and his "leaving sin unpunished" (see Carson, "Atonement in Romans 3:21–26," 136–38).

12.   Moo, *Romans*, 240.

than penal substitution, *this* problem does not arise in the same way, given their uncoupling of the God-law-sin relationship. But in biblical thought the unpaid nature of our sin is a major problem! In the OT era, when God "postponed" and forgave the people's sins *without a full satisfaction of his own moral demand*, ultimately God's integrity, justice, and moral character were at stake. If God justifies the ungodly without exact retribution, is he not arbitrary? But if God does demand the full satisfaction required by his holy and just character, then how does he justly forgive the sins of OT believers? Under the old covenant this is a huge problem that cannot be ignored. In fact, this is precisely why God promises through the prophets that a new covenant is coming by the work of a greater priest (Ps 110; Isa 53) who will bring the full forgiveness of our sin (Jer 31:34).

Now it is precisely in *this* context that the *rationale* for Christ's cross is given, and it is only penal substitution that adequately accounts for it. *Why* must the divine Son become man and die? *Why* is Christ alone able to save, and apart from him, no salvation is possible? The answer: it was *absolutely necessary* for our Lord to come and die to render full satisfaction of *God's* own righteous demand. In the past, God had forgiven sin without full payment for sin. God was only justified in doing so grounded in what would occur in the future, namely, that our sin would be paid for completely in Christ. Thus, in the present, when God justifies those who have faith in Christ, he is declaring the ungodly righteous (Rom 4:5), not by overlooking their sin or relaxing his retributive demand but by paying for their sins in full in Christ. Our salvation is holy and just because in Jesus, we have a Savior who perfectly meets our need, and in his divine-human work, *he alone* secures our redemption, reconciliation, and justification before God.

Hebrews 9:15–28

Another crucial text, similar to Romans 3:21–26, that explains *why* the cross was *necessary* is Hebrews 9:15–28. As noted previously, the book of Hebrews uniquely unpacks Christ's work as our great high priest, and it beautifully unites Christ's person and work. As Hebrews 2:5–18 explains, God the Son took on our humanity to undo the work of Adam and restore us to the purpose of our creation, and he did so by becoming our merciful and faithful high priest.

In Hebrews, the priestly theme is developed in a twofold manner, tied to typological fulfillment, thus underscoring the greater nature of Christ's identity and work. First, Christ is a *greater* priest because he *transcends* the entire Levitical order: Christ comes in a *new* order, i.e., in the order of Melchizedek (Heb 7; see Ps 110), which requires a change in covenants, given the organic covenant-priesthood relationship in biblical thought (Heb 7:11–12). Second, Christ is a *greater* priest because he *fulfills* all that the Levitical priests typified (Heb 5:1–10; 8:1–10:18). For example, if the Levitical priest was selected by God, then so was Christ; if they offered a sacrifice, then so did he; and if they functioned as mediators of a covenant, then so did he, but in a far greater and more glorious way.

In Hebrews 9:1–10:18, the specific focus turns to Christ's better sacrifice compared to the Levitical sacrifices. Yet in contrasting the old sacrifices with Christ's new covenant sacrifice, the rationale and necessity for Christ's cross is given, rooted in covenant inauguration. As Hebrews 9:1–14 explains, the old covenant sacrifices were never intended by God to be the final sacrifice. The tabernacle-temple served many purposes in the old covenant, but one of its primary tasks was to reveal, instruct, and point forward to Christ's coming and the entire new covenant era (9:8–10).[13] The limitations of the old system were apparent within the system. For example, the Levitical priest offered *daily* sacrifices but the repetitious nature of the sacrifice revealed they were never sufficient. Or, the Levitical priest could *never* enter the holy of holies, and even the high priest could only enter the holy of holies *once* a year and only by first offering a sacrifice for *his own sins*, thus revealing that the high priest too needed redemption. In all of these ways, the old system was incomplete and insufficient in paying for our sin and giving us full access to God's covenantal presence. Ultimately, as the author states, the Levitical priest and his sacrifice "were not able to clear the conscience of the worshiper. They are only a matter of food and drink and various ceremonial washings—external regulations applying

---

13. On this point, see Thomas R. Schreiner, *Commentary on Hebrews* (Nashville: B&H, 2015), 262.

until the time of the new order" (9:9b–10, emphasis added). But Christ and the sacrifice of himself is greater. As Hebrews 9:11–14 reminds us, Christ did not serve in the shadow but in the reality. He did not offer anything for himself since he was perfect, and he did not offer the "blood of goats and calves"; instead he offered *himself* "once for all by his own blood, thus obtaining eternal redemption" (9:12b). By *his* one-time sacrifice, *eternal* redemption is accomplished, which at its heart requires the complete forgiveness of sins (Jer 31:34; Heb 10:1–18).

But the author does not stop here. He explains the *reason* why Christ had to die. By setting Christ's death in its new covenant context, he argues from covenant inauguration for the *necessity* of Christ's cross (9:15–22). In verse 15, he states, "for this reason" (*kai dia touto*), which establishes a strong causal relationship between verses 11–14 and verse 15. Jesus not only fulfilled the priesthood-sacrifices of the old covenant, but he also fulfilled the *covenant* itself, thus bringing it to its God-appointed *telos*. Jesus's death is viewed as a *covenant sacrifice*, a representative death first for those under the penalties of the old covenant—"as a ransom to set them free from the sins committed under the first covenant" (v. 15)—and second as the judicial grounds for the inauguration of the new covenant which is bound up with the full forgiveness of sin. In an important way, verse 15 is very similar in thought to Romans 3:25–26, except now Christ's death is explained in terms of covenant inauguration. In Romans 3, the rationale for Christ's cross was due to God's "postponement" of the full payment of human sin, even though God had already declared OT believers just. In doing so, God's integrity was at stake unless the full satisfaction of sin was ultimately met. In a similar way, Hebrews argues that the people's sins were not fully paid for under the old system. Thus, for the new covenant to be inaugurated, which promised the permanent forgiveness of sin, a greater priest-sacrifice must pay for the sin of God's people completely.[14]

This truth is reinforced in the parenthesis of verses 16–22. These verses explain further *why* it was necessary for Christ to die. The cross's necessity is *rooted in covenant practice* based on patterns from the OT. To inaugurate a covenant, it was necessary for animals to be cut in two

---

14. See Peter T. O'Brien, *The Letter to the Hebrews*, PNTC (Grand Rapids: Eerdmans, 2010), 326–35.

and the parties of the covenant to walk between the pieces. In this way, the blood of the animal was brought forward and the legal grounding of the covenant was established. With this in mind, Hebrews argues that the legal basis for the new covenant was not established by the blood of animals but by the blood of God's own dear Son. Why is the new covenant better? Because it is legally grounded in the person and work of God the Son incarnate, who in his life, death, and resurrection paid for our sin and so is now "able to save completely those who come to God through him" (Heb 7:25a).[15]

Why, then, must Christ become one *with* us and die *for* us? Why is *his* cross necessary? Without the payment of sins under the first covenant, and the full satisfaction of God's moral demand in the present, the new covenant that promises the full forgiveness of sin is not possible. Given the relationship between God-law-sin, a covenant relationship with God requires covenant ratification in blood by God's Son, who alone is able to meet God's own righteous demand. Thus, Romans 3:21–26 and Hebrews 9:1–28 establish the same rationale for Christ's death—a rationale that is only accounted for by penal substitution.

Explaining Coherently the Diversity of Biblical Language of the Cross

The true *biblical* test of any theology is whether it accounts for *all* of the biblical data. It is our contention that penal substitution best accounts for *all* the biblical language describing the cross. In current discussion, however, many, like Joel Green and Mark Baker, insist that penal substitution is reductionistic in terms of the richness of the biblical material. They contend that penal substitution has distorted the biblical data since it views the cross only through the lens of one or two biblical metaphors at the expense of others. They insist that the cross is not monochrome and that the biblical authors do *not* explain with precision *how* Jesus's death was effective in bringing about the salvation of the world, as penal substitution does.[16] Instead, in the NT, the saving effect of Jesus's death is represented primarily through five

---

15. See O'Brien, *Hebrews*, 333–42.
16. See Joel B. Green and Mark D. Baker, *Recovering the Scandal of the Cross: Atonement in New Testament and Contemporary Contexts*, 2nd ed. (Downers Grove, IL: IVP Academic, 2011), 31–38.

images: the court of law (justification); the world of commerce (redemption); personal relationships (reconciliation); worship (sacrifice); and the battleground (triumph over evil), and within these categories, there are clusters of terms, leading them to conclude that the portrait of Jesus's death *cannot* be painted with a single color. They conclude that given "the horizons of God's purposes, the Scriptures of Israel, and Jesus's life and ministry, and in relation to the life worlds of those for whom its significance was being explored, the death of Jesus proved capable of multiple interpretations."[17] However, they lament that with the passing of time and the aging of the Christian faith, "the many-hued mural interpreting Jesus's death has lost its luster, the theological soil becomes almost barren, capable of supporting only one or two affirmations concerning the cross."[18]

This is a serious charge that cannot be ignored. No theologian who is committed to *sola scriptura* wants to neglect any portion of Scripture in our theological formulations. To be *biblical* entails that we listen to *all* of Scripture, not just one portion of it. In theology, one must always beware of reductionism; no biblical evidence is to be de-emphasized or, even worse, eliminated in one's theological construction. Is this what advocates of penal substitution do? There are at least two reasons to say no.

First, when one considers all the rich and diverse language of Scripture, set within the biblical framework of God, humans, sin, and so on, and unpacked along the Bible's own covenantal storyline, John Stott is far more accurate in concluding that *substitution* is not only central to but also makes coherent all of the biblical data. As Stott says, "Substitution is not a 'theory of the atonement.' Nor is it even an additional image to take its place as an option alongside the others. It is rather the essence of each image and the heart of the atonement itself."[19]

Second, as diverse as the biblical language is regarding the cross, diversity of presentation does *not* lead to divergence. Rather, what is striking about the Bible's diverse presentation of the cross is how interconnected are its words, imagery, and concepts. Scripture gives us eight

17. Ibid., 34–35.
18. Ibid., 35.
19. John R. W. Stott, *The Cross of Christ*, 20th Anniversary Edition (Downers Grove, IL: InterVarsity Press, 2006), 199.

ways of thinking about the cross: obedience, sacrifice, propitiation, redemption, reconciliation, justice, conquest, and moral example. Yet none of these themes, especially when placed in the Bible's covenantal categories and storyline, is isolated and random. The biblical language flows naturally together, and it is simply not the case that diverse biblical language regarding the cross obscures its meaning. Instead, the entire biblical description of the cross brings to light its meaning, and when all the data is considered, it is penal substitution which best makes sense of the nature of Christ's cross work for us, as the Bible presents it in all of its glorious achievement.

For example, think of Romans 3:21–26. In this one paragraph, diverse language about the cross is given—righteousness-justice, redemption, and propitiation—and all of it placed in the larger presentation that Christ's cross is the better new covenant sacrifice (Rom 3:21). Or think of Colossians 2:14–15. This wonderful text brings together judicial and conquest images, but it does so by locating the victory of Christ in his payment of sin within the covenantal demand and provision. Or think of Hebrews 2:14–17. The entire person and work of Christ is set within the context of Adam-Last Adam, obedience, conquest, and new creation. He is our great high priest who acts as our representative and substitute. Furthermore, later in Hebrews Christ's death is viewed in light of the biblical covenants, Christ as the fulfillment and antitype of the Levitical sacrifices, and the inauguration of the new covenant rooted in sacrificial imagery set within the context of Christ bearing our covenantal curse and penalty. Or think of Galatians 3:10–13. This text is set within the context of covenantal shifts from old to new covenant, and the underlying logic is that under the old covenant, everyone is under God's curse since no one offers the perfect obedience God requires of his image bearers and covenant members. But Christ, the incarnate and perfectly righteous Son, dies in our place, bearing the curse we deserve and redeeming us from the curse of sin, death, and God's judgment.

In addition, the unity, coherence, and interlocking nature of the biblical presentation of the cross are best demonstrated by unpacking the eight ways the cross is presented. As the themes of obedience, sacrifice, propitiation, redemption, reconciliation, justice, conquest, and moral example are unpacked in their canonical context, it is only penal substitution that accounts for the richness of the data. Here are some examples to establish this point.

Obedience

This word and concept expresses Christ's perspective of the cross, and as such, it is one of the categories Scripture employs to explain Christ's work.[20] The word obedience is developed in Romans 5:19, Philippians 2:8, and Hebrews 5:8–9, while its concept is found in many places in the NT—for example, the servant theme (Mark 10:45; Matt 20:28; see Isa 42:1; 52:13–53:12); the purpose of Jesus's coming to do his Father's will (John 5:30; 10:18; 12:49; Heb 10:5–10; see Ps 40:7); the perfected-in-suffering theme (Heb 2:10–18; 5:8–10); and Christ's submission to the law as our covenant representative (Matt 3:15; Luke 2:51–52; Gal 4:1–4).

In Romans 5, it is set in the covenantal context of the two heads of the human race—Adam and Christ—which underscores Christ's active/representative obedience for us and his passive/substitutionary death on our behalf by paying our penalty in our place. In addition, in Hebrews, one cannot think about Christ's obedience apart from his incarnation and identification with us (Heb 2:5–18) for the purpose of dying on our behalf as our great high priest (Heb 2:17–18; 5–10). Here we see how covenants, representation-substitution, obedience, priest, and sacrifice are linked together as Christ is presented as the new covenant head who identifies with us and dies for his people.

Sacrifice

The NT clearly interprets Jesus's death as a *sacrifice* to be interpreted through the OT sacrificial system use of this language (see e.g., Acts 20:28; 1 Cor 5:7; 11:25; Eph 5:2; Rom 8:3; 1 Pet 1:19; 3:18; Gal 1:4; Rev 5:8–9; 7:14). As noted, probably the greatest treatment of Jesus's sacrificial death is the book of Hebrews, which sets the entire discussion within the larger context of the biblical covenants, priesthood, sin and guilt, and the need for divine forgiveness. One cannot think of Christ's

---

20. See John Murray, *Redemption Accomplished and Applied* (Grand Rapids: Eerdmans, 1955), 19–24.

death as a *sacrifice* without thinking of priestly representation *and* penal substitution. As Macleod observes, "The most fundamental argument in favour of substitution is that it is implicit in the very fact that Christ's death was a sacrifice."[21] But sacrifice is more than representation, since in the case of our Lord he does not merely offer the sacrifice on our behalf but becomes the sacrifice. "He is not only priest but victim; not only offerer but offering, doing for us what needed to be done but which we could not do, and which, once done, we need never do for ourselves."[22]

In current discussion, it is common to downplay the substitutionary nature of Christ's death as a "sacrifice."[23] For example, Green and Baker acknowledge that the backdrop of the sacrificial language is the OT sacrificial system.[24] However, they attempt to downplay the substitutionary significance of these sacrifices in two ways. First, they argue that the setting of the sacrificial language in the gospels is the exodus, which they interpret merely in terms of deliverance.[25] Second, and more crucially, they appeal to the *diversity* of OT sacrifices as proof that they are not *primarily* concerned with sin, and thus when this language is applied to the cross it does not necessarily demand a penal substitutionary view. In fact, they contend that most sacrifices "had nothing to do with sinful activity consciously committed or with its consequences."[26] No doubt some of the sacrifices were directed in this way, particularly the sin and guilt offerings; however, as they state: "The map of Israel's sacrificial system is more complex than even the designation 'sin offering' might suggest."[27]

But this appeal to the *diversity* of OT sacrifices is not enough to dismiss the substitutionary focus of the system. The number and kinds of sacrifices are diverse in the OT.[28] However, when one investigates how

---

21. Donald Macleod, *Christ Crucified: Understanding the Atonement* (Downers Grove, IL: InterVarsity Press, 2014), 85.

22. Ibid., 85–86.

23. For example, see Green and Baker, *Recovering the Scandal of the Cross*, 64–83, 128–33; Darrin W. Snyder Belousek, *Atonement, Justice, and Peace: The Message of the Cross and the Mission of the Church* (Grand Rapids: Eerdmans, 2012), 171–91.

24. See Green and Baker, *Recovering the Scandal of the Cross*, 64–68.

25. See ibid.

26. Ibid., 66.

27. Ibid.

28. See Stott, *Cross of Christ*, 134–49.

these sacrifices function within the covenant and the book of Leviticus, much more needs to be said, especially in regard to the payment for sin.[29] At the heart of the sacrificial system is the issue of sin, guilt, God's judgment, and the need for the payment of sin. To downplay this central theme, and especially to de-emphasize how the sacrificial theme is developed in the NT, especially in Hebrews 9–10, is to miss the point of the texts. In fact, three interlocking truths may be noted in terms of the relationship between the sacrificial system and its substitutionary significance.

First, the clearest statement that the OT blood sacrifices had a substitutionary intent is Leviticus 17:11.[30] Here we have God's explanation as to why the eating of the blood was prohibited: "For the life of a creature is in the blood, and I have given it to you to make atonement for yourselves on the altar; it is the blood that makes atonement for one's life." Interestingly, there is no discussion of this text by Green and Baker. However, John Stott rightly insists that this text teaches the vicarious nature of the sacrifices—life was given for life, the life of the victim for the life of the offerer—and the God-given nature of the system as the means by which God satisfies his own righteous requirements.[31] Second, in the book of Leviticus, the Day of Atonement (Leviticus 16) is no minor event; rather it is the theological center that binds the two halves of the book together. Thus, as David Peterson observes: "The Day of Atonement ritual is designed to make atonement for the sanctuary, the tent of meeting, the altar, the priests and 'all the people of the assembly' (16:33). Without atonement, Israel cannot function as God's holy people in a sinful and fallen world."[32] Third, it is impossible to sever the link between sin, punishment, and the role the sacrifices play in removing guilt and defilement and also in averting the wrath of God by offering the life of a substitute (see Lev 16:22).

In light of these points, when the sacrificial imagery is applied to the

---

29. For example, see Richard E. Averbeck, "Leviticus: Theology of," *NIDOTTE* 4:907–23; R. T. Beckwith and M. J. Selman, eds., *Sacrifice in the Bible* (Grand Rapids: Baker, 1995); G. J. Wenham, *The Book of Leviticus*, NICOT (Grand Rapids: Eerdmans, 1979).

30. On Lev 17:11, see Emile Nicole, "Atonement in the Pentateuch," in Hill and James, *Glory of the Atonement*, 35–50.

31. See Stott, *Cross of Christ*, 137–38.

32. David Peterson, "Atonement in the Old Testament," in *Where Wrath and Mercy Meet: Proclaiming the Atonement Today*, ed. David Peterson (Carlisle, UK: Paternoster, 2001), 7.

cross, one must view the cross in representational and substitutionary categories. Christ as our "sacrifice" can only mean that he stood in our place, bearing our sin for us (1 Pet 2:24–25).[33] Thus, in his sacrificial death for us, he acted as our substitute, expiating our sin and averting God's wrath.

Propitiation

The NT also describes Jesus's death as a *propitiatory* sacrifice (Rom 3:24–26; Heb 2:17; 1 John 2:2; 4:10), thus linking the imagery of sacrifice with priest and covenant. "Propitiation" is a word derived from the *hilaskesthai* word group, and its basic meaning is to turn aside a person's wrath or anger (in this case God's wrath) by taking away sin.[34]

What is important about the use of "propitiation" is that it presents the object of the cross as God himself, a point that is central to penal substitution. As argued above in our discussion of Romans 3:25–26, Paul insists that the first consideration is *not* our being justified but the demonstration of God's justice. Because God is just, our salvation must be compatible with God's own justice and character. Thus, Christ's death involves turning back the Father's wrath that is directed against us. In our place, God the Son endured what we deserve as he bore our sin and satisfied God's own righteous requirements.

In current discussion, talk about God's wrath is widely rejected, but that rejection cannot be sustained. Many, like Green and Baker,[35] reject the idea of God's personal wrath against sin and sinners by arguing that God's wrath in Scripture has nothing to do with an "emotion-laden God" who is against sinners, nor does it convey any notion of retributive punishment.[36] They insist that there is nothing in God's own self that must be altered, or any sense in which God's holiness must be requited. Instead, God's wrath is more a description of an inevitable process of

---

33. That is why Scripture proclaims that he died "in our place" (Matt 20:28; Mark 10:45), "for us" (Matt 26:28; Rom 8:3; 1 Pet 3:18; 1 John 2:2; 4:10), and "on our behalf" (Mark 14:24; Luke 22:19–20; John 6:51; 10:11, 15; Rom 5:6, 8; 8:32; 14:15; 1 Cor 11:24; 15:3; 2 Cor 5:15, 21; Gal 1:4; 2:20; 3:13; Eph 5:2, 25; 1 Thess 5:10; 1 Tim 2:6; Tit 2:14; Heb 2:9; 10:12; 1 Pet 2:21; 3:18; 1 John 3:16).

34. On the debate regarding "propitiation," see Morris, *Apostolic Preaching of the Cross*, 144–213.

35. See Green and Baker, *Recovering the Scandal of the Cross*, 70–83.

36. See ibid., 72, 174.

cause and effect in a moral universe.[37] As they argue in a number of places:

> Thus, in Paul's argument in Romans 1, sinful activity is the consequence of God's letting the human family go its own way—and this "letting the human family go its own way" constitutes God's wrath. . . . Our sinful acts do not invite God's wrath but prove that God's wrath is already active. Needed, then, is not a transformation of God's disposition toward the unrighteous and the ungodly but rather a transformation on the human side of the equation. . . . God's righteousness is effective in the present to save, but as men and women resist it, they experience God's righteousness as condemnation. Whatever else can be made of Paul's understanding of the death of Jesus, his theology of the cross lacks any developed sense of divine retribution. Quite the contrary, according to such texts as Romans 5:6–8, the death of Christ is the ultimate expression of the boundless love of God.[38]

Certainly, talking about God's wrath must be carefully done. As with *all* talk about God, we do so analogically and not univocally. But sadly, much of the current rejection of God's wrath caricatures historic Christian theology on this point. Who affirms an angry, emotion-laden God who strikes out against his creatures? No responsible treatment of either the wrath of God in Scripture or penal substitution affirms such a thing.[39] Nor is it legitimate to "depersonalize" God's wrath and merely say that God's wrath is simply "letting the human family go its own way."[40]

Yes, part of God's judgment against sin is to "let us go our own way," but there is much more to divine judgment and wrath than this.

---

37. This is a similar position to C. H. Dodd, *The Bible and the Greeks* (London: Hodder & Stoughton, 1935); A. T. Hanson, *The Wrath of the Lamb* (London: SPCK, 1959). Also see, Stephen Travis, "Christ as Bearer of Divine Judgement in Paul's Thought about the Atonement," in *Atonement Today*, ed. John Goldingay, Gospel and Cultures (London: SPCK), 21–38.

38. Green and Baker, *Recovering the Scandal of the Cross*, 79, 82.

39. See Morris, *Apostolic Preaching of the Cross*, 147–54, 179–84; Stott, *Cross of Christ*, 104–11, 124–32, 166–73; D. A. Carson, *The Gagging of God* (Grand Rapids: Zondervan, 1996), 232–34; John M. Frame, *The Doctrine of God* (Phillipsburg: P&R, 2002), 446–68; Moo, *Romans*, 99–103.

40. Green and Baker, *Recovering the Scandal of the Cross*, 79.

The holy God stands personally against sin and evil (e.g., Rom 1:18–32; 2:5; John 3:36), and so his wrath has a strong affective element to it. Moreover, God's wrath is not some peripheral part of the Bible's storyline. As D. A. Carson reminds us, "Theologically, God's wrath is not inseparable from what it means to be God. Rather, his wrath is a function of his holiness as he confronts sin. But insofar as holiness is an attribute of God, and sin is the endemic condition of this world, this side of the Fall divine wrath cannot be ignored or evaded. It is not going too far to say that the Bible would not have a plot-line at all if there were no wrath."[41]

It is God's wrath that is stressed in the term "propitiation," as applied in the OT sacrificial system and the NT understanding of the cross. Many have followed C. H. Dodd and argued that "propitiation" should really be translated "expiation," thus removing from the concept the idea that in Christ's death the Father's wrath was averted. But as Leon Morris and Roger Nicole have convincingly demonstrated, this is not correct.[42] What propitiation conveys, then, is the sense that in the cross God is simultaneously both the subject and object of the cross. Our sin is against God, and God must, if we are going to be redeemed, act in grace and provide the propitiatory sacrifice to meet our need. Stott nicely captures the NT presentation of the cross as a propitiatory sacrifice when he states:

> It is God himself who in holy wrath needs to be propitiated, God himself who in holy love undertook to do the propitiating, and God himself who in the person of his Son died for the propitiation of our sins. Thus God took his own loving initiative to appease his own righteous anger by bearing it his own self in his own Son when he took our place and died for us. There is no crudity here to evoke our ridicule, only the profundity of holy love to evoke our worship.[43]

It is only penal substitution which does justice to this Godward

---

41. Carson, *Gagging of God*, 233.

42. See Morris, *Apostolic Preaching of the Cross*, 144–213; Stott, *Cross of Christ*, 166–73; Robert Letham, *The Work of Christ*, Contours of Christian Theology (Downers Grove, IL: InterVarsity Press, 1993), 140–43; Robert Yarbrough, "Atonement," *NDBT* 388–93; Moo, *Romans*, 230–37.

43. Stott, *Cross of Christ*, 172–73.

aspect of the cross and only penal substitution that can undergird a proper understanding of the God-law-sin relationship.

Redemption

"Redemption" and "ransom" are also words which capture the achievement of Christ's cross (see Mark 10:45; Rom 3:24–25; 1 Cor 6:19–20; Gal 3:13; 4:4–5; Eph 1:7; Col 1:13–14; 1 Tim 2:6; Titus 2:14; 1 Pet 1:18–19; Heb 9:12, 15). As a term/concept, "redemption" conveys the idea of being liberated, or "bought back," either as a purchase or a ransom. In the latter use of "ransom," it also conveys the idea of "deliverance" or "liberation" from a state of bondage and captivity *by the payment of a price*, not merely an act of deliverance. Inevitably, as John Stott reminds us, "the emphasis of the redemption image is on our sorry state—indeed our captivity—in sin which made an act of divine rescue necessary."[44]

In current discussion, some attempt to interpret "redemption" merely as an act of deliverance devoid of any concept of the payment of a price.[45] Hence, when Scripture says that Christ's death was our "redemption," it does not entail that the cross must be interpreted in light of the problem of sin and thus the need for a sacrifice to pay for our sin before God. Rather, what is at stake are "images of deliverance" viewed in light of the backdrop of the mighty rescue mission of Israel in the exodus.[46] Thus, for example, Green and Baker claim that Jesus only speaks twice of his death as an atonement, in Mark 10:45 (Matt 20:28) and Mark 14:22–25 (Matt 26:26–29; Luke 22:19–20; see 1 Cor 11:23–25). They say that in both texts Jesus is speaking of his death in light of the exodus, which has nothing to do with the need for a sacrifice to pay for our sins. Jesus is instead concerned about issues of power and status. Jesus's disciples often struggled with the question of who among them was the greatest. Jesus's response was to reject such maneuvering and to insist that status in the community must be measured by one's role as a servant.[47] On this basis, Green and Baker

---

44. Ibid., 173.
45. For example, see Green and Baker, *Recovering the Scandal of the Cross*, 54–63, 126–28.
46. See ibid., 58–59.
47. See ibid., 54–63.

conclude that "redemption" and "ransom" must be understood first in terms of "deliverance," and second, as sayings that function in an exemplary fashion.

Green and Baker are correct that the exodus is the backdrop for the NT's use of "redemption," but they mistakenly conclude that the exodus *and* the cross are acts of deliverance that lack *substitution or payment of a price*. Repeatedly in Scripture, people, property, and persons are all "redeemed" by the payment of a price (e.g., Exod 13:13; 34:20; Num 18:14–17; Jer 32:6–8; Eph 1:7; Acts 20:28; Rev 5:9). This is also true of Christ's cross where the costly price of our redemption is nothing less than Christ's own shed blood for the forgiveness of our sins (e.g., Acts 20:28; Eph 1:7; 1 Pet 1:18–19).[48]

In addition, one cannot adequately understand the exodus as an act of deliverance without also thinking about the Passover and the tenth plague which involve *both* deliverance *and* payment for sin. The only way the firstborn can be delivered is through the shed blood of the lamb applied to the doorposts. The Passover is more than a demonstration of God's love or an act of deliverance; it also involves the idea of substitution. Moreover, as the covenantal unfolding progresses in the OT, it is difficult *not* to link the Passover with elements of the sacrificial system *and* with the suffering servant of Isaiah 53, which, as noted above, is at its core substitutionary. In Isaiah 53, the Servant not only suffers undeservedly because of sin, but he also suffers in the people's place, as a substitute, the righteous for the unrighteous (see 1 Pet 2:24–25).[49]

How, then, is the "redemption" language applied to the cross? It is difficult in light of the exodus, the Passover, the covenants, the sacrificial system, and Isaiah 53 to interpret the cross as bare deliverance; rather, it must be viewed as deliverance by the payment for our sin, on our behalf, by the God who desires to "save his people from their sins" (Matt 1:21).

---

48. See Morris, *Apostolic Preaching of the Cross*, 11–64; Murray, *Redemption Accomplished and Applied*, 42–50; Steve Jeffrey, Mike Ovey, and Andrew Sach, *Pierced for Our Transgressions: Rediscovering the Glory of Penal Substitution* (Nottingham, UK: Inter-Varsity Press, 2007), 34–42; Stott, *Cross of Christ*, 173–79.

49. On this point, see Jeffrey, Ovey, and Sach, *Pierced for Our Transgressions*, 52–67.

Reconciliation

The cross is also described as the place where "reconciliation" results in a variety of relationships: first vertically with God (Rom 5:1–2; Eph 2:17–18; 3:12; Heb 10:19–22); then horizontally with one another as the demands of the old covenant are met, a new covenant is inaugurated, and a new humanity is created (Eph 2:11–22); and finally cosmically by the inauguration of the new creation which defeats sin, death, and Satan and ushers in the new heavens and new earth (Col 1:15–20; 2:15; cf. Rom 8:18–27; Eph 1:10, 22).

While the concept of reconciliation between God and humanity is repeatedly found throughout the OT and NT, the words *katallassō*, *katallagē*, and *apokatallassō* are distinctively Pauline and found in four key texts: Romans 5:10–11; 2 Corinthians 5:18–21; Ephesians 2:11–22; and Colossians 1:19–20. Paul uses the concept more often than he uses the word—note, for example, his reference to "peace," "access," and being "brought near."

At its heart, "reconciliation" means "to restore to friendship." It is an image of family or personal relationship, in contrast to the imagery of the law court (justice, justification), temple (sacrifice), or marketplace (redemption). "To reconcile" means to bring together, or make peace between two estranged or hostile parties. It assumes that an old relationship has been broken, and now, as a result of some action, two parties who were once opposed are restored to each other. The Bible's storyline declares that humans, who were created for covenant relationship with the triune God, are now, due to their sin, in a state of hostility to God. Yet by God's gracious initiative, the Father has sent his Son to reconcile us to himself, to remove the enmity which has separated us, and to satisfy his own demand against us. By our Lord's obedient life and death, our state of enmity has been removed. Consequently we have been restored to a renewed covenant fellowship with our Creator-Redeemer God. We now have peace with and access to God and are receiving the benefits of the glorious new creation.

In current discussion, some have argued that "reconciliation" does not convey the idea that God is estranged from us, and as such, the word/concept does not teach what penal substitution affirms, namely, that God is the primary object of the cross.[50] But this is incorrect.

---

50. For example, see the essays by Greg Boyd and Joel Green in *The Nature of the*

Granted, reconciliation speaks of *our* estrangement from God. By nature *we* are "God-haters" (Rom 1:30), "hostile to God" (Rom 8:7), "alienated from God" (Col 1:21). As such *we* suppress the truth of God (Rom 1:18–23; 2:1–5) and stand opposed to him. And it is this alienation that results in all other alienations (Rom 3:10–18; Eph 4:17–19). Scripture presents "reconciliation" in universal categories, utilizing the promise from Genesis 3:15 that God will restore his fallen creation by abolishing the enmity that sin introduced between God and humanity, in human relationships, and in regard to cosmic realities (Col 1:15–20). God has brought us out of a state of enmity into a state of renewed fellowship with him by the cross. In Christ and through him alone, we now have "peace" with and "access" to the Father by the Son and Spirit. Because Christ Jesus stood in our place, obeying the Father and bearing our sin, he has now turned back God's wrath that stood against us and thus has removed all the barriers to a restored friendship with him (see Eph 2:1–18).

But reconciliation understood this way also entails that God is estranged from us. As Leon Morris and others have demonstrated, reconciliation's primary focus is Godward so that in every NT text dealing with reconciliation, the primary reference is to the removal of enmity *on God's part.*[51] In fact, our change of attitude is the consequence of a reconciliation that God himself has undergone. Our holy and righteous God is inevitably at enmity with sinners, and that is why his wrath is against us. What is needed is for God's hostility to be removed, and this has occurred at Christ's cross as Jesus died our death by bearing our sin.[52] "Reconciliation," then, does not stand against penal substitution. Indeed, it cannot be properly understood without it.

Atonement: Four Views, ed. James Beilby and Paul R. Eddy (Downers Grove, IL: IVP Academic, 2006), 43, 168; cf. Green and Baker, *Recovering the Scandal of the Cross*, 84–85, 133–34.

51. Morris, *Apostolic Preaching*, 214–50; see Murray, *Redemption Accomplished and Applied*, 33–42; David Peterson, "Atonement in the New Testament," in Peterson, *Where Grace and Mercy Meet*, 36–39.

52. Commenting on Rom 5:8, 10, Peterson explains, "The process of reconciliation did not simply involve changing our attitude towards him. Reconciliation was accomplished *for us* through the death of Jesus, even though God himself was the aggrieved party. But it must still be proclaimed and received *by us* for its benefits to be enjoyed (Rom 5:11; 2 Cor 5:19–20)" (Peterson, "Atonement in the New Testament," 39).

Justice and Justification

This image has been discussed above, but for sake of comple. it is important to state how Christ's cross is interpreted as an act justice which results in our justification (e.g., Rom 3:21–26; 5:9; see 2 Cor 5:21; Gal 3:13).[53] At the heart of this image is the picture of the law court. Before the holy and righteous Judge of the universe, God's verdict is that all sinners stand guilty and condemned (Rom 3:23; 6:23; see 8:1). Yet due to God's grace and initiative, the divine Son has become one with us in his incarnation to act as our covenant, legal representative (Rom 5:12–21) and to die for us as our penal substitute (Rom 3:24–26; Gal 3:13). As a result of his work and in faith union with him, God declares us righteous, not as a description of our present moral character but as a statement of our status/position before God, due to the representative and substitutionary work of our mediator, Jesus Christ our Lord.

God is just to declare the ungodly are just (Rom 4:5), not because we are righteous but because God's declaration takes into account a larger set of facts, namely, the atoning work of our covenant mediator who stands in our place, bears our penalty, and satisfies all of God's righteous demand against us. In union with his people, Christ, our covenant head, obeys in our place, dies our death, and satisfies divine justice which is evidenced by his victorious resurrection from the dead. As a result, by faith alone and in Christ alone, his righteousness is ours, now and forevermore (2 Cor 5:21; Gal 3:13). Once again, penal substitution best accounts for this biblical image.

Victory/Conquest

Christ's cross is also presented as the place of victory by which he defeats all of our enemies: sin, death, the principalities and powers, and Satan himself.[54] Throughout the entire storyline of Scripture, from

---

53. See the helpful discussion on justice, righteousness, and current issues, especially the New Perspective on Paul, in D. A. Carson, Peter T. O'Brien, and Mark A. Seifrid, eds., *The Paradoxes of Paul*, vol. 2 of *Justification and Variegated Nomism* (Grand Rapids: Baker, 2004); Stephen Westerholm, *Perspectives Old and New on Paul: The "Lutheran" Paul and His Critics* (Grand Rapids: Eerdmans, 2004); Guy Prentiss Waters, *Justification and the New Perspectives on Paul* (Phillipsburg, NJ: P&R, 2004); cf. Douglas J. Moo, *Galatians*, BECNT (Grand Rapids: Baker, 2013), 21–31, 156–73.

54. See Stott, *Cross of Christ*, 223–46; Macleod, *Christ Crucified*, 238–55; cf. Jeremy

divine warrior theme is a major way to understand
hrist's cross. In the NT, this theme is developed by
, Paul (Col 2:13–15), and the author of Hebrews
ly unites Christ's work as the priest-king and
emptive events in Christ's work, namely, his life, death,
on, ascension, and the pouring out of the Spirit at Pentecost.

Yet, what is often missed in thinking about *Christus Victor* is the
interrelationship between sin, death, and Satan's power over us, *and how
sin before God is our basic problem which must first be remedied*. Scripture
teaches that sin leads to death, which is the penalty for sin (Gen 2:17;
Rom 6:23). Even Satan only holds the power of death over us because
of our sin (Heb 2:14–15). Satan is a creature, and so he does not have
absolute dominion over us. The only authority he has is what he usurped
by tempting the human race into sin. Jesus came to defeat the work of
the evil one so he must deal with our root problem of sin. This is why
Scripture teaches that the defeat of the powers is first achieved in the
defeat of sin and its satisfaction before God (Col 2:13–15). Our greatest
problem is not flesh and blood, nor the powers, but our sovereign
Creator and holy Judge who stands against us due to our sin. The only
solution to God's being against us is for God to act for us by graciously
meeting the demands of his own righteous character. And thankfully,
this is exactly what he has done in Jesus Christ our Lord.

Moral Example

Scripture also presents Christ and his cross as the supreme moral
example for believers of love, obedience, and suffering. As such, it serves
as the supreme standard and example of the kind of attitude and behavior
we are to have as Christ's disciples (e.g., John 13:12–17; Eph 5:1–2,
25–27; Phil 2:5–11; 1 Pet 2:18–25; 1 John 4:7–12). However, theological
liberalism has reduced the biblical teaching to this one image
and neglected *all* of the other biblical imagery, along with the entire
theology and storyline of Scripture.

Still, it is important not to veer to the other extreme and neglect
the truth that our Lord does set for us an example in his life and death

R. Treat, *The Crucified King: Atonement and Kingdom in Biblical and Systematic Theology*
(Grand Rapids: Zondervan, 2014).

for us. In his obedience as the Son *incarnate*, Jesus demonstrates what a true image bearer looks like. In his interaction with others, he reveals how we ought to act, and even in his suffering—although it is utterly unique and unrepeatable—he shows how we are to respond to our enemies, endure unjust suffering, and esteem others higher than ourselves. Christ's life and death must move us to moral action, but it does so only because it is grounded in the unique and objective work he accomplished for us at Calvary. Without the singular, unique, and *objective* work of the cross, it would not serve as an example for us.

In a similar way, it is never enough for Christ merely to identify with us in his incarnation and show us how to live. Solidarity is not itself atonement, only its prerequisite. Scripture clearly teaches that more than a mere example is needed to redeem us. Instead, what is needed is for Christ to live and die *for* us. Ultimately our problem is not a lack of knowledge, so that all we need is a great prophet or teacher. Our problem is sin before the triune holy God, and *this* problem requires the enfleshment of God's own dear Son to represent us in his obedient life and to die for us in his obedient death as our great high priest and our covenant mediator. It is only when Christ acts for us as our propitiatory sacrifice that *God's* own righteous demand is fully met, and we, by faith alone in Christ alone, receive all the glorious benefits of his new covenant work: redemption, reconciliation, justification, and victory over all of our enemies.

Concluding Reflection: The Cross of an All-Sufficient Savior as Penal Substitution

Penal substitution—the Reformation theology of the cross—is the best way of capturing and making sense of *all* the biblical data—the "factual" presentation of the cross, *how* the divine problem of forgiveness is resolved, *why* the cross is *necessary*, and *all* of the biblical language of the cross. It is true that the Bible's description of the cross is rich and diverse, and we must never succumb to reductionism. Yet when *all* of the data is placed in the Bible's own storyline and framework, penal substitution best captures the Bible's own explanation for *why* Christ had to die as our Lord and Savior.[55]

---

55. J. I Packer, "The Atonement in the Life of the Christian," in Hill and James, *Glory of*

In fact, as one works through *all* of the data, one discovers our human need, the sovereign and gracious initiative of our triune God to redeem, and how he has done so in the representative and substitutionary work of our new covenant mediator—our glorious prophet, priest, and king. For example, think of how the biblical data highlights a different aspect of our human *need*. Obedience reminds us that we are disobedient and thus require a covenant mediator who obeys completely. Sacrifice stresses our defilement, guilt, and pollution before God, while propitiation underscores God's wrath upon us. Redemption highlights our bondage and captivity to sin, while reconciliation speaks of our enmity toward God and his enmity against us, hence the need for peaceful relations to be restored once again. Justification stresses our guilt before the sovereign Judge, while conquest speaks of our bondage to the powers.

However, just as the biblical language reminds us of our human need, it also emphasizes God's sovereign grace and initiative to save, thus highlighting the God-centeredness of the cross and our salvation. From eternity past, the triune God planned, initiated, and accomplished our salvation. In Christ alone, the Father has sent his obedient Son, who willingly obeyed and became the Lamb of God who takes away our sin to meet God's own righteous demand. In Christ, God took the initiative to satisfy his own just demand by becoming sin for us, absorbing the Father's wrath, redeeming us from sin and death, and restoring us to the purpose of our creation: to know, glorify, and serve God.

But none of this biblical data makes sense apart from viewing Christ's work, in his life and death, as the one who shed his blood as our new covenant head, our great high priest, and *as our penal substitute*. All the benefits of Christ's are ours because the Son became man, represented

---

the Atonement, 416, makes this exact point. He walks through the biblical data and then shows how it only fully makes sense in light of penal substitution. He writes: "What did Christ's death accomplish? It *redeemed* us to God—purchased us at a price, that is, from captivity to sin for the freedom of life with God (Tit 2:14; Rev 5:9). How did it do that? By being a *blood-sacrifice* for our sins (Eph 1:7; Heb 9:11–15). How did that sacrifice have its redemptive effect? By making *peace*, achieving *reconciliation*, and so ending *enmity* between God and ourselves (Rom 5:10; 2 Cor 5:18–20; Eph 2:13–16; Col 1:19–20). How did Christ's death make peace? By being a *propitiation*, an offering appointed by God himself to dissolve his judicial wrath against us by removing our sins from his sight (Rom 3:25; Heb 2:17; 1 John 2:2; 4:10). How did the Savior's self-sacrifice have this propitiatory effect? By being a vicarious enduring of the retribution declared due to us by God's own law (Gal 3:13; Col 2:13–14)—in other words, by *penal substitution*."

us in his life and death, and died in our place. Everything that is ours in salvation is due to *him* and the application of his work to us in faith union with him. Christ alone took our wretchedness, sin, and death, and in so doing, he has given us his righteousness and life. Philip Bliss captures the Reformation and biblical view of penal substitution beautifully in these famous words:

> Bearing shame and scoffing rude
> In my place condemned he stood,
> Sealed my pardon with his blood—
> Hallelujah! What a Savior!

PART 3

Christ Alone in the Reformation and Today

Chalcedonian Unity: Agreement on Christ's Exclusive Identity in the Reformation

Jesus of Nazareth has been and still is an enigma to many people. Even though he has been the dominant figure in the history of Western culture for almost twenty centuries,[1] a majority of people are still confused regarding his identity.

Whom do we say that Jesus is? Why is he important? Why has the church confessed that *Christ alone* is Lord and Savior? These questions are not new; they have been asked ever since Jesus's earthly ministry. The writers of the four Gospels labored to impress upon us the revelation of Jesus of Nazareth—the Gospels persist in pressing the point of his identity: Who is this Jesus? Who is he who is born the son of David, the son of Abraham (Matt 1:1)? Who is he who announces the dawning of the kingdom (Matt 4:12–17)? Who is he who commands wind and water and turns water into wine (Luke 8:22–25; John 2:6–11)? Who is he who forgives sin (Mark 2:1–12)? Who is he who raises the dead and rises from the grave (John 11:38–44; 20:1–18)?

Even Jesus himself asked his disciples, "Who do people say that the Son of Man is?" (Matt 16:13). Similar to our own day, the responses of the people then were diverse and confused. Some identified him superstitiously with John the Baptist come back from the dead, while others thought of him as one of the great OT prophets. So Jesus asked

---

1. This is the assessment of Jaroslav Pelikan, *Jesus through the Centuries: His Place in the History of Culture* (New Haven: Yale University Press, 1999), 1.

his disciples, "Who do you say I am?" (Matt 16:15). Speaking for them, Peter answered correctly, "You are the Messiah, the Son of the living God" (Matt 16:16). But even then, Peter did not fully grasp Jesus's identity. Immediately after his confession, Peter objected to Jesus's explanation of his own suffering and death. Peter could not yet conceive of a suffering Messiah; he thought only of a victorious king. It was not until after the resurrection that Peter and the disciples began to understand who Jesus truly is as the Son and the Messiah who had to die in order to accomplish our salvation.

The disciples' pre-Easter confusion continued among many people throughout the centuries and into our own day. And so remains the challenge of confessing and professing *solus Christus*. From a Christian view, this kind of confusion and uncertainty is serious. As parts 1 and 2 have argued, Scripture presents Jesus as Christ the Lord, the Word made flesh, the Lord of Glory, who existed as God the Son from all eternity and who at a specific point in time took to himself our human nature to accomplish our redemption and to judge the living and the dead. Thus, confusion about who Christ is and what he has done is a matter of life and death. Yet, it is crucial to note that the nature of the confusion has differed over time, especially in the Christian West. This is important to remember when comparing the Reformation era to our present day.

Keep in mind that Trinitarian and christological orthodoxy was held in common by the Roman Church and the Reformers. So what precisely were the Reformers confessing in their affirmation of *Christ alone*? Before we answer that question, let us first describe what the Reformers and Rome shared in common in their confession of Christ. Then, in the next chapter we will delineate their central differences, thus gaining clarity on what the Reformer's meant by *Christ alone* and why that meaning is still important for us to confess and profess today.

Christological Orthodoxy in the Reformation

There is much that Protestants share in common with Roman Catholic theology in regard to christological orthodoxy. From the patristic through the Reformation eras, all segments of the church spoke in a unified voice regarding Christ's identity, namely, the same Nicene and Chalcedonian view that our Lord Jesus Christ is nothing

less than God the Son incarnate, the only unique and exclusive Lord
and Savior. This common christological orthodoxy is represented by the
Chalcedonian Definition.[2]

The Chalcedonian Identity of Christ

The Chalcedonian Definition is the touchstone of orthodox
Christology. It arises out of the Council of Chalcedon, which began in
October 451. At that time, 520 bishops gathered to wrestle with the
ongoing christological disputes within the church. Most of the church's
bishops were from the East and only four came from the West—two
from North Africa and two who were legates of Leo of Rome. Yet
Western influence was significant due to Leo's *Tome*—a letter which
was written prior to the council and which was incorporated into the
Chalcedonian Creed.[3] As the earlier Nicene Creed established orthodox Trinitarian theology, so the Chalcedon Definition established the
standard for orthodox Christology. Harold O. J. Brown notes that while
some have disputed the Chalcedonian Creed, it was never set aside.
Chalcedon became "the second great high-water mark of early Christian
theology: it set an imperishable standard for orthodoxy"[4] as it confessed
the deity and humanity of Christ in the classic formulation of "two
natures, one person."

Chalcedon rejected false christological views and presented a positive understanding of Christ's identity. It followed earlier Trinitarian
formulations and distinguished "person" from "nature."[5] In terms of
"person," Chalcedon asserted that the active subject of the incarnation,
"the one and the same Christ," is none other than the eternal Son, who
is of the same nature (*homoousios*) with the Father and the Spirit but

2.   For a discussion of pro-Nicene Trinitarian theology and Chalcedonian Christology,
see Lewis Ayres, *Nicaea and Its Legacy: An Approach to Fourth-Century Trinitarian Theology*
(Oxford: Oxford University Press, 2004); Aloys Grillmeier, *From the Apostolic Age to
Chalcedon (451)*, vol. 1 of *Christ in Christian Tradition*, trans. John Bowden, 2nd rev. ed.
(Atlanta: John Knox, 1975); Gerald Bray, *God Has Spoken: A History of Christian Theology*
(Wheaton, IL: Crossway, 2014).

3.   For a discussion of the events surrounding Chalcedon and its theology, see Grillmeier,
From the Apostolic Age to Chalcedon (451), 520–57, and Bray, *God Has Spoken*, 350–65.

4.   Harold O. J. Brown, *Heresies: The Image of Christ in the Mirror of Heresy and
Orthodoxy from the Apostles to the Present* (Garden City, NY: Doubleday, 1984), 181.

5.   For a full discussion of the nature-person distinction in Christology, see Stephen
J. Wellum, *God the Son Incarnate: The Doctrine of Christ* (Wheaton, IL: Crossway, 2016),
255–465.

who has now assumed a complete human nature so that *he* now subsists
in two natures—natures which are *not* confused or changed but retain
all of their attributes. The Creed reads as follows:

> In agreement, therefore, with the holy fathers, we all unanimously
> teach that we should confess that our Lord Jesus Christ is one and
> the same Son, the same perfect in Godhead and the same perfect
> in manhood, truly God and truly man, the same of a rational soul
> and body, consubstantial with the Father in Godhead, and the same
> consubstantial with us in manhood, like us in all things except sin;
> begotten from the Father before the ages as regards His Godhead,
> and in the last days, the same, because of us and because of our
> salvation begotten from the Virgin Mary, the *Theotokos*, as regards
> His manhood; one and the same Christ, Son, Lord, only-begotten,
> made known in two natures without confusion, without change,
> without division, without separation, the difference of the natures
> being by no means removed because of the union, but the property
> of each nature being preserved and coalescing in one *prosopon* and
> one *hypostasis*—not parted or divided into two *prosopa*, but one and
> the same Son, only-begotten, divine Word, the Lord Jesus Christ, as
> the prophets of old and Jesus Christ Himself have taught us about
> Him and the creed of our fathers has handed down.[6]

The Exclusivity of Christ

As with the previous Nicene Creed, Chalcedon was significant
because it addressed every problem that had so far plagued the church
in regard to Christ's identity, and it presented us with an utterly unique
and exclusive Lord and Savior.[7] It sought to curb speculation, clarify
the use of language between East and West, and function as a definitive statement and road map for all later christological reflection. The
Chalcedonian Definition argued against the following theological
errors:

- *Docetism*—Christ only appeared to be man. The Lord Jesus was

---

6. Cited from J. N. D. Kelly, *Early Christian Doctrines*, 5th rev. ed. (London: A & C
Black, 1977), 339–40.
7. See Jean Galot, *Who Is the Christ? A Theology of Incarnation* (Chicago: Franciscan
Herald, 1981), 243–44.

perfect in manness, truly man, consubstantial (*homoousion*) with us according to his manness, and born of Mary.

- *Adoptionism*—Jesus was not the eternal Son made flesh but a mere man empowered by the Logos. Jesus is the personal subsistence of the Logos "begotten of the Father before the ages."

- *Modalism*—Christ is not a distinct Son from the Father (and Spirit). Christ is distinguished as the Son from the Father by the titles of "Father" and "Son" and by the personal distinctions between the Father and Son since the Son is begotten from the Father before all ages.

- *Arianism*—Christ is not *God* the Son and is thus merely a creature. Our Lord Jesus is God the Son, perfect in deity and truly God.

- *Apollinarianism*—Christ, in the incarnation, had an incomplete human nature. Our Lord Jesus was "truly man of a reasonable soul and body . . . consubstantial with us according to his manhood; in all things like unto us."

- *Nestorianism*—Christ, in the incarnation, had two persons, the eternal Son alongside Jesus the man. Our Lord is *not* two persons but *one* and the *same* Son, *one* person and *one* subsistence, not parted or divided into two persons, whose natures are *in union* without division and without separation.

- *Monophysitism*—Christ, in the incarnation, was a divine-human blend. Our Lord Jesus had *two* natures, not one, and those natures were not confused, changed; in fact, the properties or attributes of each nature were fully preserved and united in one person.

In addition, five points capture the heart of the Definition, which provide the foundation to christological orthodoxy from the patristic to the Reformation eras, and even to our present day.

First, Christ was truly and perfectly God *and* man. Both the deity of Christ and his humanity are equally emphasized in order for him to serve as our great high priest and mediator and to win salvation for us.[8]

Second, "person" and *hypostasis* are viewed as the same thing. In so doing, Chalcedon, building on the Nicene Creed, clearly distinguished between "person" and "nature." *Person* is seen as a principle in its own right, not deducible from *nature*, or as a third element from the union

---

8.   On this point, see Grillmeier, *From the Apostolic Age to Chalcedon (451)*, 547.

of the two natures.[9] A new *person* does not come into existence when the human nature is assumed, nor does it result in two persons. Instead, Chalcedon affirms that the *person* of the incarnation is the eternal Son, who has always been in relation to the Father and Spirit and who shares with them the divine nature. Furthermore, it is a *person*, not a nature, who becomes flesh. The incarnation is a personal act of the Son who took "the very nature of a servant" (Phil 2:7) in a deliberate and sacrificial way.[10] It is the *person* of the Son who is the *one* acting agent and suffering subject. Does this imply change in the Son? Not in the sense that the person of the Son changed his identity or ceased to be what he always was. Even as the incarnate Son, he continued to possess all the divine attributes and perform all his divine functions and prerogatives. Nevertheless, as Macleod rightly notes,

> [T]here is real change: change in the sense that in Christ God enters upon a whole new range of experiences and relationships. He experiences life in a human body and in a human soul. He experiences human pain and human temptations. He suffers poverty and loneliness and humiliation. He tastes death. . . . Before and apart from the incarnation, God knew such things by observation. But observation, even when it is that of omniscience, falls short of personal experience. That is what the incarnation made possible for God: real, personal experience of being human.[11]

Third, Christ's human nature did not have a *hypostasis* (person) of its own (*anhypostasia*). Jesus of Nazareth would not have existed had the Son not entered the womb of Mary. There was no "man" apart from this divine action, but as a result of this action, the Son, who possessed the divine nature from all eternity, now added to himself a human nature with a full set of human attributes. This enabled him to live a fully human life in and through his human nature, yet he is not completely circumscribed by his human nature because Christ has two natures.

---

9. In truth, Chalcedon is still slightly ambiguous on this point, and it is not clarified until Constantinople in 553. See Aloys Grillmeier, *From the Council of Chalcedon (451) to Gregory the Great (590–604)*, vol. 2:2 of *Christ in Christian Tradition*, trans. Pauline Allen and John Cawte (Louisville: Westminster John Knox, 1995), 277.

10. See Donald Macleod, *The Person of Christ* (Downers Grove, IL: InterVarsity Press, 1998), 185–86.

11. Ibid., 186.

[handwritten annotations: "one person" / "God man"; "1 Person / 2 Natures"]

This is why, as Donald Fairbairn reminds us, the fathers of the church spoke of God the Son doing some things *qua God* and doing other things *qua man*. "The same person did things that were appropriate for humanity and other things that were appropriate, or even possible, only for God. But the person who did these things was the same, God the Son."[12] Thus, Jesus is far more than a man who is merely indwelt by God the Son; he is God the Son living on earth as a man, accomplishing our redemption as the Lord.

One of the entailments of Chalcedon is that whenever we look at the life of Christ and ask, *Who* did this? *Who* said this? *Who* suffered death for us? The answer is always the same: God the Son. Why? Because it is not the divine or human nature which acts and thus does things; rather it is the *person* of the Son acting in and through his divine and human natures. It is the *Son* who was born, baptized, tempted, transfigured, betrayed, arrested, condemned, and who died. It was the *Son* who shed his blood for us to secure our salvation. It is in the *Son* that all of God's righteous demands are met so that our salvation is ultimately of God. It is the *Son* who also rose from the dead and who now reigns as King of kings and Lord of lords. Once again, Macleod beautifully captures this truth: "In him [the Son], God provides and even becomes the atonement which he demands. In him (in his flesh, within the finitude of his life-time, the finitude of his body and the finitude of his human being) God dealt with our sin. He is a man: yet the man of universal significance, not because his humanity is in any sense infinite but because it is the humanity of God. . . . In him, God lives a truly human existence."[13]

Fourth, the union of Jesus's two natures does not obscure the integrity of either. Within God the Son incarnate, the Creator-creature distinction is preserved; there is no blend of natures or "transfer of attributes" (*communicatio idiomatum*) that produces some kind of third thing (*tertium quid*). Yet this does not entail that the two natures are merely juxtaposed, lying side by side without contact or interaction. Instead, there is a "transfer of attributes" in the sense that the attributes

12. Donald Fairbairn, *Life in the Trinity: An Introduction to Theology with the Help of the Church Fathers* (Downers Grove, IL: IVP Academic, 2009), 140. Cf. Gerald Bray, *God Is Love* (Wheaton, IL: Crossway, 2012), 129.

13. Macleod, *Person of Christ*, 190. Cf. Wellum, *God the Son Incarnate*, 316–24. After Chalcedon, this emphasis gets picked up in the language of *enhypostasia*, which clarifies *anhypostasia*.

of both natures coexist *in the one person*. This is why Scripture can say that God the Son incarnate can simultaneously uphold the universe (Col 1:17), forgive sin (Mark 2:10), become hungry, thirsty, grow in wisdom and knowledge (Luke 2:52), and even die. This is why the Son, as the subject of the incarnation, acts always in the fullness of both natures, each in its own distinct way.

Fifth, the Son took to himself a complete human nature which was comprised of a "rational soul and body." Chalcedon insists that Jesus's humanity, in order to be a complete humanity, had to be more than a body; it had to consist of a full human psychology similar to our own. Chalcedon, then, clearly distinguishes "person" from "soul," *and* it locates the "soul" as part of the human nature. It rejects the idea that the Son replaces the human soul, and it implicitly asserts that Christ had a human will and mind, thus two wills (a divine and human will), even though this latter affirmation is not formalized until the sixth ecumenical council in 681.[14]

In a nutshell, these five points capture the heart of the Chalcedonian Definition, which present us with our Lord Jesus Christ who is utterly unique, incomparable, and in a category all by himself as God the Son incarnate. After Chalcedon, further clarification of these points resulted in greater christological precision, yet these basic points give us christological orthodoxy up to our own day, which the Reformers *and* the Roman Church held in common.

So where does the disagreement arise between them? *Christ alone* cannot be a debate over the uniqueness and exclusivity of Christ's identity since they both agree on this point. What, then, are the Reformers confessing in their affirmation of *solus Christus*? The answer to this question involves two aspects: the first was central in the Reformers' recovery of the gospel against the theology of Rome, while the second was an incipient but growing problem which would later reach full bloom in the Enlightenment. In the next chapter, let us clarify both aspects to grasp better what the Reformers were confessing in their affirmation of *Christ alone*, with the goals of appreciating anew the glory of Christ and of standing with the Reformers today.

---

14. See Grillmeier, *From the Apostolic Age to Chalcedon (451)*, 547.

CHAPTER 10

The Sufficiency of Christ: The Reformation's Disagreement with Rome

The Reformers' main disagreement with Rome was their rejection of its sacramental theology, which they insisted undermined the *sufficiency* of Christ's work. As Timothy George notes, Calvin, along with the other Reformers, affirmed Chalcedonian orthodoxy, but "he recognized that adherence to correct doctrine was not sufficient to prevent the abuses he saw about him in the dependence on relics, indulgences, the rosary, and the Mass."[1] Rome confessed the exclusivity of Christ, but it lacked an equal emphasis on the sufficiency of his work, especially Christ *alone* as the *sole ground* of our justification which we receive through faith alone (*sola fide*), apart from works. Philipp Melanchthon captures this point well: "When we say that we are justified by faith, we are saying nothing else than that for the sake of the Son of God we receive remission of sins and are accounted as righteous."[2]

Some of the problem bequeathed by the medieval era, as noted in chapter 6, was filling the gap between the achievement of Christ's work and our appropriation of it. Was Christ's work appropriated by believing the gospel promises or through the sacraments of the church? Partly why this was disputed in the Reformation was due to Anselm's silence on *how* Christ's cross is appropriated by us. Into this silence, Thomas Aquinas (1224–1274) spoke, and he spoke by making more explicit the relationship between Christ's cross and our appropriation of it via the sacraments as mediated by the church. As Aquinas states, "Christ's

---

1. Timothy George, *The Theology of the Reformers* (Nashville: Broadman, 1998), 219.
2. Philipp Melanchthon, *The Chief Theological Topics: Loci Praecipui Theologici*, 2nd English ed., trans. J. A. O. Preus (St. Louis: Concordia, 2011), 157.

passion [suffering] works its effect in them to whom it is applied, through faith and charity [love] and the sacraments of the faith."[3] As this relationship was developed in medieval theology, the sacraments were viewed as *necessary* for our salvation because it is through them that Christ's work becomes ours and we are infused with Christ's righteousness. Specifically, by the sacrament of baptism, Christ's work is applied by infusing grace into us that "eradicates both the guilt and corruption of original sin,"[4] regenerates us, and incorporates us into the church. The grace that is communicated through the sacraments is infused so that our very nature is transformed, and by this infusion, we are enabled to cooperate with God to merit eternal life.[5] In addition, by this application of Christ's work we are delivered from eternal punishment and from guilt. But subsequent sins after our baptism also demand satisfaction, which is paid for either in purgatory or "through the power of the keys exercised in the sacrament of penance."[6] The sacrament of penance, then, becomes one of the most important ways Christ's cross is applied to us in our daily lives, given the necessity of additional satisfaction to be made by Christians due to ongoing sin. In this way, the exclusivity of Christ's work is affirmed but the sufficiency of it as the sole ground of our justification is compromised. Christ, plus the church in applying Christ's work to us through the sacraments and our cooperation with God to merit eternal life, are necessary for our salvation.[7]

It is at *this* precise point that the Reformers reject Rome's sacramental theology and unequivocally affirm that we are justified by faith *alone* and in Christ *alone*. For the Reformers, *solus Christus* entails the confession of Christ's exclusive identity *and* his perfect, complete, and all-sufficient work as our covenant head and mediator. In Christ alone, given *who* he is and *what* he has done as our representative and

---

3.   Thomas Aquinas, *Summa Theologica*, 5 vols., Christian Classics (Notre Dame, IN: Ava Maria, 1981), pt. 3, Q. 49, Art. 3 (4:2284).

4.   Michael Horton, *The Christian Faith: A Systematic Theology for Pilgrims On the Way* (Grand Rapids: Zondervan, 2011), 622.

5.   On this point, see ibid, and Gregg R. Allison, *Historical Theology: An Introduction to Christian Doctrine* (Grand Rapids: Zondervan, 2011), 398.

6.   Gwenfair M. Walters, "The Atonement in Medieval Theology," in *The Glory of the Atonement: Biblical, Theological, and Practical Perspectives*, eds. Charles E. Hill and Frank A. James III (Downers Grove, IL: InterVarsity, 2004), 249.

7.   See, for example, Aquinas, *Summa Theologica*, pt. 3, Q. 61, Art. 1 (4:2347, Christian Classics).

substitute, there is nothing more we can add to his work. Christ's work is sufficient in its accomplishment, and by faith alone we are declared righteous on the basis of Christ's righteousness imputed to us. Due to God's grace alone, believers are complete in Christ, and all the benefits and gifts of Christ's glorious work are ours which grounds our confidence that nothing can ever separate us from God's love in Christ Jesus our Lord (Rom 8:1–4, 28–39).

To understand better the Reformation's affirmation of *solus Christus* in opposition to the sacramental theology of Rome, let us first describe Rome's sacramental theology and why it undercuts the sufficiency of Christ's work, and then describe some areas in Rome's practice that the Reformers opposed in affirming *Christ alone*.[8]

The Sacramental Theology of Rome

As Gregg Allison rightly reminds us, Rome's sacramental theology is part of an integrated theological system centered in two intertwined ideas: the "nature-grace interdependence" and the "Christ-Church interconnection."[9]

First, in Roman Catholic theology, "nature-grace" is on a continuum of lower to higher: nature (lower) is a channel of God's grace (higher), and grace is to elevate and perfect nature. In Adam's sin, the original nature-grace relationship was marred, yet "nature still possesses a capacity to receive, transmit, and cooperate with grace."[10] God's grace, then, works in nature and stirs nature to cooperate with it, thus offering warrant for a synergistic view of the relationship between divine and human action. Also, in Roman theology, especially via Aquinas, the

---

8.   In describing Rome's sacramental theology, our focus is on what *all* the Reformers rejected as unbiblical: the church as a continuation of Christ's incarnation which mediates grace to us through its hierarchy; that the sacraments are effective *ex opere operato* ("by the work worked") and apart from the recipient's faith; that the sacraments are the means by which grace is infused in us, and that it is not the recipient's faith which is essential in receiving the sacrament but the faith of the Catholic Church which bestows the gift of faith on its people beginning in baptism. Gregg Allison and Chris Castaldo, *The Unfinished Reformation* (Grand Rapids: Zondervan, 2016), 113, summarize what *all* the Reformers rejected: "Catholics believe that the sacraments are means by which grace is infused into their recipients, transforming their nature and enabling them to merit eternal life. Moreover, they believe the sacraments are valid and effective *ex opere operato*."

9.   On this point, see Gregg R. Allison, *Roman Catholic Theology and Practice: An Evangelical Assessment* (Wheaton, IL: Crossway, 2014), 42–67.

10.   Ibid., 47. Also see, Bruce Demarest, *The Cross and Salvation: The Doctrine of Salvation*, Foundations of Evangelical Theology (Wheaton, IL: Crossway, 1997), 53–55.

nature-grace scheme results in a more positive view of human nature's *intrinsic* disposition toward the operations of grace. In Adam's sin we lost our original righteousness, viewed as a superadded gift, with a consequent disruption of reason's governance of our passions resulting in our being dominated by our lower, emotional and physical nature. But by the infusion of grace into nature, beginning in our baptism, we are able to become participants with God,[11] such that grace "divinizes" individuals and "elevates them into the divine order."[12]

By contrast, the Reformers rejected the nature-grace scheme of Rome and replaced it with a monergism built on the categories of creation, fall, redemption, and new creation. In this biblical-theological framework, nature was created good (Gen 1:31), but now, as a result of the fall, humans (and all creation) are presently corrupted (Gen 3; cf. Rom 3:23; 6:23; 8:18–25; Eph 2:1–3), thus requiring God to save us (Gen 3:15; Jonah 2:9; John 3:16; Rom 3:21–31; Eph 2:4–10).[13] For this to happen, God alone must unilaterally act to redeem us, thus accentuating God's sovereign grace to redeem us in Christ alone from beginning to the end. In Reformation theology, then, "[g]race serves, not to take up humans into a supernatural order, but to free them from sin. Grace is opposed not to nature, only to sin."[14] Grace is not viewed as an aid to humans in their pursuit of deification; rather, "grace is the beginning, the middle, and the end of the entire work of salvation; it is totally devoid of human merit."[15]

Second, and built on the nature-grace scheme, is the "Christ-Church interconnection." The church in Rome's theology is viewed as the continuation of the incarnation, mirroring Christ as a divine-human reality and acting as an *altera persona Christi*, a "second Christ."[16] It is organically linked to the nature-grace scheme by Christ's acting

---

11. See Aquinas, *Summa Theologica*, pt. 1.2, Q. 109, Art. 5 (2:1126–27, Christian Classics).

12. Michael S. Horton, *The Christian Faith: A Systematic Theology for Pilgrims On the Way* (Grand Rapids: Zondervan, 2011), 607. Also see Michael S. Horton, "What Still Keeps Us Apart?" in *Roman Catholicism: Evangelical Protestants Analyze What Divides and Unites Us*, ed. John H. Armstrong (Chicago: Moody, 1994), 245–66. Cf. B. B. Warfield, *The Plan of Salvation*, rev. ed. (Grand Rapids: Eerdmans, 1970), 52–53.

13. See Allison, *Roman Catholic Theology and Practice*, 47–48.

14. Herman Bavinck, *Sin and Salvation in Christ*, vol. 3 of *Reformed Dogmatics*, trans. John Vriend and ed. John Bolt (Grand Rapids: Baker Academic, 2006), 577.

15. Ibid., 579.

16. Allison, *Roman Catholic Theology and Practice*, 56–57.

as a mediating subject who represents "nature to grace and grace to nature, so that nature will progressively and more fully be graced and grace will eventually achieve its final goal of elevating nature."[17] The church, then, "is deemed to be co-essentially divine and human, the two aspects being intertwined and inseparable in such a way that the human aspect carries the divine and the divine aspect is embodied in human forms."[18] In addition, as a "second Christ," the church mediates God's grace to people in and through the sacraments *ex opere operato*.[19] In this way, Rome develops Augustine's concept of *totus Christus* (the whole Christ) and argues that "the whole Christ refers to Christ as head, in the totality of his divine and human natures, together with his body, the church."[20] This view is the warrant for Rome's insistence that the church can mediate divine presence and infuse grace into the recipient, and that this mediation of divine grace through the church is necessary for salvation.[21]

How are these two entwined concepts applied to Christ and his work in Catholic theology? Although the exclusivity of Christ is affirmed, Allison rightly notes that these two concepts undercut the sufficiency of Christ's work by allowing—indeed, demanding—the contribution of nature in the operation of grace. "According to the Roman Catholic nature-grace pattern, the uniqueness of the mediation of Jesus Christ needs to be qualified in terms of requiring the participation of nature in the working out of the mediation. . . . The Church, therefore, as the body of Christ and the sacrament of the intimate union with God and humanity, shares the mediatory office of Jesus Christ whose Incarnation she extends."[22] Given this understanding, Rome undercuts *solus Christus* since such an affirmation would break the organic bond between Christ and the church and weaken Rome's view that the church is given authority to dispense salvation through the church's hierarchy and practice of the sacraments by infusing grace into us which has the

---

17. Ibid., 56.
18. Ibid., 57.
19. See Warfield, *The Plan of Salvation*, 53.
20. Allison, *Roman Catholic Theology and Practice*, 58–59.
21. See ibid., 62.
22. Ibid., 65. See Warfield, *Plan of Salvation*, 53–54. As Warfield argues, in Catholic theology the church is not viewed as superseding Christ but as the continuation of Christ's incarnation and work in mediating God's grace to people.

effect of transforming our natures and enabling us to merit eternal life.[23] In Rome's theology, then, there is never *solus Christus*, but only *Christus in ecclesia* (Christ in the church) and *ecclesia in Christo* (the church in Christ).

The end result is that Rome undercuts the sufficiency of Christ's work and our justification before God by faith alone in Christ alone. In Rome's view, Christ saves us in tandem with the intervening role of the church in infusing divine grace in us via the sacraments. The Reformers did not deny the crucial role of the church in proclaiming the gospel nor that the sacraments (baptism and the Lord's Supper) were legitimate means of grace to believers. However, the Reformers did reject that the church (in its hierarchical structure), by the application of the sacraments, infuses grace into people *ex opere operato* and that the sacraments are *necessary* for our salvation. Tied to the Roman teaching, the Reformers also rejected the idea that Christ's work only pays for our past/original sin, but in terms of our present and future sin, we are saved by a *combination* of Christ's merit *and* our *sacramental* incorporation into Christ *via the church*. By receiving the sacraments, Christ's work is applied to us and our natures are infused with divine grace, thus transforming our natures and enabling us to cooperate with God to merit eternal life.[24]

Once again, it is at *this* precise point that the Reformers reject the sacramental theology of Rome for its undermining of the gospel of God's sovereign grace in and through *Christ alone*. Scripture is clear: Christ *alone* saves, and we are saved solely by his merits and *not* a combination of what Christ has done and our grace-empowered cooperation (Rom 3:21–31; 5:1–11; 8:1–4). Our Lord, precisely because he is God the Son incarnate, in obedience to his Father's will has paid for our sin finally, definitively, and completely; there is absolutely nothing we can add to his work (Gal 3:10–14; Heb 2:17–18; 5:1–10; 7:23–28; 9:15–28). And we, in covenant union with him, become the beneficiaries of his work

---

23. See *Catechism of the Catholic Church* (New York: Doubleday, 1995), section 1584.

24. On this point, see D. Clair Davis, "How Did the Church in Rome Become Roman Catholicism?," in Armstrong, *Roman Catholicism*, 45–62; S. Lewis Johnson Jr., "Mary, The Saints, and Sacerdotalism," in Armstrong, *Roman Catholicism*, 119–40. On the sacraments being necessary for our salvation, see The Council of Trent, "Decree on the Sacraments," Canons IV, VI, VIII in Philip Schaff, *The Creeds of Christendom*, 6th ed. (Grand Rapids: Baker, 1990), 2:120–21.

by faith alone because our Lord lived and died for us as our mediator and great prophet-priest-king. Thus, in Christ's obedient life and death for us, God's righteous demand has been met; Christ's righteousness is now imputed to believers because of his covenant representation and substitution for us; and the Holy Spirit, who raises us spiritually from the dead, unites us to Christ so that his work is now applied to us (Eph 2:4–10).

By faith alone we receive Christ alone. Given *who* Jesus is, *his* work for us is sufficient. His obedient, sinless life as our mediator and his substitutionary death are enough for our justification, and any "gospel" that fails to confess *solus Christus* is no gospel at all. Martin Luther beautifully captures the Reformation's affirmation of Christ alone in a letter written to his supervisor, Johann von Staupitz: "I teach that people should put their trust in nothing but Jesus Christ alone, not in their prayers, merits, or their own good deeds."[25]

Solus Christus contra Rome's Theology and Practice

As stated, the Reformers did not differ with Rome in regard to Christ's exclusive identity; instead they rejected Rome's sacramental theology, which they insisted undermined the *sufficiency* of Christ's work.[26] Yet, with that said, in stressing the sufficiency of Christ's work, the Reformers also developed, in a more biblical way, the *unity* of Christ's person *and* work and thus the perfect accomplishment *and* application of his work to us as our great prophet, priest, and king. For example, in

25. Martin Luther, "Letter to Johann von Staupitz (March 31, 1518)," in *D. Martin Luthers Werke, Kritische Gesamtausgabe: Briefwechsel*, 18 vols. (Weimar: Hermann Böhlaus Nachfolger, 1930–83), 1:160.

26. In a similar way to Anselm and Catholic theology, the Reformers argued for the unique identity of Christ as God the Son incarnate and consistent with Chalcedonian orthodoxy. For example, see Calvin, *Institutes*, 2.12.1–3; Zacharias Ursinus, *Commentary on the Heidelberg Catechism*, trans. G. W. Williard (1852; repr., Phillipsburg, NJ: P&R, 1992), 77–96; Ulrich Zwingli, "The Sixty-Seven Articles (1523)," in Lillback and Gaffin, *Thy Word Is Still Truth*, 90. Zwingli defends the exclusivity and uniqueness of Christ in these two points: "II. The sum and substance of the Gospel is that our Lord Jesus Christ, the true Son of God, has made known to us the will of his heavenly Father, and has with his innocence released us from death and reconciled God. III. Hence Christ is the only way to salvation for all who ever were, are and shall be." Cited in *Thy Word is Still Truth: Essential Writings on the Doctrine of Scripture from the Reformation to Today*, ed. Peter A. Lillback and Richard B. Gaffin Jr. (Phillipsburg, NJ: P&R, 2013), 88. Also see Francis Turretin, *Institutes of Elenctic Theology*, trans. George M. Giger and ed. James T. Dennison Jr., 3 vols. (Phillipsburg, NJ: P&R, 1994), 2:299–373.

Christ's priestly office he not only fully pays for our sin but also by the Spirit directly applies his work to us through his priestly intercession. As Ursinus writes, "All these things Christ does, obtains, and perfects, not only by his merits, but also by his efficacy. He is, therefore, said to be a Mediator, both in merit and efficacy; because he does not only by his sacrifice merit for us, but he also, by virtue of his Spirit, effectually confers upon us his benefits, which consist in righteousness, and eternal life."[27] Ursinus continues,

> In a word, Christ is our wisdom, because he is the subject, the author, and the medium. He is our *righteousness*, that is, our justifier. Our righteousness is in him, as in the subject; and he himself gives this unto us by his merit and efficacy. He is our *sanctification*, that is, sanctifier; because he regenerates us, and sanctifies us through the Holy Spirit. He is our *redemption*, that is, redeemer; because he finally delivers us: for the word that is here [1 Cor. 1:30] translated redemption, does not only signify the price, but also the effect and consummation of our redemption.[28]

In Christ alone, we have all that we need now and forevermore; he is enough.

In truth, then, although the Reformers and the Roman Catholic Church confessed a similar christological orthodoxy, in the end, Rome's Christology was deficient in fully grasping the glory of Christ in the *unity* of his person *and* work. Francis Turretin forcefully makes this point. He contends that although Rome seemingly believes in the perfection of Christ's satisfaction, "yet in reality in many ways [they] weaken and overturn it by maintaining that it must be restricted to sins committed before baptism and to the guilt of fault (*reatum culpae*) and not of punishment (*reatum poenae*), or to eternal punishment and not to temporal."[29] Rome views Christ's satisfaction, says Turretin, as one of infinite value, "yet various satisfactions are still to be made by believers, if not for guilt or eternal punishment (which they acknowledge are taken away by Christ), at least for temporal punishment."[30] But, he notes, if

---

27. Ursinus, *Commentary on the Heidelberg Catechism*, 94.
28. Ibid., 95.
29. Turretin, *Institutes of Elenctic Theology*, 2:438.
30. Ibid., 439.

taken consistently Rome's view ultimately compromises *both* Christ's unique person and work. For given *who* Christ is and *what* he accomplishes for us, we cannot think of his work other than as perfect and sufficient to fully pay for all our sins by his one offering of himself, "not only for our guilt, but also for both temporal and eternal punishment," and thus requiring "no more propitiatory offerings or satisfaction to be made for sin, either in this life or after it."[31]

The Reformers, especially Calvin and his theological heirs, drove this point home by insisting on Christ's unique person and work as the incarnate Son and our new covenant head. By focusing on Christ's active and passive obedience as our mediator, Turretin insisted that our Lord satisfied *all* the demands of God's law against us, "both as to obedience of life and the suffering of death, as to satisfactory virtue by which it has freed us from the guilt of death and the curse by enduring the punishments due to us, and as to meritorious power by which it has reconciled the Father to us, and has acquired for us a right to life."[32] The end result of such a glorious work by such a glorious person is that nothing more can be added to it. Christ's work is enough, which is evidenced in its one-time offering (Heb 7:27; 9:26; 10:10, 12, 14). Christ's obedience in life and in death is the sole ground of our justification (Rom 5:18–19), which is demonstrated by the Father's acceptance of his work by resurrection and appointment to his right hand (Phil 2:9, Heb 1:3).[33]

In addition, the Reformers, especially Calvin, not only joined Christ's person and work in his obedient life and death, but they also *united* Christ to his people in God's eternal plan and the outworking of that plan in Christ's work as our new covenant head. Calvin famously writes:

> How do we receive those benefits which the Father bestowed on his only-begotten Son—not for Christ's own private use, but that he might enrich poor and needy men? First, we must understand that as long as Christ remains outside of us, and we are separated from him, all that he has suffered and done for the salvation of the human

---

31. Ibid.
32. Ibid., 439–40. For this same emphasis in Calvin, see *Institutes*, 2.16.5.
33. See Turretin, *Institutes of Elenctic Theology*, 2:439–40, who develops these points. Michael Horton, *Christian Faith*, 504, also notes how Calvin emphasized Christ's active and passive obedience as the ground to our justification.

race remains useless and of no value for us. Therefore, to share with us what he has received from the Father, he had to become ours and to dwell within us.[34]

How does this take place? By the gracious and sovereign triune work of God—the Father in election and effectual calling, the Spirit in regeneration and uniting us to Christ as our covenant head, by faith alone. The end result of God's gracious triune action is that Christ's work in all of his perfection, fullness, and completion becomes ours by virtue of our new-covenant union in him. For this reason, Christ is enough. Our Lord Jesus has achieved the full satisfaction and payment of our sin, which includes our past, present, and future sins.

Calvin, after quoting 1 John 2:1–2, 12, which teaches that Christ is the propitiation for our sins, concludes that "there is no other satisfaction whereby offended God can be propitiated or appeased. He [John] does not say: 'God was once for all reconciled to you through Christ; now seek for yourselves another means.'"[35] Instead, Christ is presented as our perpetual advocate "in order that by his intercession he may always restore us to the Father's favor; an everlasting propitiation by which sins may be expiated. . . . He, I say, not another, takes them away [sin]; that is, since he alone is the Lamb of God, he also is the sole offering for sins, the sole expiation, the sole satisfaction."[36]

In this regard, it is important to note the crucial link between *sola fide* and *solus Christus*. In fact, *sola fide* only makes sense given faith's object. Ursinus captures this point well: We are justified by faith alone "because we are justified by the object of faith alone, that is by the merits of Christ only, without which we can have no righteousness whatever: for we are justified for Christ's sake. Nothing but the merit of Christ can be our righteousness in the sight of God, either as a whole, or a part only. We are justified only by believing, and receiving the righteousness of another, and not by our own works, or merit."[37]

Now it is in the light of *this* full-orbed theology of the glory of Christ's unique person and all-sufficient work that the Reformers confess *solus Christus*. In the strongest of terms, the Reformers reject

---

34. Calvin, *Institutes*, 3.1.1.
35. Ibid., 3.4.26.
36. Ibid.
37. Ursinus, *Commentary on the Heidelberg Catechism*, 331.

Rome's sacramental theology of infused grace, *ex opere operato* administration of the sacraments, the role of the church in bestowing faith on its people, and all of the accoutrements which are tied to the entire system. For the Reformers, what is ultimately at stake in confessing *Christ alone* is the glory of the triune God in the face of Christ and the surety of our full and complete salvation in Christ. Also, on the basis of this *theology* the Reformers rejected the *practice* of Rome, given that her *practice* was tied to her larger sacramental theology. For example, Calvin opposed the practice of indulgences, the doctrine of purgatory, and the veneration of Mary and saints precisely because it undercut Christ's all-sufficient work.[38] Likewise Turretin argued against Rome's theology of the Mass, intercession of the saints, and purgatory because it undermined the perfection of Christ's work. As he states, Scripture affirms that our sin is paid in full in Christ's death (Rom 8:1), and given that remission is deliverance from all punishment, "Christ by himself has satisfied for sin and ... there is no further satisfaction to be made by others."[39] Specifically, let us illustrate how the theology of *solus Christus* stood against two practices in the Roman Church, namely, the intercession of saints and the practice of the Mass.

The Intercession of the Saints

Given Christ's unique identity and incomparable priestly work, the Reformers argued that it was impossible to reconcile Christ's perfect intercession with the mediatorial role of human priests. No doubt Scripture commands us to pray for others. Yet as Geerhardus Vos notes, our praying for one another is "not meant [as] an official act of an office, only an intercession by brothers, who are equal, for each other. One can request the intercession of a brother but may never interpose him as a mediator between God and one's own soul. This would be deification of man. There is but one Mediator, who can bring our prayers before God."[40]

It is for this reason that the Reformers opposed any human priestly mediation which would rob Christ of his glory as our great high

38. See Calvin, *Institutes*, 3.5.1–5.
39. Turretin, *Institutes of Elenctic Theology*, 2:441.
40. Geerhardus Vos, *Christology*, vol. 3 of *Reformed Dogmatics*, trans. and ed. Richard B. Gaffin Jr. (Bellingham, WA: Lexham Press, 2014), 174.

priest. Zwingli captures this point in Article XVII of "The Sixty-Seven Articles" (1523), when he writes: "That Christ is the only eternal high priest, wherefrom it follows that those who have called themselves high priests have opposed the honor and power of Christ, yea, cast it out."[41] Or, as the Heidelberg Catechism, Q. 30, asks and then beautifully answers: "Do such then believe in Jesus the only Saviour, who seek their salvation and happiness in saints, of themselves, or anywhere else?" "They do not; for though they boast of him in words, yet in deeds they deny Jesus the only deliverer and Saviour: for one of these two things must be true, that either Jesus is not a complete Saviour, or that they, who by a true faith receive this Saviour, must find all things in him necessary to their salvation."[42]

Ursinus also captures this exact point when he asks whether there can be more than one mediator between God and man? His answer is, No! Why? "The reason of this is, because no one but the Son of God can perform the office of Mediator; and as there is only one natural Son of God, there cannot be more than one Mediator."[43] But what about the saints? Can they intercede for us? Not in the authoritative, effective way that Christ does. The saints too depend upon merits of Christ in order for their intercession to avail. Christ depends on his own merits. "And still more, Christ alone offered himself a surety, and satisfier, sanctifying himself for us, that is, presenting himself in our stead before the judgment seat of God, which cannot be said of the saints."[44] Ultimately,

---

41. Ulrich Zwingli, "The Sixty-Seven Articles (1523)," in Lillback and Gaffin, *Thy Word Is Still Truth*, 90. Zwingli continues the same thought in Article XX: "That God desires to give us all things in his name, whence it follows that outside of this life we need no mediator except himself," and Article XXI: "That when we pray for each other on earth, we do so in such fashion that we believe that all things are given to us through Christ alone."

42. Cited in Ursinus, *Commentary on the Heidelberg Catechism*, 168. Cf. the Augsburg Confession (1530), art. 21 in Philip Schaff, *The Creeds of Christendom*, 6th ed., 3 vols. (Harper and Row, 1931; repr., Grand Rapids: Baker, 1990), 3:26: "But the Scripture teacheth not to invocate saints, or to ask help of saints, because it propoundeth unto us one Christ the Mediator, Propitiatory, High-Priest, and Intercessor. This Christ is to be invocated, and he hath promised that he will hear our prayers, and liketh this worship especially, to wit, that he be invocated in all afflictions. 'If any man sin, we have an advocate with God, Jesus Christ the righteous' (1 John 2:1)."

43. Ibid., 96.

44. Ibid. For the same points, see Zwingli, "The First Zurich Disputation," in Lillback and Gaffin, *Thy Word Is Still Truth*, 31, or in "The 10 Conclusions of Berne (1528)," in Lillback and Gaffin, *Thy Word Is Still Truth*, 99–100. Zwingli writes in Article #3: "Christ is the only wisdom, righteousness, redemption, and satisfaction for the sins of the whole world. Hence it is a denial of Christ when we confess another ground of salvation and satisfaction,"

the Reformers rightly rejected the Roman practice of intercession by the saints because it undermined the glory and sufficiency of Christ.[45] Once again, Ursinus states this point powerfully: "Wherefore, inasmuch as the Papists imagine that the saints obtain favour with God, and certain good things for others on account of the worthiness of their own merits, they manifestly derogate from the office and glory of Jesus, and deny him to be an only Saviour."[46] Similarly, Turretin argues that to affirm the human mediation of saints as Rome does is also to deny Christ alone. Turretin writes: "[T]he mediation of saints casts disgrace upon Christ, as if he was not alone sufficient and needs to associate others with him in this office (which cannot be said without grievous blasphemy). . . . If Christ is a perfect Mediator, who by himself can exactly fulfil all the parts of that office, what need was there to form others for himself?"[47]

The Practice of the Mass

For similar reasons, the Reformers also opposed Rome's theology and practice of the Mass. First, the Reformers were united in rejecting Rome's view of transubstantiation, namely, that by the consecration of the elements of the Lord's Supper their substance is changed into the substance of the Christ's body and blood. Second, the Reformers rejected Rome's teaching that the Mass was a sacrifice which represented Christ's death to us by making it contemporary with us. Third, the Reformers rejected Rome's sacramental understanding of the Mass, namely, that the Mass was valid or effective *ex opere operato* as it

---

and in Article #6: "As Christ alone died for us, so he is also to be adored as the only Mediator and Advocate between God and the Father and the believers. Therefore it is contrary to the Word of God to propose and invoke other mediators."

45.   The Reformation rejection of the Roman practice of intercession to the saints is also seen in their denial of the "super-veneration" (*hyperdulia*) of Mary and Rome's elevation of Mary to the role of mediatrix alongside Christ. In Catholic theology, Mary is not only the model of faith, obedience, and love but also is a co-sufferer with Christ and a kind of co-mediator. Throughout the centuries, Marian devotion has included praying to her for help and seeking guidance from her. The Reformers and the entire Protestant tradition contend that Mary is very important in God's redemptive purposes, but in the end she needs salvation like anyone else, by faith alone in Christ alone. For current Catholic teaching on Mary, see *Catechism of the Catholic Church* (New York: Doubleday, 1995), 493–506, 964–69. Cf. Allison and Castaldo, *Unfinished Reformation*, 96–100.

46.   Ursinus, *Commentary on the Heidelberg Catechism*, 169.

47.   Turretin, *Institutes of Elenctic Theology*, 2:388.

transmits grace to its recipients, thereby transforming our nature and enabling us to merit eternal life.[48]

Ultimately the Reformers rejected Rome's teaching regarding the Mass due to their conviction that it undermined Christ's all-sufficient and perfect work. As Calvin argued, the Mass is a denial of the exclusive priesthood of Christ: only the Son of God could offer up the Son of God, because he alone was divinely appointed priest, and he had no successor. "The more detestable is the fabrication of those who, not content with Christ's priesthood, have presumed to sacrifice him anew! The papists attempt this each day, considering the Mass as the sacrificing of Christ."[49] Elsewhere Calvin writes that the Mass "inflicts signal dishonour upon Christ, buries and oppresses his cross, consigns his death to oblivion [and] takes away the benefit which came to us from it."[50] In citing John 19:30, "It is finished," Calvin declares that Scripture teaches that Christ's cross is accomplished, perfect, and final; and referring to Hebrews 9–10, Calvin writes, "In the whole discussion the apostle contends not only that there are no other sacrifices, but that this one was offered only once and is never to be repeated."[51]

Zwingli affirms the same truth in Article XVIII of "The Sixty-seven Articles": "That Christ, having sacrificed himself once, is to eternity a certain and valid sacrifice for the sins of all faithful, wherefrom it follows that the mass is not a sacrifice, but is a remembrance of the sacrifice and assurance of the salvation which Christ has given us," and in Article XIX: "That Christ is the only mediator between God and us."[52]

Once again, the concern of the Reformers in their rejection of many of Rome's practices was due to their *solus Christus* conviction. The Reformers contended that this was no mere debating point; life and death hangs upon faith in Christ alone. And what is ultimately lost in Rome's sacramental theology is the glory of Christ and our assurance

---

48. See Martin Luther, *Luther's Works*, 55 vols. (St. Louis: Concordia, 1955–86), 37:187; Calvin, *Institutes*, 4.18; Ursinus, *Commentary on the Heidelberg Catechism*, 389–408, 416–24.

49. Calvin, *Institutes*, 2.15.6.

50. Ibid., 4.18.1. See this emphasis in Luther's the *Babylonian Captivity of the Church* in *Luther's Works*, 36:51.

51. Ibid., 4.18.3. For a development of this argument, see Ursinus, *Commentary on the Heidelberg Catechism*, 416–24.

52. Zwingli, "The Sixty-Seven Articles (1523)," in Lillback and Gaffin, *Thy Word Is Still Truth*, 90.

that before God we stand justified in Christ, and that his work is complete, perfect, and sufficient to save me, now and forevermore.[53] To affirm Christ alone in all of his uniqueness and sufficiency is life, but to affirm anything else is ultimately a compromise of the gospel.

Centuries later, Charitie Bancroft in her hymn "The Advocate" (1863), beautifully captured the Reformation sentiment of *solus Christus*. She locates our total hope and confidence in the promises of the gospel and the glory of Christ:

> Before the throne of God above
> I have a strong and perfect plea.
> A great high Priest whose name is Love
> Whoever lives and pleads for me.
> My name is graven on His hands,
> My name is written on His heart.
> I know that while in Heaven He stands
> No tongue can bid me thence depart.
>
> When Satan tempts me to despair
> And tells me of the guilt within,
> Upward I look and see Him there
> Who made an end of all my sin.
> Because the sinless Savior died
> My sinful soul is counted free.
> For God the just is satisfied
> To look on Him and pardon me.
>
> Behold Him there the risen Lamb,
> My perfect spotless righteousness,
> The great unchangeable I AM,
> The King of glory and of grace,
> One in Himself I cannot die.
> My soul is purchased by His blood,
> My life is hid with Christ on high,
> With Christ my Savior and my God!

---

53. On the denial of our assurance of salvation in Christ, see The Council of Trent, "On Justification," Canon XVI in Schaff, *Creeds of Christendom*, 2:115–16.

Standing with the Reformers on *Christ Alone* Today

In affirming *Christ alone*, the Reformers opposed Rome's sacramental theology that compromised Christ's all-sufficient work as God the Son incarnate and our new covenant head. Yet it is important to recognize that the Reformation confession also served to oppose other theological errors. At key points, the Reformers not only opposed Roman Catholic theology, but they also opposed the rise of various heretical movements that advocated theological views which rejected Christian theology as an entire theology, regardless of whether it was Protestant or Roman Catholic. The seeds of these ideas and movements were sown in the Renaissance but now were beginning to bloom in the Reformation period, and eventually would reach their fruition in the era of the Enlightenment and beyond.[54]

For example, people like Michael Servetus (1511–53) and movements such as Socinianism (sixteenth–seventeenth centuries) not only rejected the sufficiency of Christ's work but also his unique and exclusive identity. [55] And, of course, along with their rejection of orthodox Christology, they also rejected the doctrinal entailments which logically followed, namely, the Trinity, penal substitutionary atonement, and in truth the entire doctrinal understanding of Christian theology. In many ways, the rise of these ideas and movements was a throwback to the patristic era when the church had to stand against heresy and defend the biblical truth regarding the triune nature of God and the exclusive identity of Christ as God the Son incarnate.

Along with their defense of orthodoxy over against a rising denial of historic Christianity, the Reformers and their heirs also had to respond to ongoing debates *within* Protestant theology regarding Christ's person and work. Andreas Osiander, for example, was a Lutheran theologian who taught a distorted Christology that denied Christ's imputed righteousness to believers in our justification. Osiander argued that in

---

54. For a discussion of this time period and the development of these ideas and movements, see John M. Frame, *A History of Western Philosophy and Theology* (Phillipsburg, NJ: P&R, 2015), 123–291; W. Andrew Hoffecker, ed., *Revolutions in Worldview: Understanding the Flow of Western Thought* (Phillipsburg, NJ: P&R, 2007), 140–280.

55. For Reformation responses to Michael Servetus, for example, see Ursinus, *Commentary on the Heidelberg Catechism*, 187, and Calvin, *Institutes*, 2.14.7–8, who both argue against Servetus's heretical Christology. In response to Socinianism, for example, see Turretin, *Institutes of Elenctic Theology*, 2:310–17, 364–66.

Christ's human nature, our Lord brings with him his eternal and essential divine righteousness, infuses this righteousness into his own people by faith, and thus justifies them.[56] Osiander's view denied Christ's imputed righteousness to believers since it insists that our salvation lies not in what Christ does outside of and for us, but in what he does in and through us, in mystical communion with Jesus. Osiander mistakenly taught we are justified not by the imputation of Jesus's active obedience but by the infusion of his essential nature.

In the end, the Reformation affirmation of *solus Christus* sought to counter *all* of these variant views. It predominantly rejected Rome's sacramental theology, but also the errors *within* Protestant theology and those *outside* historic Christianity. The positive result of the Reformers' fight against *all* of these biblical departures was a greater theological clarity and precision, which resulted in a faithful confession and proclamation of *Christ alone*.

However, with the rise of attacks on orthodoxy in the Reformation era, a new era dawned that would require not only the confession of *solus Christus* but also its larger theological framework. The Reformers only began to respond to these kinds of attacks since it was not until the rise of the Enlightenment that the full frontal attack upon historic Christianity took place. As the Enlightenment era unfolded, the need to confess and defend *solus Christus* shifted from a defense of Christ's sufficiency to a complete defense of *both* Christ's exclusive identity *and* his all-sufficient work. What the Reformers and Roman Church held in common, namely, Christ's unique and exclusive identity, was rejected by the Enlightenment as nonfactual. Today, in our postmodern era, it is viewed as inconceivable. This reminds us that our challenge of confessing *Christ alone* is similar to yet different from the Reformation era. In standing with the Reformers, we must remember that *our* proclamation of *Christ alone* will require an entire worldview defense of Christ's glorious person and work.

---

56. See Bavinck, *Sin and Salvation in Christ*, 346, for a helpful discussion and rejection of Osiander's view.

CHAPTER 11

The Loss of Christ's Exclusivity: Our Current Challenge

In every era, the church must confess and proclaim *Christ alone*; yet each era provides its own set of challenges. The challenge for the Reformers was confessing and proclaiming the sufficiency of Christ in the midst of Rome's sacramental theology. The Reformers and the Roman Catholic Church agreed on Christ's exclusive identity as God the Son incarnate. Some heretical movements arose later to deny the Trinity and the deity of Christ, causing the Reformers to defend the unique identity of Christ. But in regard to the Chalcedonian identity of Christ and his exclusivity as our Savior, the Reformers and Catholic theology agreed. The Reformers and Rome, however, disagreed on the sufficiency of Christ for salvation. As we saw in the previous chapter, Roman Catholic theology separated the believer from Christ by inserting the church and the seven sacraments as the means by which God applies his grace to us. Christ's death paid for our original sin, but our present and future sin is forgiven by a *combination* of Christ's work *and* the sacraments, which infuse grace into us as applied by the church through its priests. Christ achieved a superabundance of merit that is insufficient for our salvation unless mediated to us through the mediatorial role of the church, its saints, and its sacraments.

The Reformers assumed Christ's exclusivity along with Rome. But the Reformers also argued for an all-sufficient Savior against Rome's sacramental theology. The Reformers did not deny an important role for the church, but over against Rome, they argued from Scripture that our Lord Jesus Christ achieved a perfect and comprehensive salvation work as our mediator and new covenant head. And this sufficient work of Christ is applied to us *directly* as the Spirit applies the word of the gospel, effectually giving us new life by uniting us to our glorious Savior in covenant union, reconciling us to the Father, and making us part of God's new covenant community, the church. So that now, in Christ, *all* that Christ has achieved in his life, death, and resurrection is applied to those who believe by God's grace through faith alone. Christ's work is sufficient because of his exclusive identity. As God the Son incarnate, his substitutionary life and death accomplishes all of God's purposes and plans without remainder. As fallen creatures, we contribute nothing. We merely raise the empty hands of faith and find our complete salvation in Christ alone.

But what about today? Do we face the same challenges that the Reformers faced in confessing and proclaiming *Christ alone*? Yes and no. We must still contend for Christ's all-sufficient work over against any attempt to add human works or merit to it. Sinful human pride resists the unmerited grace of a divine-human Savior. And so many groups today proclaim a variety of false gospels that call us to contribute in some way to our own salvation. We must, therefore, stand with the Reformers and proclaim *Christ alone*, declaring and delighting in the sufficiency of his work.

The challenge of proclaiming *Christ alone*, however, has changed. Today, we must argue for the *exclusivity* of Christ's identity, something the Reformers assumed along with Rome. What was secondary in priority (not importance!) for the Reformers has become primary for us. Before we can get to the issue of sufficiency, we must first fight the denial of Christ's unique identity and exclusivity. If Christ is not God the Son incarnate, then of course his work would be insufficient. If he does not bear the unique divine-human identity, then of course he cannot accomplish divine-human reconciliation. The church has always confessed that Jesus Christ is God the Son incarnate, the only God-man and thus the only one who can save us. But today's religious pluralism does not allow for such exclusivity. At most, Jesus was merely an important man and a masterful teacher. Proclaiming Christ alone in today's intellectual context requires careful exposition and defense. We need to grasp the nature and significance of our particular challenge in confessing *Christ alone* so that we can avoid the pitfalls of our own day. Our ultimate goal is to encourage the church and call it to stand with the Reformers and proclaim *Christ alone* with renewed conviction, urgency, and fullness of joy.

Christological Confusion in Our Postmodern World

The times have changed. We no longer live in the theological world of the sixteenth century, and as a result, the confession and proclamation of *Christ alone* must be waged on a different front. But what has brought about this change? Although the answer is complex, it is primarily due to a radical shift in epistemology tied to entire worldview shifts. In the last five-hundred years, we have seen the unfolding of the old adage that "ideas have consequences."[1] After the Reformation era, certain ideas arose that challenged and then rejected the way the Reformers and the majority of people in the West had thought about God and his relationship with the world he created. More specifically, ideas about the ability of human reason and the nature of reality and our knowledge of it led to a massive shift in plausibility structures. Beginning with the Enlightenment and continuing through modernity and into postmodernity today, the intellectual rules that determine how the world works and what is possible in it have shifted away from orthodox Christianity to deny its basic presuppositions.

To confess and proclaim *Christ alone* today, then, we first must admit and seek to understand how the secularization and pluralization of the West has altered the way people think. The belief conditions of the Reformation have been eclipsed today by an entirely different set of plausibility structures. Our age does not begin with the basic truths of Christian theology because the rules that warrant belief have changed. In his magisterial work on the impact of secularization, Charles Taylor traces these epistemological changes over three distinct time periods, pivoting around the Enlightenment. Before the Enlightenment, people found it *impossible not to believe* the Christian worldview; starting with the Enlightenment, it became *possible not to believe* in the basic truths of Christianity; three hundred years after the Enlightenment and the rise of postmodern pluralism, most people find it *impossible to believe* in the objective truths and ultimate concerns of the Christian worldview.[2]

---

1. For this phrase, see Richard M. Weaver, *Ideas Have Consequences* (Chicago: University of Chicago Press, 1948).
2. See Charles Taylor, *A Secular Age* (Cambridge, MA: Belknap, 2007).

Most people in the West, then, find the church's confession of *Christ alone* to be incredulous because it is viewed as implausible. They assume such a person could not exist nor do the supernatural work that the Bible teaches. This *a priori* determination against the *Christ alone* of the Reformation has led to much christological confusion as the church tries to proclaim Christ today. David Wells acknowledges this point in his helpful book *Above All Earthly Pow'rs*. He contends that Christology today is done within a twofold reality: first, "the disintegration of the Enlightenment world and its replacement by the postmodern ethos," and second, the increase of religious pluralism.[3] These two cultural developments have posed a number of serious implications for doing orthodox Christology. How can we plausibly defend Christ's uniqueness-exclusivity in a day of philosophical pluralism?[4] As Wells notes, our theology must not remain inside the church and academy; it must also help the church meet the challenges we face in presenting Christ to a skeptical age that regards the uniqueness of Christ as highly implausible or outright impossible.[5]

How did we get to this point and where should we go from here? Confessing *Christ alone* in the context of an entire system of thinking that rejects the basics of the Christian faith might seem impossibly complex. But a brief tour through the intellectual history of the Enlightenment up to our postmodern times will help us understand how the plausibility structures have changed and give us a clear direction forward. In short, we will see that (1) the seeds of skepticism sown in the Enlightenment and cultivated in modernity and postmodernity (2) have produced a rejection of the Bible's reliability under the authority of human reason

---

3.   David F. Wells, *Above All Earthly Pow'rs: Christ in a Postmodern World* (Grand Rapids: Eerdmans, 2005), 5. For a development of this point in his previous books, see *No Place for Truth, or Whatever Happened to Evangelical Theology?* (Grand Rapids: Eerdmans, 1993); idem, *God in the Wasteland: The Reality of Truth in a World of Fading Dreams* (Grand Rapids: Eerdmans, 1994); idem, *Losing Our Virtue: Why the Church Must Recover its Moral Vision* (Grand Rapids: Eerdmans, 1999).

4.   "Philosophical pluralism" can mean different things. I am using it (along with "religious pluralism") as D. A. Carson uses it, namely, to denote that it is "necessarily wrong" to assert that a "particular ideological or religious claim is intrinsically superior to another." He continues: "The only absolute creed is the creed of pluralism. No religion has the right to pronounce itself right or true, and others false, or even (in the majority view) relatively inferior" (D. A. Carson, *The Gagging of God: Christianity Confronts Pluralism* [Grand Rapids: Zondervan, 1996], 19).

5.   See Wells, *Above All Earthly Pow'rs*, 6–12.

(3) that denies a divine-human Jesus in history and (4) denies that one man's life and death could have any real significance for the rest of humanity.

How will we proceed? When considering hundreds of years of intellectual history, we must avoid reductionism. The story of the shifts in history from the Enlightenment into postmodernity is complicated. But we can follow the basic contours of change and remain true to the content with the goal of better understanding our own day and the challenge before us. In this chapter, we will focus on key shifts that occurred in the Enlightenment, which set the stage for the loss of Christ's exclusivity. Then, in chapter 12 we will finish our story by discussing how Enlightenment ideas sown have now blossomed into today's postmodern skepticism regarding Christ's exclusivity, before we conclude with some suggestions for the way forward.

Enlightenment Ideas and the Roots of Skepticism regarding Christ's Exclusivity

Until the Enlightenment era, Christian orthodoxy unanimously affirmed that Jesus Christ is God the Son incarnate. More importantly for the current discussion, however, is *why* the church made this confession. These material understandings of the faith (along with the other tenets of orthodox Christology) follow from certain theological and methodological convictions. Traditionally, the biblical text in its final form has served as the warrant for our christological constructions. Orthodoxy has been established by a "Christology from above," from the vantage point of divine revelation. The Scriptures provide not only the raw data for our doctrine but also the structure, categories, and theological framework for understanding Jesus's identity. The church has argued that we can rightly identify Christ only by finding him in the context of the biblical storyline. Any attempt to find Jesus by some other means or in some other place leads only to a Jesus of our own imagination. Since the rise of the Enlightenment, however, orthodoxy and its methodology are no longer viewed as credible and coherent. Why? Let us look at some of the epistemological and theological turns that explain why this is the case.

The Enlightenment (1560–1780) was the hinge that swung the

medieval-Reformation era into the modern age, opening the door to what is now called "modernism." In noting the significance of this era, Alister McGrath observes, "With the benefit of hindsight, the Enlightenment can be said to have marked a decisive and irreversible change in the political, social, and religious outlook of Western Europe and North America."[6] For our interest in the challenges to *Christ alone*, we will limit our investigation to the Enlightenment's displacement of the Reformation worldview and the gradual secularization of thought and theology.[7]

Many scholars today use "Age of Reason" to describe the *nature* of the Enlightenment. But we must not imagine that reason was inoperative in the Reformation and prior to it. Reason played an important part in the way the Reformers understood the world and humanity and God's relationship with his creation. In the Enlightenment, however, reason was elevated from a ministerial instrument to a magisterial rule, especially over Scripture and tradition.[8] Immanuel Kant, for instance, viewed the "enlightened" person as one who reasons autonomously, without dependence upon the authorities of the past. The theological mindset of "faith seeking understanding" yielded to the Enlightenment motto "I believe what I can understand."[9]

By raising human reason to a position of supreme authority, the Enlightenment began to undermine Christian orthodoxy. The new ways of thinking simply would not support even the basic Christian view that God has revealed himself and the truth about us and the world in Scripture. Regarding Christology in particular, we can see the

---

6. Alister E. McGrath, *The Making of Modern German Christology 1750–1990*, 2nd ed. (Eugene, OR: Wipf & Stock, 2005), 14.

7. For a discussion of the intellectual changes in Western Europe and their impact, see W. Andrew Hoffecker, "Enlightenment and Awakenings: The Beginning of Modern Culture Wars," in *Revolutions in Worldview: Understanding the Flow of Western Thought*, ed. W. Andrew Hoffecker (Phillipsburg, NJ: P&R, 2007), 240–80.

8. McGrath makes this same point, noting that the Middle Ages were just as much an "Age of Reason" as the Enlightenment (McGrath, *Making of Modern German Christology*, 15). However, "the crucial difference lay in the manner in which reason was used, and the limits which were understood to be imposed upon it. . . . Most medieval theologians insisted that there was a set of revealed truths, to which access could not be gained by human reason" (ibid.). On the distinction between the ministerial and the magisterial use of reason, see William Lane Craig, "Classical Apologetics," in *Five Views on Apologetics*, ed. Stanley N. Gundry and Steven B. Cowan (Grand Rapids: Zondervan, 2000), 36–38.

9. Stanley J. Grenz, *A Primer on Postmodernism* (Grand Rapids: Eerdmans, 1996), 62.

significance of this challenge by considering the epistemology of the Reformers and their theological framework.

First, the Reformers emphasized a revelational epistemology in which the ministerial use of reason served theology under the magisterial authority of Scripture. On the basis of Scripture, the Reformers grounded objective truth and knowledge in the comprehensive plan of God and argued that as his image bearers we come to know truth by reasoning from divine revelation (both general and special). The Bible is the lens by which we rightly interpret who God is, who we are, and the way the world works. The Word of God gives us a true (even if not exhaustive) "God's-eye point-of-view." Without this external and authoritative revelation, we would be left with only human nature and subjectivity as the basis for theology. The Reformers believed, however, that the human creature is dependent upon God for being and believing; we are never autonomous, neither metaphysically nor methodologically.[10]

Second, the Reformers constructed their Christology from a theological framework grounded in the centrality and sovereignty of God as he is revealed in Scripture. Emphasizing *sola Scriptura*, the Reformers followed the biblical presentation to form and test all beliefs, creeds, and doctrines, including *Christ alone*. This commitment to Scripture meant that the Reformers constructed their Christology "from above," accepting the biblical presentation of Christ as God's own interpretation. As a result, they had no problem affirming the exclusive identity of Christ as the eternal Son in the flesh with all authority and power to accomplish the works of God and establish his kingdom on earth. They did not deny that the biblical authors gave us an interpreted Jesus. Rather, the Reformers believed that the interpretive framework of the biblical authors is God's own interpretive framework for the identity of Jesus—what Scripture says about Jesus, God says about Jesus.

This solid epistemological-theological ground for Reformation Christology, however, was broken and tilled by new ways of thinking in the Enlightenment. Change did not come overnight; seeds were

---

10. For this point, see Kevin J. Vanhoozer, "Human Being, Individual and Social," in *The Cambridge Companion to Christian Doctrine*, ed. Colin E. Gunton (Cambridge: Cambridge University Press, 1997), 158–59.

planted by various intellectual movements over many years.[11] But in the Enlightenment, these seeds germinated into theories about human knowledge and the nature of God that challenged the way the church and the world had thought about these things for centuries. For our purposes, we can focus on two ideas in particular that became dominant and impacted the church's confession of *Christ alone*: (1) only human reason is necessary for human knowledge; (2) the world makes sense without God's personal involvement.

1. "My Thoughts Are Not Your Thoughts": From a Revelational to a Rational Epistemology

The church should be comfortable with and comforted by the fact that God is not like us. God is uncreated and infinite; we are created and finite. This is good news. Because God transcends humanity, he can come to humanity in perfect freedom to do as he pleases, unburdened and unlimited by us. This sovereign transcendence and free immanence is part of the basis for God's encouragement to Israel. Speaking through the prophet Isaiah, the Lord called Israel to repent and trust in his compassion and pardon, declaring, "'For my thoughts are not your thoughts, neither are your ways my ways'" (Isa 55:8). In promising to restore rebellious Israel—something they could not imagine in their unrighteousness—God reminded them, "'As the heavens are higher than the earth, so are my ways higher than your ways and my thoughts than your thoughts'" (Isa 55:9). In short, God reminded Israel that their knowledge of him was dependent upon his own self-revelation.

The point is both simple and significant for our current investigation: we do not have access to the thoughts of God, who created and sustains all things and who, knowing the end from the beginning, orders all things to the *telos* he has determined. The biblical worldview gives us a revelational epistemology. For true knowledge of God, the self, and the world, we depend upon revelation from the Creator-Covenant Lord. The Reformers accepted this theocentric worldview and taught that without God's interpretation of things, we will see only a sin-distorted

11. In particular, Humanism played a significant role in preparing the intellectual culture for the coming shifts in epistemology and theology. See James A. Herrick, *The Making of the New Spirituality* (Downers Grove, IL: InterVarsity Press, 2003), 49–54; also cf. Carl Trueman, "The Renaissance," in Hoffecker, *Revolutions in Worldview*, 178–205.

image that is ultimately false, including a false estimation of our ability to know the truth.

Near the beginning of the Enlightenment, however, a particular turn occurred that shifted the common worldview from theocentric to anthropocentric. Starting with René Descartes (1596–1650), a method was developed to discover truth and establish a certainty in knowledge that did not directly rely upon divine revelation. In his "turn to the subject," Descartes displaced God with the human subject or self as the ground for his philosophy. Often called the father of modern philosophy, Descartes launched the whole project of modernity into rational self-sufficiency by his famous *cogito*, "I think, therefore I am." True knowledge would now be authenticated and demonstrated by human reason, which might or might not correspond to biblical revelation.[12] In effect, the turn to the human subject turned the word of the Lord on its head. Shifting from a revelational to a rational epistemology, man tells God, "My thoughts are not (necessarily) your thoughts." Now known as "classical foundationalism," the Enlightenment schools of epistemology—continental rationalism and British empiricism[13]— taught that we are only rational in our beliefs if our beliefs are justified by a limited number of "basic beliefs." And those basic beliefs, when consistently applied, began to undercut the basis for divine revelation.[14] Rather than receiving revelation from above with the aid of reason, the new epistemology constructed knowledge and beliefs from the ground up based on a limited set of basic beliefs, independent of God's Word-revelation.

Near the end of the Enlightenment era, Immanuel Kant (1724–1804) took another "turn to the subject," but in an even more radical direction. In his famous "Copernican revolution," Kant reversed the traditional relationship between subject (mind) and object (world).

---

12. See Hoffecker, "Enlightenments and Awakenings," in Hoffecker, *Revolutions in Worldview*, 254.

13. Continental rationalism is identified with Descartes (1596–1650), Spinoza (1632–77), and Leibniz (1646–1716); British empiricism is identified with Locke (1632–1704), Berkeley (1685–1753), and Hume (1711–76).

14. See e.g., Nicholas Wolterstorff, *Reason within the Bounds of Religion*, 2nd ed. (Grand Rapids: Eerdmans, 1988); John S. Feinberg, *Can You Believe It's True? Christian Apologetics in a Modern and Postmodern Era* (Wheaton, IL: Crossway, 2013), 37–76, 143–94. It is important to note that under this system, many beliefs would not qualify as knowledge, including beliefs from memory and logical induction and belief in God.

Instead of the mind conforming to objective reality, knowing became a creative process in which the mind actively schematizes sense data from the world, conforming external objects to internal *a priori* categories. In his *Critique of Pure Reason*, then, Kant limited knowledge to objects as they appear to us, which exclude the knowledge of God.[15] Kant made a strict distinction between objects present in our experience (*phenomena*) and objects lying beyond our experience (*noumena*). We can know only the *phenomena*; we have no direct knowledge of the *noumena*. Since God, the self, and all ultimate realities remain in the realm of the noumena beyond our direct experience, we must remain metaphysically and theologically agnostic.

As the Enlightenment worked out the consequences of these ideas, it ultimately constrained *knowledge in* the world to our *experience of* the world. As John Feinberg has noted, many moderns functioned in the world as if the only beliefs truly capable of being justified are the beliefs of science.[16] Theology became a *sub*-rational discipline open to critical assessment and subject to the canons of science and the new rationalistic epistemology.[17] As we will see, the Enlightenment idea that human reason is both necessary and sufficient for human knowledge would have devastating effects on theology in general and *Christ alone* in particular.

2. "There Is Nothing New under the Sun": From Christian Theism to Naturalistic Deism

The second Enlightenment idea that became dominant and impacted the church's confession of *Christ alone* is that the world makes sense without God's personal involvement.

The world seems to be set on repeat. The sun rises and sets day after day. And on earth under the sun, life repeats day after day with such regularity that we can be tempted to forget the Creator-Covenant Lord. Yet without him, life holds no ultimate meaning. Addressing this perspective, the book of Ecclesiastes uses the refrain "under the sun" to describe the toil and vanity (meaninglessness) of a completely horizontal

---

15. Immanuel Kant, *Immanuel Kant's Critique of Pure Reason*, trans. Norman K. Smith (London: Macmillan, 1929).

16. John S. Feinberg, *No One Like Him: The Doctrine of God* (Wheaton, IL: Crossway, 2001), 88.

17. See ibid., 84–95.

life (e.g., see Eccl 1:9; 2:11; 4:3; 6:12; 9:3). The point of the Preacher is that if we do not look beyond the sun, we will miss the whole point of life under the sun: "Now all has been heard; here is the conclusion of the matter: Fear God and keep his commandments, for this is the duty of all mankind" (Eccl 12:13). While this is the conclusion to Ecclesiastes, the progressive revelation of Scripture explains that God works continuously and intimately in and through all parts of his creation to manifest his glory. And the final goal of his creation care is that in a renewed heaven and earth, God will dwell with a renewed people in covenant peace and righteousness (see Rev 21:1–8).

In the Enlightenment, however, the order and regularity of the world was used against the notion that God was involved in the world. Although he was a theist, Isaac Newton (1642–1727) advanced a view of the physical universe that led to a shift from the Christian theism of the Reformation to a naturalistic deism in modernity. Newton's universe was a grand, orderly machine; its movements were known and measurable because they followed certain observable laws. But interpreted according to the new rationalistic epistemology, the same orderly universe must be explained naturally. Supernatural involvement by God is rejected *a priori* as unnecessary or even irrational. As Andrew Hoffecker explains, the universe was viewed as "a vast machine or a watch designed so wisely by a watchmaker that it runs on its own without outside intervention. Nature no longer was an organism; now it had a mechanical nature and operated according to Newton's laws."[18] According to naturalistic deism, if God acts at all in the world, it is only by upholding the laws of nature that he established in the first place. God does not act *extra*ordinarily in the world. James Edwards summarizes the theological effect of the combination of a rationalistic epistemology with a naturalistic methodology:

> Committed to explaining all reality by means of the scientific method, the Enlightenment reduced all reality to naturalism, empiricism, and rationalism. Committed to naturalism as the sum of reality, the Enlightenment could not admit the possibility of a God (if there was one) who would "violate the laws of nature" by

---

18. Hoffecker, "Enlightenments and Awakenings," in Hoffecker, *Revolutions in Worldview*, 247.

breaking into the natural order. Things that could not be explained by the scientific method—whether historical events, morality, human affection, or the existence of God—were explained *away* by it.[19]

Belief in "God" remained, but only in the sense of a generic deism. Belief in the triune Creator-Covenant God of the Scriptures was rejected, along with the church's confession of him. The intellectual shifts from the Reformation era through the Enlightenment provided no grounding for a personal God who creates, upholds, and acts in the world to accomplish his plan of redeeming humanity by works that are beyond our reason and ability.

Enlightenment Consequences on *Christ Alone*: The Loss of Christ's Exclusivity

The Enlightenment, then, brought a particular combination of ideas that challenged the validity of the church's confession. The idea that (1) only human reason is necessary for human knowledge entailed (2) the idea that we can make sense of the world without God's personal involvement. And this combination resulted in the application of the scientific method to all disciplines of knowledge, including theology.[20] The new rules of a rationalistic epistemology and naturalistic deism made no allowance for the revelational epistemology of Scripture or the basic tenets of orthodox Christianity, including unique divine action in the world. It seems the scientific method was pitted against Scripture and the church's confession, and the new science was declared the winner by default.[21]

Regarding our specific concern with Christology, the effect of the Enlightenment was, of course, devastating to the teaching of the

19. James R. Edwards, *Is Jesus the Only Savior?* (Grand Rapids: Eerdmans, 2005), 13 (emphasis original).

20. James Sire aptly describes the attitude of the Enlightenment: "If this way of obtaining knowledge about the universe was so successful, why not apply the same method to knowledge about God?" (James W. Sire, *The Universe Next Door: A Basic Worldview Catalogue*, 4th ed. [Downers Grove, IL: InterVarsity Press, 1997], 47).

21. Historic Christianity is not against science, properly understood. In fact, one can make a strong case that Christian theology provides the necessary presuppositions for an empirical science (see Nancy Pearcey and Charles Thaxton, *The Soul of Science: Christian Faith and Natural Philosophy* [Wheaton, IL: Crossway, 1994]).

Reformers. The magisterial rise of reason resulted in the loss of *solus Christus*. The emergence and ostensible victory of the "enlightened" man resulted in a loss for all humanity because it lost the most important man in all of history. To appreciate the consequences more specifically, we need to consider two ways in which the Enlightenment cast a shadow over *Christ alone*: the loss of Christ's exclusivity and the loss of Christ's historicity.

1. The Loss of Christ's Exclusivity

The loss of Christ's exclusivity and his historicity are really two sides of the same coin. You cannot have *Christ alone* without both. But to learn what we should do about the loss of both, it will help to alternate our focus. This section will consider the loss of Christ's exclusivity by examining the impact caused by two of the most prominent and influential Enlightenment thinkers: Immanuel Kant and Gotthold Lessing.

As noted above, Immanuel Kant confined all knowledge to the human subject's experience of the world according to *a priori* categories of the mind. To be sure, Kantianism changed through criticism and reconsideration.[22] But even as revised, Kantianism today remains true to its antimetaphysical bias: human autonomy is primary; knowledge of metaphysics is impossible apart from experience. In one move, Kantianism undercuts theology in general and the claims of Christology in particular. Revelation, miracles, direct divine activity in human history, statements regarding the substances and the nature of things, including the natures of Christ, are all ultimately unknowable. Since God is a *noumenal* reality, we can *never know him* apart from the categories and active construction of the human mind. And this creative knowledge proceeds only according to the rules of methodological naturalism.[23]

Concerning Christ, Kantianism restricts his identity to an entirely

---

22. For example, his critics have noted that Kant overstepped his own philosophy by claiming to know that all of us have the same mental categories. And many post-Kantian philosophers influenced by Darwinian theory now argue that our mental categories cannot be the same because they are the product of evolution and social construction.

23. Methodological naturalism is the view that all scientific and historical study assumes a closed causal nexus, which from the outset eliminates the ability to warrant all divine action in history. It is important to note that some "theistic" views, such as deism and panentheism, adopt the view of methodological naturalism.

natural interpretation. Applying the rules of the Enlightenment's strictly rational, naturalistic epistemology, Kantianism rejects *a priori* even the possibility that Christ is metaphysically God the Son incarnate.[24]

Gotthold Lessing (1729–1781) contributed to the shift in Christology by questioning the epistemic value of history. Prior to the Enlightenment, the church argued that the identity and significance of Jesus was tied to specific historical events, like his virgin conception, miracles, death and resurrection, and his second coming. All of these events bear witness to the uniqueness and *exclusive identity* of Christ because these events testify to *who* he is within God's universal plan given to us by divine revelation. However, if divine revelation is denied, and human reason alone becomes the basis to ground our knowledge, then how is it possible to establish *universal* truths from merely contingent historical events? Or, in the words of Lessing's famous "ugly ditch," within the restrictions of Enlightenment epistemology, "accidental truths of history can never become the proof of the necessary truths of reason."[25]

As applied to Christology, it becomes implausible to think that we can say anything metaphysically unique and universally significant about Christ merely from historical facts. For unless Christ is interpreted from the standpoint of a divine revelation which correctly explains *who* he is, set within the overall plan of the Creator-Covenant Lord of Scripture, then very little can be said about Christ's uniqueness and exclusivity. Following Lessing's argument, then, we simply have no warrant to draw the metaphysical conclusion that Jesus Christ is God the Son incarnate from historical facts, especially when those facts are both recorded and interpreted by merely human testimony apart from a divine authoritative revelation.

According to the Enlightenment, Jesus—if he really existed—was a mere man. Even if he was somehow special, being *quantitatively* superior in knowledge, wisdom, ability, and influence, Christ was *not qualitatively* different than the rest of humanity. Following the rules of the Enlightenment's rationalistic epistemology and naturalistic

---

24. See Immanuel Kant, *Religion within the Limits of Reason Alone*, trans. Theodore M. Greene and Hoyt H. Hudson (New York: Harper & Row, 1960).

25. G. E. Lessing, "On the Proof of the Spirit and Power," in *Lessing's Theological Writings*, comp. and trans. Henry Chadwick, Library of Modern Religious Thought (Stanford: Stanford University Press, 1956), 53; see also 53–55.

methodology, Christ could never be God in a way that other humans were not. The Enlightenment simply declared it impossible that Jesus could be God the Son incarnate.

2. The Loss of Christ's Exclusive History

Turning from the loss of Christ's exclusivity, we now need to consider an even more fundamental problem caused by Enlightenment epistemology. The church must confess *Christ alone* as a basic tenet of the Christian faith. But we cannot confess Christ without the Bible's revelation of Christ as part of human history. If the Bible does not or cannot establish that Jesus Christ did in fact live as a real person at a certain point in history, then our confession becomes impossible. Moreover, if Scripture does not or cannot establish that Jesus is the promised God-man of our salvation, then our confession becomes irrelevant. *In short, the church's confession of Christ's exclusivity depends upon his historicity*: that he really did walk this earth as God the Son incarnate and that his words and works in history are given to us accurately and authoritatively in Scripture.

The Enlightenment shift from a revelational to a rationalistic epistemology, however, cast doubt on the Bible's ability to give us the true historical and theological identity of Jesus Christ. In particular, the Enlightenment brought two hermeneutical changes that blurred the real and revealed person of Christ: an *extratextual* reading instead of an *intratextual* reading of Scripture; and the separation of the "Jesus of history" from the "Christ of faith."[26]

Traditional Christology has always approached the Bible on its own terms with an *intratextual* reading. Scripture demands to be received with divine authority and read according to its own structure and categories and within its own worldview framework. This means that the Bible identifies Christ through various connections within (not outside of) the texts of Scripture, which connections are governed by the Bible's own internal rules of interpretation.

---

26. "Jesus of history" refers to the "real" Jesus who actually lived and whom we come to know by historical methods. The "Christ of faith" refers to the Bible's presentation of Jesus. Orthodoxy has never separated the two, but in the Enlightenment a wedge was created between them. Why? Because given the Enlightenment worldview, the Bible's Jesus cannot be the "Jesus of history" given his uniqueness, exclusivity, and deity.

290 Christ Alone in the Reformation and Today

Quite oppositely, the Enlightenment placed external rules on the Bible for an *extratextual* reading.[27] Instead of finding the real Christ revealed according to the Bible's own presentation, the Enlightenment reading would permit only a reconstructed identity. Claims to the identity of Christ were valid only if they fit the *extratextual* scheme and constraints of the new rational epistemology and deistic understanding of the God-world relationship. And this extratextual reading was paired with the separation of the "Jesus of history" from the "Christ of faith," or better, the Bible's presentation of Jesus. The church has always confessed that Scripture reveals one Lord and Savior, the person of Jesus Christ. The Enlightenment, however, demanded that if the historical Jesus did exist, he could not be who the Bible says he is. In short, the Bible gives us not the real Jesus but only the church's faulty interpretation him.

The rise of reason in the Enlightenment, then, changed biblical hermeneutics and lost the true historical and theological identity of Christ. The eighteenth century brought an openly critical examination of the Bible, especially the four Gospels. In the Reformation era and before, differences between the Gospels were acknowledged and harmonized. But with the epistemological revolution of the Enlightenment, many abandoned their trust in the Bible as God's Word and viewed Scripture with suspicion. And this biblical suspicion grew into higher criticism, a discipline that would treat the Bible "like any other book."[28] For example, one of the discipline's most significant proponents, Herman Reimarus (1694–1768), advanced a formal criticism of the Bible by treating the Gospels "as ordinary historical documents, with no presumption of divine inspiration or even reliability."[29] He approached the text with suspicion, assuming that "to learn what really happened one must look through the texts and not take them at face value."[30]

---

27. On the distinction between *intratextual* and *extratextual*, see Stephen J. Wellum, *God the Son Incarnate: The Doctrine of Christ* (Wheaton, IL: Crossway, 2016), 79–106; cf. Hans W. Frei, *Types of Christian Theology*, ed. George Hunsinger and William C. Placher (New Haven: Yale University Press, 1992).

28. See Benjamin Jowett (1817–93) for this expression in his essay, "On the Interpretation of Scripture," in *The Interpretation of Scripture and Other Essays* (London: George Routledge & Sons, 1907), 1–76.

29. C. Stephen Evans, *The Historical Christ and The Jesus of Faith: The Incarnational Narrative as History* (Oxford: Oxford University Press, 1996), 18.

30. Ibid.

As the Enlightenment epistemology pressed further into hermeneutics, the general work of biblical criticism hardened into the "rules" of the historical-critical method that rejected the plausibility of a God-given, accurate, and authoritative interpretation of the historical Jesus.[31]

Taken as a whole, the historical-critical method functions on the basis of three Enlightenment principles.[32] As they became rules for interpretation, these principles replaced three pillars of orthodox theology in general and Christology in particular. The table below will help us appreciate the significance of this hermeneutical shift.

Interpreting the Identity of Christ from Scripture from the Reformation Era into the Enlightenment Era

Pillars of Christian Orthodoxy (Revelational Epistemology)	Principles of the Historical-Critical Method (Rational Epistemology)
(1) The truths of Scripture are given by God himself as the accurate and authoritative interpretation of history.	(1) Methodological Doubt: all historical (including biblical) judgments are statements of probability, open to criticism and revision.
(2) Divine revelation concentrates on a single supernatural incursion into the world that is qualitatively unique.	(2) Principle of Analogy: all historical events are in principle qualitatively similar.
(3) Our finitude and fallenness prevents an appeal to general revelation as a sufficient basis for knowledge.	(3) Principle of Correlation: all historical phenomena exist in a closed causal nexus.

---

31. Scholars developed and used various tools (e.g., source, form, and redaction criticism) to subject the Gospels to historical-critical analysis. But they all assumed that the Gospels do not accurately record history and that the "Jesus of history" is not the "Jesus of the Bible." For a discussion of the critical tools and their use, see e.g., I. Howard Marshall, ed., *New Testament Interpretation: Essays on Principles and Methods* (Exeter: Paternoster, 1977).

32. See Ernst Troeltsch, "Historical and Dogmatic Method in Theology (1898)," in *Religion in History*, trans. James Luther Adams and Walter E. Bense (Minneapolis: Fortress, 1991), 11–32.

In the Reformation (and the eras before it), the Bible was received for what it is and claims to be: the reliable word of God himself that rightly interprets all historical events in its scope. For Christology, the pillars of orthodox interpretation held up the Bible as the one and only place to identify the real historical Jesus. The principles of interpretation in the Enlightenment, however, reduced the Bible to just another historical artifact filled with errors and myths. The historical-critical method begins by doubting all that the Bible says about historical events. Nothing in Scripture is an historical fact; it is a collection of merely human historical opinions. The principles of analogy and correlation then combine to determine a particular text's historical accuracy. Because all historical events are interrelated, interdependent, and qualitatively similar, the biblical events and persons that do not fit our present experience must be rejected.

By application of its first principles, then, the historical-critical method is incapable of identifying the historical Jesus in Scripture. Under the new rules, there is only one legitimate question that can lead to a proper judgment regarding a text's historical accuracy: Is the supposed historical event analogous with our present experience? Because we do not presently witness virgin conceptions, people walking on water, and resurrections from the dead, we must judge that these and all other supernatural signs and works that identify Christ are implausible and the biblical texts are in error. In the Enlightenment, the historical-critical method reduced Christ to just another mere human who might or might not have been important in some circles at some point in time, but who certainly was not someone with an exclusive and universally significant history as God the Son incarnate.

Unfortunately, this hermeneutical skepticism continues today. To see the current effects of the historical-critical method, we can look briefly at the so-called "Quests for the historical Jesus."[33] The goal of the Quests has been to recover the "Jesus of history" by using the

---

33. The specific developments within and individuals associated with the Quests are detailed in many places. For example, see McGrath, *Making of Modern German Christology*; N. T. Wright, *Who Was Jesus?* (Grand Rapids: Eerdmans, 1993); idem, *Jesus and the Victory of God* (Minneapolis: Fortress, 1997). For the present taxonomy of the Quests, I am following N. T. Wright's description in *Jesus and the Victory of God*, 1–124.

historical-critical method to peel back the biblical layers of legend and myth.[34]

The Old Quest (1778–1906)[35] assumed that the Bible is wholly unreliable and proceeded to reconstruct the "historical" Jesus without reliance upon and almost without reference to the biblical presentation. During an interim period (1906–1953),[36] which some call the No Quest, theologians disregarded historical facts, including a historical Jesus, as unnecessary for the Christian faith.[37] The New Quest (1953 to present)[38] focuses on the sayings of Jesus in Scripture. These theologians agree with the other Quests that the Gospels contain the subjective interpretations of the early church. But they argue that we can sift through the subjectivity using *extratextual* rules (e.g., consistency and multiple attestation; the criteria of dissimilarity; various linguistic and cultural tests) to determine what the historical Jesus really said. Finally, at the same time, the Third Quest (early 1980s to present)[39]

---

34. On this point, see Albert Schweitzer, *The Quest of the Historical Jesus: A Critical Study of its Progress from Reimarus to Wrede*, trans. William Montgomery (New York: Macmillan, 1968), 3. N. T. Wright, *Jesus and the Victory of God*, 17–18, agrees: "Let us be clear. People often think that the early 'lives of Jesus' were attempting to bring the church back to historical reality. They were not. They were attempting to show what historical reality really was, in order that, having glimpsed this unattractive sight, people might turn away from orthodox theology and discover a new freedom. One looked at the history in order then to look elsewhere, to the other side of Lessing's 'ugly ditch,' to the eternal truths of reason unsullied by the contingent facts of everyday events, even extraordinary ones like those of Jesus."

35. As the first, the Old Quest received its name from the English title of Schweitzer's book, *The Quest of the Historical Jesus*. For the most part, the Old Quest starts with Reimarus, ends with Schweitzer, and includes a veritable who's who in biblical studies and classical liberal theology: e.g., David Strauss (1808–74); F. C. Baur (1792–1860); Albrecht Ritschl (1822–89); Adolf von Harnack (1851–1930); William Wrede (1859–1906); Wilhelm Bousset (1865–1920).

36. W. Barnes Tatum, *In Quest of Jesus: A Guidebook* (Atlanta: John Knox, 1982), 71.

37. Probably the best example, Rudolf Bultmann simply replaced (demythologized) the NT's mythological framework with an existential structure. (Rudolf Bultmann, *New Testament and Mythology and Other Basic Writings*, ed. and trans. Schubert Miles Ogden [Philadelphia: Fortress, 1984], 5–6; cf. idem, *Jesus Christ and Mythology* [New York: Scribner, 1958], 11–21).

38. For example, see Ernst Käsemann, "The Problem of the Historical Jesus," in *Essays on New Testament Themes*, trans. W. J. Montague (1964; repr., London: SCM, 2012), 15–47; Günther Bornkamm, *Jesus of Nazareth*, trans. Irene McLuskey, Fraser McLuskey, and James M. Robinson (Minneapolis: Fortress, 1995); James M. Robinson, *A New Quest of the Historical Jesus and Other Essays* (Minneapolis: Augsburg Fortress, 1983).

39. See Ben F. Meyer, *The Aims of Jesus*, Princeton Theological Monograph Series 48 (Eugene, OR: Wipf & Stock, 2002); E. P. Sanders, *Jesus and Judaism* (Minneapolis: Fortress, 1985); J. D. G. Dunn, *Jesus Remembered*, vol. 1 of *Christianity in the Making* (Grand Rapids: Eerdmans, 2003).

applies its own version of historical-critical criteria that take the NT texts more seriously as literary documents. But these conciliatory efforts still come with Enlightenment commitments that do not necessarily embrace the full reliability of Scripture and, thus, its ability to identify the historical Jesus with complete accuracy and authority.

The Quests, then, tell us that the hermeneutical shift in the Enlightenment continues into the present, obscuring the "real" and revealed Jesus of history, who is the Christ of faith. The trend today assumes that the historical Jesus is *not* who the church says he is according to the Scriptures and attempts to find him some other way.[40]

To grasp the depth of the problem posed by the Enlightenment, we need to close this discussion by focusing on the power of its presuppositions. The power of presuppositions lies in their precognitive nature: once adopted, presuppositions control our thinking, and thus how we act, often with little or no reflection. More specifically, we think and act within the limits of what we determine is plausible, which is governed by assumptions we make about how the world works. For our present concern with the exclusivity of Christ, this means that we must follow the Reformers and allow the Bible to set our presuppositions that Jesus is God the Son incarnate and the hope of the world.

The new Enlightenment presuppositions, however, made it impossible to accept this biblical presentation of Christ. In their large shifts in epistemology, their understanding of the God-world relationship, and their specific changes in hermeneutics the Enlightenment thinkers departed from Reformation thinking by making different assumptions. The various philosophers and theologians did not argue that the teaching of the Reformation and the rest of orthodox Christianity was unable to explain the world and the purpose of humanity in it. The new thinking, rather, simply determined different rules of explanation and interpretation and then declared that orthodoxy did not fit. This meant

---

40. In the last thirty years, this trend is famously epitomized by John Hick, ed., *The Myth of God Incarnate* (Philadelphia: Westminster, 1977) and the Jesus Seminar. For helpful overviews and critiques of the Jesus Seminar, see Michael J. Wilkins and J. P. Moreland, eds., *Jesus Under Fire: Modern Scholarship Reinvents the Historical Jesus* (Grand Rapids: Zondervan, 1995); see also Craig A. Evans, *Fabricating Jesus: How Modern Scholars Distort the Gospels* (Downers Grove, IL: InterVarsity Press, 2006); Ben Witherington, *The Jesus Quest: The Third Search for the Jew of Nazareth* (Downers Grove, IL: InterVarsity Press, 1995), 42–57.

that the unique identity and history of Christ was not just conceptually difficult but categorically denied.[41]

In the next chapter, we will finish our survey of intellectual history by discussing how our postmodern era has not turned back Enlightenment skepticism regarding the uniqueness, exclusivity, and sufficiency of Christ. Understanding why this is the case will allow us to reflect on the way forward as we learn to confess and proclaim with the Reformers, *Christ alone.*

---

41. See e.g., Rudolf Bultmann, "Is Exegesis Possible without Presuppositions?," in *Existence and Faith: Shorter Writings of Rudolf Bultmann*, comp. and trans. Schubert M. Ogden (New York: Meridian Books, 1960), 289–96. The principles of the historical-critical method are the necessary rules of a rationalistic epistemology combined with a deistic worldview. These enlightenment rules of interpretation reject Christian theism without examination or analysis. Yet the principles underneath historical criticism are not demonstrably true and can be assumed only by first adopting a naturalistic (even if deistic) worldview that denies the possibility of unique, extraordinary, supernatural events in history. On this point, see Van A. Harvey, *The Historian and the Believer: The Morality of Historical Knowledge and Christian Belief* (Philadelphia: Westminster, 1966), 29–30.

CHAPTER 12

Reaffirming Christ Alone Today

The times have indeed changed. We do not live in the same kind of era as the Reformation. Our current context is full of widespread christological confusion, yet our confession and proclamation of *Christ alone* must continue with the same urgency and conviction.

In this chapter, we turn from the key Enlightenment epistemological and theological shifts that help explain why *Christ alone* is viewed with such suspicion to a discussion of our postmodern era. We will discover that although much of the Enlightenment mindset has been rejected, ironically, ideas sown in the Enlightenment have now blossomed into a more skeptical outlook regarding Christ's exclusivity. This is one of the main reasons why our postmodern society has embraced religious pluralism with a vengeance. As in the Enlightenment, so today, Jesus is not as Scripture and the church confess: God the Son incarnate. Instead, Jesus is viewed in diverse ways, primarily only as a man and one religious leader among many.

Our goal in thinking through this intellectual history is to explain why our primary task today in confessing and proclaiming *Christ alone* is to argue for Christ's exclusive identity and then his all-sufficient work. Obviously, Christ's exclusivity *and* sufficiency cannot be separated, but given our postmodern context, the basis for both must be clearly articulated and defended. With that in mind, we will conclude our discussion by offering a few reflections on how to stand today with the Reformers and joyously declare *Christ alone*.

Postmodern Ideas and the Fruit of Skepticism regarding Christ's Exclusivity

Most scholars acknowledge that Western culture has shifted from a modern to a postmodern mindset. The intellectual shifts of the Enlightenment continued to shape the way modernity thought about the world. But by the early part of the twentieth century, changes appeared in the presuppositional structure of the intellectual culture. The exact nature of the shift and its implications for theology remain hotly debated.[1] Even the term *postmodernism* is difficult to define because of its diverse use. For our purposes, however, we require not an exact definition but only the basic principles regarding what has changed.

In short, postmodernity breaks from modernity's confidence in the reality of objective truth and our ability to know it. The French sociologist Jean-François Lyotard first used the term *postmodernism* to signal an important shift in epistemology.[2] Lyotard described the postmodern condition as bearing a certain kind of skepticism: "Incredulity toward metanarratives."[3] "Post" refers to a move away from the "modern" and Enlightenment ideals of rationality and progress.[4] Specifically, postmodernism rejects at least three conditions of modern knowledge: "(1) the appeal to metanarratives as a foundationalist criterion of legitimacy, (2) the outgrowth of strategies of legitimation and exclusion, and (3) a desire for criteria of legitimacy in the moral as well as the epistemological domain."[5] Put more simply, postmodernism eschews "grand narratives" and universal, objective truth by which we can validate some things (e.g., ideas, events, people) and invalidate others.

While these shifts from the previous eras might sound like a radical departure, postmodernism actually bears the fruit of skepticism from

---

1.   For example, see six evangelical approaches to postmodernism in Myron B. Penner, ed., *Christianity and the Postmodern Turn: Six Views* (Grand Rapids: Brazos, 2005). In my view, postmodernism ought to be viewed as the logical end of modernism's assumptions, not as distinct and conceptually *beyond* modernism.

2.   James W. Sire, *The Universe Next Door: A Basic Worldview Catalogue*, 4th ed. (Downers Grove, IL: InterVarsity Press, 1997), 213.

3.   Jean-François Lyotard, *The Postmodern Condition: A Report on Knowledge*, trans. Geoff Bennington and Brian Massumi, Theory and History of Literature 10 (Minneapolis: University of Minnesota Press, 1984), 24.

4.   Kevin J. Vanhoozer, "Theology and the Condition of Postmodernity: A Report on Knowledge (of God)," in *The Cambridge Companion to Postmodern Theology*, ed. Kevin J. Vanhoozer (Cambridge: Cambridge University Press, 2003), 7.

5.   Ibid., 9.

its roots in the Enlightenment. Even though it rejects Enlightenment-modern methodology, postmodernism begins with the same "turn to the subject/self" and ends with an increased skepticism toward theology in general and Christology in particular.

Similar to the Enlightenment, postmodernism combines two ideas that have become dominant and impacted the church's confession of *Christ alone*: (1) "knowledge" is merely a subjective opinion based on a local perspective; (2) "God" is merely the non-personal and developmental dynamics of a changing world. As with the Enlightenment changes in epistemology and theology, these postmodern ideas have consequences for the ability of most people to accept the plausibility of Christ's exclusivity. Let us look at each of these in turn.

1. From a Rational to a Contextual Epistemology

As noted in the previous chapter, the Reformers and the premodern era in the West functioned with a revelational epistemology: truth is universal and objective because it is grounded in the triune God and Creator-Covenant Lord of the universe. He is the source and standard of all knowledge because his sovereign plan encompasses all things. In the language of Reformed orthodoxy, God's knowledge is *archetypal* and, as his finite image bearers, our knowledge is *ectypal*. This does not mean, however, that we cannot know truth. Our knowledge, though limited, is a subset of God's own knowledge, such that as we "think his thoughts after him" in nature and in Scripture, it is possible to have finite but still objective and true knowledge.

In the modern era, philosophy continued its Enlightenment "turn to the subject." Rooted in classical foundationalism, human reason sought to operate apart from divine revelation, with the goal of achieving a universal, unified explanation of all reality. Modernism believed that if human reason simply followed the correct methods, starting in human autonomy, reason could arrive at a grand theory or "metanarrative." This grand narrative would ultimately explain all reality, albeit a reality now constrained by the limits of Enlightenment thought. And this epistemological rationalism brought with it a methodological naturalism to form a whole mindset at odds with the premodern worldview. This modern mindset has led to a massive distrust of Scripture, including a denial of the biblical Jesus and a rejection of christological orthodoxy and its metaphysical commitments.

Now in its own turn (to the subject-self), postmodernism rejects modern foundationalism, not by returning to a premodern revelational epistemology but by pressing forward in the assumptions of rationalism. Postmodernism actually takes the Enlightenment presuppositions to their more consistent conclusion. An epistemology that depends upon an autonomous subject can never provide a universal understanding of its object, whether the workings of the world itself or its history of people and events. Kant had argued that the mind is active in structuring knowledge and concluded that our minds are not objective in the knowing process. Postmodernism extends this modern principle, but only to deny the modern claim to a common and correct set of mental categories. The foundationalism of the Enlightenment that continued into modernity maintained the ability of autonomous reason to make sense of objective reality. Postmodernism now clearly critiques and openly rejects this rule. With subjective minds thinking in what could be very different mental categories, we are unable to gain anything close to universal, objective truth.[6]

This is not to say that postmodernism rejects all rationality—far from it. Rather, it simply concedes that a universal explanation is not reasonable because universal reason does not exist. Postmodernism rejects not rationality but *reason*. As Vanhoozer concludes, "They deny the notion of universal rationality . . . reason is rather a contextual and relative affair. What counts as rational is relative to the prevailing narrative in a society or institution."[7] This is why postmodernism is often associated with the attempt to deconstruct the thinking of anyone who claims to have a universal viewpoint or metanarrative.

In postmodernity, we have another shift in plausibility structures but the same implausibility of Christ's exclusivity. Postmodernism gives us a completely *contextual epistemology* by promoting a *radical pluralism* of knowledge. The notion of "knowledge" becomes a particular articulation from one local perspective that will necessarily differ and even

---

6.   See John S. Feinberg, *Can You Believe It's True? Christian Apologetics in a Modern and Postmodern Era* (Wheaton, IL: Crossway, 2013), 37–76, for a discussion of shifts from modernism to postmodernism.

7.   Vanhoozer, "Theology and the Condition of Postmodernity," 10.

diverge from other local perspectives. Knowledge in postmodernity, then, is not objective and universal but subjective and local. Knowledge can never exceed its immediate context—chronological, geographical, cultural, relational, etc. We simply cannot aspire to God's interpretation of history or his own identification of Christ in it. In fact, this contextual epistemology questions whether we can have anything other than our own individual interpretations and identifications.

Specifically, postmodernism attempts to break the link between language and reality, a *logocentrism* that once characterized Western thought. In the premodern era, this *logocentrism* was grounded in Christian theology and then carried over into the modern era as borrowed capital from Christianity. This referential view of language shifted to a constructivist view with the rise of Darwinism and the attendant self-conscious rejection of Christian theism.[8] Rather than conceiving of the mind as a "mirror of nature" consistent with a correspondence theory of truth, postmodernism argues that human beings view reality through the lens of language and culture. As a result, all of our theorizing is perspectival, provisional, and incomplete. In place of comprehensive theories we now have relative confessions about how things look to us. In the end, it is all about interpretation, not about what is real, true, or good.

Such a completely contextual epistemology has obvious and disastrous implications for hermeneutics and the Bible's identification of Christ. Postmodernism agrees with modernism's rejection of the Bible's universal authority. Modernism denies the text's truthfulness and therefore rejects its authoritativeness. Postmodernism takes the Scriptures as authoritative, but only according to the reader's or community's interpretive experience. Rather than taking the text as the objective and universally true word of God written, the postmodern hermeneutic transforms the text into "an echo chamber in which we see ourselves and hear our own voices."[9] The modernist critic reads the Bible according to the author's intent but then rejects the Bible's factual and theological claims. The postmodernist interpreter, says Vanhoozer, argues that "the text has no stable or decidable meaning, or that what meaning is

---

8.　See Kevin J. Vanhoozer, *Is There a Meaning in This Text? The Bible, the Reader, and the Morality of Literary Knowledge* (Grand Rapids: Zondervan, 1998), 43–147.
9.　Ibid.

there is biased and ideologically distorted. The result is that the Bible is either not recognized as making claims or, if it is, that these claims are treated as ideologically suspect."[10] If not completely meaningless, the Bible has become entirely insufficient to provide anything other than isolated opinions from divergent local perspectives.

Postmodernity has a new contextual epistemology, but it gives us the same modern skepticism toward the Bible's presentation of Christ, namely, that Jesus is the exclusive and all-sufficient Lord and Savior because he is God the Son incarnate.

2. From Naturalistic Deism to Evolutionary Panentheism

The movement from a modern to a postmodern outlook has also brought a corresponding change in science: "It is naturalism, but. . . ."[11] According to the predominant scientific paradigm of modernism, the world is a closed system of causal laws. Today, however, science switched paradigms to quantum and relativity theories that view the world as integrated, contingent, and continuously changing. John Feinberg helpfully summarizes this change in perspective:

> [I]n contrast to Newtonian physics, which saw the universe as composed of static, changeless bits of matter that interact according to set natural laws, the new science claims that things in our world are interrelated in a continuous process of change and becoming. Even in the most solid bits of matter (at the atomic and subatomic levels) things are not static but in motion. . . . Moreover, as opposed to Newtonian physics which held that physical things interact according to set physical laws, quantum physics claims that there is a certain indeterminacy at least at the atomic and sub-atomic levels of existence.[12]

At the same time that scientific paradigms have changed, however, the view of evolution remains entrenched. As in the modern era, the establishment of evolution as a basic presupposition comes as a necessary

---

10. Ibid., 24.
11. This phrase and concept is taken from John S. Feinberg, *No One Like Him: The Doctrine of God* (Wheaton, IL: Crossway, 2001), 104.
12. Ibid., 104–5.

part of the larger move to an *a priori* definition of science that rules out any consideration of the supernatural and nonmaterial. With the acceptance of quantum mechanics and relativity theory, however, some believe the door has opened for a return to an affirmation of God's acting in our world.[13] But even so, most postmoderns still view the universe as a basically closed system and thus assume a methodological naturalism in their approach to all academic disciplines. The primary reason for this adherence to naturalism is a refusal to return to a full-blown Christian theism, which alone can provide the proper underpinnings for the miraculous. For its conception of God, rather, postmodernism adopts a more panentheistic alternative.[14]

Although panentheism comes in many varieties, the most rigorous theological view sees God as the universe in constant progression (opposed to permanence), with historical events as the basic building blocks (instead of substances).[15] This kind of panentheism pictures all reality as a series of events, each of which has two poles. The mental or primordial pole is all the possibilities that actual entities can become; the physical or consequent pole is the world, God's body, which is the progressive realization of the various possibilities. In this metaphysical scheme, God is viewed as an event who is *in* everything. There is, then, no Creator-creature distinction. God and the world are not identical but they are inseparable; they are mutually dependent without one being subordinate to the other. The world is viewed as a moment within the divine life. In fact, because God is not only connected with but immanent to the world, he is undergoing a process of self-development and growth. God is not the supernatural, transcendent Creator of the world and Lord of history; he is (in) the natural processes of evolution by which the world and history take shape.

This evolutionary view of God in the world not only fits well with

---

13. See e.g., C. Stephen Evans, *The Historical Christ and the Jesus of Faith: The Incarnational Narrative as History* (Oxford: Oxford University Press, 1996), 137–69; cf. Gregory A. Boyd, *God of the Possible: A Biblical Introduction to the Open View of God* (Grand Rapids: Baker, 2000), 107–12.

14. See John W. Cooper, *Panentheism, the Other God of the Philosophers: From Plato to the Present* (Grand Rapids: Baker Academic, 2006); also see Kevin J. Vanhoozer, *Remythologizing Theology: Divine Action, Passion, and Authorship* (Cambridge: Cambridge University Press, 2010), 81–138.

15. See John B. Cobb Jr. and David R. Griffin, *Process Theology* (Philadelphia: Westminster, 1976).

current scientific conceptions of the world, but it also supports many familiar postmodern confessions: e.g., "a God who is merely immanent and relational; a God whose very being interpenetrates all things and hence underscores the connectedness of all things; a God who is not static but is constantly changing as he responds to our needs; and a God to whom we can contribute value as well as one who enhances our existence."[16] Feinberg rightly reminds us that this "process" conception of God "poses a formidable threat to a traditional Christian understanding of God, and it also offers a way to synthesize various non-evangelical postmodern notions about God."[17] In fact, process theology predominates in non-evangelical theology today. Yet even within evangelicalism, movements such as "open theism" have embraced some tenets of panentheism.[18]

Postmodernity has a new dominant theology, but it comes as a repackaged form of the same evolutionary assumptions of modernity— still undercutting the possibility of unique, divine extraordinary action in the world, undermining a traditional understanding of metaphysical categories, weakening even the possibility of an authoritative revelation to interpret the universal significance of Christ, and thus denying even the possibility of Christ's exclusive divine-human identity.

Postmodern Consequences: The Rise of Confusion and the Loss of *Christ Alone*

Previously we saw that two ideas intersected in the Enlightenment to challenge the church's confession of *Christ alone*: (1) a strictly rationalistic epistemology, claiming that only human reason is necessary for human knowledge, and (2) a naturalistic deism, claiming that the world makes sense without God's personal involvement. These ideas combined to change the plausibility structures against orthodox Christology. The rise of human reason deposed the divine revelation and presence in the world. Yet this rise of reason came at a high cost: the loss of the divine-human identity of Christ. For many, the Enlightenment-modern way of

---

16.   Feinberg, *No One Like Him*, 142.
17.   Ibid.
18.   For example, see Clark H. Pinnock, et al. *The Openness of God: A Biblical Challenge to the Traditional Understanding of God* (Downers Grove, IL: InterVarsity Press, 1994). It is important to acknowledge crucial differences between open theism and panentheism, specifically the former's affirmation of the Creator-creature distinction.

thinking still operates to produce an *a priori* skepticism of the Bible and the biblical presentation of Christ.

But a new epistemology and theology has become dominant. Postmodernism now combines the ideas that (1) "knowledge" is merely a subjective opinion based on a local perspective, and (2) the idea that "God" refers only to the nonpersonal and developmental dynamics of a changing world. Yet as with the Enlightenment, these postmodern ideas have consequences for the plausibility of Christ's exclusivity. Rather than bringing any clarity to Christology, these ideas combine to increase the confusion regarding the identity of Christ.

Postmodernism demands a radical pluralism in every endeavor, including Christology.[19] Every Christology is constructed upon a presupposed conception of God, self, and the world.[20] In previous eras, Enlightenment rationalism and deism denied that Jesus could be different in kind than the rest of humanity. So modern Christians looked for other ways to privilege Christ as a religious figure.[21] For example, classical liberalism rejected the historic confession that Christ is God the Son incarnate, but it still tried to maintain that Jesus was exceptional in degrees of morality. Today, however, postmodernism denies that Jesus can be different *in kind or in degree*. According to postmodern epistemology, knowledge is only perspectival opinion. So all interpretations of Jesus are valid. According to postmodern panentheism, we are all in the process of development as some part of the divine. None of us are more divine than another. So according to this pluralistic paradigm, Jesus can be only one religious figure among many.

Even more fundamentally, postmodern pluralism denies the ability

---

19. Postmodernism also encourages an embrace of inclusivism, even though inclusivism has been held as a minority position throughout church history. Although there are a variety of inclusivisms, the evangelical version affirms that Christ alone is Savior but then denies that saving faith in Christ is necessary in this life for those who have never heard the gospel. At least two problems result for Christ alone. First, saving faith is redefined to a generalized faith instead of a specific faith *in Christ* (and prior to Christ's coming in terms of specific covenant promises given by special revelation). Second, the inseparable link is cut between Christ's work in paying for our sin *and* securing the Spirit's work to bring us to faith *in him*. On these points, see Christopher W. Morgan and Robert A. Peterson, eds., *Faith Comes by Hearing: A Response to Inclusivism* (Downers Grove, IL: IVP Academic, 2008).

20. For a helpful elaboration on this point, see David F. Wells, *The Person of Christ: A Biblical and Historical Analysis of the Incarnation* (Wheaton, IL: Crossway, 1984), 7, 148–54.

21. Examples include the work of Friedrich Schleiermacher (Christ exhibits the highest order of God-consciousness) and the entire view of classical liberalism (Christ is the highest ideal of ethical teaching).

of Scripture to give us the real identity of Christ. Modernism believed that it could reconstruct history in an objective manner, peeling off the layers of myth to rediscover the real Jesus of history. Postmodernism takes this skepticism of Scripture even further: there is "no historical Jesus nor indeed a Christ of faith, nor any historical evidence for a clear delineation of the relationship between them. There is only Bultmann's, Schweitzer's, Käsemann's, Pannenberg's, Wright's or Crossan's constructed histories of the narratives, stories and loose causal identities that form our perception of the past."[22] By rejecting all metanarratives, postmodernism rejects even the possibility of a Christology from Scripture. The Bible cannot be received as God's word written because such a transcendent, universal perspective is *a priori* impossible. And without such an interpretive word grounded in God's comprehensive knowledge and plan for the world, we cannot judge between true and false, right and wrong.

According to postmodernism, then, we *still* cannot say anything unique or even definitive about Christ.[23] The Reformers relied on biblical presuppositions and the Bible's presentation to teach the exclusive identity of Christ as part of *Christ alone*. But the new Enlightenment presuppositions changed the rules of interpretation and made it impossible to accept the biblical presentation of Christ. From the Enlightenment through the modern period, the prevailing plausibility structures formed by a strict rationalism, naturalism, and deism led to one conclusion: Even if Jesus did exist, he simply could not be God the Son incarnate. Regardless of his importance in his time, Jesus could not be, say, or do anything that would have significance for all humanity throughout all history.

In our own day postmodernism still leaves us on the wrong side of Lessing's ditch. Postmodernism rejects even the possibility of objective, universal truth, limiting the identity of Jesus not just to a particular time but also to a specific location. Moreover, postmodernism brings

---

22. Colin J. D. Greene, *Christology in Cultural Perspective: Marking Out the Horizons* (Grand Rapids: Eerdmans, 2003), 167.

23. For examples of pluralism worked out in Christology, see John Hick, *God Has Many Names* (Philadelphia: Westminster, 1982); idem, *The Metaphor of God Incarnate: Christology in a Pluralistic Age*, 2nd ed. (Louisville: Westminster John Knox, 2006); John H. Hick and Paul F. Knitter, eds., *The Myth of Christian Uniqueness: Toward a Pluralistic Theology of Religions* (Maryknoll, NY: Orbis, 1987).

God from a deistic distance beyond the world to a developmental dependence upon the world. God is in all things, progressing with the natural evolution of the world. No one man, then, can claim a unique identity as God the Son who came into the world to save it. In short, we are still unable to say anything certain or unique about Jesus.

The exclusivity of Christ remains just as implausible as it has been since the Enlightenment, just for different reasons.

Establishing *Christ Alone* Today: Where Do We Go from Here?

Ideas in epistemology and theology have consequences for establishing the identity of Christ. The Reformation focused primarily on the sufficiency of Christ's work and only secondarily on the exclusivity of his identity. Today, however, we cannot get to the work of Christ before first confronting the loss of his exclusivity that makes his sufficiency possible. Moreover, we must admit that this loss comes by the powerful operation of radically different worldview presuppositions. The roots of skepticism in the Enlightenment-modern period produced the fruit of pluralism in postmodernity. The changes and the impact on *Christ alone* have been dramatic and the challenge is great. Yet in the face of such massive shifts in epistemology and theology, our task remains the same: to confess and proclaim *Christ alone*. The Reformation teaching must be articulated, defended, and proclaimed anew today.

What is the way forward? Our comments must be brief, but three points require emphasis, especially in light of the lessons learned from our survey of intellectual history.[24]

First, the way forward is not working within the contemporary views on the nature of knowledge and the relationship between the autonomous individual, the world, and the divine. To do so will only lead to a "Christology from below," i.e., the attempt to do Christology from the vantage point of historical-critical research and the current thought of the day, independent of a commitment to Scripture and a Christian-theistic view of the universe. Where such a Christology leads is to a Jesus

---

24. For a development of these points, see Stephen J. Wellum, *God the Son Incarnate: The Doctrine of Christ* (Wheaton, IL: Crossway, 2016), 79–104.

who is a "larger-than-life religious figure,"[25] but *not* the Jesus who is God the Son incarnate, our unique and all-sufficient Lord and Savior.

Second, the way forward is to do a "Christology from above," i.e., establishing Christ alone by starting with Scripture, its revelational epistemology, and the truth of the biblical worldview. Our previous survey of intellectual history illustrated the power and importance of worldviews for Christology. Every interpretation of Christ's identity depends upon and derives from a presuppositional nexus of philosophical and theological commitments. Any attempt to say who Jesus is and define his significance for the world presupposes an entire *a priori* understanding regarding the nature of God, the world, humanity, and how we warrant these beliefs. To begin reclaiming *solus Christus*, we first need to stand with the Reformers in a knowledge of the world that depends on revelation by its Creator. The strictly *rational epistemology* of the Enlightenment restricted knowledge of the world to our experience of the world. The completely *contextual epistemology* of postmodernity then further restricted knowledge of the world to individual circumstances in the world. But to know Christ, we need to return to a *revelational epistemology* and the truth of the *biblical worldview.*

Orthodox Christology is rooted in a specific conception of God, Scripture, humans, sin, and so on, and apart from that worldview it cannot stand.[26] Thus, in reclaiming *Christ alone*, we must simultaneously articulate and defend the basic tenets and coherence of the entire theological system of orthodox Christianity. To that end, the church today will need to defend Trinitarian theism and an authoritative Scripture not only as basically credible but also as absolutely necessary. Orthodox Christology receives specific truths necessary for its rationality and plausibility from Scripture—a Scripture which does not give us implausible accounts of history (contra the Enlightenment) or mere opinions

---

25. Wells, *Person of Christ*, 172.

26. On this point, see ibid., 7. Lesslie Newbigin, *Proper Confidence: Faith, Doubt, and Certainty in Christian Discipleship* (Grand Rapids: Eerdmans, 1995), 93, helpfully observes that the *reasonableness* of Christianity, specifically Christology, must be understood in *Christian* terms. He states: "The story the church is commissioned to tell, if it is true, is bound to call into question any plausibility structure which is founded on other assumptions. The affirmation that the One by whom and through whom and for whom all creation exists is to be identified with a man who was crucified and rose bodily from the dead cannot possibly be accommodated within any plausibility structure except one of which it is the cornerstone. In any other place in the structure it can only be a stone of stumbling."

from limited perspectives within history (contra postmodernism). In Scripture, rather, "prophets, though human, spoke from God as they were carried along by the Holy Spirit" (2 Pet 1:21) to give us God's own conceptual scheme and intellectual framework.

The biblical worldview, then, is God's own worldview that guides our interpretation of his work in the world, including his self-revelation through the incarnate life of his Son. Apart from grounding *Christ alone* in this worldview rooted in God's Word-revelation *from above*, Christology loses its integrity, uniqueness, and truthfulness, and it is set adrift in our day to wander in the mire of pluralism. We must *not* travel this path if we are to reclaim the basis for the confession and proclamation of the glory, exclusivity, and sufficiency of Christ and his work.

Third, the way forward to reclaiming solus Christus *today is to build on* sola Scriptura. Scripture alone gives us the epistemology and worldview that we need to identify Jesus Christ as God the Son incarnate. The exclusivity of *solus Christus* depends upon the epistemic-interpretive power of *sola Scriptura*. A truly biblical Christology, then, must proceed self-consciously, explicitly, and obediently from the Bible's self-presentation of Christ as the only way to rightly identify him. A *biblical* Christology is one that constructs the identity of Jesus from the Bible and on the Bible's own terms. Apart from doing this, the Jesus constructed will not be the biblical Jesus, and as a result there will be nothing unique or exclusive about him.

In addition, to recapture *sola Scriptura*, we must also read Scripture as an entire canon and take seriously what it says about God's mighty acts *and* how it interprets them, especially in regard to Christ. This means that Scripture describes the facts of history with accuracy *and* explains those facts so we can rightly know Christ and formulate correct doctrine regarding his identity. In establishing *solus Christus, sola Scriptura* demands that we move carefully from Scripture's own teaching (first-order) to theological formulation (second-order).[27]

Submitting to Scripture alone does not mean that we ignore the aid of tradition and historical theology. But we must remain clear that these hermeneutical servants merely help us apply the rule of faith as we

---

27. See Richard Lints, *The Fabric of Theology* (Grand Rapids: Eerdmans, 1993), 259–336.

read the authoritative Word of God in Scripture. So we must confess that Scripture alone has *magisterial authority* and always reigns over tradition; but we must also say that tradition functions in a *ministerial capacity* to aid our interpretation and application of Scripture. Stating the relationship between Scripture and tradition this way does not deny that reading the Bible involves what is famously called a "hermeneutical spiral." No one approaches Scripture as a *tabula rasa*; we all interpret Scripture with viewpoints, assumptions, and even biases inherited from our various traditions, cultures, and backgrounds. But Scripture is able to confirm or correct our views as needed precisely because Scripture itself is not the interpretation of the church but the written Word of God himself that interprets his own acts in history and their significance for his church and the world.

Ultimately, it is not overstating the case that to reclaim *Christ alone* we must *submit to the Scriptures* to know Christ's true identity. More specifically, the church's confession requires that we *trust God himself* and that he has revealed who Christ is by way of the particular storyline, categories, and coherence of Scripture. We reclaim the Reformation doctrine of *Christ alone* by receiving the revealed identity of Christ *from above* through a revelational reading of Christ in the Bible. By trusting the Scriptures, we can know Jesus in truth and formulate correct doctrine regarding his unique and exclusive identity and his all-sufficient work, and thus stand today with the Reformers of old.

Conclusion

To capture the heartbeat of the Reformation confession of *solus Christus*, one can do no better than to meditate deeply on these words by John Calvin. In a nutshell, he not only depicts what is central to *Christ alone*, namely our Lord's unique and exclusive identity and his all-sufficient work, but also how *Christ alone* ought to function in our Christian lives.

We see that our whole salvation and all its parts are comprehended in Christ [Acts 4:12]. We should therefore take care not to derive the least portion of it from anywhere else. If we seek salvation, we are taught by the very name of Jesus that it is "of him" [1 Cor. 1:30]. If we seek any other gifts of the Spirit, they will be found in his anointing. If we seek strength, it lies in his dominion; if purity, in his conception; if gentleness, it appears in his birth. . . . If we seek redemption, it lies in his passion; if acquittal, in his condemnation; if remission of the curse, in his cross [Gal. 3:13]; if satisfaction, in his sacrifice; if purification, in his blood; if reconciliation, in his descent into hell; if mortification of the flesh, in his tomb; if newness of life, in his resurrection; if immortality, in the same; if inheritance of the Heavenly Kingdom, in his entrance into heaven; if protection, if security, if abundant supply of all blessings, in his Kingdom; if untroubled expectation of judgment, in the power given to him to judge. In short, since rich store of every kind of good abounds in him, let us drink our fill from this fountain, and from no other. Some men, not content with him alone, are borne hither and thither from one hope to another; even if they concern themselves chiefly with him, they nevertheless stray from the right way in turning some part of their thinking in another direction. Yet such distrust cannot creep in where men have once for all truly known the abundance of his blessings.[1]

---

1.   John Calvin, *Institutes*, 2.16.19.

Throughout this work we have sought to present our Lord Jesus Christ in all of his glory, splendor, and majesty. From thinking through the biblical and theological grounding of *solus Christus*, to contending for his centrality in God's eternal plan now worked out on the stage of history, and to grasping why Christ alone is absolutely necessary for our salvation, we have sought to account for why the Reformers confessed *Christ alone* and why we must still do so today. In the Reformation, a proper comprehension of *solus Christus* was central to all the other *solas*, and thus crucial for the recovery of the gospel of God's sovereign grace. Despite the differences between the Reformation era and our day, to be faithful to the Word of the Lord and the Lord of the Word, we must continue to confess, defend, and proclaim with the same vigor, confidence, and conviction that our Lord Jesus Christ is the unique and exclusive Lord and all-sufficient Savior. In a day of rampant pluralism, our voice must be clear and strong: Jesus Christ is Lord, and apart from faith alone in Christ alone there is no salvation.

However, it is not enough for us merely to confess the wonderful truth of *solus Christus*. As Calvin reminds us, our confession of the wonder and glory of Christ must also properly function in our daily lives. Doctrinal truth must affect the entirety of who we are. As Calvin says, it is possible for us, "even if [we] concern [ourselves] chiefly with [Christ]" to nevertheless "stray from the right way in turning some part of [our] thinking in another direction." There are many good things in life which legitimately demand our attention. Yet, it is far too easy to forget who is central to everything, namely our Lord Jesus. Given *who* our Lord is as God the Son incarnate; given *what* he has done for us as our new covenant head and incomparable Redeemer; given the absolute necessity of his work; given that *he* has represented us in obedient life and stood in our place in substitutionary death to pay for our sin and accomplish our eternal salvation; given that he is the all-sufficient Savior who meets *all* of our needs as our great prophet, priest, and king; given all of this, our only reasonable response is to submit ourselves to him in complete trust, confidence, love, joy, worship, and obedience. He demands *and* deserves nothing less.

How do we continue to grow in our knowledge, love, and devotion to our Lord Jesus Christ? In truth, the Reformation *solas* help to answer this question. Without *sola Scriptura*, it is impossible to grow in the knowledge of Christ. We must continue to feed upon Scripture and learn more about the glory of Christ in his person and work. Scripture is foundational to knowing Christ, thinking through how he is presented in Scripture, seeing his glory displayed before our eyes, and learning anew why he alone is Lord and Savior and worthy of all of our love and devotion. But growing in Christ requires more than mere knowledge. By God's grace, we must also experience our deep need for Christ, that apart from him our condition before God is desperate, and that in ourselves we cannot save ourselves.

In this regard, grasping rightly and experiencing deeply *sola gratia* and *sola fide* is also crucial for growing in Christ and not drifting away. Christianity is rightly described as a "sinner's religion." It is not until, by God's grace and by the convicting work of the Spirit, we come to realize our own lostness and sin before God that we gladly, joyfully, and with abiding conviction embrace *Christ alone*. Scripture is clear: our greatest need as humans is to be reconciled and justified before our holy, righteous, triune Creator-Covenant God. This is something that fallen humans do not grasp, regardless of whether it is the Reformation era or our own secular, postmodern time. To rejoice and glory in *Christ alone*, then, we must first know something about our own guilt before God and our helpless condition outside of Christ; we must know that before God we deserve nothing but condemnation and judgment. When we know and experience this to be true, then we gladly affirm that our only hope now and forevermore is the triune God redeeming us by sovereign grace (*sola gratia*), in and through Christ alone (*solus Christus*), which we receive by raising the empty hands of faith (*sola fide*).

It is not until we grasp these great Reformation truths, rooted in biblical truth, that Christ will become increasingly precious to us in our daily lives, and that we will desire to fulfill the purpose of our creation: to live for the glory of God (*soli Deo gloria*). As these truths are impressed upon our minds and hearts, our love for Christ will grow, and our desire to live for him and to make him known will increase.

C. S. Lewis illustrates this growth in Christ in his Narnia series. In *Prince Caspian*, he describes an encounter between Lucy and Aslan. As Lucy is lying between Aslan's front paws and looking up at him in glowing adoration, we hear this interchange:

"Welcome, child," he said.

"Aslan," said Lucy, "you're bigger."

"That is because you are older, little one," answered he.

"Not because you are?"

"I am not. But every year you grow, you will find me bigger."[2]

Lewis has nicely captured something of how Christ becomes increasingly precious to us. As we grow in our Christian lives through the study of Scripture, gathering with God's people, and walking daily with our Lord, *he* grows bigger before us, not because he has changed, but because we are being transformed by the Spirit who bears witness to Christ.

This book has sought to confess with the Reformers that Christ Jesus our Lord bears the exclusive identity of God the Son incarnate and has accomplished an all-sufficient work to fulfill God's eternal plans and establish God's eternal kingdom on earth. My prayer is that *Christ alone* will become more precious to us, and that in our individual lives and in our churches, we will commit ourselves anew to believing, living out, and proclaiming the unsearchable riches of Christ, as we cry with the church in all ages, "Come, Lord Jesus" (Rev 22:20b).

---

2.   C. S. Lewis, *Prince Caspian: The Return to Narnia* (New York: HarperCollins, 1994), 141.

Bibliography

Alexander, T. Desmond, et al. *New Dictionary of Biblical Theology*. Downers Grove, IL: InterVarsity Press, 2000.

Allison, Gregg R. *Historical Theology: An Introduction to Christian Doctrine*. Grand Rapids: Zondervan, 2011.

———. *Roman Catholic Theology and Practice: An Evangelical Assessment*. Wheaton, IL: Crossway, 2014.

Allison, Gregg R., and Chris Castaldo. *The Unfinished Reformation: What Unites and Divides Catholics and Protestants after 500 Years*. Grand Rapids: Zondervan, 2016.

Anselm. *Why God Became Man*. In *Anselm of Canterbury: The Major Works*. Edited by Brian Davies and G. R. Evans. Oxford World's Classics. Oxford: Oxford University Press, 1998.

Ante-Nicene Fathers. Edited by Alexander Roberts and James Donaldson. 1885–1887. 10 vols. Repr., Peabody, MA: Hendrickson, 1994.

Aquinas, Thomas. *Summa Theologica*. 5 vols. Christian Classics. Notre Dame, IN: Ava Maria, 1981.

Athanasius. *On the Incarnation of the Word*. Translated and edited by Penelope Lawson. New York: Macmillan, 1946.

Augustine of Hippo. *On the Trinity*. Translated by Edmund Hill. Brooklyn: New City, 1991.

Augustine. *Letters*. Translated by Wilfrid Parsons. Volume 3. Washington, DC: Catholic University Press of America, 1953.

Aulén, Gustav. *Christus Victor: An Historical Study of the Three Main Types of the Idea of the Atonement*. Translated by A. G. Herbert. London: SPCK, 1965.

Averbeck, Richard E. "Leviticus: Theology of." *NIDOTTE* 4: 907–23.

Ayres, Lewis. *Nicaea and Its Legacy: An Approach to Fourth-Century Trinitarian Theology*. Oxford: Oxford University Press, 2004.

Bauckham, Richard. *Jesus and the God of Israel: God Crucified and Other Studies on the New Testament's Christology of Divine Identity*. Grand Rapids: Eerdmans, 2008.

Bavinck, Herman. *God and Creation*. Vol. 2 of *Reformed Dogmatics*. Edited by John Bolt. Translated by John Vriend. Grand Rapids: Baker Academic, 2004.

———. *Sin and Salvation in Christ*. Vol. 3 of *Reformed Dogmatics*. Edited by John Bolt. Translated by John Vriend. Grand Rapids: Baker Academic, 2006.

Beale, G. K. *A New Testament Biblical Theology: The Unfolding of the Old Testament in the New*. Grand Rapids: Baker Academic, 2011.

———. *The Temple and the Church's Mission*. NSBT 17. Downers Grove, IL: InterVarsity Press, 2004.

Beckwith, R. T., and M. J. Selman, eds. *Sacrifice in the Bible*. Grand Rapids: Baker, 1995.

Beilby, James, and Paul R. Eddy, eds. *The Nature of the Atonement: Four Views*. Downers Grove, IL: InterVarsity Press, 2006.

Belousek, Darrin W. Snyder. *Atonement, Justice, and Peace: The Message of the Cross and the Mission of the Church*. Grand Rapids: Eerdmans, 2012.

Blocher, Henri. "Agnus Victor: The Atonement as Victory and Vicarious Punishment." In *What Does It Mean to Be Saved? Broadening Evangelical Horizons of Salvation*. Edited by John G. Stackhouse Jr. Grand Rapids: Baker, 2002.

Block, Daniel I. "My Servant David: Ancient Israel's Vision of the Messiah." In *Israel's Messiah in the Bible and the Dead Sea Scrolls*. Edited by Richard S. Hess and M. Daniel Carroll. Grand Rapids: Baker, 2003.

Boersma, Hans. *Violence, Hospitality, and the Cross: Reappropriating the Atonement Tradition*. Grand Rapids: Baker Academic, 2004.

Bornkamm, Günther. *Jesus of Nazareth*. Translated by Irene McLuskey, Fraser McLuskey, and James M. Robinson. Minneapolis: Fortress, 1995.

Bowman, Robert Jr., and J. Ed. Komoszewski. *Putting Jesus in His Place: The Case for the Deity of Christ*. Grand Rapids: Kregel, 2007.

Boyd, Gregory A. *God of the Possible: A Biblical Introduction to the Open View of God*. Grand Rapids, MI: Baker, 2000.

Bray, Gerald. "Christology." Page 137 in *New Dictionary of Theology*. Edited by Sinclair B. Ferguson, David F. Wright, and J. I. Packer. Downers Grove, IL: InterVarsity Press, 1988.

———. *God Has Spoken: A History of Christian Theology*. Wheaton, IL: Crossway, 2014.

———. *God Is Love: A Biblical and Systematic Theology*. Wheaton, IL: Crossway, 2012.

Brown, Harold O. J. *Heresies: The Image of Christ in the Mirror of Heresy and Orthodoxy from the Apostles to the Present*. Garden City, NY: Doubleday, 1984.

Bruce, F. F. *The Epistle to the Hebrews*. NICNT. Grand Rapids: Eerdmans, 1964.

Brunner, Emil. *The Mediator*. Translated by Olive Wyon. 1927. Repr., Philadelphia: Westminster, 1947.

Bultmann, Rudolf. "Is Exegesis Possible without Presuppositions?" In *Existence and Faith: Shorter Writings of Rudolf Bultmann*. Compiled and translated by Schubert M. Ogden. New York: Meridian Books, 1960.

———. *Jesus Christ and Mythology*. New York: Scribner, 1958.

———. *New Testament and Mythology and Other Basic Writings*. Edited and translated by Schubert M. Ogden. Philadelphia: Fortress, 1984.

Calvin, John. *Commentary on Philippians, Colossians, and Thessalonians*. 1844–1856. Repr., Grand Rapids: Baker, 1993.

———. *Institutes of the Christian Religion*. Edited by John T. McNeill. Translated by Ford Lewis Battles. Library of Christian Classics. Philadelphia: Westminster, 1960.

Campbell, John McLeod. *The Nature of the Atonement.* 2nd ed. 1897. Repr., Edinburgh: Handsel, 1996.

Carson, D. A. "Atonement in Romans 3:21–26: God Presented Him as a Propitiation." In *The Glory of the Atonement: Biblical, Historical, and Practical Perspectives.* Edited by Charles E. Hill and Frank A. James III. Downers Grove, IL: InterVarsity Press, 2004.

———. *The Difficult Doctrine of the Love of God.* Wheaton, IL: Crossway, 2000.

———. *The Gagging of God: Christianity Confronts Pluralism.* Grand Rapids: Zondervan, 1996.

———. *The Gospel According to John.* PNTC. Grand Rapids: Eerdmans, 1991.

———. *Jesus the Son of God: A Christological Title Often Overlooked, Sometimes Misunderstood, and Currently Disputed.* Wheaton, IL: Crossway, 2012.

———. *Matthew.* EBC 8. Grand Rapids: Zondervan, 1984.

Carson, D. A., Peter T. O'Brien, and Mark A. Seifrid, eds. *The Paradoxes of Paul.* Vol. 2 of *Justification and Variegated Nomism.* Grand Rapids: Baker, 2004.

Catechism of the Catholic Church. New York: Doubleday, 1995.

Chalke, Steve, and Alan Mann. *The Lost Message of Jesus.* Grand Rapids, MI: Zondervan, 2003.

Cobb, John B. Jr., and David R. Griffin. *Process Theology.* Philadelphia: Westminster, 1976.

Cooper, John W. *Panentheism, the Other God of the Philosophers: From Plato to the Present.* Grand Rapids: Baker Academic, 2006.

Cowan, Steven B., and Stanley N. Gundry, eds. *Five Views on Apologetics.* Grand Rapids: Zondervan, 2000.

Crisp, Oliver. "Penal Non-Substitution." *Journal of Theological Studies* 59.1 (2008): 140–53.

Crisp, Oliver D. *Divinity and Humanity.* Cambridge: Cambridge University Press, 2007.

Cullmann, Oscar. *The Christology of the New Testament.* London: SCM, 1959.

Davis, D. Clair. "How Did the Church in Rome Become Roman Catholicism?" In *Roman Catholicism: Evangelical Protestants Analyze What Divides and Unites Us.* Edited by John H. Armstrong. Chicago: Moody, 1994.

Demarest, Bruce. *The Cross and Salvation: The Doctrine of Salvation.* Foundations of Evangelical Theology. Wheaton, IL: Crossway, 1997.

Dempster, Stephen. *Dominion and Dynasty: A Biblical Theology of the Hebrew Bible.* Downers Grove, IL: InterVarsity Press, 2003.

DeWeese, Garrett. "One Person, Two Natures: Two Metaphysical Models of the Incarnation." In *Jesus in Trinitarian Perspective.* Edited by Fred Sanders and Klaus D. Issler. Nashville: B&H Academic, 2007.

Dodd, C. H. *The Bible and the Greeks.* London: Hodder & Stoughton, 1935.

Dumbrell, William. *Covenant and Creation: A Theology of the Old Testament Covenants.* 2nd edition. Milton Keynes: Paternoster, 2002.

Dunn, J. D. G. *Christology in the Making: A New Testament Inquiry into the Origins of the Doctrine of the Incarnation.* 2nd ed. Grand Rapids: Eerdmans, 1996.

———. *Jesus Remembered.* Vol. 1 of *Christianity in the Making.* Grand Rapids: Eerdmans, 2003.

———. *Romans 1–8.* WBC 38A. Dallas: Word, 1988.

Edwards, James R. *Is Jesus the Only Savior?* Grand Rapids: Eerdmans, 2005.

Eusebius of Caesarea. *The Proof of the Gospel.* Trans. W. J. Ferrar. New York: Macmillan, 1920.

Evans, C. Stephen. *The Historical Christ and the Jesus of Faith: The Incarnational Narrative as History.* Oxford: Oxford University Press, 1996.

Evans, Craig A. *Fabricating Jesus: How Modern Scholars Distort the Gospels.* Downers Grove, IL: InterVarsity Press, 2006.

Fairbairn, Donald. *Life in the Trinity: An Introduction to Theology with the Help of the Church Fathers.* Downers Grove, IL: IVP Academic, 2009.

Fee, Gordon D. *Paul, the Spirit, and the People of God.* Peabody, MA: Hendrickson, 1996.

———. *Pauline Christology: An Exegetical-Theological Study.* Peabody, MA: Hendrickson, 2007.

Feinberg, John S. *Can You Believe It's True? Christian Apologetics in a Modern and Postmodern Era.* Wheaton, IL: Crossway, 2013.

———. *No One Like Him: The Doctrine of God.* Foundations of Evangelical Theology. Wheaton, IL: Crossway, 2001.

Ferguson, Sinclair B. *The Holy Spirit.* Contours of Christian Theology. Downers Grove, IL: InterVarsity Press, 1996.

Ferguson, Sinclair B., and David F. Wright, eds. *New Dictionary of Theology.* Downers Grove, IL: InterVarsity Press, 1988.

Frame, John M. *A History of Western Philosophy and Theology.* Phillipsburg, NJ: P&R, 2015.

———. *The Doctrine of God.* Phillipsburg, NJ: P&R, 2002.

———. *The Doctrine of the Word of God.* Phillipsburg, NJ: P&R, 2010.

France, R. T. *The Gospel of Matthew.* NICNT. Grand Rapids: Eerdmans, 2007.

Frei, Hans W. *Types of Christian Theology.* Edited by George Hunsinger and William C. Placher. New Haven: Yale University Press, 1992.

Gaffin, Richard B., Jr. *Resurrection and Redemption: A Study in Paul's Soteriology.* Phillipsburg, NJ: P&R, 1987.

Galot, Jean. *Who Is Christ? A Theology of the Incarnation.* Translated by M. Angeline Bouchard. Chicago: Franciscan Herald, 1981.

Gamble, Richard. *God's Mighty Acts in the Old Testament.* Vol. 1 of *The Whole Counsel of God.* Phillipsburg, NJ: P&R, 2009.

Gathercole, Simon. *Defending Substitution: An Essay on Atonement in Paul.* Grand Rapids: Baker, 2015.

————. *The Preexistent Son: Recovering the Christologies of Matthew, Mark, and Luke.* Grand Rapids: Eerdmans, 2006.

Gentry, Peter J., and Stephen J. Wellum. *Kingdom through Covenant: A Biblical-Theological Understanding of the Covenants.* Wheaton, IL: Crossway, 2012.

George, Timothy. "The Atonement in Martin Luther's Theology." In *The Glory of the Atonement: Biblical, Historical, and Practical Perspectives.* Edited by Charles E. Hill and Frank A. James III. Downers Grove, IL: InterVarsity Press, 2004.

————. *The Theology of the Reformers.* Nashville: Broadman, 1998.

Gibson, David, and Jonathan Gibson, eds. *From Heaven He Came and Sought Her: Definite Atonement in Historical, Biblical, Theological, and Pastoral Perspective.* Wheaton, IL: Crossway, 2013.

Goldsworthy, Graeme. *According to Plan: The Unfolding Revelation of God in the Bible.* Downers Grove, IL: InterVarsity Press, 1991.

————. *The Son of God and the New Creation.* Wheaton, IL: Crossway, 2015.

Green, Joel B., and Mark D. Baker. *Recovering the Scandal of the Cross: Atonement in New Testament and Contemporary Contexts.* 2nd ed. Downers Grove, IL: InterVarsity Press, 2011.

Greene, Colin J. D. *Christology in Cultural Perspective: Marking Out the Horizons.* Grand Rapids: Eerdmans, 2003.

Grenz, Stanley J. *A Primer on Postmodernism.* Grand Rapids: Eerdmans, 1996.

Grillmeier, Aloys. *From the Apostolic Age to Chalcedon (451).* Vol. 1 of *Christ in Christian Tradition.* Translated by John Bowden. 2nd rev. ed. Atlanta: John Knox, 1975.

————. *From the Council of Chalcedon (451) to Gregory the Great (590–604).* Vol. 2:2 of *Christ in Christian Tradition.* Translated by Pauline Allen and John Cawte. Louisville: Westminster John Knox, 1995.

Gunton, Colin E. *The Actuality of Atonement: A Study of Metaphor, Rationality, and the Christian Tradition.* London: T&T Clark, 1988.

Guthrie, George H. *Hebrews.* NIVAC. Grand Rapids: Zondervan, 1998.

Habets, Myk. *The Anointed Son: A Trinitarian Spirit Christology.* Eugene, OR: Pickwick, 2010.

Hanson, A. T. *The Wrath of the Lamb.* London: SPCK, 1959.

Harris, Murray J. *Prepositions and Theology in the Greek New Testament.* Grand Rapids, MI: Zondervan, 2012.

————. *Three Crucial Questions about Jesus.* Grand Rapids: Baker, 1994.

Harvey, Van A. *The Historian and the Believer: The Morality of Historical Knowledge and Christian Belief.* Philadelphia: Westminster, 1966.

Hawthorne, Gerald F. *The Presence and the Power: The Significance of the Holy Spirit in the Life and Ministry of Jesus.* Eugene, OR: Wipf & Stock, 2003.

Heim, S. Mark. *Saved by Sacrifice: A Theology of the Cross.* Grand Rapids: Eerdmans, 2006.

Hengel, Martin. *Crucifixion*. Translated by John Bowden. Minneapolis: Fortress, 1977.

Herrick, James A. *The Making of the New Spirituality*. Downers Grove, IL: InterVarsity Press, 2003.

Hick, John. *God Has Many Names*. Philadelphia: Westminster, 1982.

———. *The Metaphor of God Incarnate: Christology in a Pluralistic Age*. 2nd ed. Louisville: Westminster John Knox, 2006.

———, ed. *The Myth of God Incarnate*. Philadelphia: Westminster, 1977.

Hick, John, and Paul F. Knitter, eds. *The Myth of Christian Uniqueness: Toward a Pluralistic Theology of Religions*. Maryknoll, NY: Orbis, 1987.

Hill, Charles E., and Frank A. James III, eds. *The Glory of the Atonement: Biblical, Theological, and Practical Perspectives*. Downers Grove, IL: InterVarsity Press, 2004.

Hoekema, Anthony A. *The Bible and the Future*. Grand Rapids: Eerdmans, 1979.

Hoffecker, W. Andrew, ed. *Revolutions in Worldview: Understanding the Flow of Western Thought*. Phillipsburg, NJ: P&R, 2007.

Horton, Michael S. *The Christian Faith: A Systematic Theology for Pilgrims on the Way*. Grand Rapids: Zondervan, 2011.

———. *Covenant and Eschatology: The Divine Drama*. Louisville: Westminster John Knox, 2002.

———. *Lord and Servant: A Covenant Christology*. Louisville: Westminster John Knox, 2005.

———. "What Still Keeps Us Apart?" In *Roman Catholicism: Evangelical Protestants Analyze What Divides and Unites Us*. Edited by John H. Armstrong. Chicago: Moody, 1994.

Hurtado, Larry W. *Lord Jesus Christ: Devotion to Jesus in Earliest Christianity*. Grand Rapids: Eerdmans, 2003.

Issler, Klaus. "Jesus's Example: Prototype of the Dependent, Spirit-Filled Life." In *Jesus in Trinitarian Perspective*. Edited by Fred Sanders and Klaus D. Issler. Nashville: B&H Academic, 2007.

Jeffery, Steve, Mike Ovey, and Andrew Sach. *Pierced for Our Transgressions: Recovering the Glory of Penal Substitution*. Nottingham, UK: Inter-Varsity Press, 2007.

Jeremias, Joachim. *The Prayers of Jesus*. Philadelphia: Fortress, 1989.

Jersak, Brad, and Michael Hardin, eds. *Stricken by God? Nonviolent Identification and the Victory of Christ*. Grand Rapids: Eerdmans, 2007.

Johnson, S. Lewis, Jr. "Mary, the Saints, and Sacerdotalism." In *Roman Catholicism: Evangelical Protestants Analyze What Divides and Unites Us*. Edited by John H. Armstrong. Chicago: Moody, 1994.

Jones, Mark. *Knowing Christ*. Carlisle, PA: Banner of Truth, 2015.

Kähler, Martin. *The So-Called Historical Jesus and the Historic, Biblical Christ*. Philadelphia: Fortress, 1964.

Kant, Immanuel. *Critique of Pure Reason.* Translated by Norman K. Smith. London: Macmillan, 1929.

———. *Religion within the Limits of Reason Alone.* Translated by Theodore M. Greene and Hoyt H. Hudson. New York: Harper & Row, 1960.

Käsemann, Ernst. "The Problem of the Historical Jesus." In *Essays on New Testament Themes.* Translated by W. J. Montague. 1964. Repr., London: SCM, 2012.

Kelly, J. N. D. *Early Christian Doctrines.* 5th rev. ed. London: A & C Black, 1977.

Köstenberger, Andreas J. John. BECNT. Grand Rapids: Baker, 2004.

———. *A Theology of John's Gospel and Letters: The Word, the Christ, the Son of God.* Biblical Theology of the New Testament. Grand Rapids, MI: Zondervan, 2009.

Köstenberger, Andreas J., and Scott R. Swain. *Father, Son, and Spirit: The Trinity and John's Gospel.* NSBT 24. Downers Grove, IL: InterVarsity Press, 2008.

Kruger, Michael J. *Canon Revisited: Establishing the Origins and Authority of the New Testament Books.* Wheaton, IL: Crossway, 2012.

Kruse, Colin G. *Paul's Letter to the Romans.* PNTC. Grand Rapids: Eerdmans, 2012.

Kuyper, Abraham. "Sphere Sovereignty." In *A Centennial Reader.* Edited by James D. Bratt. Grand Rapids: Eerdmans, 1998.

Ladd, George Eldon. *A Theology of the New Testament.* Grand Rapids: Eerdmans, 1974.

Lane, William. *Hebrews 1–8.* WBC 47A. Dallas: Word, 1991.

———. *Hebrews 9–13.* WBC 47B. Dallas: Word, 1991.

Lessing, G. E. "On the Proof of the Spirit and Power." In *Lessing's Theological Writings.* Compiled and translated by Henry Chadwick. Library of Modern Religious Thought. Stanford: Stanford University Press, 1956.

Letham, Robert. *The Holy Trinity: In Scripture, History, Theology, and Worship.* Phillipsburg, NJ: P&R, 2004.

———. *The Work of Christ.* Contours of Christian Theology. Downers Grove, IL: InterVarsity Press, 1993.

Lewis, C. S. *Prince Caspian: The Return to Narnia.* New York: HarperCollins, 1994.

Lints, Richard. *The Fabric of Theology: A Prolegomenon to Evangelical Theology.* Grand Rapids: Eerdmans, 1993.

Lloyd-Jones, D. Martyn. *Romans: Atonement and Justification—An Exposition of Chapters 3.20–4.25.* Grand Rapids: Zondervan, 1970.

Luther, Martin. D. *Martin Luthers Werke, Kritische Gesamtausgabe: Briefwechsel.* 18 vols. Weimar: Hermann Böhlaus Nachfolger, 1930–83.

———. "Epistle Sermon: Twenty-Fourth Sunday after Trinity." In *The Precious and Sacred Writings of Martin Luther.* Edited by John Nicholas Lenker. Volume 9. Minneapolis: The Luther Press, 1909.

———. *Luther's Works.* Edited by Jaroslav Pelikan and Helmut Lehmann. 55 vols. St. Louis: Concordia, 1955–86.

Lyotard, Jean-François. *The Postmodern Condition: A Report on Knowledge.* Translated by Geoff Bennington and Brian Massumi. Theory and History of Literature 10. Minneapolis: University of Minnesota Press, 1984.

Machen, J. Gresham. *Christianity and Liberalism*. Grand Rapids: Eerdmans, 1923. Repr., Grand Rapids: Eerdmans, 1981.

Macleod, Donald. *Christ Crucified: Understanding the Atonement*. Downers Grove, IL: IVP Academic, 2014.

———. *The Person of Christ*. Contours of Christian Theology. Downers Grove, IL: InterVarsity Press, 1998.

Marshall, I. Howard, ed. *New Testament Interpretation: Essays on Principles and Methods*. Exeter: Paternoster, 1977.

———. *New Testament Theology*. Downers Grove, IL: InterVarsity Press, 2004.

Martin, Hugh. *The Atonement: In Its Relations to the Covenant, the Priesthood, the Intercession of Our Lord*. Edinburgh: James Gemmell, 1882.

Martin, R. P. *Carmen Christi*. Cambridge: Cambridge University Press, 1967.

McDonald, H. D. *The Atonement of the Death of Christ: In Faith, Revelation, and History*. Grand Rapids: Baker, 1985.

McGrath, Alister E. *The Making of Modern German Christology 1750–1990*. 2nd ed. Eugene, OR: Wipf & Stock, 2005.

McKnight, Scot. *A Community Called Atonement*. Nashville: Abingdon, 2007.

Melanchthon, Philipp. *The Chief Theological Topics: Loci Praecipui Theologici*. Translated by J. A. O. Preus. 2nd ed. St. Louis: Concordia, 2011.

Meyer, Ben F. *The Aims of Jesus*. Princeton Theological Monograph Series 48. Eugene, OR: Wipf & Stock, 2002.

Meyers, Carol. *Exodus*. New York: Cambridge University Press, 2005.

Miley, John. *Systematic Theology*. 2 vols. 1893. Repr., Peabody, MA: Hendrickson, 1989.

Moo, Douglas J. *The Epistle to the Romans*. NICNT. Grand Rapids: Eerdmans, 1996.

———. *Galatians*. BECNT. Grand Rapids: Baker, 2013.

———. *The Letters to the Colossians and to Philemon*. PNTC. Grand Rapids: Eerdmans, 2008.

Morgan, Christopher W., and Robert A. Peterson, eds. *Faith Comes by Hearing: A Response to Inclusivism*. Downers Grove, IL: IVP Academic, 2008.

Morris, Leon. *The Apostolic Preaching of the Cross*. 3rd ed. Grand Rapids: Eerdmans, 1965.

———. *The Atonement: Its Meaning and Significance*. Downers Grove, IL: InterVarsity Press, 1983.

Motyer, J. Alec. *Isaiah*. TOTC. Downers Grove, IL: InterVarsity Press, 1999.

Moule, C. F. D. *The Origin of Christology*. Cambridge: Cambridge University Press, 1977.

Mozley, J. K. *Doctrine of Atonement*. London: Duckworth, 1915.

Muller, Richard A. *Post-Reformation Reformed Dogmatics: The Rise and Development of Reformed Orthodoxy, ca. 1520 to ca. 1725*. 4 vols. Grand Rapids: Baker, 2003.

Murray, John. "The Atonement." In *Collected Writings of John Murray, Volume 2: Lectures in Systematic Theology*. Carlisle, PA: Banner of Truth, 1977.

———. *Redemption Accomplished and Applied.* Grand Rapids: Eerdmans, 1955.

Nelson, Richard. *Raising Up a Faithful Priest.* Louisville: Westminster John Knox, 1993.

Newbigin, Lesslie. *Proper Confidence: Faith, Doubt, and Certainty in Christian Discipleship.* Grand Rapids: Eerdmans, 1995.

Nicene and Post-Nicene Fathers, First Series. Edited by P. Schaff and H. Wace. 1886–89. 14 vols. Repr., Grand Rapids, MI: Eerdmans, 1994.

Nicene and Post-Nicene Fathers, Second Series. Edited by P. Schaff and H. Wace. 1886–89. 14 vols. Repr., Grand Rapids, MI: Eerdmans, 1994.

Nicole, Emile. "Atonement in the Pentateuch." In *The Glory of the Atonement: Biblical, Historical, and Practical Perspectives.* Edited by Charles E. Hill and Frank A. James III. Downers Grove, IL: InterVarsity Press, 2004.

O'Brien, P. T. *The Epistle to the Philippians.* NIGTC. Grand Rapids, MI: Eerdmans, 1991.

———. *The Letter to the Hebrews.* PNTC. Grand Rapids, MI: Eerdmans, 2010.

Oswalt, John. *Isaiah 40–66.* NICOT. Grand Rapids, MI: Eerdmans, 1998.

Owen, John. *The Priesthood of Christ: Its Necessity and Nature.* Fearn, Ross-shire, UK: Christian Focus, 2010.

Packer, J. I. "The Atonement in the Life of the Christian." In *The Glory of the Atonement: Biblical, Historical, and Practical Perspectives.* Edited by Charles E. Hill and Frank A. James III. Downers Grove, IL: InterVarsity Press, 2004.

———. *The J. I. Packer Collection.* Compiled by Alister McGrath. Downers Grove, IL: InterVarsity Press, 1999.

———. *Keep in Step with the Spirit.* Old Tappan, NJ: Revell, 1984.

———. *Knowing God.* 20th Anniversary Edition. Downers Grove, IL: InterVarsity Press, 1993.

Packer, J. I., and Mark Dever. *In My Place Condemned He Stood.* Wheaton, IL: Crossway, 2007.

Parker, Rebecca, and Joanne Carlson Brown. "For God So Loved the World." In *Christianity, Patriarchy and Abuse.* Edited by Joanne Carlson Brown and Carole R. Bohn. New York: Pilgrim, 1989.

Pearcey, Nancy, and Charles Thaxton. *The Soul of Science: Christian Faith and Natural Philosophy.* Wheaton, IL: Crossway, 1994.

Penner, Myron B., ed. *Christianity and the Postmodern Turn: Six Views.* Grand Rapids: Brazos, 2005.

Peterson, David. "Atonement in the Old Testament." In *Where Wrath and Mercy Meet: Proclaiming the Atonement Today.* Edited by David Peterson. Carlisle, UK: Paternoster, 2001.

———. *Hebrews and Perfection: An Examination of the Concept of Perfection in the "Epistle to the Hebrews."* SNTSMS 47. Cambridge: Cambridge University Press, 1982.

Peterson, Robert A. *Calvin and the Atonement.* Fearn, Ross-shire, UK: Mentor, 1999.

Peterson, Robert A., and Christopher W. Morgan, eds. *The Deity of Christ*. Wheaton, IL: Crossway, 2011.

Pinnock, Clark H., et al. *The Openness of God: A Biblical Challenge to the Traditional Understanding of God*. Downers Grove, IL: InterVarsity Press, 1994.

Pugh, Ben. *Atonement Theories: A Way through the Maze*. Eugene, OR: Cascade, 2014.

Reeves, Michael. *Rejoicing in Christ*. Downers Grove, IL: IVP Academic, 2015.

Reeves, Michael, and Tim Chester. *Why the Reformation Still Matters*. Wheaton, IL: Crossway, 2016.

Reymond, Robert L. *Jesus, Divine Messiah: The New and Old Testament Witness*. Fearn, Ross-shire, UK: Mentor, 2003.

Ridderbos, Herman. *Paul: An Outline of His Theology*. Grand Rapids: Eerdmans, 1975.

Robinson, James M. *A New Quest of the Historical Jesus and Other Essays*. Minneapolis: Augsburg Fortress, 1983.

Sanders, E. P. *Jesus and Judaism*. Minneapolis: Fortress, 1985.

Schaeffer, Francis A. *A Christian View of Philosophy and Culture*. Vol. 1 of *The Complete Works of Francis A. Schaeffer*. Westchester, IL: Crossway, 1982.

———. *Escape from Reason*. London: Inter-Varsity, 1968.

Schaff, Philip. *The Creeds of Christendom*. 6th ed. 3 vols. Harper and Row, 1931. Repr., Grand Rapids: Baker, 1990.

Schreiner, Thomas R. *Commentary on Hebrews*. Nashville: B&H, 2015.

———. *New Testament Theology: Magnifying God in Christ*. Grand Rapids: Baker, 2008.

———. *Romans*. BECNT. Grand Rapids: Baker, 1998.

Schweitzer, Albert. *The Quest of the Historical Jesus: A Critical Study of Its Progress from Reimarus to Wrede*. Translated by William Montgomery. New York: Macmillan, 1968.

Sire, James W. *The Universe Next Door: A Basic Worldview Catalogue*. 4th ed. Downers Grove, IL: InterVarsity Press, 1997.

Stott, John R. W. *The Cross of Christ*. 20th Anniversary Edition. Downers Grove, IL: InterVarsity Press, 2006.

Tatum, W. Barnes. *In Quest of Jesus: A Guidebook*. Atlanta: John Knox, 1982.

Taylor, Charles. *A Secular Age*. Cambridge: Belknap, 2007.

Tidball, Derek. *The Message of the Cross*. Downers Grove, IL: InterVarsity Press, 2001.

Travis, Stephen. "Christ as Bearer of Divine Judgement in Paul's Thought about the Atonement." Pages 21–38 in *Atonement Today*. Edited by John Goldingay. Gospel and Cultures. London: SPCK.

Treat, Jeremy R. *The Crucified King: Atonement and Kingdom in Biblical and Systematic Theology*. Grand Rapids: Zondervan, 2014.

Troeltsch, Ernst. "Historical and Dogmatic Method in Theology (1898)." In *Religion in History*. Translated by James Luther Adams and Walter E. Bense. Minneapolis: Fortress, 1991.

Trueman, Carl. "The Renaissance." In *Revolutions in Worldview: Understanding the Flow of Western Thought*. Edited by W. Andrew Hoffecker. Phillipsburg, NJ: P&R, 2007.

Turner, Max. "Holy Spirit." In *NDBT* 551–58.

———. *The Holy Spirit and Spiritual Gifts: In the New Testament Church and Today*. Peabody, MA: Hendrickson, 1997.

Turretin, Francis. *Institutes of Elenctic Theology*. Translated by George M. Giger. Edited by James T. Dennison Jr. 3 vols. Phillipsburg, NJ: P&R, 1994.

Ursinus, Zacharias. *Commentary on the Heidelberg Catechism*. Translated by G. W. Williard. Phillipsburg, NJ: 1852. Repr., Phillipsburg, NJ: P&R, 1992.

Van Til, Cornelius. "Nature and Scripture." In *Thy Word is Still Truth: Essential Writings on the Doctrine of Scripture from the Reformation to Today*. Edited by Peter A. Lillback and Richard B. Gaffin Jr. Phillipsburg, NJ: P&R, 2013.

VanGemeren, Willem. *New International Dictionary of Old Testament Theology and Exegesis*. 5 vols. Grand Rapids: Zondervan, 1997.

Vanhoozer, Kevin J. "The Atonement in Postmodernity: Guilt, Goats and Gifts." In *The Glory of the Atonement: Biblical, Historical, and Practical Perspectives*. Edited by Charles E. Hill and Frank A. James III. Downers Grove, IL: InterVarsity Press, 2004.

———. "Exegesis and Hermeneutics." In *NDBT* 52–64.

———. *First Theology: God, Scripture and Hermeneutics*. Downers Grove, IL: InterVarsity Press, 2002.

———. "Human Being, Individual and Social." In *The Cambridge Companion to Christian Doctrine*. Edited by Colin E. Gunton. Cambridge: Cambridge University Press, 1997.

———. *Is There a Meaning in This Text? The Bible, The Reader, and the Morality of Literary Knowledge*. Grand Rapids: Zondervan, 1998.

———. *Remythologizing Theology: Divine Action, Passion, and Authorship*. Cambridge: Cambridge University Press, 2010.

———. "Theology and the Condition of Postmodernity: A Report on Knowledge (of God)." In *The Cambridge Companion to Postmodern Theology*. Edited by Kevin J. Vanhoozer. Cambridge: Cambridge University Press, 2003.

Vidu, Adonis. *Atonement, Law, and Justice: The Cross in Historical and Cultural Contexts*. Grand Rapids: Baker Academic, 2014.

Vos, Geerhardus. *Biblical Theology*. Carlisle, PA: Banner of Truth, 1975.

———. *Christology*. Vol. 3 of *Reformed Dogmatics*. Translated and Edited by Richard B. Gaffin Jr. Bellingham, WA: Lexham, 2014.

———. "The Eschatological Aspect of the Pauline Conception of the Spirit." In *Redemptive History and Biblical Interpretation*. Edited by Richard B. Gaffin Jr. Phillipsburg, NJ: P&R, 1980.

Walters, Gwenfair M. "The Atonement in Medieval Theology." In *The Glory of the Atonement: Biblical, Theological, and Practical Perspectives*. Edited by Charles E. Hill and Frank A. James III. Downers Grove, IL: InterVarsity Press, 2004.

Waltke, Bruce K. "Atonement in Psalm 51: My Sacrifice, O God, Is a Broken Spirit." In *The Glory of the Atonement: Biblical, Historical, and Practical Perspectives*. Edited by Charles E. Hill and Frank A. James III. Downers Grove, IL: InterVarsity Press, 2004.

Warfield, B. B. "The Emotional Life of Our Lord." In *The Person and Work of Christ*. Edited by Samuel G. Craig. Philadelphia: P&R, 1980.

———. *The Lord of Glory*. Grand Rapids: Baker, 1974.

———. *The Plan of Salvation*. Rev. ed. Grand Rapids: Eerdmans, 1970.

Waters, Guy Prentiss. *Justification and the New Perspectives on Paul*. Phillipsburg, NJ: P&R, 2004.

Watts, Rikki E. "The New Exodus/New Creational Restoration of the Image of God: A Biblical-Theological Perspective on Salvation." In *What Does It Mean to Be Saved? Broadening Evangelical Horizons of Salvation*. Edited by John G. Stackhouse Jr. Grand Rapids: Baker, 2002.

Weaver, J. Denny. *The Nonviolent Atonement*. Grand Rapids: Eerdmans, 2001.

Weaver, Richard M. *Ideas Have Consequences*. Chicago: University of Chicago Press, 1948.

Wells, David F. *Above All Earthly Pow'rs: Christ in a Postmodern World*. Grand Rapids: Eerdmans, 2005.

———. *God in the Wasteland: The Reality of Truth in a World of Fading Dreams*. Grand Rapids: Eerdmans, 1994.

———. *God the Evangelist*. Grand Rapids: Eerdmans, 1987.

———. *Losing Our Virtue: Why the Church Must Recover Its Moral Vision*. Grand Rapids: Eerdmans, 1999.

———. *No Place for Truth, or Whatever Happened to Evangelical Theology?* Grand Rapids: Eerdmans, 1993.

———. *The Person of Christ: A Biblical and Historical Analysis of the Incarnation*. Westchester, IL: Crossway, 1984.

Wellum, Stephen J. *God the Son Incarnate: The Doctrine of Christ*. Foundations of Evangelical Theology. Wheaton, IL: Crossway, 2016.

Wenham, Gordon J. *The Book of Leviticus*. NICOT. Grand Rapids: Eerdmans, 1979.

Westerholm, Stephen. *Perspectives Old and New on Paul: The "Lutheran" Paul and His Critics*. Grand Rapids: Eerdmans, 2004.

Wilkins, Michael J., and J. P. Moreland, eds. *Jesus Under Fire: Modern Scholarship Reinvents the Historical Jesus*. Grand Rapids: Zondervan, 1995.

Williams, David. *The Office of Christ and Its Expression in the Church*. Lewiston: Mellen, 1997.

Williams, Garry. "A Critical Exposition of Hugo Grotius' Doctrine of the Atonement in De Satisfactione Christi." D. Phil. Thesis. Oxford University, 1999.

———. "The Cross and the Punishment of Sin." In *Where Wrath and Mercy Meet*. Edited by David Peterson. Carlisle, UK: Paternoster, 2001.

Witherington, Ben, III. *The Jesus Quest: The Third Search for the Jew of Nazareth*. 2nd ed. Downers Grove, IL: InterVarsity Press, 1997.

Wolterstorff, Nicholas. *Reason within the Bounds of Religion*. 2nd ed. Grand Rapids: Eerdmans, 1988.

Wright, Christopher J. H. *Knowing the Holy Spirit through the Old Testament*. Downers Grove, IL: InterVarsity Press, 2006.

Wright, N. T. *The Challenge of Jesus: Rediscovering Who Jesus Was and Is*. Downers Grove, IL: InterVarsity Press, 1999.

———. *The Climax of the Covenant: Christ and the Law in Pauline Theology*. Minneapolis: Fortress, 1992.

———. *Colossians and Philemon*. TNTC. Grand Rapids: Eerdmans, 1986.

———. *How God Became King: The Forgotten Story of the Gospels*. New York: HarperOne, 2012.

———. "Jesus." *NDT* 348–51.

———. *Jesus and the Victory of God*. Christian Origins and the Question of God 2. Minneapolis: Fortress, 1997.

———. *The New Testament and the People of God*. Christian Origins and the Question of God 1 Minneapolis: Fortress, 1992.

———. *The Original Jesus: The Life and Vision of a Revolutionary*. Grand Rapids: Eerdmans, 1996.

———. *The Resurrection of the Son of God*. Christian Origins and the Question of God 3. Minneapolis: Fortress, 2003.

———. *Simply Jesus: A New Vision of Who He Was, What He Did, and Why He Matters*. New York: HarperOne, 2011.

———. *Who Was Jesus?* Grand Rapids: Eerdmans, 1993.

Yarbrough, Robert. "Atonement." In *NDBT* 388–93.

Yeago, David S. "The New Testament and Nicene Dogma: A Contribution to the Recovery of Theological Exegesis." *Pro Ecclesia* 3.2 (1994): 152–64.

Young, Edward J. *My Servants the Prophets*. Grand Rapids: Eerdmans, 1952.

Zwingli, Ulrich. "The 10 Conclusions of Berne (1528)." In *Thy Word Is Still Truth: Essential Writings on the Doctrine of Scripture from the Reformation to Today*. Edited by Peter A. Lillback and Richard B. Gaffin Jr. Phillipsburg, NJ: P&R, 2013.

———. "The First Zurich Disputation." In *Thy Word Is Still Truth: Essential Writings on the Doctrine of Scripture from the Reformation to Today*. Edited by Peter A. Lillback and Richard B. Gaffin Jr. Phillipsburg, NJ: P&R, 2013.

———. "The Sixty-Seven Articles (1523)." In *Thy Word Is Still Truth: Essential Writings on the Doctrine of Scripture from the Reformation to Today*. Edited by Peter A. Lillback and Richard B. Gaffin Jr. Phillipsburg, NJ: P&R, 2013.

Scripture Index

Genesis

1–2 . . . . 36, 112, 177
1:2 151
1:3 134
1:26–31 . . . . . . 131, 145
1:28 128
1:31 . . . . 43, 260
2–3 116
2:1–3 37
2:16–17 . . . . . . 128, 130
2:17 . . . . 210, 242
2:18 . . . . 146, 207
3 260
3:6 43
3:8 134
3:15 . . . . 42, 46, 85, 113,
     133, 163, 240, 242
3:21–24 43
3:22 42
5:5 146
6:5 43
8:1 . . . . 48, 144
12:1 134
15:1 134
15:6 . . . . 223, 224
18:25 . . . . . . 40, 71, 218
49:8–12 133

Exodus

3:2–5 37
4:4 87
4:22 98
12:12–13 200
12:50–13:16 200
13:13 238

19–24 131
24:6–8 202
28:17–21 138
28:30 138
29:9 137
29:44 137
32:19–20 139
33–34 . . . . 56, 134
34:20 238

Leviticus

10:10–11 138
11–15 138
11:44 37
16 233
16:15–19 139
17:11 . . . . . 122, 202, 233
18:8 138
18:25–28 44
20:22–23 44
21:16–23 137

Numbers

3:5–10 . . . . 138, 139
3:10 137
12:6–8 . . . . 133, 135
18:1–7 . . . . 137, 139
18:14–17 238
23:19 74
25:1–9 139

Deuteronomy

1:17 63
4:17–20 65
18:15–18 135

18:15–19 132
21:23 196
27–30 131
27:26 207
32:4 40
33:10 138
34:10–12 133

1 Samuel

1:19 . . . . 48, 144
2:6 63
16:13–14 151

2 Samuel

7 146
7:18–21 145

1 Kings

8:27 36
11:1–11 65
17:19–24 71

2 Kings

5:7 71

2 Chronicles

35:3 138

Job

9:2 109
9:8 63
25:6 74

Psalms

2 . . . . . . 47, 111, 145, 146
2:7 . . . . . . 60, 86, 89, 103

2:7–8 104
7:17 36
8 . . . . . 75, 113, 131, 145
8:4 74
8:4–6 112
9:2 36
9:8 . . . . .36, 177
14:1 132
21:7 36
22 208
32:1–2 224
33:5 . . . . .36, 177
33:6 134
40:7 231
45 . . . . 47, 111
50:12–14 . . . .36, 39, 177
62:2 79
62:6 79
62:7 79
65:7 63
72 . . . . 145, 146
75:8 203–204
77:19 63
89:27 . . . . .56, 98
93:2 . . . . .36, 39, 177
97:9 36
107:23–31 63
110 . . . . . . 47, 111, 202,
                225, 226
110:1 49
119:9 134
119:25 134
119:28 134
119:65 134
119:89 134
130:3 140
139:1–4 . . . . . . .36, 177
139:1–10 36
139:16 . . . . . .36, 39, 177
147:15–18 134

Proverbs
1:7 132

Ecclesiastes
1:9 285
2:11 285
4:3 285
6:12 285
9:3 285
12:13 285

Isaiah
1:4–20 . . . . . 37, 178, 214
6:1 36
6:1–3 37
6:5 . . . . .44, 56, 109, 134
7:14 . . . . 47, 85, 145
9:6 49
9:6–7 . . . . 47, 50, 51, 60,
               85, 88, 145
9:7 49
11 . . . . 49, 146
11:1–5 . . . . .50, 151
11:1–16 . . . . .51, 145
11:42 85
11:49 85
11:53 85
11:61 85
22:11 39
25:6–9 . . . . .48, 63, 144
29:18–19 62
32:15–17 152
35:5–6 . . . . .62, 77
35:8 . . . . . . 37, 178, 214
40:3–5 49
41:4 78
42:1 . . . . .60, 231
42:1–8 151
42:1–9 145
42:8 . . . . .65, 72
43:10 78
43:25 78
44:3–4 152
45:8 78
45:18 78
45:19 78

45:20–25 96
45:22 78
46:4 78
46:9 78
46:9–11 . . . . .36, 177
46:13 223
48:11 72
48:12 78
48:17 78
49:1–7 145
50:5–8 223
51:9 49
51:9–10 63
51:12 74
52:10 49
52:13 201
52:13–53:12 145
53 . . . . .225, 238
53:1 49
53:4 77
53:5 201
53:8 198
53:10 211
53:10–12 201
53:11 50
53:12 . . . . 175, 207, 231
55:1 134
55:8 282
55:9 282
56:2 74
57:15 37
59:1–4 44
59:15–21 51
59:16 201
59:16–17 49
59:20–21 152
61 198
61:1 . . . . .62, 77
61:1–2 59
61:1–3 151
63:7–14 151

Jeremiah

23:1–6 51
23:5–6 50
25:15–29 204
25:31 63
31:29–34 152
31:31–34 202
31:34 . . . . . . 48, 77, 108,
        144, 203, 225, 227
32:6–8 238
49:18 74
49:33 74
50:40 74
51:43 74

Ezekiel

22:26 138
23:32–34 204
34 . . . . . . .47, 49, 50, 51,
        59, 76, 85, 88
34:1–9 79
34:1–24 145
34:11–13 79
36:25–27 152
37 63
37:1–23 . . . . .48, 63, 144
37:13 71
37:14 152
39:29 152

Daniel

7 . . . . 47, 198
12:2 . . . . .48, 63, 144

Hosea

11:9 . . . . 37, 178, 214

Joel

2:2 207
2:28–32 152

Amos

8:9, 10 207

Jonah

2:9 . . . . 59, 79, 260

Micah

7:9 223

Habakkuk

1:12–13 . . . . 37, 178, 214

Haggai

2:11–13 138

Zechariah

12:10 152

Malachi

2:5–9 138

Matthew

1–2 62
1:1 . . . . .85, 249
1:18–25 60
1:21 . . . .77, 85, 108, 149,
        157, 197, 202, 205,
                 207, 238
1:23 77
2:5–12 64
3:15 . . . . 59, 231
3:16–17 59
3:17 68
4:3 151
4:4 132
4:6 151
4:12–17 249
4:23 . . . . 61, 63
5–7 61
5:17 76
5:17–20 62
5:22 133
6:9 67
7:22–23 63
8–9 61
8:17 77

8:20 75
8:26 62
9:13 76
9:35 . . . . 61, 63
10:1 61
10:1 135
10:7–8 63
10:23 75
10:34 76
10:35 76
11:1–15 50
11:25–27 . . . . 60, 67–69,
                           72
12:28 151
12:40 198
12:41–42 50
13:16–17 50
14:22–33 63
14:25 62
14:28–30 62
14:33 65
16:13 249
16:14 133
16:15 250
16:16 250
16:17 69
16:21 198
16:21–23 64
16:27 63
17:1–8 60
17:5 68
17:9 75
19:28 75
20:28 . . . . . 76, 231, 234,
                         237
21:15–16 65
22:41–46 49
24:30 75
25:29–31 150
25:31 75
25:31–33 63
25:41 63
25:46 63

26:26–29 237
26:28 234
26:29 69
26:39 67
26:42 67
26:54 198
27:46 208
27:51 208
28:9 65
28:17 65
28:18 150
28:18–20 . . . . 37, 61
28:19 68
28:20 61

Mark
1:1 . . . . .56, 68
1:10 . . . . .60, 151
1:11 . . . . .60, 68
1:38 76
2:1–12 . . . . . . .216, 249
2:7 65
2:10 . . . . .75, 256
2:20 198
2:28 75
3:11 68
3:13–19 135
5:7 68
6:45–52 63
8:31–32 198
8:38 75
9:2–8 60
9:7 . . . . .56, 68, 199
9:31 198
10:32–34 198
10:45 . . . . . 64, 75, 163,
             231, 234, 237
12:6 56
13:26 75
14:22–25 237
14:24 234
14:33–34 203
14:36 . . . . . .67, 204, 208

14:61 68
14:62 75
15:26 207
15:34 208
15:38 208
15:39 68

Luke
1:26–38 60
1:31 151
1:32 68
1:35 151
2:47 151
2:49 69
2:51–52 231
2:52 256
3:22 56
3:32 68
4:9 68
4:16–21 . . . . 59, 151
4:17–21 151
4:18 163
4:21 198
5:20–26 64
5:21 65
6:12–16 135
7:16 133
7:18–22 50
7:22–23 62
7:34 75
8:22–25 249
9:8 133
9:11 63
9:28–36 60
9:31 199
9:35 . . . . .56, 68
9:58 75
10:9 63
10:17 63
10:21 67
10:23–24 50
11:2 67
11:20 63

12:8–10 75
12:40 75
12:49 76
17:22–30 75
17:24–25 75
18:8 75
18:31 . . . . .64, 198
19:10 . . . . .75, 76
20:13 56
22:19–20 . .199, 234, 237
22:20 . . . . .143, 202
22:22 198
22:28 69
22:31–32 143
22:37 . . . . .198, 207
22:42 . . . . .67, 204
22:43 203
22:48 75
23:4 206
23:13–14 206
23:15 206
23:16 206
23:20–22 206
23:22 206
23:25 206
23:34 . . . . .67, 208
23:39–40 206
23:43 208
23:45 208
23:46 . . . . . .67, 69, 209
23:47 206
24:7 75
24:24–27 133
24:25–27 199
24:26–27 21
24:26 198
24:44–47 . .133, 198, 199
24:46 198
24:50–53 150

John
1:1 . . . . 38, 69, 108,
            133, 134, 208

1:1–3 . . .50, 85, 104, 208
1:1–4 37
1:1–18 . . . . .55, 134
1:4 48
1:12 68
1:14 . . . . 38, 69, 85,
        108, 120, 133, 134
1:14a 55
1:14–18 . . . . . 37, 50, 133
1:18 . . .56, 133, 134, 208
1:29 199
1:33–34 151
2:6–11 249
3:14 . . . . .75, 198
3:16 39, 68, 209, 211, 260
3:17 68
3:35–36 68
3:36 236
4:19 133
5:16–30 . . . . 37, 69
5:19–20 71
5:19–23 . . . . .68, 72
5:21 64
5:22–23 . . . . 21, 63
5:23 65
5:25 64
5:26 . . . . .48, 72
5:29 63
5:30 231
5:39–40 21
5:45–47 133
6:20 78
6:40 68
6:51 234
6:53 75
7:24–25 143
7:30 198
7:39 153
8:12 79
8:20 198
8:24 78
8:28 . . . . .75, 78
8:36 68

8:58 78
9:17 133
10:7 79
10:9 79
10:11 . . . . .79, 234
10:14 79
10:15 234
10:17–18 64
10:18 . . . . .198, 206, 231
11:7–15 198
11:25 . . . . .48, 64, 79
11:38–44 249
11:41 69
12:23 . . . . .75, 198
12:27 . . . . .80, 204
12:28 69
12:30–33 64
12:31–33 242
12:44 80
12:49 231
13:1 198
13:12–17 242
13:21 80
13:31 75
14:1 . . . . .79, 80
14:6 . . . . . .48, 56, 68, 79
14:9 133
14:13 68
15:1 79
15:5 79
15:8 69
15:13 211
15:26–27 152
17:1 . . . . .68, 198
17:1–5 37
17:3 . . . . .50, 52, 208
17:5 69
17:6–26 143
17:26 68
18:6 78
18:11 211
19:7 207
19:15 65

19:26–27 208
19:30 . . . . .208, 270
20:1–18 249
20:9 198
20:17 67
20:28 65
20:31 68

Acts

1:6–11 150
1:11 150
2:22–36 196
2:23 196
2:36 153
2:42 135
3:6 61
3:13–15 196
3:18 196
3:22–26 . . . . . . .132, 133
4:10 61
4:12 . . . . .80, 196, 311
4:25–26 88
4:27–28 . . . . 37, 177
4:28 196
5:30–31 196
7:37 133
7:56 74
9:34 61
10:25–26 65
10:43 . . . . .79, 80
12:24 60
13:32–33 86
13:33 . . . . .88, 104
14:14–15 65
16:31 . . . . .79, 80
16:34 80
17:24–25 . . . .36, 39, 177
17:28 36
17:31 149
20:28 . . . . .231, 238

Romans

1:1–4 . . . . . . .86, 89, 90

1:3-4 . . . . . . 69, 83, 103, 104, 146, 153
1:4 151
1:18 132
1:18-3:20 . . . . . 222, 223
1:18-23 . . . . . 37, 65, 240
1:18-32 236
1:24-32 223
1:25 43
1:30 240
2:1-5 240
2:3 63
2:5 236
2:5-6 63
3:9-12 145
3:10 43
3:10-18 240
3:21-26 . . . . 38, 51, 178, 194, 222-225, 228, 230, 241
3:21-31 . . . . 260, 262
3:23 . . . . . . 43, 140, 145, 175, 241, 260
3:24-25 237
3:24-26 . . . . . . 234, 241
3:25 244
3:25-26 . . . . . . 141, 227
4 223
4:3 80
4:5 . . . . 80, 225, 241
4:17 80
4:24 80
4:25 150
5:1-2 239
5:1-8:39 51
5:1-11 262
5:6 234
5:6-8 235
5:8 . . . . 234, 240
5:9 241
5:10-11 . . . 239, 240, 244
5:12 146

5:12-21 . . . 42, 113, 128, 129, 210, 222, 241
5:14 41
5:15-19 146
5:18-19 265
5:19 . . . . 122, 231
6:1-23 150
6:4 71
6:23 . . . . . . 43, 109, 116, 140, 146, 175, 207, 210, 241, 242, 260
8:1 . . . . . . 109, 146, 241
8:1-4 . . . . 259, 262
8:3 . . . 207, 208, 231, 234
8:7 240
8:7-8 140
8:11 153
8:14-27 153
8:15 68
8:18-25 260
8:18-27 239
8:23 153
8:28-39 259
8:32 . . 176, 208, 211, 234
8:32-34 143
8:34 150
10:9-11 80
10:12-13 79
11:33-36 37
12:19 218
13:1 205
14:10 63
14:15 234
16:20 163
16:25-27 51
121:33-36 177

1 Corinthians
1:2 80
1:18 196
1:30 . . . . 264, 311
2:1-2 196
5:7 . . . . 199, 231

6:14 150
6:19-20 237
8:5-6 37
11:23-25 237
11:24 234
11:25 . . . . 143, 231
15:1-34 51
15:3 . . . . 196, 234
15:3-4 157
15:12-58 . . . . . . 129, 150
15:20 . . . . . 100, 149, 153
15:23 . . . . 100, 153
15:27 150
15:42-44 . . . . . . 149, 153
15:45 151
15:47 107
15:55-57 . . . . . 117, 149

2 Corinthians
1:22 153
3:17-18 151
4:4 . . . . 117, 132
4:14 150
5:5 153
5:10 63
5:15 234
5:17 . . . . 129, 149
5:18-20 244
5:18-21 239
5:21 . . . . . 121, 123, 176, 205, 207, 209, 210, 234, 241
13:14 37

Galatians
1:4 . . . . 231, 234
2:20 234
3:6 80
3:10-13 230
3:10-14 262
3:13 . . . . . 175, 176, 197, 207, 234, 237, 241, 244, 311

4:1–4 231
4:4–5 . . . . 153, 237
4:6 68

Ephesians
1:3–4 37
1:4 39
1:7 . . . . . . 237, 238, 244
1:7–10 . . . . 51, 57
1:9–10 . . . . . 22, 103, 135
1:10 . . . . 161, 239
1:11 . . . . 36, 205
1:13 153
1:14 153
1:18–22 . . . . . . 146, 150
1:22 239
2:1–3 . . . . . 109, 117, 140, 146, 260
2:1–4 175
2:1–18 240
2:1–22 129
2:4–10 . . . . 260, 263
2:6 . . . . 71, 150
2:11–22 239
2:13–16 244
2:17 135
2:17–18 239
3:11 39
3:12 239
4:1–4 132
4:6 36
4:8–12 150
4:17–19 240
4:30 153
5:1–2 242
5:2 . . . . 231, 234
5:25 234
5:25–27 242

Philippians
2:5–11 . . . 83, 86, 90–96, 188, 242
2:6–11 . . . . 51, 69, 97

2:7 254
2:8 . . . . 211, 231
2:8–9 150
2:9 265
2:9–11 . . . . 72, 146, 150, 211

Colossians
1:12 20
1:13 117
1:13–14 237
1:15 56
1:15–17 . . . 50, 104, 105, 208
1:15–20 . . . . . 57, 83, 86, 96–101, 146, 239, 240
1:16–17 22
1:17 256
1:19–20 244
1:21 240
1:28 24
2:9 . . . . 50, 100
2:13–14 244
2:13–15 . . . 149, 163, 242
2:14–15 . . . . . . 146, 230
2:15 239
3:1 . . . . 71, 150

1 Thessalonians
1:8 80
5:10 234

1 Timothy
2:6 . . . . 234, 237
3:16 . . . . 150, 151

2 Timothy
1:9 39

Titus
2:14 . . . . . . 234, 237, 244
3:8 80

Hebrews
1–3 50
1:1–3 . . . . . . 83, 86, 134
1:1–3a 22, 133
1:1–4 . . . . 101–106, 110
1:3 . . . . . . 150, 208, 265
1:3b 111
1:4–14 101
1:5 . . . . 88, 104
1:5–14 111
1:8–9 104
1:13 . . . . 104, 105
2:5–8 101
2:5–18 . . . . . 51, 98, 110, 112, 121, 129, 142, 149, 225, 231
2:6 74
2:9 . . . . 113, 234
2:10 . . 102, 114, 115, 117
2:10–13 113
2:10–18 231
2:14 164
2:14–15 . . . . . . 146, 242
2:14–16 . . . . . . 116, 163
2:14–17 230
2:17 . . . . 234, 244
2:17b 119
2:17–18 . . . 118, 120, 262
2:18 119
3:1–6 . . . . 104, 135
4:14 150
4:14–5:10 118
4:14–10:39 101
4:14–15 120
4:15 . . . . 102, 210
4:16 150
5:1 . . . 128, 137, 138, 142
5:1–10 . . . 104, 119, 226, 262
5:5 . . . . 88, 104
5:5–10 142
5:6 105

5:7 203
5:8 102
5:8–10 . . . . . . .205, 231
6:1 80
6:20 105
7. 226
7–8. 202
7–10. . . . . .102, 143
7:1–8:13. 105
7:1–10:25. 118
7:11 202
7:11–12 143
7:14 102
7:23–28 . . . . . . .143, 262
7:25 . . . . . .119, 142, 150
7:25a 228
7:25–27 142
7:26 102
7:26–28 145
7:27 265
8–10. . . . . .141, 143
8:1–3 51
8:3 142
9–10. . . . . .233, 270
9:1–10:18. 226
9:1–28 228
9:11–10:18. 51
9:11–14 227
9:11–15 . . . . . .142, 244
9:12 . . . . .142, 237
9:13 144
9:14 212
9:15 237
9:15–28 . . . . . 194, 222,
             225–228, 262
9:22 122
9:24 150
9:26 265

9:28 176
10:1–4 142
10:1–18 . . . . . .139, 227
10:4 224
10:5–10 231
10:10 265
10:12 . . . . .234, 265
10:14 265
10:15–18 142
10:19–22 239
12:29 44
13:6–8 150
13:9 19

1 Peter
1:3 150
1:8–9 27
1:10–12 . . . . . .133, 135
1:17 63
1:18–19 . . . . . .237, 238
1:19 231
1:20 . . . . .39, 198
1:21 80
2:9b 24
2:18–25 242
2:21 234
2:24 208
2:24–25 . . .201, 234, 238
3:18 . . . . .151, 176, 207,
             231, 234
3:22 150

2 Peter
1:21 309

1 John
1:5 44
2:1–2 . . . . .143, 266

2:2 . . . . .234, 244
2:12 266
3:16 234
3:23 80
4:7–12 242
4:8 38
4:10 . . . . .234, 244
5:11–12 48
5:13 80

Revelation
1:13 74
1:17b–18 117
1:17–18 149
2:7 88
4:3 36
4:8 38
5:8–9 231
5:9 . . . . .238, 244
7:14 231
12:1–12 163
12:5 88
13:8 196
14:10 204
14:14 74
16:1–21 204
18:6 204
19:10 65
19:15 88
20:11–15 71
21–22. 129
21:1–8 285
21:3–4 . . . . .48, 144
22:8–9 65
22:20b 314

Subject Index

Abba, 67–68, 208
Abelard, Peter, 182
adoptionism, 253
"Age of Reason," 280
Allison, Gregg, 166, 182, 259, 261
all-sufficient savior
   Christ as, 32, 130, 145, 193–219, 221,
     243–45, 312
   cross of, 193–219, 243–45
   penal substitution and, 193–219,
     243–45
all-sufficient work. *See also* cross-work
   of Christ, 20–22, 107–23, 127–55,
     193–219
   cross and, 193–219
   threefold office of, 127–55
Anselm, 32, 107, 110, 165–75, 177–78,
   257
apollinarianism, 253
apostolic witness, 21–22, 83–106
Aquinas, Thomas, 171–72, 257
arianism, 253
Arminius, James, 183
ascension, 61, 75, 135, 143, 150–57
Athanasius, 161–63, 165
atonement
   biblical rationale for, 110–23
   cross and, 23–26
   cross-work and, 158–67, 190–92
   debates on, 177–80, 190–92
   doctrine of, 23–26, 160–61, 173
   governmental views of, 183–90
   incarnation and, 23–25, 107–23
   as penal substitution, 26
   Reformation and, 158–67, 175–79

Socinian view of, 181–83
theologies of, 26, 158–67, 176–97,
   216, 224–25
Augustine, 94, 165–66, 261

Baker, Mark, 213, 216–17, 228, 232–34,
   237–38
Bancroft, Charitie, 271
baptism of Christ, 25, 59–61, 68, 81,
   205
Bavinck, Herman, 22, 196, 198
Belousek, Darrin, 216–17
biblical identity, 31–53. *See also* Christ
biblical worldview, 282–83, 308–9
Brown, Harold O. J., 251
Bruce, F. F., 116
Brunner, Emil, 195

Calvin, John, 19, 127, 157, 173–74, 177,
   205, 257, 265–67, 270, 311–12
Carson, D. A., 62, 70–72, 77, 152, 236
centrality
   of Christ, 20–23, 157–58, 195–96, 312
   of cross, 158, 194–97, 213, 221
   of God, 170, 177, 191, 281, 312
   of Trinitarian theology, 21–23
Chalcedonian Definition, 84, 251–52, 256
Chalcedonian identity, 251–52, 275
Chalcedonian Unity, 249–73
Christ
   as all-sufficient savior, 32, 130, 145,
     193–219, 221, 243–45, 313
   all-sufficient work of, 20–22, 107–23,
     127–55, 193–219
   apostolic witness to, 21–22, 83–106
   baptism of, 25, 59–61, 68, 81, 205

biblical identity of, 31–53
centrality of, 20–23, 157–58, 195–96, 312
covenantal development of, 25, 35, 46, 64, 127–37
cross and, 157–219, 221–45
cross-work of, 157–92
crucifixion of, 41, 75, 80, 100, 114–17, 196–97, 204–5
death of, 21–26, 59–69, 113–18, 154–89, 193–205, 209–15, 221–22, 227–38, 254, 263, 267–70, 275, 312
exclusive identity of, 20, 25–27, 107–23, 249–73, 275–95, 304–12
faith in, 79–80
healings of, 61–64, 69, 77
"I am" statements of, 78–79
identity of, 19–27, 31–53, 107–23, 275–95
incarnation of, 23–27, 45–53, 55–81, 83–110, 127–34, 143–45, 207–12, 255–63, 275–276, 288–94, 305–14
kingdom of God and, 65–67
kingly work of, 128–30, 145–55
life of, 61–64
loss of identity, 275–95
ministry of, 60–64, 135–36
miracles of, 61–64, 66, 73, 76, 287–88
natures of, 83–106, 287
necessity of, 32–35
Passion of, 172, 311
priestly work of, 128–30, 136–45, 157–58
prophetic work of, 128–36
Reformation and, 249–73, 312–13
resurrection of, 33–34, 63–66, 71–72, 75, 79, 148–53
sacrifice of, 26, 160–65, 189, 199–200, 207–16, 226–27, 231–37
salvation and, 23, 32–35, 39, 58, 128–29, 151, 171–74, 179
self-consciousness of, 58–59

self-identity of, 58–81, 107
self-witness of, 21, 55–81
as Son of God, 68–76, 83–106
substitutionary death, 24–26, 69, 129, 182, 231, 263, 312
sufficiency of, 26–27, 257–73
sufficient work of, 20–27, 107–23, 127–55, 193–219
teachings of, 61–64
threefold office of, 127–55
trial of, 205–7
triunity of God and, 38, 85, 212–13
understanding of cross, 197–209
unique identity of, 27, 34–35, 51–58, 83–86, 107–23, 251–63, 275–95, 304–12
worship of, 65
Christ alone (solus Christus)
affirmation of, 102, 250, 256–59, 263, 272–73, 297–314
biblical rationale for, 52–53, 83–106, 157–58, 187
identifying, 52–53
listening to, 81
reaffirming, 297–310
understanding of, 19–27, 83–106
Christian theism, 284–86, 301–5, 308
christological confusion, 277–79, 297, 304–12
christological orthodoxy
doctrine of, 20–26, 159, 173
Reformation and, 20, 250–56, 264
rejection of, 251–52, 299–300
Trinitarian theology and, 159, 173, 250–51
Christus Victor, 116, 163, 174–80, 190, 242
Chrysostom, John, 165
Cicero, 196
Collins, Robin, 216
confusion, 277–79, 297, 304–12
contextual epistemology, 299–302, 308

covenantal development, 25, 35, 46, 64,
127–37
covenantal obedience, 40–43
covenantal storyline, 31, 35, 49–52, 80,
85, 229
covenantal-typological development,
127–37, 145
Creator-Covenant Lord, 36–40, 43, 52,
109, 114, 123, 129, 145, 177, 286,
313
Crisp, Oliver, 184, 188
cross. *See also* cross-work
of all-sufficient savior, 193–219, 243–45
atonement and, 23–26
biblical language of, 228–31
centrality of, 158, 194–97, 213, 221
Christ and, 157–219, 221–45
as conquest, 241–42
doctrine of, 23
"facts" of, 194, 209–13, 221
forgiveness and, 213–19, 221
justice and, 241
as moral example, 242–43
necessity of, 221–28
obedience and, 231–32
as penal substitution, 23, 160–61,
165–67, 179–219, 221–45
as ransom, 160–61, 163–65, 237–38
as recapitulation, 160–63
reconciliation and, 239–40
redemption and, 237–38
sacrifice and, 159–60, 231–37
scandal of, 215–17
understanding of, 197–209
as victory, 160–65, 241–42
views of, 209–13
cross-work. *See also* cross
atonement and, 158–67, 190–92
of Christ, 157–92
historical perspectives on, 157–92
medieval era and, 167–73
patristic era and, 160–67

penal substitution and, 160–61,
165–67, 179–92
Reformation era and, 158–67, 173–79
crucifixion, 41, 75, 80, 100, 114–17,
196–97, 204–5
Cyril of Alexandria, 164

Darwinism, 301
deism, 36, 284–86, 302–6
Descartes, René, 283
divine forgiveness, 43–53, 139, 184,
231–32
docetism, 252–53
Dodd, C. H., 236
Dunn, James, 86, 91

Edwards, James R., 285
empiricism, 283, 285–86
Enlightenment era, 27, 180, 256,
272–73, 279–300, 304–8
eternal redemption, 39, 69, 95, 114–15,
142, 218–19, 227. *See also* redemption
Eusebius of Caesarea, 165
evolutionary panentheism, 302–4
exclusive identity, 20, 25–27, 107–23,
249–73, 275–95, 304–12. *See also*
identity

Fairbairn, Donald, 255
faith alone (*sola fide*), 19–20, 191, 313
fatalism, 33, 64
Feinberg, John S., 284, 302, 304
forgiveness
cross and, 213–19, 221
divine forgiveness, 43–53, 139, 184,
231–32
problem of, 44–45, 51, 141, 170,
179–82, 194, 213–22, 243
of sin, 43–53, 76–78, 139, 144,
157–59, 184, 202, 218–19, 227–32
Frame, John, 39–40
France, R. T., 77

Gathercole, Simon, 76

George, Timothy, 171, 257
Gethsemane, 203–5, 208, 211, 221
God
　centrality of, 170, 177, 191, 281, 312
　divine purpose of, 43, 75–79
　glory of, 19–20, 24, 43, 72, 90, 105,
　　191, 195, 313
　justice of, 33–34, 164–65, 173–78,
　　182–89, 216–18, 221–22, 234
　kingdom of, 25–27, 44–53, 57, 61–67,
　　74–77, 89–90, 157, 197, 281
　obedience to, 40–52, 91, 129, 151–55,
　　199–212, 262–63
　revelation of, 21, 25, 35, 56–57, 97–103,
　　129–35, 155–57, 195, 223, 282–83
　of Scripture, 36–40, 191
　Son of, 68–76, 83–106
　sovereignty of, 34–37, 72–73, 98–99,
　　281
　as triune Creator-Covenant Lord,
　　36–40, 43, 52, 109, 114, 123, 129,
　　145, 177, 286, 313
　triunity of, 23, 36–40, 85, 212–13
　Word of God, 55–59, 131–34, 157–63,
　　250–52, 281–83, 309–12
　work of God, 57, 63–66, 75–79, 145,
　　228–29, 266
　worship of, 65
God's glory alone (*soli Deo gloria*),
　19–20, 191, 195, 313
governmental views, 183–90
grace alone (*sola gratia*), 19–20, 191, 313
Green, Joel, 213, 216–17, 228, 232–34,
　237–38
Gregory of Nyssa, 164
Grotius, Hugo, 183

Harris, Murray, 61, 101
healings, 61–64, 69, 77
historical theologies, 158–67, 193, 309
Hodge, Charles, 216
Hoffecker, Andrew, 285

"I am" statements, 78–79
identity
　of Christ, 19–27, 31–53, 107–23,
　　275–95
　conclusions on, 311–14
　exclusive identity, 20, 25–27, 107–23,
　　249–73, 275–95, 304–12
　loss of, 275–95
　unique identity, 27, 34–35, 51–58,
　　83–86, 107–23, 251–63, 275–95,
　　304–12
incarnation
　atonement and, 23–25, 107–23
　biblical rationale for, 83–106, 109–23,
　　157–58
　of Christ, 23–27, 45–53, 55–81,
　　83–110, 127–34, 143–45, 207–12,
　　255–63, 275–76, 288–94, 305–14
　reason for, 107–10
intercession of saints, 267–69

John of Damascus, 164
justice
　concept of, 216–18
　cross and, 241
　enactment of, 182–89, 216–18, 241
　of God, 33–34, 164–65, 173–78,
　　182–89, 216–18, 221–22, 234
　justification and, 241
　retributive justice, 173–77, 182–89,
　　216–18
　standard of, 187
justification
　cross and, 241
　justice and, 241
　need for, 129, 139, 150, 171–73, 186–89
　obedience and, 171–73, 244, 263–65

Kähler, Martin, 195
Kant, Immanuel, 280, 283–84, 287, 300
kingdom of God, 25–27, 44–53, 57,
　61–67, 74–77, 89–90, 157, 197, 281
kingly work, 128–30, 145–55

Köstenberger, Andreas, 55
Kuyper, Abraham, 147

Ladd, George, 73
Last Supper, 199–203
Lessing, Gotthold, 287–88, 306
Letham, Robert, 136, 188
Lewis, C. S., 313–14
life of Christ, 61–64. *See also* Christ
Lloyd-Jones, Martyn, 222
logocentrism, 301
logos, 55, 134, 253
lordship, 24–26, 36–40, 45, 96–105,
    145–48
Luther, Martin, 173, 222, 263
Lyotard, Jean-François, 298

Machen, J. Gresham, 189
Macleod, Donald, 92, 94, 120, 122, 159,
    179, 188–90, 203–5, 209–12, 218,
    232, 254–55
magisterial authority, 281, 310
Martin, Hugh, 138, 158
Martyr, Justin, 197
Mass, practice of, 269–71
McGrath, Alister, 280
mediation for salvation, 137–45
mediation of saints, 267–69
medieval era, 167–73, 257–58, 279–80
Melanchthon, Philipp, 257
Miley, John, 183–84
ministerial capacity, 280–81, 310
ministry of Christ, 60–64, 135–36. *See
    also* Christ
miracles, 61–64, 66, 73, 76, 287–88
modalism, 253
modernism, 280, 299–302, 306
monogenēs, 56, 134
monogenēs theos, 56, 134
monophysitism, 253
Moo, Douglas, 88–89, 100, 224
moral example, 230–31, 242–43
moral naturalism, 217–18

Morris, Leon, 236, 240
Mozley, J. K., 163
Muller, Richard, 182
Murray, John, 32, 136–37, 189–90

naturalism, 217–18, 284–86, 288, 302–6
nestorianism, 253
Newton, Isaac, 285, 302
Nicene Creed, 98, 251–52
Nicole, Roger, 194, 236

obedience
    covenantal obedience, 40–43
    cross and, 231–32
    to God, 40–52, 91, 129, 151–55,
        199–212, 262–63
    justification and, 171–73, 244, 263–65
O'Brien, Peter T., 92, 100, 114–15, 117
optionalism, 33
Origen, 164, 165
Osiander, Andreas, 272–73
Oswalt, John, 201

Packer, J. I., 22, 107
panentheism, 36, 302–5
Passion of Christ, 172, 311
Passover, 199–203, 238
patristic era, 160–67, 272
penal substitution
    all-sufficient savior and, 193–219,
        243–45
    as atonement theory, 26
    cross as, 23, 160–61, 165–67,
        179–219, 221–45
    cross-work and, 160–61, 165–67,
        179–92
    reactions to, 179–92
    rejection of, 181
    substitutionary death and, 24–26, 69,
        129, 182, 231, 263, 312
    Trinity and, 209, 213
    views of, 166–68, 177–93
Pentecost, 147, 150–53, 195–96, 242
Peterson, David, 200–201, 233

pluralism, 33, 131, 180–83, 276–78,
    297–301, 305
postmodernity, 277–79, 297–308, 313
priestly work, 128–30, 136–45, 157–58
problem of forgiveness, 44–45, 51, 141,
    170, 179–82, 194, 213–22, 243. *See
    also* forgiveness
problem of sin, 108, 117, 130, 237, 242.
    See also sin
prophetic work, 128–36
propitiation, 119, 122, 138, 188, 212,
    230, 234–37, 244, 266
protevangelium, 46, 48–49, 113, 144

radical pluralism, 300–301, 305
ransom, cross as, 160–61, 163–65, 237–38
rational epistemology, 282–86, 291,
    299–300, 305–8
recapitulation, cross as, 160–63
redemption
    cross and, 237–38
    eternal redemption, 39, 69, 95,
        114–15, 142, 218–19, 227
    history of, 20–21
Reeves, Michael, 21, 22
Reformation
    atonement and, 158–67, 175–79
    christological orthodoxy and, 20,
        250–56, 264
    cross-work and, 158–67, 173–79
    Enlightenment and, 280–91
    identity of Christ and, 249–73, 312–13
    principle of, 19–20
    Rome and, 257–73
    solas of, 19–20
    theology of, 19, 33–34, 81, 158, 162,
        175–77, 243–44, 260
    Trinitarian theology and, 173, 250–51
Reimarus, Herman, 290
resurrection
    of Christ, 33–34, 63–66, 71–72, 75,
        79, 148–53
    eyewitnesses of, 135–36

importance of, 63–64, 71–72, 148–50
power of, 63–64, 71–72
uniqueness of, 148–50
retributive justice, 173–77, 182–89,
    216–18. *See also* justice
revelation
    of God, 21, 25, 35, 56–57, 97–103,
        129–35, 155–57, 195, 223, 282–83
    for salvation, 130–32
    source of, 103, 133
    sufficiency of, 132–36
revelational epistemology, 35, 281–91,
    299–300, 308–10
Reymond, Robert, 73, 87
Roman Church, 250, 256, 267, 273
Rome
    Mass and, 269–71
    Reformation disagreement, 257–73
    sacramental theology of, 259–66
    saints and, 267–69
    theology of, 259–71

sacrifice
    of Christ, 26, 160–65, 189, 199–200,
        207–16, 226–27, 231–37
    cross and, 159–60, 231–37
    propitiatory sacrifice, 234–37
saints, intercession of, 267–69
salvation
    Christ and, 23, 32–35, 39, 58,
        128–29, 151, 171–74, 179
    doctrine of, 23
    of humanity, 21–23, 27, 32–35,
        128–29, 206, 228–29, 265–66
    lordship for, 145–46
    mediation for, 137–45
    plan of, 33–34, 39, 58, 151
    revelation for, 130–32
Schaeffer, Francis, 35
Schreiner, Thomas, 75, 87, 93, 98, 100,
    113
Scripture alone (*sola Scriptura*), 19–20,
    191–92, 229, 281, 309–13

self-consciousness of Christ, 58–59
self-identity of Christ, 58–81, 107
self-witness of Christ, 21, 55–81. *See also*
    Christ
Servetus, Michael, 272
sin
    forgiveness of, 43–53, 76–78, 139, 144,
        157–59, 184, 202, 218–19, 227–32
    nature of, 178, 186, 200–203, 207–14,
        221
    problem of, 108, 117, 130, 237, 242
skepticism, 131, 278–83, 292–99, 302,
        305–7
Socinianism, 181–83
Socinus, Faustus, 181
sola fide (faith alone), 19–20, 191, 313
sola gratia (grace alone), 19–20, 191, 313
sola Scriptura (Scripture alone), 19–20,
        191–92, 229, 281, 309–13
solas, 19–24, 27, 191, 312–13
soli Deo gloria (God's glory alone),
        19–20, 191, 195, 313
solus Christus (Christ alone)
    affirmation of, 102, 250, 256–59, 263,
        272–73, 297–314
    biblical rationale for, 52–53, 83–106,
        157–58, 187
    identifying, 52–53
    listening to, 81
    reaffirming, 297–310
    understanding of, 19–27, 83–106
"Son of God," 68–76, 83–106
sovereignty of God, 34–37, 72–73,
        98–99, 281
Staupitz, Johann von, 263
Stott, John, 23, 44, 64, 203–4, 214–15,
        229, 233, 236–37
substitutionary death, 24–26, 69, 129,
        182, 231, 263, 312
sufficiency of Christ, 26–27, 257–73
sufficient work of Christ, 20–27, 107–23,
        127–55, 193–219. *See also* Christ

Swain, Scott, 55
Synoptics, 60, 64–68, 78

Taylor, Charles, 277
Tertullian, 165
trial of Christ, 205–7
Trinitarian theology
    centrality of, 21–23
    Christ and, 38, 85, 212–13
    christological orthodoxy and, 159,
        173, 250–51
    defense of, 308–9
    doctrine of, 23, 159, 173
    Reformation and, 173, 250–51
Trinity
    doctrine of, 23, 159
    penal substitution and, 209, 213
    rejection of, 272, 275
Trypho, 196
Turretin, Francis, 264–65, 267, 269

Ursinus, Zacharias, 264, 266, 268–69

Vanhoozer, Kevin J., 300, 301
victory, cross as, 160–65, 241–42
Vos, Geerhardus, 267

Walters, Gwenfair, 171–72
Warfield, B. B., 73
Wells, David, 51, 56, 60, 278
Williams, Garry, 217
witness
    apostolic witness, 21–22, 83–106
    of Christ, 21, 55–81
    of resurrection, 135–36
    self-witness, 21, 55–81
Word of God, 55–59, 131–34, 157–63,
        250–52, 281–83, 309–12
work of God, 57, 63–66, 75–79, 145,
        228–29, 266. *See also* God
Wright, N. T., 98

Zwingli, Ulrich, 173, 268, 270

THE **5 SOLAS** SERIES

Faith Alone—The Doctrine of Justification

What the Reformers Taught ... and Why It Still Matters

Thomas Schreiner; Matthew Barrett, Series Editor

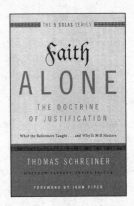

Historians and theologians have long recognized that at the heart of the sixteenth-century Protestant Reformation were five declarations, often referred to as the five "solas": *sola Scriptura, solus Christus, sola gratia, sola fide,* and *soli Deo gloria.* These five statements summarize much of what the Reformation was about, and they distinguish Protestantism from other expressions of the Christian faith. Protestants place ultimate and final authority in the Scriptures, acknowledge the work of Christ alone as sufficient for redemption, recognize that salvation is by grace alone through faith alone, and seek to do all things for God's glory.

In *Faith Alone—The Doctrine of Justification,* renowned biblical scholar Thomas Schreiner looks at the historical and biblical roots of the doctrine of justification. He summarizes the history of the doctrine, looking at the early church and the writings of several of the Reformers. Then he turns his attention to the Scriptures and walks readers through an examination of the key texts in the Old and New Testament. He discusses whether justification is transformative or forensic and introduces readers to some of the contemporary challenges to the Reformation teaching of *sola fide,* with particular attention to the new perspective on Paul.

Five hundred years after the Reformation, the doctrine of justification by faith alone still needs to be understood and proclaimed. In *Faith Alone* you will learn how the rallying cry of *"sola fide"* is rooted in the Scriptures and how to apply this *sola* in a fresh way in light of many contemporary challenges.

Available in stores and online!

God's Glory Alone—The Majestic Heart of Christian Faith and Life

What the Reformers Taught ... and Why It Still Matters

David VanDrunen; Matthew Barrett, Series Editor

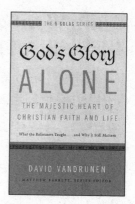

Historians and theologians have long recognized that at the heart of the sixteenth-century Protestant Reformation were five declarations, often referred to as the "*solas*": *sola Scriptura, solus Christus, sola gratia, sola fide,* and *soli Deo gloria.* These five statements summarize much of what the Reformation was about, and they distinguish Protestantism from other expressions of the Christian faith. Protestants place ultimate and final authority in the Scriptures, acknowledge the work of Christ alone as sufficient for redemption, recognize that salvation is by grace alone through faith alone, and seek to do all things for God's glory.

In *God's Glory Alone—The Majestic Heart of Christian Faith and Life,* renowned scholar David VanDrunen looks at the historical and biblical roots of the idea that all glory belongs to God alone. He examines the development of this theme in the Reformation, in subsequent Reformed theology and confessions, and in contemporary theologians who continue to be inspired by the conviction that all glory belongs to God. Then he turns to the biblical story of God's glory, beginning with the pillar of cloud and fire revealed to Israel, continuing through the incarnation, death, and exaltation of the Lord Jesus Christ, and culminating in Christ's second coming and the glorification of his people. In light of these stunning biblical themes he concludes by addressing several of today's great cultural challenges and temptations—such as distraction and narcissism—and reflecting on how commitment to God's glory alone fortifies us to live godly lives in this present evil age.

Available in stores and online!

God's Word Alone—The Authority of Scripture

What the Reformers Taught ... and Why It Still Matters

Matthew Barrett

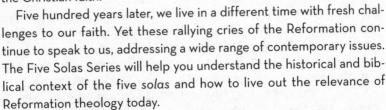

Historians and theologians alike have long recognized that at the heart of the sixteenth-century Protestant Reformation were five declarations (or "*solas*") that distinguished the movement from other expressions of the Christian faith.

Five hundred years later, we live in a different time with fresh challenges to our faith. Yet these rallying cries of the Reformation continue to speak to us, addressing a wide range of contemporary issues. The Five Solas Series will help you understand the historical and biblical context of the five *solas* and how to live out the relevance of Reformation theology today.

In *God's Word Alone—The Authority of Scripture*, scholar and pastor Matthew Barrett looks at the historical and biblical roots of the doctrine that Scripture alone is the final and decisive authority for God's people. He examines the development of this theme in the Reformation and traces the crisis that followed resulting in a shift away from the authority of Scripture. Barrett shows that we need to recover a robust doctrine of Scripture's authority in the face of today's challenges and why a solid doctrinal foundation built on God's Word is the best hope for the future of the church.

Available in stores and online!

Grace Alone—Salvation as a Gift of God

What the Reformers Taught ... and Why It Still Matters

Carl Trueman; Matthew Barrett, Series Editor

Historians and theologians alike have long recognized that at the heart of the sixteenth-century Protestant Reformation were the five "solas": *sola Scriptura, solus Christus, sola gratia, sola fide,* and *soli Deo gloria.* These five *solas* do not merely summarize what the Reformation was all about but have served to distinguish Protestantism ever since. They set Protestants apart in a unique way as those who place ultimate and final authority in the Scriptures, acknowledge the work of Christ alone as sufficient for redemption, recognize that salvation is by grace alone through faith alone, and seek to not only give God all the glory but to do all things vocationally for his glory.

The year 2017 will mark the 500th anniversary of the Reformation. And yet, even in the twenty-first century we need the Reformation more than ever. As James Montgomery Boice said not long ago, while the Puritans sought to carry on the Reformation, today "we barely have one to carry on, and many have even forgotten what that great spiritual revolution was all about." Therefore we "need to go back and start again at the very beginning. We need another Reformation."[1] In short, it is crucial not only to remember what the *solas* of the Reformation were all about but also to apply these *solas* in a fresh way in light of many contemporary challenges.

[1] James Montgomery Boice, "Preface," in *Here We Stand: A Call from Confessing Evangelicals* (Grand Rapids: Baker, 1996), 12.

Available in stores and online!